CRESCENT OVER ANOTHER HORIZON

CRESCENT OVER ANOTHER HORIZON

Islam in Latin America, the Caribbean,
and Latino USA

EDITED BY MARÍA DEL MAR LOGROÑO NARBONA,
PAULO G. PINTO, AND JOHN TOFIK KARAM

UNIVERSITY OF TEXAS PRESS   *Austin*

Requests for permission to reproduce material from this work should be sent to:
  Permissions
  University of Texas Press
  P.O. Box 7819
  Austin, TX 78713-7819
  http://utpress.utexas.edu/index.php/rp-form

♾ The paper used in this book meets the minimum requirements of ANSI/NISO
Z39.48-1992 (R1997) (Permanence of Paper).

LIBRARY OF CONGRESS CATALOGING-IN-PUBLICATION DATA
Crescent over another horizon : Islam in Latin America, the Caribbean, and
Latino USA / edited by María del Mar Logroño Narbona, Paulo G. Pinto, and
John Tofik Karam. — First edition.
    pages   cm
    Includes index.
    ISBN 978-1-4773-0229-3 (cloth : alk. paper) — ISBN 978-1-4773-0230-9 (library
e-book) — ISBN 978-1-4773-0231-6 (nonlibrary e-book)
    1. Muslims—Latin America—Ethnic identity.   2. Muslims—Caribbean Area—Ethnic
identity.   3. Muslims—United States—Ethnic identity.   4. Islam—Latin America.
5. Islam—Caribbean Area.   6. Islam—United States.   I. Logroño Narbona, María
del Mar, editor.   II. Pinto, Paulo Gabriel Hilu da Rocha, editor.   III. Karam, John
Tofik, editor.
    F1419.M87C74   2015
    305.6′9708—dc23

                                                            2015009519

doi:10.7560/302293

الى كل المسلمين الذين ساهموا في كل الاقطار الاميركية

PARA LOS MUSULMANES Y LAS MUSULMANAS
QUE HICIERON Y HACEN LAS AMÉRICAS

PARA OS/AS MUÇULMANOS/AS QUE FIZERAM
E FAZEM AS AMÉRICAS

CONTENTS

ACKNOWLEDGMENTS

CRESCENT OVER ANOTHER HORIZON is a collaborative volume in which multiple efforts have coalesced. A research and dissemination grant from the Social Science Research Council (SSRC)–Carnegie Foundation provided the opportunity to help formulate this volume more than three years ago. Its funding of a project to disseminate information about Islam in Latin America together with the support of the Latin American and Caribbean Center (LACC) at Florida International University (FIU) in 2009–2010 were instrumental in providing the editors and some of the contributors to this volume the opportunity to meet and share the results of their research on different occasions. The project built on an informal network of scholars from Latin American and US institutions and aimed at sharing and popularizing their cutting-edge work beyond academic circles. The editors want to thank Tom Asher and the team at the SSRC for their support in yet another intellectual endeavor. John Stack, director of the School of International and Public Affairs; Cristina Eguizabal, then director of LACC at FIU; and Mohiaddin Mesbahi, then director of the Middle East Studies Center at FIU, have been avid supporters of this project since its inception.

However, as Evelyn Alsultany and Ella Shohat have acknowledged in *Between the Middle East and the Americas: The Cultural Politics of Diaspora*, this project "was probably in the making long before we actually" started it. The editors met more than ten years ago for the first time in Niteroi, Brazil, on the occasion of the opening of the Center for Middle Eastern Studies at the Universidade Federal Fluminense. Paul Amar and Paulo Gabriel Hilu da Rocha Pinto were then two young scholars who set the ground for many years of intellectual collaborations to come, including this volume.

The editors are particularly indebted to the staff of the University of Texas Press and particularly senior editor Jim Burr for their continuous support and encouragement in making this volume possible. Likewise, the editors want to thank all scholars in this volume, as this project would not have been possible without their contributions. We also wish to thank Hanna AlShaikh for her editing of an earlier draft. Last, but not least, we have dedicated this volume to Muslims in the Americas, many of whom have had the generosity to let researchers enter their lives. We all sincerely hope they feel satisfied with the analyses and representations contained in these pages.

CRESCENT OVER ANOTHER HORIZON

LATINO AMERICA IN THE *UMMA*/
THE *UMMA* IN LATINO AMERICA

JOHN TOFIK KARAM, MARÍA DEL MAR LOGROÑO NARBONA, AND PAULO G. PINTO

La ilaha illa Allah . . .
[There is no god but God . . .]

IN THE 1660S a *morisco*, a nominal Muslim convert, stated aloud the above opening refrain of the *shahada* (profession of faith) at the request of Spanish inquisitors in Veracruz, Mexico.[1] In the 1750s a "Mandingo servant" repeated it alongside his British master in Jamaica, and a century later in Panama another recaptured West African inferred it in his manuscript.[2] Starting in the mid-nineteenth century, indentured laborers mostly from Bihar and the United Provinces would have referenced the *shahada* as Muslim "Hindustanis" in Dutch-ruled Suriname and elsewhere in the Caribbean.[3] Likewise after the 1870s, Arab migrants in Buenos Aires and Rio de Janeiro would have inflected it in the founding of charity and civic associations in Argentina, Brazil, and other South American nation-states.[4] Today, US Latinas/os[5] as well as increasing numbers of *latinoamericanos* marked their journey into Islam through this same profession of faith, as they selectively engaged with such histories and institutions.

In establishing a direct relationship with his or her sole creator, the *shahada* positions the speaker in a community of believers (*umma*), which is shaped by and helps to shape history and geography. Secretly, forcibly, and voluntarily stemming from five regions around the world, the aforementioned Muslims who professed their faith were stamped by historically specific processes in the hemisphere, including the Inquisition, slavery and indentured servitude, as well as civil society and nationalist ideology. At the same time, whether undertaken by *moriscos*, Mandingos, Hindustanis, Arabs, Latin American or Caribbean subjects, or US Latinos, the profession of faith informed the imperial, national, and ethnic politics of this same hemisphere. Just as the *shahada* enables one to affirm God's uniqueness and confirms one's membership in the *umma*, its recitation in the moments referenced above also serves as the starting point to rethink the very geographies of these Americas and an Islamic world.

This book positions Latin America, the Caribbean, and Latino USA within a wider Islamic world and at the same time situates Muslims within this hemisphere. The twelve chapters in this volume reveal the longue durée of the interplay between these "Americas" and an "Islamic world," two world areas usually misconstrued as distant or even separate from one another. But instead of focusing on doctrinal or theological dynamics, we address how the unity of Islam took shape through thoroughly plural formulations of identity, power, and belonging in Latin America, the Caribbean, and Latino USA. The contributors to this volume collectively ask, "How did Muslims shape Latin America, the Caribbean, and Latino USA, and, in turn, how were they shaped by this hemisphere?" Our main point is not only that Islam helped define Latin America, the Caribbean, and Latino USA, but also that an Islamic *umma* was imagined and constructed by this hemisphere. By bringing together the study of Iberian colonists, enslaved Africans, indentured South Asians, migrant Arabs, as well as Latino and Latin American converts, this volume reveals the global breadth of Islam and its plural configuration in the making of these Americas. We show that the crescent, the symbol that has come to represent Islam, inhabits a far more expansive horizon than has been heretofore examined.

Building on the work of Zidane Zeraoui,[6] this volume counteracts the widespread assumption that Islam is new or foreign to these Americas. Constructed through Iberians, Africans, South Asians, Arabs, as well as Latin American, Caribbean, and US Latino converts, Islam helped to animate and in turn was constructed in particular ways by imperial powers and colonial societies as well as ethnic, national, and transnational publics in this hemisphere. Our volume demonstrates the formative role Islam plays in a region that allegedly holds a numerically small Muslim population. Indeed, the Pew Center recently conducted a study that claimed there are only 1.486 million Muslims in present-day Latin America and the Caribbean,[7] less than .003 percent of the total population. This sort of quantitative, ahistorical study erases, or, as Edward Said put it, "covers,"[8] a wide range of cultural and social facets of an Islam present in the very conception of a New World and the very pulse of this hemisphere ever since. The twelve historically and qualitatively grounded contributions to our volume reveal that these Americas are part of an Islamic world and that Muslims are integral to these Americas.

Our lens on Islam in Latin America, the Caribbean, and Latino USA endeavors to rethink the construction of "world areas" as well as the normative categorization between "minorities" and "majorities" in them. This introduction situates our book's aims in two corresponding bodies of scholarship: area and ethnic studies. In the remaining pages of this chapter, we first explore the ways that knowledge about these Americas and an Islamic world has been carved up and authorized in the United States since the early twentieth century to the present. Following the hemispheric turn in Latin American and Latino studies, we reconceptualize the study of these historically specific geographies based on their mutual intersection through what we call a Latino American architecture (or model) of a wider Islamic world. Our second goal here is to reframe the study of Muslim "minorities" in Spanish and Portuguese colonies and the nation-states that emerged from them. Such countries' mainstream histories, written as some Muslim migrants arrived in them during the late nineteenth and twentieth centuries, often claim a special relationship to Islam through the Iberian Peninsula. By situating Islamic difference within ethnic, national, and wider sociocultural dynamics, the goal is to show that while national and state powers often configured Islam in contradictory agendas, actual Muslims sought to forge their own identities, affinities, and detachments in multiple ways as well.

REMODELING AREA STUDIES: TOWARD A LATINO AMERICAN ARCHITECTURE OF AN ISLAMIC WORLD

How do we study the interface between "American" and "Islamic" spaces? Although identifying with history and the social sciences, we conceptualize such regional formations over any single (or multi-) disciplinary vision. Our purpose in doing so is to "disturb the disciplinary claim to universality and the particular place this assigns to areas," as critically observed by Timothy Mitchell.[9] In the past the intertwined spaces that we now explore were split up into more abstract categories by the US model of "area studies," which includes Africa, Latin America, the Middle East, South Asia, and Southeast Asia, among other spaces. Growing in the interwar years and becoming institutionalized during the next half century, these area studies naturalized what Arjun Appadurai criticized as "trait geographies,"[10] creating and disseminating knowledge about the world as a handful of discrete cultural territories with seemingly distinct, enduring features of human life. Rather than wholly dismissing the enterprise, Appadurai calls for a more processual approach. He proposes a "new architecture of area studies" that outlines "how others, in what we still take to be certain areas as we define them, see the rest of the world in regional terms."[11] From a Latino American subject position, what does an Islamic world, one that is more "global" than conventionally assumed, look like? Our work answers this question by building a "globalized Latino American" architecture of an Islamic world.[12]

We emphasize our commitment to area studies, though well aware of its trajectory "within the liberal culture of the US academy in the latter half of the twentieth century."[13] Since we return to this question of the past and present political stakes of area studies later on, suffice it to say that US academic and government authorities institutionalized the study of "world areas" in efforts to not only deprovincialize US postsecondary curricula but also to advance US "styles of learning."[14] Several specialists of the previously mentioned areas, in fact, delineated how Islam was to be studied. Anthropologist Clifford Geertz characterizes this approach in *Islam Observed*,[15] which compares religious meaning in Indonesia and Morocco. Approaching Southeast Asia and North Africa as two given parts of the world, Geertz not only "overidealized" the two Islamic-majority countries "through myriad contrasting pairs,"[16] but also privileged the "primacy of meaning without regard to the processes by which meanings are constructed."[17] In avoiding questions of power and knowledge, Geertz and other social scientists sought to build a universal understanding of religion by reducing the range of Islamic belief and practice to the making of meaning as well as by minimizing or ignoring the historically specific ties across a more expansive Islamic *umma*. The contributors to this volume move beyond these limitations through foregrounding the power-laden processes that construct Islam and the Americas in a broader Islamic world. In the three parts to this volume, we unevenly trace the forced, secretive, coerced, or voluntary migration of Muslims from Africa, Iberia, the Middle East, and South Asia into this hemisphere, as well as map the imagined and institutional ties cultivated between these Muslim Americas and Islamic-majority states.

As another testing ground for universal claims in the twentieth century, the area of Latin America served an array of US social scientific disciplines. It was most deeply marked by efforts to establish generalizable knowledge about "culture." Many Latin American or Caribbean intellectuals simultaneously sought to theorize and legitimize their own seemingly exceptional national cultures in terms of hybridity among African, Amerindian, or European peoples.[18] As shown later on, their definitions of "mixed" or "creole" cultures reserved a special place for Islam. Even though these key thinkers spent some time in the United States, area studies scholars based in the United States generally sidestepped their characterizations in order to build general theories of "culture," at least through World War II. For anthropologist Oscar Lewis, the study of Mexico or Puerto Rico fitted into his idea of a "culture of poverty."[19] Likewise, anthropologist Melville Herskovits studied Haiti, Trinidad, and Brazil to theorize cultural retention and change.[20] Although US academics held universalistic pretensions and their counterparts in the rest of the Americas staked more particular claims, these historical trajectories suggest that ideas of culture took shape across the continent. In structuring our volume through a more evenhanded hemispheric framework, part 1 of our volume situates Muslims in relation to Iberian or northern European colonial powers across the Americas, while parts 2 and 3, respectively, focus on their shifting positions within Latin America and the Caribbean as well as Latino USA.

Whether drawn from Latin American settings to conceptualize culture or the aforementioned North African and Southeast Asian contexts to theorize religion, these field-based studies were "integral to the larger attempt to create a sovereign structure of universal knowledge" in the United States.[21] Anthropologists, economists, political scientists, and others studied presumably discrete world areas in order to gather and construct ethnographic, historical, and demographic "data" that could be used to test and hypothesize comprehensive theories about culture, religion, or other facets of an allegedly universal human condition particular to the West and especially the United States. In this manner, the myriad forms of knowledge produced about allegedly distinct areas in the world served to universalize provincial US social sciences and, in turn, provide US government officials with the kinds of blanket categories needed to manage both domestic and foreign differences. As the contributors to this volume are social scientists and historians themselves, our point is not to rail against such disciplines but rather to map geographies that are more historically relevant to the actual persons and powers circulating to, from, and across them: these Americas and an Islamic world.

Of course, there is nothing really new or necessarily liberating about either area. At least since the nineteenth century, Latin American intellectuals—including Cuban writer and activist José Martí—critically reflected upon *nuestra América* (our America) in light of Iberian colonial legacies and US neocolonialism.[22] In contrast, contemporaneous US-based academics and statesmen spoke of the "American hemisphere" or inter-American relations with civilizing and modernizing pretensions.[23] Not unlike Martí, equally active and mobile Muslim intellectuals, such as Jamal al-Din al-Afghani, critically reflected upon the *ʿasabiyya* ("bonds" or "solidarity," in Arabic) of the *umma* as part of the wider struggle against European imperialism.[24] Yet again, European scholarly and colonial authorities framed a Muslim world within the long-standing conception of an Orient that should be ruled and represented by the West.[25] *América* and the *umma* thus not only serve as historically specific geographies for those who wrote about unifying and inhabiting them under foreign powers. Whether through North-South or East-West binaries, distinct imperial projects could also co-opt such imaginaries for their own cross-purposes. Though their content may shift depending on one's perspective, the model of "world areas" takes shape through competing and contradictory agendas.

Constituted by parallel histories in their encounters with different empires, knowledge production about these Americas and an Islamic world in the United States underwent dramatic change during the late twentieth and early twenty-first centuries. Although media and popular culture engaged in "Latino spin"[26] and the "good Muslim/bad Muslim" distinction,[27] academics thought about the making of peoples and regions in novel ways. Since the 1990s, Caribbean, Latin American, and US Latino scholars conceived of these Americas as a novel unit of analysis that highlights connections across the hemisphere.[28] Whether through circular migration,[29] Spanish-language media flows,[30] or overlapping US and Latin American border policies,[31] scholars combined analyses of persons, images, and ideas in movement with critiques of US power domestically and hemispherically. By focusing on transnational Muslim societies, anthropologists and historians likewise began to grasp the making of regional spaces that are not only marked by several imperial histories but also more meaningful for the actual Muslims who inhabit and move across them, including the Indian Ocean,[32] the Mashriq and the Mahjar,[33] as well as the Malay world.[34] As noted by Gayatri Spivak,[35] studying this vast "range and diversity of Islamic diaspora" helps "undo the politically monolithized view of Islam that rules the globe today." The three parts of *Crescent over Another Horizon* build on these contributions and insights by placing Latin America, the Caribbean, and Latino USA within a broader Islamic world and by locating Muslims of varied genealogies within this hemisphere over the longue durée.

What is at stake in this kind of area studies architecture, especially now, during the War on Terror? It must be remembered that the original model of area studies was institutionalized during the Cold War, but the knowledge it created was "not simply a reaction" to US desires to know purported threats, but rather advanced "the project of a globalized American modernity to which the Cold War also belonged."[36] As mentioned earlier, area studies helped to "nourish" the social science disciplines and "bring them in better touch with the 'real world.'"[37] In turn, social scientific theories of "culture, the state, the economy, or society" reinforced the US "liberal pluralist" style of governing domestic and foreign affairs.[38] But at the end of the Cold War, these objects of inquiry became harder to theorize in a given territory precisely at the time that the US style of governing seemed unrivaled in an allegedly "new world order." Consequently, in the 1990s many social scientists deemed area studies to be "the source of the trouble" and made repeated calls to dismantle such programs.[39] In the midst of this "so-called crisis of area studies," which was actually part of a wider "crisis . . . to delimit and legitimate a field of scholarship,"[40] scholars conceived of several "alternative" or "new" geographies, such as the Black Atlantic,[41] the Pacific Rim,[42] as well as several others mentioned earlier. Our volume is part of this current moment, and since history is messier for those living it, we are not sure whether this conjuncture signals the limits of a "globalized American modernity" or its insidious reach into realms heretofore unexplored. What we can say with greater certainty is that the main point of this volume—the long-standing past and present of Islam in this hemisphere, and this hemisphere in an Islamic world—challenges some of the most deeply held assumptions on the part of the liberal pluralist establishment today. But then again, as Vicente Rafael reminds us,[43] this kind of critique has been part of area studies since its very institutionalization.

ARE WE ALL MOORS? REFRAMING ISLAM IN LATINO AMERICA

Parallel to the historic way that area studies construed the United States as a "nonregional center" around which "all regions orbited," ethnic studies traditionally made whiteness "the unmarked center" against which knowledge about minorities was produced.[44] In studies of Muslims in the West,[45] scholars critically engaged with that center by calling attention to the making of "Muslim minorities" amid a usually implicit "non-Muslim majority." However, due to their focus on the North Atlantic, such categories themselves were not sufficiently problematized. This section aims to reframe the study of Muslims, non-Muslims, and their interplay through ethnic, national, and wider struggles. We ask what it means to be Muslim in Ibero-American nations whose ideologies and intellectual trends often uphold what Andrew Shryock,[46] in another context, called "Islamophilia," or the "generalized affection for Islam and Muslims . . . with its own political costs." Nineteenth- and twentieth-century Latin American and Caribbean intellectuals, as shown by Ella Shohat, selectively identified with Spanish or Portuguese "Moors" in writing anti-imperialist and nationalist narratives.[47] Here in this introductory chapter, we address the making of such narratives, but our wider concern is with the processes of ethnicity and nation making that encompass them.

Building on the insights of Fredrik Barth[48] and Thomas Eriksen,[49] we consider ethnicity as the construction and marking of boundaries between identities and groups through perceptions of cultural difference. These boundaries can be produced in interactions between Muslims and non-Muslims, or they can emerge among Muslims themselves, despite the fact that the Qur'an and hadith make limited passing references to what we would call ethnic or racial difference and rather emphasize religiosity as the key definition to belonging in the imagined community of the *umma*.[50] In certain cases Islam can be the cultural diacritic that defines the ethnic boundary, creating forms of Muslim ethnicity, as it could be argued about the *moriscos/mouriscos*, Iberian Muslims who were forcibly converted to Catholicism and their descendants, in the colonial Spanish and Portuguese Americas, or *malês* (a term used to refer to African Muslims) in nineteenth-century Brazil. Another fitting example of this ethnic configuration is Muslim community formation in Brazil from the late nineteenth century to the 1990s. During this time Muslims in Brazil were generally considered Arabs, and Islam was seen to be an ethnic religion by both Muslims and non-Muslims. However, after the last decade of the twentieth century, with the influx of immigrants and students from Africa and the conversion of non-Arab Brazilians, new ethnic categories emerged within Muslim communities, with "Arab," "African," and "Brazilian" being used to designate discrete groups of Muslims within the religious landscape of Islam in Brazil. As a relation between persons who see themselves as distinctive, and are regarded as such by persons of other groups with whom they interact, ethnicity is shaped by wider colonial, national, and transnational politics.

The shifting relation between Muslim identities and ethnicity can be traced through the plural histories of the Islamic presence in Latin America and the Caribbean. There are roughly three periods that express the continuities and discontinuities in the historical and cultural dynamics of Islam in the Americas. The first is the colonial period from the fifteenth to the nineteenth centuries, defined by the influx of Iberian *moriscos/mouriscos*, Muslim African slaves, and Javanese and Indian indentured workers to the Americas. During these centuries, it can be generally stated that Islam was an ethnic religion and, even, defined a discrete ethnic identity beyond the actual religious practices of the agents. The second period is linked to Middle Eastern migration to the Americas from the late nineteenth century to the early twenty-first century, which resulted in the creation of many of the Islamic institutions and community formations in Latin America and the Caribbean today. During this period, Islam was linked to Palestinian or Syrian-Lebanese immigrants and their descendants, being primarily seen as an ethnic religion. The most recent period began in the last decade of the twentieth century, with the growing conversion to Islam of non-Arabs in Latin America, the Caribbean, and Latino USA. These new Muslims reject the ethnic overtones that Muslim identities had acquired in the Americas, claiming and advancing a more universal definition and understanding of Islam. Nevertheless, new ethnic classifications appeared, not as markers of the boundaries between Muslim and non-Muslims, as was the case in the previous periods, but rather as indexes of the discrete histories and cultural identifications of the various groups that compose the *umma* in this part of the world.

These plural histories, which unfolded in multilingual and multiethnic societies that were heterogeneous themselves, created a wide range of understandings and ways of practicing and living Islam in the Americas. That is, Muslims in the Americas claim and strive to be part of the *umma*, but they do so in a variety of ways. Besides the steady stream of religious authorities and texts that move across, to, and from the Middle East, Africa, India, or Indonesia, the Internet is an increasingly influential source of religious knowledge and an arena for debating and affirming one's Muslim identity. The recent trend of having Muslims born in Brazil and Argentina trained as imams in the Middle East and then returning to lead communities back home will further the process of localizing Islamic religious authority in the Americas.

While immigrants and older Muslims in the Americas may use more Arabic as the linguistic context for acquiring religious knowledge, the newer generations are more prone to seek religious information in English on the Internet or debate the tenets of Islam and how to live them in the many Islamic forums in Spanish, Portuguese, or French, bringing global debates into a variety of local or national idioms. Particular issues, such as how to negotiate one's Muslim identity in a non-Muslim family context, connect with globalized aspects of Islam, such as the debate over the use of the *hijab*, creating processes of creolization[51] that reshape Islam in these Americas as well as include these Americas in an Islamic religious cartography.

Transnational religious practices, such as pilgrimage, also connect Muslim communities to global Islamic spaces, which have in Mecca a point of convergence. However, the practices of hajj vary enormously, creating a plurality of sacred geographies that ground the religious imagination of Muslims in these Americas. Immigrants and their descendants tend to go to Mecca through their ancestral homeland, such as Lebanon, Syria, or Palestine, and usually stay with pilgrims from these same countries during the hajj, renewing their multiple diasporic links. Converts to Islam tend to engage in similar detours to spiritual homelands, such as Turkey, Cyprus, or Algeria in the case of the Sufis, or to centers of religious knowledge, such as Cairo or Damascus. These converts incline toward transnational Islamic movements, such as the Jamʿat Tablighi, tracing other sacred geographies that connect Brazil or Argentina to South Africa, England, India, Pakistan, and Mecca. Finally, non-Sunni traditions in the Americas create sacred topographies with multiple centers through transnational religious practices. ʿAlawis from Brazil and Argentina regularly do pilgrimage to the tombs of holy men in Syria, while Brazilian

Shi'is have the holy cities of Iraq as the focal center for major pilgrimages during 'Ashura and Arba'in. The *umma* imagined, produced, and experienced through these Muslim religious practices in the Americas has a plurality of symbolic and spatial configurations.

Of course, Muslims were part of the socioeconomic, political, and cultural fabric of much of the Iberian Peninsula for nearly a millennium. In Spanish and Portuguese they were called *moros* and *mouros* (Moors) and in Arabic *al-andalusiyyun* (Andalusians). Their histories of coexistence, conflict, and blurring with Christians and Jews varied. However, after the fall of the caliphate of Córdoba in the early eleventh century, and in the emerging context of the European Crusades, Portuguese and Spanish Catholic rulers increasingly targeted Muslims of *Al-Andalus* as "enemies of the faith," in a process that culminated with the capitulations of the Nasrid emirate of Granada in 1492, the 1496 royal order of the Portuguese Crown that expelled Muslims who had not adopted Catholicism in the period of a year, the forced conversion of Muslims from 1500 to 1524, and the final expulsion of most Muslims from Spain to North Africa and elsewhere between 1609 and 1614.[52] In *We Are All Moors*, Anouar Majid explores the significance of this past for present-day Europe and the United States. He affirms that in a "symbolic or metaphorical sense . . . minorities living in the West after 1492 are descendants of the Moors."[53] His framing is our point of departure into a more literal exploration of the relationship between the Muslim presence in Iberia that Catholic crowns tried to purge from the peninsula and the "competing visions" of Islam that developed in the Americas.[54] Since the nineteenth century, romanticized versions of an Iberian Moorish heritage coexisted in popular and intellectual minds with less than welcoming attitudes toward Muslim and Arab migrants. The special place reserved for Islam in what came to be their anti-imperialist and nationalist agendas in Latino America represented only one of many possibilities for actual Muslims to create their own identities, affinities, or detachments. However, as pointed out in this introduction and shown in the following chapters, actual Muslims generally steered clear of such narratives, though their own configurations of Muslimness in Latino America occasionally reproduced ambiguous or derogatory representations of Islam together with ethnicized and sometimes positive views of the Moorish past or a Muslim world.

The starting points to understand these dynamics are the fifteenth-century battles that Catholic Spain led against Muslims as well as the sixteenth-century wars that it waged against Amerindians. Gibson finds little evidence that the Catholic kingdom's so-called reconquest of Muslim Iberia fed into the conquest of indigenous peoples in the Americas. He did, however, reveal that the Spanish military, crown, and church officials who were living at the time themselves debated the relationship between their colonization of the Old and New Worlds.[55] In his letter to the Spanish king Carlos V, for instance, the conquistador Fernando Cortés compared his victory over the province of Tlaxcala in Mexico in 1519 with the province of Granada that Fernando and Isabel took over in 1492. Many other soldiers likewise tended "to interpret their own conquest activities in Reconquista terms, as if the conquests were analogues or continuations of the wars against the Moors."[56] Other allegations that "would have made America too a part of the Reconquista" were refuted by none other than Bartolomé de las Casas. Gibson explains that "for Las Casas, it was imperative that America not be part of the Reconquista, that Indians never be confused with Moslems [*sic*]."[57] For sixteenth-century Spaniards, "Indians" who survived the wars of conquest could be converted into loyal Catholic subjects, while Muslims continued as "enemies of the faith." As Karoline P. Cook and John Tofik Karam show in their respective chapters, *moriscos*, actual Muslims from both Iberia and Africa, as well as anti-Islamic fears held by Iberian crowns helped to define and in turn were animated by imperial projects in the New World during the sixteenth and seventeenth centuries.

In the context of Enlightenment ideas about the progression of history as human and not divine, nineteenth-century Spanish intellectuals began to think about the Muslim peninsular past in unprecedented but distinct ways. Take, for example, José Antonio Conde's *Historia de la dominación de los árabes en España sacada de varios manuscritos y memorias arábigas* (The history of Arab domination in Spain taken from various Arabic manuscripts and memories).[58] As a liberal, Conde aimed to clarify the history of Muslim Spain between 711 and 1492 not from the perspective of "one party" but rather by comparing "both" sides. With opposite intentions, his conservative contemporaries in the Royal Academy of History formally approved *Reconquista* (Reconquest) "as a word in good standing."[59] Unknown to the Christian soldiers who fought Muslims in conflicts that had ended three centuries previously, the term "Reconquest" originated in the eighteenth century to refer to the alleged "recuperation" of land "taken" by Muslims. Whether undermining or defining Spain as "Catholic," both historical reconstructions of the Moorish past on the peninsula were imagined at a time when Iberian empires broke down in the Americas. In 1808 the very seat of the Portuguese empire was transferred to Brazil, and fourteen years later this former colony became an independent monarchy. Meanwhile, the Spanish Crown was inundated by two bloodier waves of rebellion that resulted in the formation of several independent republics by 1828. As Iberian rule was decisively challenged in the Americas, Spanish intellectuals wrote about its much longer past on the peninsula.

José Martí, the Cuban intellectual mentioned earlier, might not have appreciated this irony. After all, Spain not only held on to two Caribbean colonies, Cuba and Puerto Rico, but also expanded its colonization of North Africa through the second half of the nineteenth century. Martí was uniquely positioned to grasp these ongoing Spanish imperial designs. Born in mid-nineteenth-century Havana and exiled several times, Martí lived throughout the Americas and southern Europe. Shortly before his premature death in Cuba in 1895, he expressed solidarity with a mass uprising against Spanish rule in the region of Rif, present-day Morocco in North Africa. As noted by Hisham Aidi, Martí twice proclaimed "¡Seamos moros!" (Let us be Moors!) and reflected that "the revolt in the Rif . . . is not an isolated incident, but an outbreak of the change and realignment that have entered the world. Let us be Moors . . . we who will probably die by the hand of Spain."[60] In urging Cubans, and perhaps Puerto Ricans, to identify as "Moors," Martí made the connection among "oppressed people who will never cede to those who occupy it." Whereas his counterparts in Spain romanticized or vilified the Moorish past in their reconstructions of Spanish rule, the Cuban writer called for solidarity with present-day "Moors" who endured Spanish imperialism not only during his own lifetime but also for "four centuries" after their historic expulsion from the Iberian Peninsula to North Africa.

Just after Martí expressed this commonality with "Moors" in North Africa, Cuba gained independence in 1898, while Puerto Rico was colonized by the United States. Around this time migrants arrived from what are today Syria, Lebanon, and Palestine. Muslims represented up to 30 percent of Arabs settling in Cuba.[61] Especially in the early twentieth century, they "prayed at home," privately observed religious fasts and holidays such as "Ramadán Karim [*sic*]," "Eid-el-Kebir (la gran fiesta [*sic*])," as well as "Eid-el-Adha (fiesta del sacrificio [*sic*])," as well as quietly oversaw Islamic rites for newborns, newlyweds, and the deceased.[62] These early-twentieth-century Muslims were marked as *turco* (Turk), *sirio* (Syrian), or *árabe* (Arab), and their upward economic mobility furthered ethnic, and not necessarily religious, differentiation. This simultaneous downplaying of Islam in Arab difference and foregrounding of Islamophilia in anti-imperialist stances speak to the respective chapters of Luis Mesa Delmonte and Hjamil A. Martínez-Vázquez. Delmonte points out that today, Islam attracts not Arabs but rather Afro-Cuban and other converts, while the Cuban state selectively fosters diplomatic and commercial ties with Islamic counterparts. Martínez-Vázquez shows how Puerto Rican and Dominican converts in the United States emphasize their link to romanticized versions of Muslim Iberia and Africa. Blurring clear-cut divisions between "minority" and "majority" categories, Islam and Islamophilia among Caribbean subjects can be best conceptualized through ethnic, nationalist, and anti-imperialist politics.

Argentine elites sought to define their nation through an affective tie with Muslim Spain. For the century following its declaration of independence from the Spanish Crown in 1816, statesmen such as Domingo Sarmiento[63] and writers including Leopoldo Lugones[64] embarked upon separate projects to define Argentine identity. As demonstrated by Christina Civantos,[65] they did so through the cowboy-like figure of the gaucho who roamed the Argentine pampas. While Sarmiento likened gauchos to Arabs and Bedouins, Lugones, in a more celebratory tone, reflected upon the alleged Moorish descent of the gaucho himself.[66] Together, these works elevated the *gaucho moro* (gaucho Moor) as "that which is most Argentine."[67] The authors did so not only to distance Argentine national identity from former Spanish rulers. Most important, for *criollos* (Euro-Argentines), they also aimed to minimize the place of Amerindians, Africans, and others in the nascent nation. The connection that Sarmiento, Lugones, and other Euro-Argentines traced to Muslim Spain was thus employed to marginalize "darker," "non-European" Argentines and bolster elite efforts to "civilize" Argentina.

Civantos goes on to show how these exclusionary, orientalist politics of Argentine nationalism were taken up by two Arab Argentines, Ibrahim Hallar (of Muslim Lebanese descent) and Juan Yaser (of Christian Palestinian origins). Hallar and Yaser were part of the some 180,000 Arabs, Christian and Muslim, who settled in Argentina by 1929.[68] After World War II, Hallar and Yaser claimed the gaucho not only as a "national hero," but as the primordial, essential connection between Argentines and Arabs. This enabled them to stake "a central place in Argentine culture."[69] Hallar and Yasser empowered their ethnic claims to the nation by complying with the status quo that downplayed the indigenous and African background of the gaucho and that of Argentina itself. In counterdistinction to this narrow embrace of Argentine Islamophilia, however, Muslim migrants to Argentina before the end of World War I also debated Ottomanist, emergent nationalist, as well as colonialist forms of belonging to an ever-changing "homeland."[70] In this regard, Silvia Montenegro demonstrates that while Arab Muslims in Argentina similarly cultivated long-distance nationalist ties with Syrian or Arab homelands, non-Arab converts deepened their connection to Islam by studying in Saudi Arabia and Iran. Muslim affinities in the Southern Cone extend beyond national narratives idealizing Muslim Spain and reveal the ongoing (re)formulation of the ties between these Americas and a greater Islamic world.

José Vasconcelos, a highly influential Mexican statesman and writer in the first half of the twentieth century, likewise referenced Muslim Spain in his work *La Raza Cósmica*.[71] As a supporter of an uprising against Porfírio Díaz that turned into the Mexican revolution (1910–1920), Vasconcelos's essay proclaimed the rise of a "cosmic race" centered around the mestizo, or mixed subject, who traced his or her lineage to both Amerindians and Iberians (as well as potentially other peoples). In this *mestizaje* (mixture), however, Vasconcelos expressed ambivalence about the contribution of Spain as a once great empire and a debilitated power in Mexico. As part of this empowerment and abjection, Vasconcelos mentioned that the "Castilian blood" of Spain possesses "Arabian melancholy, as a reminder of the sickly Muslim sensuality. Who has not a little of all this, or does not wish to have all?"[72] Much later, Octávio Paz attributed a more felicitous phrase to Vasconcelos: "We are the prodigal sons of a homeland which we cannot even define but which we are beginning at last to observe. She is Castilian and Moorish, with Aztec markings."[73] Whether ambivalent or hopeful of the Moorish legacy, this ideologue of *mestizaje* included it in the Mexican nationalist narrative.

Arab Muslims settled in Mexico since the start of Porfírio Díaz's rule, but they did not claim a place in this "mixture" and elites did not distinguish them through an Islamophilic lens. Although Christian counterparts vastly outnumbered Muslims,[74] Middle Easterners were ethnicized as *turcos* (Turks), and the extensive economic networks they developed underlay such differentiation, "independent of the religion practiced."[75] As illustrated by Theresa Alfaro-Velcamp,[76] Middle Easterners used ethnic ties with one another to supply "various revolutionary factions" during the 1910s and, in turn, became xenophobic targets. Although Christian Lebanese responded to such exclusion with a "discourse that largely excluded Arabs, Muslims, and Druzes,"[77] everyday Mexicans associated Middle Easterners, whether Christian or Muslim, with economic and social power. This "distinction" of being Muslim, as shown by Camila Pastor de Maria y Campos in her chapter, draws non–Middle Easterners to convert to Islam as a way to maneuver around their subordination in postcolonial Mexican hierarchies.

Perhaps more than any of his contemporaries, Brazilian writer and essayist Gilberto Freyre most explicitly reimagined a special relationship with Moors. As the key work constructing national identity in twentieth-century Brazil, his *Casa-grande e senzala* was published as a sociohistorical study, but it became a "founding fiction" for the nation.[78] Not unlike his counterparts across Latin America, Freyre endeavored to study the formation of Brazil out of three peoples, Africans, Amerindians, and Europeans. But the Portuguese colonizer, for Freyre, was different from other northern European settlers, not only because Portugal served "as a kind of bi-continentality between Europe and Africa," but also due to the Moorish imprint on Iberia that shaped the Portuguese colonization of Brazil.[79] For Freyre, Portuguese men's interactions with Moorish women on the Iberian Peninsula fueled their desire for and miscegenation with enslaved women of color in colonial Brazil. According to Freyre, Moorish Iberia predisposed Portuguese men to mix with African, Indian, and dark-skinned women, resulting in a mixed Brazilian society that supposedly "balanced racial antagonisms."[80] Freyre's celebration of mixture (*mescla* or *mistura*) and racial democracy (*democracia racial*) came to serve as tenets of twentieth-century Brazilian nationalism. However, despite his positive portrait of the Moors, Freyre wrote harshly about Islam and its influence on the African slaves.

These negative images of Islam were informed by the Brazilian state's repression of African Muslims that intensified after the 1835 slave rebellion.[81] They could also be found among twentieth-century Brazilian elites who questioned the belonging of Arab Muslims suspected of avoiding mixture by "marrying among themselves."[82] Although African Muslims were forced to hide their religious practices in the nineteenth century, their Arab counterparts, especially in the first half of the twentieth century, founded many charity groups, including the Associação Druza Beneficente in Minas Gerais in 1929, Sociedade Beneficente Muçulmana de São Paulo in 1929, Sociedade Beneficente Muçulmana Alauíta in Rio de Janeiro in 1931, and Sociedade Muçulmana Beneficente Muçulmana do Rio de Janeiro in 1951.[83] Rather than imagine themselves in the Freyrian narrative, Arab Muslims participated as active agents in emergent civil society and sometimes "ethnicized" Islam as an "Arab religion."[84] Building on his earlier work, Paulo G. Pinto's chapter explores the relationship between Arab ethnicity and Muslim identity in these local, national, and transnational dimensions.

Though heretofore focused on Iberian colonial projects and legacies in the Americas, this introductory chapter's aim to shift the study of Muslims and their images from minority or majority categories toward ethnic, national, as well as wider struggles is relevant to Caribbean spaces marked by British, Dutch, and French powers as well. We agree with John Voll when he states that "the case of Muslims in the Caribbean region is a strong reminder that minority . . . identities may have many different dimensions and are not simply monolithic."[85] His reflection that Muslims in the Caribbean "may *not* be 'Muslim minorities'" must be taken seriously. Are Muslims there necessarily drawn to "pan-Islamic" associations? Likewise, are Islamic traditions significant only to Muslims themselves? In Suriname's ethnic politics, for instance, Muslims of Indian and Javanese origins steer clear of "common Islamic programmes and institutions."[86] Yet in the self-defined Creole nation of Trinidad, the Hosay tradition that began with the South Asian Shiʿi observance of Mu-harram now appeals to Afro-Trinidadians and non-Muslim South Asians too.[87] Muslims in the Caribbean may not be minorities in the European or US American sense, but they certainly are situated within ethnic, national, and wider politics. In such ways, the chapter by Ellen Bal and Kathinka Sinha-Kerkhoff as well as that of Halima-Saʿadia Kassim, respectively, address the historical and current trajectories of Muslim South Asians from subverting partition in Suriname to their use of social media today in Trinidad. Liliane Kuczynski's chapter, based in Martinique, likewise inquires into the making of Islam among believers from different parts of the world through the island's own plurality.

Attending to these ethnic, national, and transnational politics widens our understanding of Muslim identity negotiations and practices in Latino USA as well. When he explained his own reversion to Islam some time ago, Ibrahim Gonzalez, a Puerto Rican in the Bronx and cofounder of the Alianza Islámica, called attention to the aforementioned Muslim Atlantic histories: "I was in-spired by the history of Andalusia, the kingdoms of Muslim Spain, and our African ancestry also has elements of Islam—the Wolof [Jolof] and Fulani brought the faith."[88] Not long after the first attack on the World Trade Center in 1994, however, Gonzalez was paid a visit by Federal Bureau of Investigation (FBI) agents, who were "looking for terrorists." His experience speaks to the paradox between a growing number of Muslims in this Latino America—well aware of their long history here—and an increasingly repressive governmental apparatus that erases such a history in order to construe them as threats. On the one hand, conversion to Islam, or what believers consider to be a return, and hence a reversion to the rightful faith, gained momentum in the late twentieth century and continues today. On the other hand, the same period witnessed the increased targeting of Islamic institutions and individuals by counterterrorist modes of surveillance. Yesenia King and Michael P. Perez chart how Latina converts to Islam navigate this and other marginalities, not only the gender and racial politics of US society, but also the ethnic hierarchies maintained by Arab and South Asian Muslims. Reframing these ethnically diverse Muslims in Miami from the 1970s to the post-9/11 era, Mirsad Krijes-torac's chapter asks what it means to be Muslim in a Latino-majority city, re-vealing the blurred categories of "minority" and "majority" in these Americas.

THE LAYOUT OF *CRESCENT OVER ANOTHER HORIZON*

The volume's twelve chapters are divided into three main parts: part 1, "Re-considering History"; part 2, "Contemporary Cartographies"; and part 3,

"Islam Latina/o." Focusing on varied imperial histories, the three chapters in part 1 explore *moriscos* under Spanish rule in the New World, West African Muslims challenging or enduring multiple empires, as well as Muslim South Asian laborers mobilizing in Dutch-controlled Suriname. The six chapters in part 2 attend to the late-twentieth- and early-twenty-first-century Muslim presence through case studies on Arab identity politics amid plural Islamic community configurations in Argentina and Brazil, South Asian Internet use in Trinidad and Tobago, conversion in Cuba during the crisis of the 1990s, as well as the multiethnic relations among Muslim migrants and converts in Martinique and Mexico. The three chapters in part 3 reveal not only the emergence of an Islam Latina/o among Puerto Ricans, Dominicans, Mexicans, and others in major US cities from the East to the West Coasts but, equally as important, the making of Islam among ethnically diverse subjects in the Latino city of Miami in South Florida.

NOTES

1. Karoline Cook, "Forbidden Crossings: Morisco Emigration to Spanish America, 1492–1650" (PhD diss., Princeton University, 2008), 69.

2. Moustafa Bayoumi, "Moving Beliefs: The Panama Manuscript of Sheikh Sana See and African Diasporic Islam," *Interventions* 5, no. 1 (2003): 70; Bryan Edwards, *The History, Civil and Commercial, of the British Colonies in the West Indies* (London: Printed for Crosby and Letterman, 1799), John Carter Brown Library, 4:61, http://www.archive.org/details/historycivilcommo6edwa.

3. Raymond S. Chickrie, "Muslims in Suriname: Facing Triumphs and Challenges in a Plural Society," *Journal of Muslim Minority Affairs* 31, no. 1 (2011): 84, 93; Muhammed Abdulah al-Ahari, "The Caribbean and Latin America," in *Islam Outside the Arab World*, edited by Ingvar Svanberg and David Westerlund (New York: Routledge, 1999), 443–461.

4. María del Mar Logroño Narbona, "The Development of Nationalist Identities in French Syria and Lebanon: A Transnational Dialogue with Arab Immigrants to Argentina and Brazil, 1915–1929" (PhD diss., University of California, Santa Barbara, 2007); Paulo Gabriel Hilu da Rocha Pinto, *Árabes no Rio de Janeiro: Uma identidade plural* (Rio de Janeiro: Cidade Viva Editora, 2010).

5. "Latinos" will be henceforth used to stand for "Latinas/os."

6. Zidane Zeraoui, ed., *El Islam en América Latina* (Monterrey: Editorial Limusa, 2010). See also Raymond Delval, *Les musulmans en Amérique latine et aux Caraibes* (Paris: Dominique Guéniot, 1992).

7. Pew Research Center, *Mapping the Global Muslim Population: A Report on the Size and Distribution of the World's Muslim Population* (Washington, DC: Pew Forum on Religion and Public Life, 2009), 32–33.

8. Edward Said, *Covering Islam* (New York: Pantheon Books, 1981).

9. Timothy Mitchell, "The Middle East in the Past and Future of Social Science," in *The Politics of Knowledge: Area Studies and the Disciplines*, edited by David Szanton (Berkeley: University of California Press, 2004), 98.

10. Arjun Appadurai, "Grassroots Globalization and the Research Imagination," in *Globalization*, edited by Arjun Appadurai (Durham, NC: Duke University Press, 2001), 7.

11. Ibid., 8.

12. Juan Poblete, ed., *Critical Latin American and Latino Studies* (Minneapolis: University of Minnesota Press, 2003), xxxiii.

13. Vicente Rafael, "The Cultures of Area Studies in the United States," *Social Text* 41 (1994): 92.

14. Ibid.; David Szanton, "The Origin, Nature, and Challenges of Area Studies in the United States," in *Politics of Knowledge*, edited by Szanton, 1–33.

15. Clifford Geertz, *Islam Observed: Religious Development in Morocco and Indonesia* (Chicago: University of Chicago Press, 1968).

16. Daniel Martin Varisco, *Islam Obscured: The Rhetoric of Anthropological Representation* (New York: Palgrave-Macmillan, 2005), 30–31.

17. Talal Asad, *Genealogies of Religion: Discipline and Reasons of Power in Christianity and Islam* (Baltimore: Johns Hopkins University Press, 1993), 43.

18. Gilberto Freyre, *Casa-grande e Senzala* (1933; reprint, Rio de Janeiro: José Olympio Editora, 1977); C. L. R. James, *The Case for West-Indian Self-Government* (London: Hogarth Press, 1933); Leopoldo Lugones, *El Payador* (1916; reprint, Buenos Aires: Stock Cero, 2004); José Vasconcelos, *La Raza Cósmica* (1925; reprint, Baltimore: Johns Hopkins University Press, 1997).

19. Oscar Lewis, *The Children of Sanchez: Autobiography of a Mexican Family* (1961; reprint, New York: Vintage Books, 2011); Oscar Lewis, *La Vida: A Puerto Rican Family in the Culture of Poverty—San Juan and New York* (New York: Random House, 1966); Susan Rigdon, *The Culture Façade: Art, Science, and Politics in the Work of Oscar Lewis* (Urbana: University of Illinois Press, 1988).

20. Jerry Gershenhorn, *Melville J. Herskovits and the Racial Politics of Knowledge* (Lincoln: University of Nebraska, 2004); Melville Herskovits, *Trinidad Village* (New York: Alfred A. Knopf, 1947); Melville Herskovits, *The Myth of the Negro Past* (Boston: Beacon Press, 1941); Melville Herskovits, *Life in a Haitian Valley* (New York: Alfred A. Knopf, 1937).

21. Mitchell, "Middle East in the Past," 86.

22. Jeffrey Belnap and Raúl Fernández, eds., *José Martí's "Our America": From National to Hemispheric Cultural Studies* (Durham, NC: Duke University Press, 1998); Camilla Fojas, *Cosmopolitanism in the Americas* (Bloomington: Indiana University Press, 2005).

23. Thomas O'Brien, *Making the Americas: The United States and Latin America from the Age of Revolutions to the Era of Globalization* (Albuquerque: University of New Mexico Press, 2007).

24. John Esposito, *The Islamic Threat: Myth or Reality?* (New York: Oxford University Press, 1999); Nikki Keddie, *An Islamic Response to Imperialism: Political and Religious Writings of Sayyid Jamal ad-Din "al-Afghani"* (1968; reprint, Berkeley: University of California Press, 1983).

25. Edward Said, *Orientalism* (New York: Pantheon Books, 1978).

26. Arlene Dávila, *Latino Spin: Public Image and the Whitewashing of Race* (New York: New York University Press, 2008).

27. Mahmood Mamdani, *Good Muslim, Bad Muslim: America, the Cold War, and the Roots of Terror* (New York: Pantheon Books, 2004).

28. Pedro Cabán, "The New Synthesis of Latin American/Latino Studies," in *Borderless Borders: U.S. Latinos, Latin Americans, and the Paradox of Interdependence*, edited by Frank

Bonilla et al. (Philadelphia: Temple University Press, 1998); Juan Flores and Renato Rosaldo, eds., *A Companion to Latina/o Studies* (New York: Blackwell, 2007); Juan Flores and George Yúdice, "Living Borders/Buscando America: Languages of Latina/o Self-Formation," *Social Text* 24 (1990): 57–84; Alberto Moreiras, "A Storm Blowing from Paradise: Negative Globality and Critical Regionalism," in *The Latin American Subaltern Studies Reader*, edited by Ileana Rodríguez (Durham, NC: Duke University Press, 2001); José David Saldívar, *The Dialectics of Our America: Geneaology, Cultural Critique, and Literary History* (Durham, NC: Duke University Press, 1991).

29. Jorge Duany, *The Puerto Rican Nation on the Move: Identities on the Island and in the United States* (Chapel Hill: University of North Carolina Press, 2001).

30. Elizabeth Fox and Silvio Waisbord, *Latin Politics, Global Media* (Austin: University of Texas Press, 2002).

31. Saskia Sassen, "The Transnationalization of Immigration Policy," in *Borderless Borders*, edited by Bonilla et al.

32. Engseng Ho, "Empire through Diasporic Eyes," *Comparative Studies in Society and History* 4 (2004): 210–235; Engseng Ho, *The Graves of Tarim: Genealogy and Mobility across the Indian Ocean* (Berkeley: University of California Press, 2006).

33. Andrew Arsan, Akram Khater, and John Tofik Karam, "Editorial Foreword," *Mashriq & Mahjar: Journal of Middle East Migration Studies* 1, no. 1 (2013): 1–7. This essay introduced the inaugural issue of the peer-reviewed journal, which can be found at http://faculty.chass.ncsu.edu/akhater/Mashriq/index.html.

34. Joel Kahn, *Other Malays: Nationalism and Cosmopolitanism in the Modern Malay World* (Singapore: Singapore University Press, 2006).

35. Gayatri Chakravorty Spivak, *Death of a Discipline* (New York: Columbia University Press, 2003), 87.

36. Mitchell, "Middle East in the Past," 86.

37. Rafael, "Cultures of Area Studies," 95.

38. Mitchell, "Middle East in the Past," 99; Rafael, "Cultures of Area Studies," 91.

39. Mitchell, "Middle East in the Past," 98.

40. Ibid., 86–87.

41. Paul Gilroy, *The Black Atlantic: Modernity and Double Consciousness* (London: Verso, 1993); Jacqueline Brown, "Black Liverpool, Black America, and the Gendering of Diasporic Space," *Cultural Anthropology* 13, no. 3 (1998): 291–335.

42. Arif Dirlik, *What Is in a Rim? Critical Perspectives on the Pacific Region Idea* (Boston: Rowman and Littlefield, 1998).

43. Rafael, "Cultures of Area Studies," 91.

44. Poblete, *Critical Latin American and Latino Studies*, xii.

45. Akbar Ahmed and Hastings Donnan, eds., *Islam, Globalization, and Postmodernity* (New York: Routledge, 1994); Yvonne Yazbeck Haddad, ed., *Muslims in the West: From Sojourners to Citizens* (New York: Oxford University Press, 2002); Yvonne Yazbeck Haddad and Jane Smith, eds., *Muslim Minorities in the West: Visible and Invisible* (Boston: Rowman and Littlefield, 2002); Barbara Daly Metcalf, ed., *Making Muslim Space in North America and Europe* (Berkeley: University of California Press, 1996); Olivier Roy, *Globalized Islam: The Search for a New Umma* (New York: Columbia University Press, 2004).

46. Andrew Shryock, "Introduction: Islam as an Object of Fear and Affection," in *Islamophobia/Islamophilia: Beyond the Politics of Enemy and Friend*, edited by Andrew Shryock (Bloomington: Indiana University Press, 2010), 9.

47. Ella Shohat, "The Sephardi-Moorish Atlantic: Between Orientalism and Occidentalism," in *Between the Middle East and the Americas: The Cultural Politics of Diaspora*, edited by Evelyn Alsultany and Ella Shohat (Ann Arbor: University of Michigan Press, 2013), 54. See also Freyre, *Casa-grande e Senzala*; James, *Case for West-Indian Self-Government*; Lugones, *El Payador*; and Vasconcelos, *La Raza Cósmica*.

48. Fredrik Barth, introduction to *Ethnic Groups and Boundaries*, edited by Fredrik Barth (Prospect Heights, IL: Waveland Press, 1998).

49. Thomas Eriksen, *Common Denominators: Ethnicity, Nation-Building and Compromise in Mauritius* (Oxford: Berg, 1998).

50. James Jankowski, "Ethnicity and Race: Islamic Views," in *New Dictionary of the History of Ideas*, edited by Maryanne Cline Horowitz (New York: Charles Scribner's Sons, 2005), vol. 6.

51. Ulf Hannerz, *Transnational Connections: Culture, People, Places* (London: Routledge, 1996).

52. L. P. Harvey, *Muslims in Spain, 1500–1614* (Chicago: University of Chicago Press, 2005).

53. Anouar Majid, *We Are All Moors: Ending Centuries of Crusades against Muslims and Other Minorities* (Minnesota: University of Minneapolis Press, 2009), 5.

54. Kambiz GhaneaBassiri, *Competing Visions of Islam in America: A Study of Los Angeles* (Westport, CT: Greenwood Press, 1997).

55. Charles Gibson, "Reconquista and Conquista," in *Homage to Irving A. Leonard* (East Lansing: Latin American Studies Center at Michigan State University, 1977), 19–28.

56. Ibid., 19.

57. Ibid., 26.

58. José Antonio Conde, *Historia de la dominación de los árabes en España sacada de varios manuscritos y memorias arábigas* (Barcelona: Imprenta de D. Juan Oliveres, 1844), vols. 1–3.

59. Gibson, "Reconquista and Conquista," 21.

60. Cited by Hishaam Aidi, "Let Us Be Moors: Race, Islam, and 'Connected Histories,'" *MERIP: Middle East Report* 229 (2003): 42–43.

61. Rigoberto Menéndez Paredes, *Los árabes en Cuba* (Havana: Publicaciones de la Oficina del Historiador de la Ciudad, 2007), 113.

62. Ibid., 115–116.

63. Domingo Faustino Sarmiento, *Facundo: Civilization and Barbarism* (1845; reprint, Berkeley: University of California Press, 2004).

64. Lugones, *El Payador*.

65. Cristina Civantos, *Between Argentines and Arabs: Argentine Orientalism, Arab Immigrants and the Writing of Identity* (Albany: State University of New York Press, 2006).

66. Ibid., 55, 59.

67. Ibid., 21.

68. Logroño Narbona, "Development of Nationalist Identities," 16; Silvia Montenegro, "Panorama sobre la inmigración árabe en Argentina," in *Los árabes en América Latina: Historia de una emigración*, edited by Abdeluahed Akmir (Madrid: Siglo XXI, 2009), 71–72.

69. Civantos, *Between Argentines and Arabs*, 68.

70. Steven Hyland Jr., "'Arisen from Deep Slumber': Transnational Politics and Competing Nationalisms among Syrian Immigrants in Argentina, 1920–1922," *Journal of Latin American Studies* 43 (2011): 547–574.

71. Vasconcelos, *La Raza Cósmica*, 62.

72. Ibid.

73. Octávio Paz, *The Labyrinth of Solitude* (1951; reprint, New York: Grove Press, 1985), 153.

74. Theresa Alfaro-Velcamp, "Mexican Muslims in the Twentieth Century: Challenging Stereotypes and Negotiating Space," in *Muslims in the West*, edited by Haddad, 278; Zidane Zeraoui, "La inmigración árabe en México: Integración nacional e identidad comunitaria," in *Contra Relatos desde el Sur: Apuntes sobre África y Medio Oriente* (Córdoba, Argentina: CLACSO, 2006), 25–26.

75. Zeraoui, "La inmigración árabe," 26.

76. Theresa Alfaro-Velcamp, *So Far from Allah, So Close to Mexico: Middle Eastern Immigrants in Modern Mexico* (Austin: University of Texas Press, 2007), 70, 79–81, 109.

77. Alfaro-Velcamp, *So Far from Allah*, 133.

78. Freyre, *Casa-grande e Senzala*.

79. Ibid., 12–13, 214–216, 223–225.

80. Ibid., 126.

81. João Jose Reis, Flávio dos Santos Gomes, and Marcus J. M. de Carvalho, *O Alufá Rufino: Tráfico, escravidão e liberdade no Atlântico negro* (São Paulo: Companhia Das Letras, 2010); João José Reis, *Slave Rebellion in Brazil: The Muslim Uprising of 1835 in Bahia* (Baltimore: Johns Hopkins University Press, 1993).

82. John Tofik Karam, *Another Arabesque: Syrian-Lebanese Ethnicity in Neoliberal Brazil* (Philadelphia: Temple University Press, 2007).

83. John Tofik Karam, "Historias musulmanas en América Latina y el Caribe," *Istor: Revista de Historia Internacional* 12, no. 45 (2011): 34; Pinto, *Árabes no Rio de Janeiro*, 115, 119.

84. Paulo Gabriel Hilu da Rocha Pinto, "Ritual, etnicidade e identidade religiosa nas comunidades muçulmanas no Brasil," *Revista da USP* 67 (2005): 235–236.

85. John Voll, "Muslims in the Caribbean: Ethnic Sojourners and Citizens," in *Muslim Minorities in the West*, edited by Haddad and Smith, 265.

86. Ellen Bal and Kathinka Sinha-Kerkhoff, "Separated by the Partition? Muslims of British Indian Descent in Mauritius and Suriname," in *Global Indian Diasporas: Exploring Trajectories of Migration and Theory*, edited by Gijsbert Oon (Amsterdam: Amsterdam University Press, 2007), 135.

87. Frank Korom, *Hosay Trinidad: Muharram Performances in an Indo-Caribbean Diaspora* (Philadelphia: University of Pennsylvania Press, 2003); Gustav Thaiss, "Contested Meanings and the Politics of Authenticity," in *Islam, Globalization, and Postmodernity*, edited by Akbar Ahmed and Hastings Donnan (New York: Routledge, 1994).

88. Bill Weinberg, "Muslims in the Americas Face Scrutiny," *NACLA Report on the Americas* (May–June 2005): 25.

PART I

RECONSIDERING HISTORY

CHAPTER 1

"DE LOS PROHIBIDOS": MUSLIMS AND MORISCOS IN COLONIAL SPANISH AMERICA

KAROLINE P. COOK

FROM THE FIRST VOYAGES to conquer and settle the New World, Spanish authorities prohibited Muslims, converts from Islam (known as Moriscos), and their descendants from emigrating to the Americas. The Crown issued a series of royal decrees restricting the overseas travel of both free and enslaved Muslims and Moriscos. Moriscos constituted a diverse category—Spanish Muslims who had been forcibly converted to Catholicism as well as voluntary converts and North African Muslims, many of whom had been taken captive in the Mediterranean and were baptized before being compelled to labor on the galleys or in households in Spain.[1] In spite of the legislation prohibiting Muslims and Moriscos in Spanish America, a number of individuals were able to make the journey overseas and forge new lives thousands of miles across the Atlantic. Their presence in Spanish America points to the need to examine more closely the interconnectedness of Iberian Atlantic and Mediterranean worlds during the early modern period, specifically how peninsular experiences with Islam and the Moriscos influenced the creation of colonial ethnic and legal categories. Considering Morisco emigrants, whose presence is rendered visible through litigation, can also raise new questions for the study of colonial society by showing how they negotiated their status and identities in a land in which they were officially nonexistent.

During the sixteenth and early seventeenth centuries, Spanish authorities' anxieties about Muslims and Moriscos ran deep, prompting extensive legislation aimed at prohibiting their contact with indigenous peoples. This was a time when Spaniards were actively debating what membership in the Spanish nation meant and a time when their empire was rapidly expanding and incorporating new types of peoples into its administrative and judicial structure. Spaniards were increasingly defining their nation and empire as Catholic, whose global preeminence was supported by papal authority, and Moriscos threatened the stability of these definitions. Commentators increasingly raised questions about the Moriscos' religious and political loyalty, raising fears that they would act as a fifth column in Spain by forming alliances with Ottomans or French Protestants. Theologians such as Jaime Bleda and Pedro Aznar Cardona crafted increasingly racialized arguments that sought to excise Moriscos from the body politic. Royal officials also expressed concern that in the Americas, Morisco interaction with indigenous peoples could provide a dangerous alternative to the idealized Hispanized Catholic lifestyle they intended to promote—a model they associated with Islam and by extension rebelliousness and disloyalty to the nation. In this atmosphere of increasing tension, many peninsular Moriscos turned to the courts to claim status as "good and faithful Christians" and, in Spanish America, as loyal subjects who performed valuable services to the Crown during the conquests.

This chapter examines the movement of Moriscos to Spanish America during the sixteenth and seventeenth centuries and demonstrates that despite repeated legislation restricting their presence, they had a number of means at their disposal to emigrate. This chapter also analyzes the extension of peninsular anxieties about Muslims and Moriscos to the Americas and their impact on local communities, as individuals denounced their neighbors before the secular, ecclesiastical, and inquisitorial courts in disputes over status. Finally, it explores cases of Moriscos' experiences of religiosity in the Americas, through the testimonies of individuals who struggled with their faith, caught between Islam and Catholicism.

BRIEF PENINSULAR BACKGROUND

Despite the long history of coexistence among Christians, Muslims, and Jews in medieval Iberia, by the end of the fifteenth century, attitudes were beginning to harden, as evidenced in the decrees of expulsion of Jews in 1492 and the conquest of the Muslim kingdom of Granada in that same year. Treaties negotiated between the Catholic monarchs and the Granadan sultan allowed for Granadan Muslims to maintain their religious and cultural practices and local forms of governance. However, by 1500 campaigns to convert the Granadans to Catholicism that targeted specifically previous Christian converts to Islam led to a rebellion on the part of locals, who felt this violated the surrender treaties. After this first Alpujarras uprising was suppressed, the Granadan Muslim population was forced to choose between baptism and exile. Many remained in Granada and became known as Moriscos, thereby acquiring a new legal status as Christians who were subject to ecclesiastical discipline, including inquisitorial surveillance. Other parts of Spain had different histories. In Castile Muslims had been living alongside Christians for centuries, and many had converted to Christianity voluntarily. They were also labeled Moriscos, but fell under less suspicion and scrutiny than the Granadinos, and by the late sixteenth century they began to petition for old Christian status, as "de los antiguos."[2] By law, however, all Moriscos were subject to the same regulations that became more restrictive during the sixteenth century. This tendency was related to Spain's attempts to cast itself as a more Catholic nation, its changing relations with the Ottoman Empire, and its contested relationship with the Moriscos living along the Mediterranean coast who authorities feared would ally with the Turks.

Spanish policies toward emigration during the sixteenth and seventeenth centuries loosely followed these peninsular dynamics. With the conquest of Granada in 1492 and the expulsion of the Jews, Ferdinand and Isabel were eager to cast themselves as Catholic monarchs and negotiated treatises with the papacy in their ongoing competition with Portugal over access to Atlantic trade routes. The papal bull *Inter Caetera* (1493) recognized their role as exemplary bearers of Christianity as conquerors of Granada and made their title to the lands west and south of the Azores and Cape Verde Islands conditional on the evangelization of the peoples they encountered.[3] Because these bulls made Spanish dominion over American lands contingent upon the conversion of indigenous peoples, royal policies continued to emphasize populating the lands with settlers who would facilitate missionary efforts. Emigrants were required to obtain official licenses from the Casa de Contratación (House of Trade) in Seville, in which witnesses testified to their status as old Christians whose actions and reputation were considered irreproachable.

The earliest decrees regulating emigration to the Spanish Americas were issued by the Crown in 1501, in the instructions to Friar Nicolás de Ovando, who was sent as governor to Hispaniola. These instructions stipulated: "As we with great care have to carry out the conversion of the Indians to our holy Catholic faith: if you find persons suspect in matters of the faith present . . . it could create an impediment. Do not . . . allow Muslims or Jews, heretics, anyone reconciled by the Inquisition, or persons newly converted to our Faith to go there."[4] These restrictions were echoed in the *cédulas* (royal decrees) that regulated the colonization and settlement of the Spanish territories. In 1508 King Ferdinand ordered the Casa de Contratación to forbid the "children and grandchildren of the converts of Jews and Muslims, or the children of those executed or reconciled by the Inquisition," from traveling to or trading on the island of Hispaniola.[5] Orders for the settlement of Florida and Bimini issued by Queen Juana in 1514 specified that "new Christians [who are descendants] of Muslims and Jews can neither populate nor reside in the said islands under penalty of the loss of their goods."[6] Although complaints concerning a shortage of Spanish settlers proliferated in the newly conquered regions, the Crown maintained officially that only old Christians could settle in the Americas.

Despite an official preoccupation with both emigrants' lineage as old Christians and their public reputations for piety, these requirements were often overlooked in practice during the early years of colonization. Due to their perceived skills as artisans and interpreters, Moriscos and North African Muslims were sought out in early projects in Spanish America. Granada was well known for its silk industry during the sixteenth century, and Morisco men and women were highly skilled in trades involving silk production.[7] In 1537 Friar Juan de Zumárraga, bishop of New Spain, requested that a group of Moriscos be brought to New Spain to teach indigenous peoples the delicate art of raising silkworms on a diet of mulberry leaves from trees imported from Granada and harvesting and spinning silk from their cocoons.[8] Zumárraga hoped sericulture would provide both a civilizing activity and a source of income for the indigenous peoples congregated in the newly founded mission communities.[9] While the Crown rejected Zumárraga's proposal, others were more successful in bringing Moriscos and Muslims to work as interpreters or laborers on the construction of forts in the Caribbean.[10] Moriscos and North African Muslims also arrived as slaves, with limitations specified in their licenses on the number of years they could remain in Spanish America. Cases brought before the court at the Casa de Contratación reveal that slaveholders did not always send their slaves back to Spain within the stipulated period and were subject to penalties even if they claimed their slaves had run away and they could no longer be held accountable for them. During the 1530s a few of these Moriscos learned indigenous languages and served in New Spain as interpreters (*naguatatos*) for prominent officials such as Viceroy Antonio de Mendoza. The *naguatatos* gained some degree of authority in colonial society before they also found themselves involved in disputes. In the 1546–1547 official inspection of Viceroy Mendoza's term of office, three interpreters who served under him were cast as men who "live more like Muslims than Christians" and whose cohabitation with indigenous peoples and "scandalous" deeds rendered them untrustworthy, dishonorable, and potentially treacherous.[11] The language that shaped these accusations, and the assumptions it carried, was echoed in later disputes involving suspected Moriscos in Spanish America. Restrictions on emigration generally appear to have been less carefully observed prior to Philip II's reign, and some fortunate Moriscos accompanied expeditions of conquest and acquired *encomiendas*, or grants of indigenous tributaries.[12]

Attitudes toward the Moriscos in Spain began to harden by the mid-sixteenth century. No longer considered neophytes, Moriscos were increasingly cast as unrepentant Muslims and a threat to the Spanish nation. With the growth of the Ottoman Empire and the emergence of Protestantism in Europe, Spanish authorities increasingly linked religious identity to political loyalty.[13] Spanish jurists and theologians became concerned that Moriscos would ally with the Ottoman Turks to invade Spain. Consequently, Spanish officials began to propose policies that promoted assimilation or exile, depending on their opinions of the Moriscos.[14] In 1567 the Royal Council in Madrid passed a series of laws increasing restrictions on the Granadan Morisco population. These laws included prohibiting Moriscos from observing religious practices such as performing ritual ablutions, fasting during Ramadan, and butchering meat in the manner permitted in Islam. These laws also prohibited everyday activities such as speaking in the Arabic language, giving their children Muslim names, and wearing traditional clothing, including the veil (*almalafa*). Authorities closed the bath houses in Granada, and they prohibited Morisco doctors and midwives from exercising their professional duties, stemming from fears that they would circumcise Morisco babies.[15] Even foods such as couscous became stigmatized, alongside local Morisco dances (*zambras*) and music (*leilas*).[16] Leaders of the Granadan Morisco community such as Francisco Núñez Muley complained to the Royal Audiencia and Chancery Court of Granada that these were customary practices, similar to those in other regions across Spain, rather than religious practices. As a result, they were not incompatible with Catholicism.[17] Nonetheless, petitions on their behalf produced few practical results, and many Granadan Moriscos experienced increasing surveillance and repression.[18] In 1569 a group rose up in protest and moved into the Alpujarras mountain towns to resist Spanish Catholic authorities. Fighting continued until 1571, when their efforts were finally overcome by royal forces. Some Moriscos were enslaved as rebels and apostates, despite legally being baptized Christians. Others were forcibly resettled in Christian communities across Spain, while Granada continued to be "repopulated" with old Christian settlers.[19] After this second Alpujarras rebellion, Moriscos were increasingly viewed with suspicion, and their position in Spain was debated at court by those who urged Philip II to expel them from the peninsula, as Philip III eventually did.

Royal policies concerning emigration also reflected changing attitudes toward the Moriscos. Philip II reissued the royal decrees of Charles V regulating emigration, but their tone changed to emphasize the spread of heresy and symbolic pollution of the commonwealth as well as the obsessive desire to protect Spanish America from the spread of Protestantism and Islam that were seen as threatening Europe. Spanish American authorities became more likely to enforce these policies, and more individuals were denounced for emigrating illegally and practicing Islam in secret than they had been previously. Philip II also established the first inquisitorial tribunals in Mexico City (1571) and Lima (1570) that formalized the prosecution of cases that previously had been subject to the jurisdiction of local bishops.[20] In 1570 the king ordered the royal courts to aid inquisitors in their efforts to uphold Catholicism in the "provinces that God has entrusted to [the Spanish Crown]."[21] This decree stated: "It is very necessary to take special care and vigilance in the preservation of the devotion, and the good name, reputation, and fame of its settlers . . . as faithful and Catholic Christians, and natural and true Spaniards."[22] By restricting settlement to individuals who could trace their lineage as "old Christians," Spanish authorities hoped to limit indigenous peoples' exposure to beliefs they considered heretical. The language of these decrees reinforced the connection between loyalty and Catholicism, as they pertained to definitions of Spanishness and membership in the nation. In towns across Spanish America, officials read aloud inquisitorial edicts that asked individuals to come forward to denounce anything they had witnessed or committed that could be considered contrary to the faith. These edicts of faith included specific mentions of "Morisco ceremonies" that included praying five times daily, observing Ramadan, and performing ritual ablutions.[23] As in Spain, inquisitorial tribunals in Spanish America tried a range of cases of baptized Christians practicing Judaism and Islam, in addition to blasphemy, bigamy, and witchcraft. Indigenous peoples were not subject to the tribunals established in this period, as they remained under the authority of the bishops and ecclesiastical courts. The Inquisition presented itself as a confessional that had the sole power to absolve the sin of heresy, thereby encouraging scrutiny of individual and communal beliefs and practices. A third tribunal was established in the port city of Cartagena de Indias in 1610, as Spanish authorities became increasingly worried that those whose faith was questionable would cross over from Portuguese Brazil to the Spanish territories.[24]

LEGISLATION, CIRCUMVENTION, DISCUSSION OF NUMBERS

Diego Herrador's case exemplifies these changes in jurisdiction and how individuals attempted to emigrate clandestinely. In 1577 Herrador stood accused before the Mexican Inquisition of "being of the caste and lineage of Moriscos and the grandson of a *quemado* on his mother's side, [who] made a false report that he is an old Christian of pure blood and ancestry, and that no one of his lineage has been punished by the Holy Office."[25] During his trial Herrador admitted that he had obtained a false license to travel, and he told inquisitors how he did it. In his birthplace of Mérida, Extremadura, Herrador and his brother-in-law summoned four witnesses to testify that they were old Christians who possessed the requisite purity of blood (*limpieza de sangre*) to emigrate. After providing a physical description of Herrador, the witnesses testified that the two men and their families were all legitimate children of pure old Christian lineage and were "calm and peaceful, of good lifestyle and reputation."[26] Herrador had also adopted the surname of his paternal grandfather, instead of those of his parents, Hernández and Céspedes, who were reputed to descend from the Moriscos of Hornachos and were also rumored to have had a relative executed by the Inquisition.[27] Then, instead of processing his papers at the Casa de Contratación in Seville, Herrador sailed to the Canary Islands from the port of Lisbon. On the island of Palma, Herrador was able to embark for New Spain. Inquisitors eventually determined they did not have the authority to prosecute him because he was accused of the falsification of a license to emigrate rather than heresy.[28]

The route from Lisbon to the Canary Islands was well traveled among individuals wishing to avoid controls when engaging in contraband trade or emigrating to Spanish America.[29] A royal decree issued by Charles V in 1540 described the strategies that foreigners (*estrangeros*) used after loading their ships with unregistered merchandise: "They pretend to load their ships for the Canary Islands, and go secretly to Hispaniola, and other parts of our Indies."[30] In 1558 another *cédula* mentioned ships leaving Portuguese ports with clandestine passengers and unregistered goods: "They pretend to be going to Brazil, but [claim] that due to a storm, they reached these parts."[31] In 1560 Philip II issued a royal decree ordering the deportation of settlers who

> pass to our Indies secretly, some as sailors, others as soldiers, and others pretending to be merchants or their agents and others go through the Canary Islands, and find other routes and ways to pass. Under these guises men pass who are thugs and of sinful life and poor example, and prohibited persons. . . . Some people leave from ports that are outside of these kingdoms, in foreign and domestic ships, so that they go to some parts of the kingdom where they depart and pretend that with bad weather they docked in the Indies. . . . With this deceit they pass . . . [and] acquire goods and estates.[32]

In this way, Moriscos could enlist as soldiers and sailors, who were not subject to the same scrutiny as emigrants because it was assumed they would return to Spain. They could then jump ship once they reached ports in the Caribbean or the mainland. Spanish authorities complained repeatedly of the difficulties in locating "prohibited persons" who had arrived with false licenses, due to the vast distances separating the viceregal centers from the towns and settlements on the edges of empire where they feared Moriscos and *conversos* would settle. Inquisitors lacked qualified commissioners to cover all those areas. Furthermore, jurisdictional disputes also created confusion as to who held the authority to prosecute heresy—local bishops in ecclesiastical hearings or the newly established inquisitorial tribunals in Mexico City and Lima. In this context it was possible for individuals to escape unnoticed, unless they had the misfortune of encountering someone from their hometown in Spain who recognized them.

SUSPICIONS AND DENUNCIATIONS

Alongside the earlier examples of interpreters, other reputed Moriscos were able to acquire status within the new towns in Spanish America as holders of local offices or grants of indigenous tributaries (*encomiendas*). Their stories come to light in royal court (*audiencia*) and inquisitorial cases detailing the disputes over their *encomiendas*, lands, or offices by others seeking to increase their own status in colonial society. Some, including Diego Romero in Santa Fe, New Granada, were able to retain their *encomiendas* successfully. During a lengthy transatlantic trial, Romero's accuser summoned witnesses in the Spanish city of Alcalá de Henares in 1554 to testify that Romero had been born in Oran to a Muslim slave woman, captured during the conquest of that city, and brought to Spain. Witnesses described how Romero was raised a slave in a royal accountant's household before running away to Seville, changing his name, and sailing off with a false license to join Gonzalo Jiménez de Quesada's expedition to conquer Santa Marta and New Granada. In response, Romero produced an account of his services to the Crown in which he claimed to have contributed as much to the conquest and maintenance of his *encomienda* and community as any of the other conquerors of the region and was therefore entitled to his *encomienda*.[33] Romero and his lawyer also successfully argued that his high status protected him from being examined for evidence of circumcision by the doctors summoned by his accuser, because this would dishonor him. After several years of heated litigation, Romero was allowed to keep his *encomienda*.

Similar to Romero, in 1611 in Santiago de Guatemala, Nicolás de Oliva stood accused of being a Morisco in a bid for his farm (*estancia*). As seen in Oliva's case, ideas about Moriscos extended beyond religiosity to occupation, dress, and physical appearance. Gaspar Bernal de Reyna described to inquisitors a conversation he had with a merchant from Gracias a Dios in the province of Honduras named Pedro de la Portilla who worked in the province of

San Salvador. In one of the pueblos he passed through, Portilla encountered Oliva, whom he called a "bad Christian and they understood he was a Morisco because he shows it in his color, and in his trade, because he was a *buñolero* (maker of buñuelos or buns), an occupation held ordinarily by Moriscos in Spain."[34] Portilla had said that Oliva owned an *estancia* with livestock and a dye works (*obraje de tinta*), and when trouble occurred, "they heard him call upon Muhammad, saying these words, 'Oh Muhammad.'" Portilla had reprimanded Oliva, urging him to invoke instead, "Our Lady or her Blessed Son, that they would favor him, and not to call on Muhammad." Portilla continued: "In this province they said he was a Morisco, and what aid could he receive from Muhammad? Therefore everything turned out badly for him."[35] To Portilla's chagrin, Oliva ignored his advice.

Bernal de Reyna also noted that Portilla and Oliva were involved in a dispute over Oliva's *estancia* and a debt. By 1613 an inquisitorial investigation against Oliva was opened in San Salvador, Guatemala. There, Portilla testified that he had stayed at Oliva's house for fifteen days to collect a debt from him. Portilla claimed to have heard Oliva, "many times during the fifteen days, say on any occasion which offered itself, 'ah Muhammad.'"[36] Portilla repeatedly admonished Oliva to stop, telling him, "Look, they say you are a Muslim," and then Nicolás Oliva replied to this witness, "I cannot."[37] Portilla added that he had heard Oliva was a man "who had little fear of God or of his conscience. . . . [He was also] a man of bad conduct who with great ease denies debts that he owes, both with his signatures and without them, under oath. . . . He did not see in the house of the said Nicolás Oliva either cross or image or . . . rosary, nor is the Christian doctrine taught in his house to the people in his service."[38] Religious identity was an important point of contention in many of the cases, because *encomenderos* and other Spaniards in charge of indigenous workers were responsible for their catechization and attendance at Mass on Sundays and Catholic feast days. As seen in the testimony against Oliva, religious identity was also increasingly connected to qualities such as trustworthiness in business relations and loyalty to the emerging Spanish nation.

Portilla also raised questions concerning Oliva's birthplace, something that could call into question the legality of Oliva's status in Spanish America. While Oliva was generally reputed to be from Valencia del Cid, one man had called him "a circumcised Muslim dog from Greece."[39] Portilla had also heard Oliva claim he was from Mallorca, "so that sometimes he says that he is from Valencia del Cid and at others from Mallorca."[40] Oliva's occupation was also charged with meaning. Portilla stated that it was common knowledge that Oliva was a *buñolero*, and he had heard the public notary say that he had seen

Oliva "making *buñuelos*, and as a result he is understood to be a Morisco."[41] Portilla ended his denunciation with a vehement proclamation: "As long as he has known him, he has not seen him cross himself or pray or do anything that resembles anything Christian."[42] In fact, Oliva wore clothes at home that Portilla associated with Moriscos, including "a dirty rag wrapped around his head in the usage and dress of a Morisco."[43]

Another witness, Pedro de Cuéllar, described how he had met Oliva in Seville in 1579 and had seen him there "in the house of a Morisco *buñolero* engaging in the same occupation of *buñolero*."[44] Cuéllar testified that Oliva had lived in the province of San Salvador for fourteen years and had been married to an indigenous woman. Cuéllar said that Diego Sánchez, who had spent a lot of time on the *estancia*, had seen Oliva "one day, naked, passing by in a canoe on the Lempa River that passes near the *estancia* . . . and he saw that he did not have foreskin on his member."[45] Sánchez had asked Oliva what had happened, and Oliva replied that it had been removed due to an illness. After relating Sánchez's account, Cuéllar added that he had heard Oliva had been a captive in North Africa, and he had heard him speaking in Arabic, although he did not understand what Oliva was saying.[46] Ideas about what made someone a Morisco circulated in Spanish America and infused the denunciations that surfaced during local conflicts. Accusations, such as those leveled against Oliva, threatened public reputations and could even result in ecclesiastical court cases, as the burden to restore reputations fell upon the accused.

The types of accusations Oliva and Romero faced reflect attitudes toward suspected Moriscos and Muslims in other cases from Spanish America. Some accusations echoed the formulaic points in the edicts of faith that were read periodically by commissioners of the Inquisition, listing "ceremonies" of Muslims such as invoking Muhammad and praying in Arabic. Inquisitors expressed concern that anyone hearing these edicts, including indigenous peoples, could learn too much about Islam. Other cases such as Oliva's reveal common conceptions of Moriscos that included dress, occupation, and "public and notorious" behavior in church or in the streets. Many accusations against suspected Moriscos involved acting out during Mass, especially when the Eucharist was brought out, in the presence of supposedly impressionable indigenous witnesses.[47] These peninsular anxieties arose in Spanish America in disputes over status, offices, and *encomiendas*.

Tensions formed between personal experiences of religiosity and the broader community's perceptions of an individual's actions. Inquisitorial edicts of faith that labeled certain actions as Muslim, when read publicly, became politically charged in the popular imagination. Customary practice was associated with a person's place in Catholic society and, therefore, with their legal status. This carried substantial consequences regarding their rights and privileges within their community. How a person dressed, whether in clothing associated with Moriscos, indigenous peoples, or old Christian Spaniards, represented not only the community's perceptions of an individual, but also an assumed position in the social hierarchy. The right to bear arms, wear silk, own slaves, or participate in the local economy was structured according to these assumed identities. Clothing and gestures displayed publicly an individual's caste, religious affiliation, social status, and gender. Whether invoked to gain privileges, or by envious accusers, clothes and customs acted as statements that rendered "public and notorious" an individual's position in society.

INDIVIDUAL EXPERIENCES OF RELIGIOSITY

Religiosity remained a contested issue in Spanish America, as individuals suspected of being Moriscos fell under their neighbors' scrutiny. In other cases, preoccupations with individual salvation and doubts about whether Christianity or Islam was the "true" faith drove individuals to denounce themselves before the Inquisition, attempting to find new meaning in religion and be reconciled within the Catholic faith.[48] Conversations about Islam and Christianity continued on an everyday level in Spanish America, as people went about their daily lives. In 1594 María Ruiz, a Morisca born in the town of Albolote in the Alpujarras mountains of Granada, denounced herself before Mexican inquisitors. She did so at the insistence of her confessor, who was required to remit cases of heresy to the Inquisition, as it claimed it was the sole institution with the power to absolve this sin.[49] Ruiz had been residing in Mexico City for approximately ten years, where she was married to an old Christian wine merchant. During her trial she provided an account of her life that included descriptions of her religious practices in both Spain and Mexico. Many of the devotions that Ruiz described during her trial parallel those in other inquisitorial testimonies of Moriscos in Spain.

Some individuals denounced themselves before the Inquisition with genuine doubts about their faith, as the Inquisition had jurisdiction over cases of heresy and could absolve this sin, while confessors could not. Anyone denouncing themselves generally received only "spiritual" penance that included reciting prayers and religious instruction in a convent or monastery. Denouncing oneself could be a strategy for staving off harsher punishment if someone else's accusation was imminent. However, other cases reveal how some individuals struggled with their beliefs in hope of salvation. Self-denunciation was the formal way in which Christian captives in the Mediterranean could be reincorporated into their communities once they returned home to Spain from captivity in North Africa.[50] If scrutinized carefully, testimonies from self-denunciations before the Inquisition provide some information on what the religious practices of Moriscos might have looked like in Spanish America. Evidence exists confirming the presence of Morisco women in Peru, who accompanied the conquerors as slaves, and in some cases married into prominent families, going on to gain status in colonial society. The documents for these women come primarily from secular sources, such as the hearings before the Audiencia of Panama in which Juana Morisca petitioned successfully for her freedom, and do not reveal much about the religious choices they would have faced.[51] Regarded with suspicion, some Moriscos like Ruiz continued to practice a limited version of Islam in the privacy of their homes, even as they moved across the viceroyalties of New Spain and Peru. These cases also reflect the diversity of Morisco experiences in Spain, as individuals professed a range of religious beliefs and practices, whether acting as Muslims or as Christians or combining elements of Islam and Catholicism.

Due to her family's fear of discovery, Ruiz's religious instruction appears to have taken place under very controlled conditions. By the mid-sixteenth century, Moriscos in many parts of Spain along the Mediterranean coast who continued to practice Islam no longer spoke the Arabic language, and there is some evidence that, because they were so actively persecuted by the Inquisition, the *alfaquíes* (religious leaders) were no longer able to carry out official teachings in Qur'anic schools.[52] At the time of the expulsion of the Moriscos from Spain, some North African Muslim commentators decried the Morisco exiles' ignorance of Islam and began a campaign to instruct the new arrivals. Ruiz noted that she possessed limited knowledge of the formal teachings of Islam before arriving in New Spain. She recalled how, when she was a child before the second Alpujarras rebellion, her mother had taught her to fast during Ramadan, which she did "two or three times, and she did not continue with [the fasts] because, as such a young girl, she became hungry and ate. . . . Her mother carried out the said fasts with other women in the neighborhood . . . and they were cautious around her. Her mother told her not to talk about the fasts . . . because if she did they would be burned in an *auto-da-fé*."[53] Ruiz's mother also taught her prayers in Arabic, and "until three years ago, after she had come to this land [Mexico], she had always practiced Islam and believed in it although she did not do the ceremonies that her mother carried out . . . because as she had said, her parents were cautious around her and were afraid she would reveal them."[54] Other Morisco parents in Spain were similarly cautious, delaying their children's religious instruction until they were old enough to be discreet around old Christians and not arouse the suspicion of inquisitors.[55]

When asked by inquisitors how she prayed, Ruiz said she always "commended herself to God in heaven, and she did not recite prayers, other than when she got out of bed, and before going to bed, [she said] 'Halamay' . . . which she saw her parents do, and when she needed something from God and found herself in trouble she commended herself to God in heaven, saying that word."[56] Upon being asked whether she "excluded the persons of the Son and Holy Spirit" when praying to God, Ruiz replied, "Yes, she excluded them because she understood that there was only one God, and she did not believe in the Son or the Holy Spirit because she thought they were things of the air, and there was nothing to them."[57] The prominent place of the Trinity in Christian-Muslim polemics in Spain led to their salience in inquisitorial inquiries as well as Morisco responses. Christian-Muslim polemics that were prevalent in Spain informed contemporaries' responses to Moriscos in Spanish America. Differing opinions about the nature of the Trinity or the virginity of Mary could become contentious topics for debate in the Spanish world.[58] These differences surfaced in verbal exchanges on both sides of the Atlantic, in politically charged conversations about Muhammad and Islam, and could result in denunciations before the Inquisition. To Ruiz, the unitary nature of God was undermined by the presence of Christ and the Holy Spirit. This led some Moriscos in Spain to claim that Christians were polytheists who worshipped three deities rather than one God or that God had both a mother and a son.[59] During the ten years she spent in New Spain, Ruiz had taken Communion only "four times, and she did this to comply with her husband who told her to go and confess and take communion, and in all the confessions she made, she confessed all her sins except this one of her belief in Muhammad."[60] Ruiz remembered one occasion when she took Communion, while "very sick in the Hospital de Nuestra Señora in this city of Mexico," soon after she had arrived from Castile.[61] Ruiz said that because she was so ill, she was told to take Communion if she had confessed, to which she replied that "yes she had confessed, and thus they brought her the holiest sacrament, and she received it, not believing in it, nor that in it was the body of our redeemer Jesus Christ, because she did it to comply and not be detected."[62] Ruiz told inquisitors that for the past three years, she had no doubts about Catholicism, but that previously when practicing Islam, "she had doubts many times" about whether Islam or Christianity was the true faith.[63] Because she had appeared voluntarily before the Inquisition, Ruiz received only a light sentence and was reconciled in private. Inquisitors noted that they did not want to punish her publicly, since this might discourage other Moriscos from also denouncing themselves. However, records of the Mexican tribunal housed in Mexico City and Madrid show that no other self-identified Moriscos came forward that year.

Other cases reveal how individuals debated about which was the true faith in which they might be saved and struggled with their beliefs in a world where Catholicism and Islam were conceived of by ecclesiastical authorities as mutually exclusive. Their testimonies depict a multiconfessional world in which members of different religious communities spoke about their beliefs with one another and attempted to make sense of a variety of attitudes toward religiosity. One of the most intriguing examples is the case of a slave born in Algiers named Cristóbal de la Cruz, who in 1660 denounced himself before Mexican inquisitors.[64] De la Cruz engaged inquisitors with his doubts about Catholicism and discussed with them the nature of the Eucharist and the role of the priest during Mass, even quoting Saint Augustine. He described beliefs and practices he claimed to have observed intermittently from the time of his childhood in Algiers and requested that inquisitors help him dispel doubts about Catholicism so that he could achieve salvation.

In one instance, De la Cruz told inquisitors how, while sailing between Cádiz and Santo Domingo, he swam in the sea "with the intention of doing the *zahala* [and] bathing in the way that is customary for the Muslims . . . although this bath should be done in water that is fresh and not of the sea."[65] Here De la Cruz refers to the *salat*, or prayer that was preceded by ritual ablutions and conducted five times a day, if circumstances allowed.[66] De la Cruz noted that he had had to be careful when performing the ritual ablutions in public: "Because those soldiers and sailors are so . . . accustomed to seeing Muslims and renegades, he did not do those ceremonies because . . . [they] could not help but see him."[67] De la Cruz then described how, while watching the swimmers, one of them had asked him, "Why don't you throw yourself into the water and remove the grease?"[68] De la Cruz ignored him initially. However, after finishing their meal, the men began to swim again. This time De la Cruz joined them, "with neither malice nor intention of stopping being a Christian, nor any other thought than washing himself."[69] While he was in the water, several of the men swimming with him began to reminisce, "we remember the old times when we did the *zahala*," to which he exclaimed, "Leave me with a thousand devils! You think you are still in Algiers."[70] Soon after this exchange, De la Cruz claimed to have bathed again, this time "with the desire to be a Muslim . . . and saying while washing himself . . . *abdecader silali* which means powerful lord remember me. In this way he did the *zahala*."[71] On the island of Santo Domingo, De la Cruz confided his thoughts to another Muslim, who asked him, "If he had these doubts, why had he become a Christian?"[72] Like the earlier example of Ruiz, De la Cruz was given a light sentence. He was effectively removed from harsh labor in the galleys and required to perform less arduous work, exercising his profession as a cook in a monastery in order to be better instructed in Catholicism. His testimony reveals one of many conversations taking place about Islam in Spanish America in which individuals discussed their beliefs and attempted to make sense of their relationships to each other, in ways that could lead to conflicts both internal and external.

CONCLUSION

Due to prohibitions on Moriscos' and Muslims' emigration to Spanish America, many histories of the Iberian Atlantic world have overlooked the possibility that Moriscos and Muslims played a role in colonial society. Because their passage was clandestine, the sources we have on Moriscos in the New World reveal only the cases in which individuals were caught traveling with false licenses, while escaping enslavement and being sent back to Spain, or entangled in disputes over status and possessions. They reveal only a segment of the total number of emigrants, as we will never know how many were lucky enough to escape unnoticed and forge new lives for themselves overseas. The Americas would have drawn emigrants for whom North African destinations would have seemed unfamiliar, who were Spaniards like the old Christians, with strong ties to their regions of birth, but for whom only religious faith, or even only ancestry, remained a marker of difference. In a society preoccupied with tracing lineage in order to establish purity of blood, thereby excluding new Christians from holding prestigious offices and attending universities, some individuals promoted actions and services to the Crown as indicators of status that bore more importance than descent.

During the sixteenth century, the Spanish Crown was invested in creating and maintaining a Catholic empire. Royal officials and administrators considered faith and membership in a religious community critical to the Crown's jurisdiction over the Americas and its power and authority on an international stage. The religiosity of indigenous peoples acted as the foundation on which Spanish claims to empire and dominion rested. Anxieties over the incomplete conversion of native communities persisted into the seventeenth and eighteenth centuries, and Spanish ecclesiastical and secular authorities proposed numerous policies to ensure their Christianization. These anxieties were compounded with the real and imagined presence of Africans, Protestants, Jews, Muslims, *conversos*, Moriscos, and their descendants in colonial society. Fears of indigenous alliances with maroon communities and with French or English Protestants in the borderlands and fears of rebellion against Spanish authority surfaced at various times across the Americas. This produced an environment in which the status of people of mixed backgrounds who crossed ethnic and religious boundaries was increasingly debated and labeled suspect. Moriscos on both sides of the Atlantic also fell under these suspicions, as their conversion to Catholicism was increasingly deemed incomplete and they were described as rebels in an atmosphere that rendered religious identity synonymous with loyalty to the Crown. Debates over the legal status of peoples across the empire turned on this concept of political and religious loyalty, as close attention was paid to various forms of public behavior—customary practices, religious rituals, reputation, and exemplary actions in a variety of contexts. Public behavior carried weight in the courtroom and influenced an individual's status, but was also open to negotiation with the summoning of new witnesses, testimony, and evidence to build and support new interpretations of that individual's behavior. In contrast to this emphasis on actions, some Spanish commentators invoked descent, lineage, and genealogy to counter social and legal claims, reinforcing the malleability of status. They crafted new arguments that became increasingly racialized over time, believing that descent determined one's social standing and membership in the nation. Similar arguments connecting religiosity with loyalty were applied to Moriscos, *conversos*, and Protestants, but the historical position of Moriscos across the empire was different. In Spain, prior to the expulsion and following both Alpujarras uprisings, Moriscos were more frequently cast as a threat to the nation—as rebels who could ally with North African corsairs or with the Ottomans.

In order to govern a vast empire, stretching from the Mediterranean to the Atlantic to the Philippines, Spanish authorities became increasingly concerned with defining religious identity and customary practices. In conjunction with this aim, royal officials, lawyers, and litigants continued to develop a series of legal practices on both sides of the Atlantic. Officials were concerned with describing and categorizing the peoples within their jurisdiction, whose ethnic ties, associations, and identifications remained fluid. Individuals turned to the courts to negotiate their status, when faced with accusations that they lacked purity of blood, descended from Muslims and Moriscos, or practiced Islam. They joined many other individuals who were actively negotiating their status in the colonial period, including mestizos, *mulatos*, Spaniards, and indigenous peoples. Religious identity was only one component of a complex series of ascriptions and identifications, but it remained a pervasive one during the sixteenth and seventeenth centuries. Anxieties about the presence of Muslims and Moriscos in Spanish America posed exceptional challenges for individuals accused of possessing Muslim ancestry. Despite growing attempts to categorize peoples, the Spanish Empire functioned because a degree of fluidity was tolerated, even if this was contrary to the interests of some. Through this process, definitions of peoples became increasingly racialized, as ideas about nation and belonging were developed and articulated over time and applied to new settings. Ideas about reputation and honor were intimately connected to this process, as were an insistence on tracing lineage and genealogical constructs of identity that placed emphasis on bloodlines and were informed by imagined familial connections to biblical ancestors such as Ham, Ishmael, Shem, or Japheth. Religious identity was critical to this process, as attitudes toward religiosity informed early modern Spanish ideas about lineage, public reputation, and, increasingly, belonging to the nation.

The Inquisition in the New World, with specific interest in upholding indigenous evangelization and Spanish policies toward conversion, by indirect means, worked to police and define community in the Americas. Although it could not try Amerindians, the Inquisition's focus on "heretics"—whether converts from Judaism, Islam, or Protestants—reflected implicit assumptions about their political loyalty and ability to influence indigenous faith and faithfulness. This categorization involved not only spiritual matters, but also membership in the broader Catholic community and, by extension, nation and empire. Many Moriscos were viewed in this context as crypto-Muslims, as dangerous and disloyal individuals whose assimilation was impossible. By questioning witnesses in what it likened to the private space of the confessional, the Inquisition collected a body of information about their beliefs and practices that could then be used to transform their status publicly following an appearance in an auto-da-fé. Through the assumptions present in the purity of blood statutes, a public sentencing could affect a family for generations. Stereotypes about Moriscos that included language, dress, and occupation cropped up in the denunciations of suspected Moriscos. Rumors played a similar role, with the occasional appearance in the Americas of former residents of a suspected Morisco's hometown in Spain who proclaimed to their new neighbors they descended from Moriscos or were runaway North African Muslim slaves. The impact of these images of Moriscos was real: the accused were subject to loss of their wealth and status, as well as deportation to Spain. Moriscos who had arrived in the Americas as slaves, and had escaped, could be reenslaved at public auction at the Casa de Contratación in Seville. It was therefore through a variety of legal contexts that individuals challenged accusations that they were Moriscos, in public and in the courts, thereby defending their status as Christians and their legitimate place as members of colonial society.

NOTES

I would like to thank my colleagues at Washington State University—Lawrence Hatter, Steven Kale, Charles Weller, and Ashley Wright—for their thoughtful feedback on a draft of this chapter.

1. On Muslim and Morisco slaves in Iberia, see Debra Blumenthal, *Enemies and Familiars: Slavery and Mastery in Fifteenth-Century Valencia* (Ithaca, NY: Cornell University Press, 2009); and Aurelia Martín Casares, *La esclavitud en la Granada del Siglo XVI* (Granada: Universidad de Granada, 2000). On African Muslim slaves in the Americas, see Sylviane A. Diouf, *Servants of Allah: African Muslims Enslaved in the Americas* (New York: New York University Press, 1998). On Muslim slaves in the Caribbean, see David Wheat, "Mediterranean Slavery, New World Transformations: Galley Slaves in the Spanish Caribbean, 1578–1635," *Slavery and Abolition* 31, no. 3 (2010): 327–344.

2. James B. Tueller, *Good and Faithful Christians: Moriscos and Catholicism in Early Modern Spain* (New Orleans, LA: University Press of the South, 2002).

3. James Muldoon, *The Americas in the Spanish World Order: The Justification for Conquest in the Seventeenth Century* (Philadelphia: University of Pennsylvania Press, 1994).

4. *Cedulario Indiano Recopilado por Diego de Encinas, Oficial Mayor de la Escribanía de Cámara del Consejo Supremo y Real de las Indias* 1 (Madrid 1945): 455.

5. Archivo General de Indias (AGI), Indiferente 1961, L. 1, f. 38v.

6. AGI, Indiferente 419, L. 5, f. 250r.

7. Mary Elizabeth Perry, *The Handless Maiden: Moriscos and the Politics of Religion in Early Modern Spain* (Princeton, NJ: Princeton University Press, 2005), 76.

8. Woodrow Borah, *Silk Raising in Colonial Mexico* (Berkeley: University of California Press, 1943), 9.

9. Karoline P. Cook, "Muslims and the Chichimeca in New Spain: The Debates over Law and Slavery," *Anuario de Estudios Americanos* 70, no. 1 (2013).

10. On Muslim slaves in Cuba, see Alejandro de la Fuente, *Havana and the Atlantic in the Sixteenth Century* (Chapel Hill: University of North Carolina Press, 2008), 102–106.

11. "Haze mas vida de moro que de cristiano," variations of which appear in the charges against Francisco de Triana, Marcos Romero, and Alonso Ortiz de Zúñiga. AGI, Justicia 260, 175r. Ida Altman discusses this *visita* in depth in *The War for Mexico's West: Indians and Spaniards in New Galicia, 1524–1550* (Albuquerque: University of New Mexico Press, 2010).

12. Auke Pieter Jacobs, "Legal and Illegal Emigration from Seville, 1550–1650," in *"To Make America": European Emigration in the Early Modern Period*, edited by Ida Altman and James Horn (Berkeley: University of California Press, 1991), 59–84. Also see the case of the *encomendero* Diego Romero in Karoline P. Cook, "'Moro de linaje y nación': Religious Identity, Race and Status in Sixteenth-Century New Granada," in *Race and Blood in the Iberian World*, edited by Max S. Hering Torres, María Elena Martínez, and David Nirenberg (Berlin: LIT VERLAG, 2012), 81–97.

13. Stephen Haliczer, "The Moriscos: Loyal Subjects of His Catholic Majesty Philip II," in *Christians, Muslims and Jews in Medieval and Early Modern Spain: Interaction and Cultural Change*, edited by Mark D. Meyerson and Edward D. English (Notre Dame, IN: University of Notre Dame Press, 1999), 265–273.

14. Grace Magnier, *Pedro de Valencia and the Catholic Apologists of the Expulsion of the Moriscos: Visions of Christianity and Kingship* (Leiden: Brill, 2010).

15. Luis García Ballester, *Los moriscos y la medicina: Un capítulo de la medicina y la ciencia marginadas en la España del siglo XVI* (Barcelona: Labor Universitaria, 1984).

16. A group of Moriscos was tried by Toledo inquisitors for throwing a party at which they danced *zambras*, sang *leilas*, ate couscous, and called each other by their Muslim names. See Louis Cardaillac, *Moriscos y cristianos: Un enfrentamiento polémico (1492–1640)* (Madrid: Fondo de Cultura Económica, 1979).

17. Francisco Núñez Muley, *A Memorandum for the President of the Royal Audiencia and Chancery Court of the City and Kingdom of Granada*, edited and translated by Vincent Barletta (Chicago: University of Chicago Press, 2007).

18. Granadan Morisco elites present a very different case. Families such as the Granada Venegas allied with Christian conquerors and later petitioned successfully for titles of nobility and old Christian status. See Mercedes García-Arenal, "El entorno de los Plomos: Historiografía y linaje," in *Los Plomos del Sacromonte: Invención y tesoro*, edited by Manuel Barrios Aguilera and Mercedes García-Arenal (Valencia: Publicacions de la Universitat de València, 2006), 51–78.

19. Antonio Domínguez Ortíz and Bernard Vincent, *Historia de los moriscos: Vida y tragedia de una minoría* (Madrid: Alianza Editorial, 2003); L. P. Harvey, *Muslims in Spain, 1500–1614* (Chicago: University of Chicago Press, 2005); Perry, *Handless Maiden*. On sixteenth-century projects to bring Christian settlers to Granada, see David Coleman, *Creating Christian Granada: Society and Religious Culture in an Old-World Frontier City, 1492–1600* (Ithaca, NY: Cornell University Press, 2003).

20. Richard Greenleaf, *The Mexican Inquisition of the Sixteenth Century* (Albuquerque: University of New Mexico Press, 1969).

21. "Provinciass por Dios a nos encomendadas." *Cedulario Indiano Recopilado por Diego de Encinas*, 1:46.

22. "Y que es tan necessario tener especial cuydado y vigilancia en la conservacion de la devocion, y buen nombre y reputacion y fama de sus pobladores como fieles y catholicos Christianos, y naturalles y verdaderos Españoles." Ibid.

23. Archivo Histórico Nacional (AHN), Inq. libro 1033, 318v and 409r–v; Archivo General de la Nación (AGN), Inq. vol. 89, 57v–58r.

24. On the establishment of the Cartagena tribunal, see Antonio Domínguez Ortíz, *Los judeoconversos en Espana y America* (Madrid: ISTMO, 1988). On Portuguese policies on settlement in Brazil, see Timothy Coates, *Convicts and Orphans: Forced and State-Sponsored Colonizers in the Portuguese Empire, 1550–1755* (Stanford, CA: Stanford University Press, 2001).

25. "Siendo de casta y generazion de moriscos e nieto de quemado por parte de madre a echo falsamente informazion de que es xpiano viejo de limpia sangre e generazion e que ninguno de su linaje aya sido castigado por el sancto off[ici]o." AGN, Inq. vol. 82, 217r. The term *quemado* referred to an individual remitted by the Inquisition to secular authorities and executed. For an analysis of the impact of the purity of blood statutes in colonial Mexico, see María Elena Martínez, *Genealogical Fictions: Limpieza de Sangre, Religion, and Gender in Colonial Mexico* (Stanford, CA: Stanford University Press, 2008).

26. "Quietos e pacificos de buen vivir e fama." AGN, Inq. vol. 82, 229v.

27. AGN, Inq. vol. 82, 219r. Hornachos had a large Morisco population during the sixteenth century that has been well studied. See Alberto González Rodríguez, *Hornachos, enclave morisco: Peculiaridades de una población distinta* (Mérida: Asamblea de Extremadura Publicaciones, 1990); and Harvey, *Muslims in Spain*.

28. AGN, Inq. vol. 82, 219v.

29. See Jacobs, "Legal and Illegal Emigration from Seville"; and José Luis Martínez, *Pasajeros de Indias: Viajes transatlánticos en el siglo XVI* (Mexico City: Fondo de Cultura Económica, 1999).

30. *Cedulario Indiano Recopilado por Diego de Encinas*, 1:442.

31. Ibid., 444–446.

32. Ibid., 443–444.

33. Cook, "'Moro de linaje y nación.'"

34. "Era mal cristiano y entendian que era morisco por que en el color la muestra, y en su trato porque a sido bunolero oficio que lo usan de ordinario moriscos en España." AGN, Inq. vol. 292, f. 194r.

35. Ibid.

36. AGN, Inq. vol. 292, f. 198v.

37. Ibid.

38. "Honbre poco themerosso de dios y de su conçiençia asi por lo que tiene dho como por ser honbre de mal trato y que con gran facilidad niega deudas que deve asi por firmas suyas como sin ellas debaxo de juramento y que demas . . . no a bisto en cassa del dho Niculas de Oliva cruz + ni ymagen ni al sussodho le a bisto rosario ni que en su cassa se enseñase la dotrina christiana a la gente de servicio." AGN, Inq. vol. 292, ff. 198v–199r.

39. "Perro moro retajado de Greçia." AGN, Inq. vol. 292, f. 199r.

40. Ibid.

41. AGN, Inq. vol. 292, f. 199v.

42. Ibid.

43. "En su cassa anda con un calçon de manta corto abierto y una camissa de lo mysmo y una toaza çuçia rebuelta en la caveça a usança y traxe de morisco." Ibid.

44. AGN, Inq. vol. 292, f. 204r.

45. Ibid.

46. AGN, Inq. vol. 292, ff. 204v–205r.

47. Karoline P. Cook, "Forbidden Crossings: Morisco Emigration to Spanish America, 1492–1650" (PhD diss., Princeton University, 2008).

48. On conversations about religiosity in Spanish America, and the expressed belief that all could be saved according to their law, see Stuart B. Schwartz, *All Can Be Saved: Religious Tolerance and Salvation in the Iberian Atlantic World* (New Haven, CT: Yale University Press, 2008).

49. AGN, Inq. vol. 151, exp. 5, f. 3r.

50. Bartolomé Bennassar and Lucile Bennassar, *Los cristianos de Alá* (Madrid: Editorial Nerea, SA, 2001).

51. Juana Morisca's case does provide testimony as to the average price at which Morisca slaves were auctioned in the Lima slave market, demonstrating that she was not the only one. Later complaints about Lima Inquisition officials from the 1620s also indicate suspicion that some of these prominent men were married to Morisco women. On these Lima complaints, see Cook, "Forbidden Crossings." On Morisca slaves, see Rukhsana Qamber, *Inquisition Proceedings against Muslims in 16th-Century Spanish America* (Islamabad: Islamic Research Institute, International Islamic University, 2007).

52. Cardaillac, *Moriscos y cristianos*, 147–148; Mercedes García-Arenal, *Inquisición y moriscos: Los procesos del Tribunal de Cuenca* (Madrid: Siglo Veintiuno Editores, 1978), 46–47.

53. AGN, Inq. vol. 151, exp. 5, ff. 3r–3v.

54. AGN, Inq. vol. 151, exp. 5, ff. 3v–4r.

55. Cardaillac, *Moriscos y cristianos*, 25.

56. "Dixo que siempre se encomendava a Dios del cielo y no dezia oraciones, mas de al levantarse de la cama y al acostar, Halamay, como tiene declarado que via hazer a los dhos sus padres, y que quando queria alcança algo de Dios, y se via en algun travajo, se encomendava a Dios del cielo diziendo la dha palabra Halamay." AGN, Inq. vol. 151, exp. 5, ff. 8v–9r. I have not found references to this invocation in other inquisitorial documents or secondary sources on the subject. In many trials, Moriscos were accused of saying "Alhanduliley" (Praise God) or "Bismillah" (In the name of God), which precedes the *shahada*, or profession of faith, in Islam.

57. "Dixo que si excluya porque entendia que no avia mas de un solo Dios, y no creya en el hijo ni en el spiritu s[an]to porque lo tenia por cosa de ayre, y que no avia nada de aquello." AGN, Inq. vol. 151, exp. 5, f. 9r.

58. While many Muslims do recognize and venerate Mary, because of the charged interactions between new and old Christians in the early modern Iberian world, a sector of the Morisco population disavowed her virginity. However, religious disagreement and variation also existed among Moriscos themselves, and David Coleman notes cases of Moriscos expressing special devotions to Mary in their wills in *Creating Christian Granada*, 46. See also Amalia García Pedraza, "La asimilación del morisco Don Gonzalo Fernández el Zegrí: Edición y análisis de su testamento," *Al-Qantara* 16 (1995).

59. Cardaillac, *Moriscos y cristianos*, 211–213. These statements are found in inquisitorial trials of Granadan Moriscos, examined by Cardaillac, as well as a polemical text in *aljamiado* by Muhammad al-Qaysi, entitled "Deskonkordamiyento de los Kiristiyanos."

60. AGN, Inq. vol. 151, exp. 5, f. 8v.

61. AGN, Inq. vol. 151, exp. 5, f. 21r.

62. Ibid.

63. "Muchas vezes se le ofreçian dubdas." AGN, Inq. vol. 151, exp. 5, f. 9r.

64. On the case of Cristóbal de la Cruz, see Karoline P. Cook, "Navigating Identities: The Case of a Morisco Slave in Seventeenth-Century New Spain," *Americas: A Quarterly Review of Inter-American Cultural History* 65, no. 1 (2008): 63–79.

65. AHN, Inq. 1729, exp. 10\4\f. 3v.

66. Diouf, *Servants of Allah*, 59.

67. AHN, Inq. 1729, exp. 10\4\f. 4r.

68. AHN, Inq. 1729, exp. 10\5\f. 17v.

69. AHN, Inq. 1729, exp. 10\5\f. 17v.

70. AHN, Inq. 1729, exp. 10\5\f. 18r.

71. AHN, Inq. 1729, exp. 10\5\f. 18r.

72. AHN, Inq. 1729, exp. 10\4\f. 16v-17r.

CHAPTER 2

AFRICAN REBELLION AND REFUGE
ON THE EDGE OF EMPIRE

JOHN TOFIK KARAM

FLAGS OF VARIED European powers flew over ships that forcibly dispersed African Muslims in the New World. The British, French, Portuguese, and Spanish, among others, competed with one another in the trading of captives mainly from Senegambia or Upper Guinea since the fifteenth century and from Lower Guinea between the late eighteenth and mid-nineteenth centuries. Bought and sold to toil in the towns and estates of the Caribbean, South America, and elsewhere, African Muslims were active agents in the same domains that enslaved them.

Their agency in overlapping imperial orders that sought to deny or inhibit its exercise should not be surprising. Islam, in fact, possesses a long history in the sociopolitical landscape of the aforementioned West African regions that extend from the Senegal River (along present-day Senegal's northern border) to what is today southern Cameroon. Although Muslims represented an estimated 15 to 20 percent of the twelve to fifteen million Africans in the transatlantic slave trade, much of the non-Muslim majority abducted from Senegambia, Upper Guinea, and Lower Guinea would have been familiar with Islam as well.[1]

Drawing on the works of Sylviane Diouf, Michael Gomez, and James Sweet, among others,[2] this chapter focuses overwhelmingly on Mande speakers, the so-called *mandingos*, through the eighteenth century and mostly Hausa and Yoruba in the first half of the nineteenth century. How were African Muslims shaped by empires, and, in turn, how did they help to shape imperial formations in the New World? Until the 1790s Iberian and northern European powers viewed the Muslimness of captives in distinct ways. Nonetheless, as part of a changing Atlantic world from the 1800s onward, these Africans marked Islam in parallel ways by mobilizing among enslaved subjects and against the prevailing status quo. In so doing, African Muslim histories reveal the tensions within and among empires in the Atlantic.

Scorned by Spanish and Portuguese officials and relatively "privileged" by the British and French,[3] African Muslim subjects provide a window into the rise and fall of Iberian powers amid the expansive authority of northern European empires in the Atlantic. More tellingly, however, Islam brought into its fold African-born believers as well as nonbelievers to confront, withstand, and expose the cracks in and between these competing imperial orders in the New World. As "an ally of power" used to justify territorial expansion in West Africa as well as a "refuge for the poor" lending "spiritual and moral strength,"[4] Islam was used for both rebellion and refuge, enabling Africans to outlast some of the empires that gave rise to their diaspora.

With broad historical brushstrokes, this chapter begins after the moment that "Columbus stumbled upon . . . the middle of this nowhere they now call the Caribbean."[5] The first two sections situate African Muslims in Iberian and northern European dominions of the New World from the 1490s to the 1790s. The last two sections look at a series of dramatic changes that transpired from the 1800s through the 1910s, including not only demographic shifts among African captives (both Muslim and non-Muslim), but also the exacerbation and dissolution of intra- and interimperial dynamics that initiated their diaspora.

CONSTRUED AS JEOPARDIZING
IBERIAN ORDERS, 1490S–1650S

In the second half of the fifteenth century, Africans began to be acquired by Portuguese and Spanish traders from the regions of Senegambia, around the Senegal and Gambia Rivers, as well as Upper Guinea, which continues southward to what is today northwest Liberia.[6] For the next 150 years, they were abducted from these regions where Islam was "the religion of merchants and rulers."[7] Between 1521 and 1639, Senegambians and Upper Guineans composed many of the 110,525 Africans in the so-called (West) Indies and New Spain.[8] Distinguishing them from other captives, Iberian rulers occasionally referred to Muslims as *mandingos*. However, these captives belonged to a range of distinct ethnolinguistic groups such as the Jolof (sometimes written as *jalof* or *geolof*), Fula, and Mandinga.[9] Their lands of origin had been governed by the Jolof Confederation, whose elites from early on incorporated Islam as a source of indigenous religiocultural practices. As the confederation broke down under external pressure and conflict after the mid-fifteenth century, its subjects were abducted by the Portuguese, who early on supplied the Spanish, and later on competed with them and other European slavers.

In 1522 "negros of jalof" participated in one of the first slave revolts of the New World.[10] They rose up on the island of Hispaniola, then governed by Columbus's own son Diego. Gomez recounts that on early Christmas morning, twenty captives took up machetes and rebelled for the next three days, practicing warfare skills that they had perhaps learned in the waning years of Jolof rule. As a result, the Spanish Crown barred from the Indies any "slaves suspected of Islamic leanings, such as the notorious *esclavos Gelofes* [Jolof slaves] of the Guinea area, many of whom not only were infidels but were prone to insubordination as well."[11] As one of many laws prohibiting the migration of Muslims to the New World, the 1532 royal decree of the Spanish Crown characterized Jolofs as "proud and disobedient, agitators and incorrigible."[12] Islam was assumed, by the Catholic rulers, to feed insubordination.

Indeed, Spanish imperial officials, settlers, and missionaries cultivated fears of a slave insurrection or conspiracy through their own peculiar view of Islam. Although Bowser characterized the aforementioned 1522 revolt as a "relatively minor affair," other uprisings through the 1500s gave pause to the Spanish Crown's importation of enslaved Africans.[13] The Spanish monarchy, however, did not know whom to blame. From the 1520s to the 1540s, the Spanish first targeted enslaved blacks transferred from Iberia. Next, they blamed Jolofs, and, finally, they settled on enslaved mulattoes "suspected of Moorish ancestry."[14] Whether or not African Muslims played a major role in this or other such uprisings, it is clear that Spanish elites presumed that Muslims would defy their rule in the New World, only decades after the fall of the Muslim kingdom of Granada on the Iberian Peninsula.

Portuguese slavers and the Crown held a similar vision of Islam in Senegambia and Upper Guinea, whose "black" adherents they compared to "white moors."[15] Mid-fifteenth-century papal bulls granted the Portuguese permission to "capture, vanquish, and subdue all Saracens [that is, Muslims] and pagans whatsoever . . . and to reduce their persons to perpetual slavery."[16] By 1641, however, the Crown reversed this policy and placed "a ban on owning Muslim slaves" in the kingdom, apparently uneasy with the growing numbers of enslaved African Muslims. A decade later the Portuguese Inquisition tried several Jolofs for holding Islamic beliefs.[17] During the sixteenth and seventeenth centuries, the Portuguese supplied these and other captives to Spanish counterparts as well as their own overseas empire, including a half-million captives to colonial Brazil.[18] For the seventeenth-century Jesuit priest Antonio Vieira, enslaved Africans—concentrated in coastal cities such as Recife, Rio de Janeiro, Salvador, and São Vicente—were very much part of a larger struggle against the "Mahometan empire."[19]

Of course, Islam was of particular concern to Iberian religious orders. In 1627 missionary Alonso de Sandoval wrote that he had detected the presence of "Mohamaden" slaves in the Caribbean port of Cartagena de Indias.[20] In endeavoring to convert the non-Christian masses, Sandoval occasionally fretted about Muslims who carried on their religious practices from their original homelands. In Guinea, where the missionary had served, he wrote that there were "orators who have the duty . . . to refer to the victories of their ancestors . . . finishing their prayers with the greatest one of all, which is to annihilate our holy faith and enhance the cursed sect of Mahoma, persuading others to persevere and not become Christians." And in Cartagena de Indias, he likewise observed that "iolofes [Jolofs], berbesies, mandingas, and fulos [who] tend ordinarily to understand one another, despite their distinct languages and castes, because the greatest communication that they have is due to all these nations having commonly received the evil sect of Mahoma." Besides his anti-Islamic zeal, Sandoval's observations imply that African Muslims commiserated and prayed together. Muslims from Upper Guinea, in this light, both outwardly fought against the slavocrat regime and turned inwardly as well.

In this regard, the Spanish Crown and church "feared that the black man would hamper the Christianization of the Indian" not only because of their alleged "idolatrous" practices but also due to the enslaved African being viewed as "an Islamic infidel."[21] While indigenous peoples were generally construed as holding the potential to be "saved" and made into "loyal subjects," Africans were seen as irredeemable and impure, due, in part, to Spaniards' own "long history of linking blackness to both servitude and Islam."[22] Such dubious distinctions in *nueva España* (new Spain), María Elena Martínez argues, were made through the wider, and much older, Iberian conception of "blood purity," once used to marginalize Jews and Muslims on the peninsula.[23] Through sexual relations or religious conversions, Indians could seek ambiguous inclusion by ostensibly becoming Christians, vassals, or mestizos. However, "blacks were by definition impure," and in so being, they not only compromised "Spanish Old Christian blood" but were also "deemed to be a threat to the purity of the Indians," too.[24] At least through the mid-seventeenth century, Iberian elites generally targeted Islam, and by extension Africanness, as potentially jeopardizing their imperial orders in the New World.

PATRONIZED IN THE BRITISH AND FRENCH CARIBBEAN, 1650S–1790S

In the British, Dutch, and French Indies, the presence of enslaved Africans increased in tandem with the expansion of the "plantation complex" from the mid-seventeenth century onward.[25] In fact, northern European colonies in the Caribbean became the destination for more than a third of the African captives between 1662 and 1867.[26] During the seventeenth century, however, enslaved Africans mostly stemmed from the west central area (present-day Angola and Congo), where Islam had a more limited presence than in other regions. Concurrently, Senegambia or Upper Guinea "supplied 6.2 percent and 15.5 percent of the total British trade" in 1700 and 1807,[27] some of whom were resettled on the British islands of Jamaica, Barbados, and elsewhere.

During this time, Upper Guinean captives were also moved to French-ruled Guadeloupe, Saint Domingue, Martinique, and elsewhere. As early as 1658, French missionary Chevillard complained that the Jolofs of Senegambia "could perpetuate their religion" on the island of Guadeloupe.[28] A century later, according to Diouf, "Mandingo, Fulani, Hausa, Nago, Mina, and Susu accounted for 15 to 19 percent of the Africans in Saint Domingue."[29] Early-eighteenth-century missionary Père Jean-Baptiste Labat had recommended that "slaves from Senegambia" raise cattle to complement sugar plantations on the nearby island of Martinique.[30] In the 1780s some French planters moved their African captives from these French colonies to then Spanish-ruled Trinidad. And after the British took control of that island in the 1790s, many Africans, some with Muslim names, ended up in Trinidad as well.[31]

Like their fellow Catholic rulers in Iberia, French agents of empire scrutinized the Islamic faith of African captives. The aforementioned mid-seventeenth-century French missionary on the islands critically reflected on proselytizing among "blacks . . . with a tint of the Mahometan," and fifty years later the vicar-general of the Dominican mission echoed complaints about "those from Mahometan countries."[32] While they were seen as less willing to accept Christianity, African Muslims also appear to have been viewed as intellectually superior to other Africans due to their ability to read and write in Arabic and their subsequent assignment "to more 'prestigious,' less back-breaking tasks."[33] However, even on the eve of "the events that shook up Saint Domingue from 1791 to 1804,"[34] a French officer failed to construe African Muslims and their alleged superiority as a threat to imperial rule.[35] Like the "unthinkable" moment of the Haitian Revolution in the framework of Western thought, the French perceived African Muslims as difficult to convert, but hardly as agents in active defiance of empire.

In this regard an intriguing figure who challenged French rule four decades before the start of the revolution is a maroon leader by the name of François Makandal.[36] Diouf suggests that Makandal was Mandingo by birth, and Gomez points out that "given the pattern of French slaving operations off the West African coast, it is probable that he hailed from . . . Sierra Leone or Senegambia." Given the lack of evidence "to connect him to the Daho-mean traditions that form the vodou's religion's framework,"[37] both Diouf and Gomez draw on sources that imply that Makandal was educated in a madrasa in West Africa and could read and write in Arabic. Incorporating in-digenous African religious traditions in his role as an African-born leader in Saint Domingue, Makandal contradicted the previous assumptions of French missionaries that African Muslims kept to themselves and their own beliefs. Makandal became a key insurgent against French plantation owners, who, in a report issued after he was "burned at the stake" in early 1758, related his role in tactics against both whites and slavery. Unlike other rebellions after 1800, African Muslims did not figure prominently in the Haitian Revolution. How-ever, Makandal's role does point to Islam as being part of a wider sea change that would occur in the early nineteenth century.

Michael Gomez writes that "patterns of privileging Muslim individuals would develop all over anglophone America."[38] As early as the 1650s, a Por-tuguese traveler observed that "English traders operating in Senegambia—a region populated by Fula agropastoralists—'buy many blacks whom they ship to Barbados,'" whose "African practice of livestock tethering was repro-duced in many plantation societies of the English Caribbean."[39] More than one hundred years later, Bryan Edwards, a British government official who lived intermittently in Jamaica, noted that one of his faithful "Mandinka ser-vants" had "not forgotten the morning and evening prayers that his father taught him" and "chants . . . 'La Illa ill illa' [there is no god but God]" as well as observed "strict fasting" during Ramadan.[40] When the British took over the island of Trinidad in 1797, Mandingos and Fulas represented nearly 10 per-cent of a regiment made up of enslaved and free peoples of African origin.[41] In Barbados, Jamaica, and Trinidad, the British characterized African Muslims as possessing greater skills or knowledge than others. However, as noted by Hisham Aidi and Manning Marable, such a quality "was rarely seen as a result of their exposure to Islam or Arabic education in West Africa but was attrib-uted to their Arab, Berber, or Moorish origin."[42]

Although "forced conversion was not the policy" in the Anglican-dominant colonies in the Caribbean, missionaries did target Muslims from Senegambia and Upper Guinea who, in response, dissimulated their beliefs.[43] Take, for instance, Muhammad Kaba, a "Mahometan" who was captured, en-slaved, and brought to Jamaica in the 1770s and later formally converted to Christianity and was given a Christian name. According to British missionary J. H. Buchner, Kaba "was by birth a Mandingo; he was taught to read and write, and early initiated into the Mahometan faith, being designed for an expounder of their law."[44] In order to observe "Mahometan fasts" before his conversion, Bucher complains, Kaba "pretended to be sick." He was even alleged to explain to a British authority, "Me say me believe in God, but not in his Son; for in me country we pray to God and his prophet Mahomet." Several decades after Kaba ostensibly converted to Christianity, Richard Robert Madden, a British magistrate and proabolitionist in Jamaica, doubted "the old African's renunciation of Islamism.[45]" As explored below, Kaba maintained correspondence with other African Muslims in Jamaica and elsewhere in the ever-changing Atlantic of the early 1800s.

CHANGING TIDES IN A BLACK ATLANTIC, 1800S–1830S

This Black Atlantic began to undergo changes in the first three decades of the nineteenth century, not the least of which were the backgrounds and points of origin of African Muslims. During the first three centuries of the transatlantic slave trade, as stated previously, many captives were Mande speakers from Upper Guinea; however, by the early 1800s, most were Hausa and Yoruba (called *nagô*, in Brazil) from Lower Guinea. Between the 1750s and 1850s, Yoruba made up half of the captives shipped from this region through the Bight of Benin.[46] Enslaved Hausa and Yoruba were transferred and "concentrated in three major areas by the end of the eighteenth and during the nineteenth centuries: Cuba; Bahia, Brazil; and Saint Domingue."[47] Diouf notes that "in 1807 alone, 8,307 Hausa, Nago, and Ewe were introduced to Bahia," precipitating the "hegemonic" role of Yoruba cultural forms in Brazil.[48]

This nineteenth-century shift in the "ethnic background" of captives in Brazil and the Caribbean was linked to political transformations in Lower Guinea.[49] Located between the Cape Palma and the Bight of Biafra,[50] this region witnessed the rise of Usuman dan Fodio and his declaration of jihad in the early 1800s. As the leader of one of several Islamic reformist movements, dan Fodio targeted other Hausa states that allegedly conjoined Islam with other indigenous beliefs. Although dan Fodio was victorious in establishing the Sokoto caliphate in present-day northern Nigeria, many Hausa captured during warfare ended up in the hands of European slavers, who sent them across the Atlantic. Not long after, many Yoruba suffered a similar fate after war erupted in the nearby Oyo Empire that disintegrated by the 1830s. The intra- and interstate warfare that precipitated the forced departure of Hausa, Yoruba, and others also served as the context of their arrival in the New World.

In the shadow of the Haitian Revolution and "the French colonial collapse" that benefited the British, Portuguese, and Spaniards,[51] African captives witnessed the rise, fall, and tensions among empires in the Americas during the early 1800s. Anti-Portuguese sentiments and disturbances marked the period during which Brazil became the seat of the Portuguese Empire in 1808 and an independent monarchy by 1822. Meanwhile, the Spanish Crown suffered two waves of rebellions that resulted in nine independent republics by 1828. The British welcomed this near dissolution of Iberian power. In 1824 its foreign secretary, George Canning, mused, "Spanish America is free, and if we do not mismanage our affairs wrongly, she is English."[52] In the next decade, another English statesman characterized the Portuguese as "inhabiting the lowest rung" of morality and Brazilians as "degenerate Portuguese."[53] Before they made plans to economically and morally dominate former Iberian colonies, the English abolished the slave trade in 1807 and consequently seized suspect vessels. Many of the "recaptured" Hausa and Yoruba in such ships were subsequently brought to Sierra Leone, Trinidad, and Brazil.[54] Such intra- and interstate conflicts among imperial powers and their (Euro-) American challengers served as the settings for actions and exchanges authored by African Muslims themselves.

In and across these increasingly unstable imperial orders, captives and ex-slaves commiserated and corresponded among themselves. "There is good evidence," writes João José Reis, "that Brazilian slaves knew about Haiti and considered it an almost mythical touchstone."[55] Drawing on Luiz Mott's work, he adds that "blacks in Rio de Janeiro wore necklaces bearing the image of Dessalines within a year of his declaring Saint Domingue's independence [1805]."[56] In addition, African Muslims in Bahia met with one another in freedmen's houses and slave quarters.[57] Together they prayed, practiced writing in Arabic and the recitation of the Qur'an, shared meals, and observed holy days. In addition to engaging in these acts of the faith, pious Muslims in British-ruled Jamaica took part in exchanges that point to the existence of an African Muslim Atlantic. The most widely examined correspondence has been a clerical or pastoral letter, a *wathiqa* (in Arabic), that "exhorted all the followers of Mahomet to be true and faithful, if they wished to go to Heaven."[58] Scholars agree that the letter originated in West Africa and circulated among Muslims in Jamaica before it was delivered to the aforementioned Muhammad Kaba and made the pages of Richard Robert Madden's 1835 account. This is to say, African Muslims upheld their faith in and across imperial domains that were shaken by a series of Muslim-led rebellions.

One of the most well-known revolts coordinated by African Muslims shook Salvador da Bahia in 1835. The rebellion is generally believed to have been led by *malês*, the generic label for African Muslims in Brazil. Some suggest that this insurrection was the culmination of Usuman dan Fodio's jihad a few decades earlier.[59] In stark contrast, Reis contextualizes the *malê* revolt in terms of Brazil's aforementioned political and military transformations during the early nineteenth century. In such circumstances, Reis argues, the 1835 slave rebellion is best grasped as an *African* uprising with Muslim leadership and African-born, non-Muslim rank and file. Based on the police and court records on the Muslim and non-Muslim African insurgents who attacked military garrisons and government buildings in Salvador, Reis concludes that Islam furnished "the predominant ideology and language" of the 1835 rebellion that attracted Africans of diverse ethnic and religious backgrounds.[60] The most visible markers of this Islamic mold of the uprising were amulets, called *mandingas*, small cloth pieces containing a paper with one or more Qur'anic verses, written in Arabic. Prepared by educated African Muslims (as was common in Lower Guinea), the pieces were used by both Muslim and non-Muslim Africans for protection. Islam thus served as the "glue" of African "ethnic solidarity" against a Luso-Brazilian order based on slavery. Ultimately, however, Brazilian authorities expelled insurgents to Africa and used the 1835 rebellion to characterize Islam as "foreign" and Christianity as Brazil's so-called native religion.

A more famous but not well-researched uprising took place on the Spanish ship *La Amistad*. In 1839 enslaved Africans mutinied after departing the port of Havana, Cuba, one of only two island colonies that remained under the Spanish Crown in the New World. Although the mutineers sought to sail back to Africa, the surviving Spaniards, José Ruíz and Pedro Montéz, steered the vessel northward, where it was captured by the US Navy. Ruíz and Montéz attempted to prosecute the Africans in a US court for the murder of a slaver. Some of these Africans were Muslim. Mentioned above, Madden testified that one captive greeted another by stating, "'salaam Aleikoum' or Peace to you and the man immediately replied 'Aleikoum Salaam' or with you be peace."[61] Likewise, an 1839 account related that "the belief of one God, and of a future state of reward and punishment, is entire and universal among them" and that "most of the prisoners . . . told the interpreter that they are from Mandingo . . . in the Senegambia country."[62] Awaiting trial for the next two years, this case attracted US abolitionists critical of not only slavery but also the Spanish slavers in terms of the Black Legend. The 1839 account purported to sympathize with the African captives as "unfortunate victims of Spanish cruelty and avarice."[63] It reasoned that the Spaniards illegally kidnapped Africans because Cuba served as a "*refugium peccatorum*" and a "nest of pirates and a den of thieves," concluding in no uncertain terms: "It is full time the United States took possession of the Island of Cuba."[64] The African mutiny and its trial thus point to the intersection of emergent and residual empires in the Atlantic.

SURVIVING THE ENDS OF EMPIRE, 1840S–1910S

The British, however, had been the rising power since the early nineteenth century. Their enforcement of the 1807 act abolishing the trade justified their seizure of suspect vessels, which were actually under the jurisdiction of the Spanish-ruled Caribbean and the Brazilian Empire (1822–1889). Nonetheless, Cuban and Brazilian slave trades "continued to flourish."[65] While the Spanish and Brazilian Crowns sought to appease England's directive to end the trade, they also cultivated the interests of domestic planter elites dependent on captive labor.[66] Each Crown claimed to prohibit the trade while large numbers of African captives entered their very domains. Despite Spain's agreement to end the trade, just over 200,000 Africans were forcibly transferred to Cuba between 1841 and 1867.[67] Between 1840–1841 and 1855–1856, estimates of captives sent to Brazil ranged between 371,615 and 384,500, despite the monarchy's prohibitions of the trade as well.[68] Whether from Upper or Lower Guinea, the forced entry of a minority of African Muslims into a trade that was simultaneously illegal and thriving took shape through the changing dynamics among Brazilian, British, Spanish, and other empires across the Atlantic.

Take, for example, Shaykh Sana See, probably a Fula from Senegambia who arrived in mid nineteenth-century Panama, or what was then the north-western province of the Republic of New Granada, founded after the collapse of the Spanish Empire. Based on an Arabic manuscript authored by this "recaptured Mohammedan," Moustafa Bayoumi relates that Sana See "would have been a youth around the time of the conflicts" in Hausaland and Yorubaland during the first half of the nineteenth century and that he would have been aware of dan Fodio's earlier declaration of jihad.[69] According to Bayoumi, Sana See states that he had traveled "to the countries of 'Dominic,' 'Seralina,' and 'Panama,'" or Dominica, Sierra Leone, and Panama. After embarking on a slave vessel, suggests Bayoumi, Sana See would have been recaptured by the British navy and then "dumped" in Sierra Leone, from which point he probably set sail for Dominica. The collapse of the sugar economy on the then British-ruled island, continues Bayoumi, perhaps led Sana See to his next destination, Panama, where cheap labor was contracted to help build a railroad in the early 1850s.[70] At this conjuncture, Sana See, a member of the Sufi Qadriyya order, composed his six-page manuscript that was "essentially an interior version of Islam," speaking not "of revolt but of remembering." Instead of criticizing the near-slavery conditions that he toiled in or his contact with imperial powers, Sana See's text "promotes the idea that the proper remembrance of Allah will assist and protect the believer." Recaptured by the British from what was most likely Spanish or Portuguese slaving ships, and arriving in Panama, Sana See articulated his inward-looking, devotional perspective amid the end of one empire (Spain) and the domination of yet another (Britain).

Such continuity and change similarly marked the journey of Rufino José Maria, also known as Abuncare (or ʿAbdul-Karim), in Brazil. João José Reis, Flávio dos Santos Gomes, and Marcus de Carvalho recount that Rufino was born into a Yoruba family and received basic education in the Oyo Empire around the time of the aforementioned Islamic reformist movements that forced many Yoruba and Hausa into the transatlantic slave trade.[71] From Rio de Janeiro, the city of disembarkation, Rufino accompanied the man who purchased him to the southern city of Porto Alegre, where he "met . . . some enslaved or already emancipated people from his homeland."[72] There Rufino bought his freedom and, not long after, returned to Rio de Janeiro, where he joined the crew of a Portuguese vessel in the transatlantic slave trade.[73] He worked as a cook on the ship, but in 1841 the English seized it near Angola and brought it to await trial in Sierra Leone. In the five months spent in a land that became home to many Yoruba like himself, Rufino "took advantage of the opportunity . . . to improve his religious education and his knowledge of Arabic."[74] After a brief return to Brazil, he again embarked to the same place in Sierra Leone to continue his training in 1844. Crisscrossing the Atlantic, this Muslim Yoruba who settled in Northeast Brazil deepened his connection to Islam and West Africa through British and Brazilian imperial tensions.

With the malé-led rebellion fresh in its memory, however, the Brazilian Empire grew increasingly paranoid about African Muslims like Rufino.[75] In 1853, as the slave trade entered into irreversible decline, Crown officials arrested Rufino in Recife, the Northeast Brazilian city (where he had been living since the mid-1840s alongside some Yoruba and mostly Congo-Angola–born subjects). Having returned to Brazil after his second stay in Sierra Leone, Rufino abandoned the trade in order to serve the local population as an *alufá* (spiritual guide). His clientele consisted not only of "people of his nation [that is, nagô], but also included other Africans, *pardos* [browns], and even some whites, for whom he would foretell the future, heal varied ailments and even remove curses.[76]" Like the presence of Islam among believers and non-believers in Lower Guinea, the amulets with Qurʾanic verses were prepared by this *alufá* to protect his clients against varied afflictions. Yet when rumors spread of a slave insurrection, local authorities went on a "witch hunt" for *malês* and quickly detained Rufino. His Arabic-language writings and books, including the Qurʾan, reminded them of the 1835 rebels and raised the suspicions of Brazilian imperial officials. Though Rufino was found innocent and released, Reis, Gomes, and Carvalho point out that, in a more profound sense, "Rufino represented another kind of threat, a sort of cultural and even psychological affront to the world of white Brazilians, for being a black man who was proud of being different, a Muslim with powers."[77] Africans' mid-nineteenth-century recourse to Islam as a refuge still animated imperial fears.

African Muslims in Brazil, however, continued to congregate and pray together. In 1865 an account of their practices was penned by Abd al-Rahman Al-Baghdadi, an Arab Ottoman subject whose ship unintentionally landed in Rio de Janeiro.[78] Wearing a turban as he toured the city, Al-Baghdadi was surprised by a black man "dressed as a Frank" (a term for Westerner, in Arabic) who greeted him with "as-salaam alaykum."[79] After they prayed together and found an Arabic-Portuguese translator, Al-Baghdadi learned that "these Blacks came from Bilad al-Sudan in Africa" and numbered "'approximately five thousand.'" Asked to evaluate their religious practices, Al-Baghdadi did not openly criticize them, but rather voiced disdain toward what he called a "corrupted" Islam in his journal. Al-Baghdadi repeated such condescension when he visited Muslim communities in Bahia, Pernambuco, and elsewhere. At the same time, he and the ship's commander stated that "Muslims hid their faith from Christians" (both whites and blacks) "and fear the Frankish communities very much because the latter know them publicly as Christians." Aside from showing a bigoted view of blacks, Al-Baghdadi's writing confirms that Africans continued to observe and hide Islam in imperial Brazil.

Notwithstanding their own dissimulation, African Muslims drew the attention of other observers after the fall of the monarchy and the declaration of the republic in 1889. In Salvador in 1896, physician Nina Rodrigues found that *mussulmis* evoked the name of Allah, having located a Yoruba inscription in front of a butcher shop near the Baixa dos Sapateiros, translated as "There is no king but God, or equal to God."[80] In Rio de Janeiro in 1904, reporter João do Rio wrote that an Afro-Brazilian guide brought him to "the residence of an alufá," and "from the door, the guide yelled 'Salamaleco' [*sic*]. No one responded. [He repeated] 'Salamaleco.' [And a man answered] 'Maneco Masalauré!' [*sic*]."[81] These references should be grasped in relation to a Protestant missionary's exaggerated estimate that, in 1916, one hundred thousand "Brazilian negroes" practiced Islam, "mostly in Bahia and Rio de Janeiro."[82] Indeed, Nina Rodrigues, João do Rio, and others at this time noted that Muslim Afro-Brazilians were moving from Bahia to Rio de Janeiro.[83] One such migrant, Carmen Teixeira da Conceição, was born in Salvador in 1877 and "continued to practice" Islam upon resettling in Rio de Janeiro in 1893.[84] As an adult she became a devout Roman Catholic, but she shed tears when toward the end of her life, she recalled "her faith as a girl and young lady and the old Muslims of Rio de Janeiro."

OF LOSS AND LEGACY

From the 1490s to the 1910s, African Muslims maintained an ongoing presence in what is now called Latin America and the Caribbean. Sometimes they openly defied the status quo or were suspected of doing so by imperial authorities. At other times, Muslims from Senegambia, Upper Guinea, and Lower Guinea coordinated with one another to commiserate, pray together, and observe holy days. In seeking rebellion and refuge, these African Muslim actions and exchanges provide a novel lens into the inner workings of and multifaceted tensions among imperial powers in the New World. Throughout the colonial period, Spanish and Portuguese Crowns viewed them as threats to the social order, while the British and French also patronized them over other captives. But in the 1800s, as the slave trade was simultaneously suppressed (by the British) and thriving (in Cuba and Brazil), the Islamic currents between the Americas and West Africa shifted and intensified. At this conjuncture, African Muslims contributed to and were shaped by the collapse of Iberian colonialism and the rise of British imperial authority.

In the early 1900s, however, direct transatlantic shipping lines ceased between, on the one hand, the Caribbean and South America and, on the other, West Africa. Moreover, the domestic policing and repression of African Muslims heightened in what became Portuguese- and Spanish-speaking republics, which, for the most part, enforced a strict version of Roman apostolic Catholicism. Despite surviving some of the empires that had given rise to their diaspora, African Muslims were denied any future as the twentieth century wore on. Ironically, most African Muslim experiences and identities filter down to us today through the writings or reports of imperial agents, including missionaries, administrators, or slavers.[85] As Moustafa Bayoumi notes, the same forces of modernity that enslaved and sought to wipe out African Muslims in the New World are the means through which we "remember these losses" today.[86]

NOTES

1. Sylviane Diouf, *Servants of Allah: African Muslims Enslaved in the Americas* (New York: New York University Press, 1998), 48; Michael Gomez, *Black Crescent: The Experience and Legacy of African Muslims in the Americas* (Cambridge: Cambridge University Press, 2005),

12; James Sweet, *Recreating Africa: Culture, Kinship, and Religion in the African-Portuguese World, 1440–1770* (Chapel Hill: University of North Carolina Press, 2003), 19.

2. Diouf, *Servants of Allah*; Gomez, *Black Crescent*; Sweet, *Recreating Africa*.

3. Gomez, *Black Crescent*, 52.

4. João José Reis, *Slave Rebellion in Brazil: The Muslim Uprising of 1835 in Bahia* (Baltimore: Johns Hopkins University Press, 1993), 95–96.

5. Michel-Rolph Trouillot, *Silencing the Past: Power and the Production of History* (Boston: Beacon Press, 1995), 178.

6. Sweet, *Recreating Africa*, 18, 87.

7. Gomez, *Black Crescent*, 11, 24; Colin Palmer, *Slaves of the White God: Blacks in Mexico, 1570–1650* (Cambridge, MA: Harvard University Press, 1976), 23.

8. Palmer, *Slaves of the White God*, 28.

9. Leslie Rout, *The African Experience in Spanish America, 1502 to the Present-Day* (Cambridge: Cambridge University Press, 1976), 16.

10. Gomez, *Black Crescent*, 1–2, 8–9; Rout, *African Experience in Spanish America*, 24.

11. Frederick Bowser, *The African Slave in Colonial Peru, 1524–1650* (Stanford, CA: Stanford University Press, 1974), 28.

12. Manuel Lucena Salmoral, *Regulación de la esclavitud negra en las colonias de América española (1503–1886)* (Murcia: Universidad de Murcia, 2005), 45.

13. Bowser, *African Slave in Colonial Peru*, 148.

14. Ibid.

15. Sweet, *Recreating Africa*, 88.

16. Francis Dutra, "Portuguese Slave Trade," in *The Historical Encyclopedia of World Slavery* (1997), 2:517.

17. A. C. de C. M. Saunders, *A Social History of Black Slaves and Freedmen in Portugal* (1982; reprint, Cambridge: Cambridge University Press, 2010), 42, 161.

18. Dutra, "Portuguese Slave Trade," 517.

19. Padre Antônio Vieira, *De Profecia e Inquisição* (Brasília: Conselho Editorial do Senado Federal, 1998), 166 167. See also Alfredo Bosi, "Antônio Vieira, profeta e missionário: Um estudo sobre a pseudomorfose e a contradição," *Estudos Avançados* 23, no. 65 (2009): 247–270.

20. Alonso Sandoval, *De instauranda aethiopum salute: El mundo de la esclavitud negra en América* (1627; reprint, Bogotá: Empresa Nacional de Publicaciones, 1956), 75, 91.

21. Bowser, *African Slave in Colonial Peru*, 27–28.

22. María Elena Martínez, "The Black Blood of New Spain: Limpieza de Sangre, Racial Violence, and Gendered Power in Early Colonial Mexico," *William and Mary Quarterly* 61, no. 3 (2004): 486.

23. Ibid.

24. Ibid., 491, 515.

25. Philip Curtin, "The Tropical Atlantic in the Age of the Slave Trade," in *Islam and European Expansion: The Forging of a Global Order*, edited by Michael Adas (Philadelphia: Temple University Press, 1993), 165–197.

26. David Eltis, David Richardson, and Stephen Behrendt, "Patterns in the Transatlantic Slave Trade, 1662–1867," in *Black Imagination and the Middle Passage*, edited by Maria Diedrich, Henry Louis Gates Jr., and Carl Pedersen (Oxford: Oxford University Press, 1999), 24.

27. Gomez, *Black Crescent*, 47.

28. Raymond Delval, *Les musulmans en Amérique latine et aux Caraibes* (Paris: Dominique Guéniot, 1992), 45.

29. Diouf, *Servants of Allah*, 47–48.

30. Judith Ann Carney and Richard Nicholas Rosomoff, *In the Shadow of Slavery: Africa's Botanical Legacy in the Atlantic World* (Berkeley: University of California Press, 2009), 172.

31. David Trotman and Paul Lovejoy, "Community of Believers: Trinidad Muslims and the Return to Africa, 1810–1850," in *Slavery on the Frontiers of Islam* (Princeton, NJ: Markus Wiener, 2004), 221–222.

32. Cited in Diouf, *Servants of Allah*, 51–52.

33. Gomez, *Black Crescent*, 83–84.

34. Trouillot, *Silencing the Past*, 82.

35. Gomez, *Black Crescent*, 86–87.

36. Diouf, *Servants of Allah*, 150–153; Gomez, *Black Crescent*, 87–90.

37. David Patrick Geggus, *Haitian Revolutionary Studies* (Bloomington: Indiana University Press, 2002), 75.

38. Gomez, *Black Crescent*, 59.

39. Judith Ann Carney and Richard Nicholas Rosomoff, *In the Shadow of Slavery: Africa's Botanical Legacy in the Atlantic World* (Berkeley: University of California Press, 2009), 174.

40. Cited by Sultana Afroz, "Invisible yet Invincible: The Muslim Ummah in Jamaica," *Journal of Muslim Minority Affairs* 23, no. 1 (2003): 213–214; Muhammed Abdullah al-Ahari, "The Caribbean and Latin America," in *Islam Outside the Arab World*, edited by David Westerlund and Ingvar Svanberg (New York: Palgrave-Macmillan, 1999), 445; Gomez, *Black Crescent*, 51–52.

41. Trotman and Lovejoy, "Community of Believers," 222.

42. Hishaam Aidi and Manning Marable, "The Early Muslim Presence and Its Significance," in *Black Routes to Islam* (New York: Palgrave-Macmillan, 2009), 6.

43. Diouf, *Servants of Allah*, 54; Gomez, *Black Crescent*, 55.

44. J. H. Buchner, *The Moravians in Jamaica: History of the Mission of the United Brethren's Church* (London: Longman, Brown, 1854), 50–51.

45. Cited in Diouf, *Servants of Allah*, 56; and Gomez, *Black Crescent*, 53.

46. Paul Lovejoy, "The Yoruba Factor in the Trans-Atlantic Slave Trade," in *The Yoruba Diaspora in the Atlantic World*, edited by Toyin Falola and Matt Childs (Bloomington: Indiana University Press, 2004), 43.

47. Toyin Falola and Matt Childs, eds., *The Yoruba Diaspora in the Atlantic World* (Bloomington: Indiana University Press, 2004), 7.

48. Diouf, *Servants of Allah*, 153; João Jose Reis, "Candomblé in Nineteenth-Century Bahia: Priests, Followers, Clients," in *Rethinking the African Diaspora: The Making of a Black Atlantic World in the Bight of Benin and Brazil*, edited by Kristin Mann and Edna Bay (Oxford: Frank Cass, 2001), 116.

49. Paul Lovejoy, "Background to Rebellion: The Origins of Muslim Slaves in Bahia," *Slavery and Abolition* 15 (1994): 178.

50. Sweet, *Recreating Africa*, 19.

51. David Eltis, *Economic Growth and the Ending of the Transatlantic Slave Trade* (Oxford: Oxford University Press, 1987), 36.

52. Cited by H. W. V. Temperley, "The Later American Policy of George Canning," *American Historical Review* 11 (1906): 796.

53. João José Reis, Flávio dos Santos Gomes, and Marcus J. M. de Carvalho, *O Alufá Rufino: Tráfico, escravidão e liberdade no Atlântico negro* (São Paulo: Companhia das Letras, 2010), 192.

54. Ibid.; Trotman and Lovejoy, "Community of Believers."

55. Reis, *Slave Rebellion in Brazil*, 48.

56. Ibid.

57. Ibid., 104–111.

58. Philip Curtin, *Africa Remembered: Narratives by West Africans from the Era of the Slave Trade* (Madison: University of Wisconsin Press, 1967), 163; Diouf, *Servants of Allah*, 58; Gomez, *Black Crescent*, 54; Trotman and Lovejoy, "Community of Believers," 202.

59. Roger Bastide, "Black Islam in Brazil," in *The African Religions of Brazil* (Baltimore: Johns Hopkins University Press, 1978), 143–154; Jack Goody, "Writing, Religion, and Revolt in Bahia," *Visible Language* 20, no. 3 (1986): 318–343; Lovejoy, "Background to Rebellion."

60. Reis, *Slave Rebellion in Brazil*, 175.

61. Cited in Diouf, *Servants of Allah*, 202.

62. *A True History of the African Chief Jingua and His Comrades with a Description of the Kingdom of Mandingo and of the Manners and Customs of the Inhabitants* (1839), 3, 22–23, General Collection, Beinecke Rare Book and Manuscript Library, Yale University, New Haven, CT.

63. Ibid., 32.

64. Ibid.

65. Leslie Bethell, *The Abolition of the Brazilian Slave Trade: Britain, Brazil, and the Slave Trade Question* (Cambridge: Cambridge University Press, 1970), 151; Franklin Knight, *Slave Society in Cuba during the Nineteenth Century* (Madison: University of Wisconsin Press, 1970).

66. Eltis, *Economic Growth*, 125.

67. Ibid., 242.

68. Bethell, *Abolition of the Brazilian Slave Trade*, 388; Eltis, *Economic Growth*, 241.

69. Moustafa Bayoumi, "Moving Beliefs: The Panama Manuscript of Sheikh Sana See and African Diasporic Islam," *Interventions* 5, no. 1 (2003): 71–72.

70. Bayoumi, "Moving Beliefs," 71, 74.

71. Reis, Gomes, and Carvalho, *O Alufá Rufino*.

72. Ibid., 52.

73. Ibid., 99–100.

74. Ibid., 232.

75. Alberto Costa e Silva, "Comprando e vendendo Alcorões no Rio de Janeiro do século XIX," *Estudos Avançados* 18, no. 50 (2004): 285–294.

76. Reis, Gomes, and Carvalho, *O Alufá Rufino*, 306.

77. Ibid., 357.

78. Abd al-Rahman Al-Baghdadi, *The Amusement of the Foreigner*, translated by Yacine Daddi Addoun and Renée Soulodre–La France (Toronto: York University, 2001).

79. Ibid., 7, 8, 11.

80. Nina Rodrigues, "O animismo fetichista dos negros bahianos," *Revista Brazilera* 2, no. 6 (1896): 165.

81. João do Rio (pen name for Paulo Barreto), *As religiões do Rio* (1906; reprint, Rio de Janeiro: Editora Companhia Nacional, 1928), 12.

82. S. M. Zwemer, "Islam in South America," *Muslim World* 6, no. 2 (1916): 150.
83. Costa e Silva, "Comprando e vendendo Alcorões," 290–291.
84. Cited in ibid., 292–293.
85. Reis, *Slave Rebellion in Brazil*, xiii; Reis, Gomes, and Carvalho, *O Alufá Rufino*, 11–12.
86. Bayoumi, "Moving Beliefs," 80.

CHAPTER 3

ETHNIC AND RELIGIOUS IDENTIFICATION AMONG MUSLIM EAST INDIANS IN SURINAME (1898–1954)

ELLEN BAL AND KATHINKA SINHA-KERKHOFF

THIS CHAPTER FOCUSES ON men who migrated from British India to work as indentured laborers in Suriname, a Dutch colony until 1975. Since the late 1870s, Dutch planters in Suriname welcomed such laborers, who replaced the liberated African slaves, in first their sugar and later their coffee and cacao plantations. Most of these migrants never returned to India, even after their contracts expired. Endowed with a small plot of land, they became independent cultivators and cattle farmers. By the 1920s some had taken up professions such as shopkeeper and teacher, and others were involved in small trade. They had also started identifying as Hindustanis, a label that originated during Mughul-governed India. The majority of these Hindustanis originated from the eastern part of India and were Hindu and Muslim by religion, though a few had converted to Christianity as well. In this chapter we illustrate that though they developed into an ethnic community based on common linguistic, regional, and sociocultural backgrounds,[1] religious differences remained a latent bone of contention among them. Though women migrated as well, we discuss ethnic and religious identification processes among only male Muslims and to a lesser extent Hindus from British Indian origin.

We start our analysis around 1898, the year in which one such Muslim migrant named Rahman Khan, at the age of twenty-four, was shipped fifteen thousand miles away from the port of Calcutta to Suriname in South America. Like most other migrants from British India, Khan never returned to the country of his birth. Yet Khan was exceptional in other ways, as he was literate. Identifying as a *munshi* (learned man), Khan became a teacher, educating both Hindus as well as Muslims in Hindi and Hinduism. Munshi Rahman Khan was also the first and to our knowledge the only indentured laborer who produced an autobiography, written between 1943 and 1945, twenty-seven years before his demise in 1972.[2] Our analysis ends around 1954, when the Dutch colony became a constituent country of the Kingdom of the Netherlands and had full autonomy except in areas of defense, foreign policy, and nationality. Related to this, free elections were in the air after 1949, though the country became fully independent only on November 25, 1975.

This chapter is based on Khan's autobiography as well as interviews with his family, friends, enemies, and their descendants. We feel that Rahman Khan embodied not only communal concord but also contradictory communal divergence. In our view Khan's life was quite representative of many other Hindustani Muslims in Suriname during 1898 and 1954. Using his autobiography and our findings from oral history projects in Suriname as well as in the Netherlands, combined with other contemporary and secondary textual sources, in this chapter we unravel the process of community formation among the indentured laborers of British Indian descent and not only describe communal friction but also try to explain why Hindu and Muslim Hindustanis in Suriname by the early 1950s still emphasized ethnic similarity rather than religious difference. This outcome was at variance with not only Mauritius, where religious dissimilarities among British Indian migrants led to the construction of discrete ethnoreligious communities,[3] but also British India, where discord between the Hindus and Muslims developed in demands for separate nations.

SURINAME: A MULTIFARIOUS SOCIETY

Wedged between British Guiana to the West, French Guiana to the East, and Brazil to the South, Suriname sets the stage for this chapter. The country offers a textbook example of a so-called polyethnic or plural society.[4] Since the Dutch arrived in 1667, ethnicity has provided the primary criterion for the organization of society in Suriname. Initially, ethnic (typically referred to as *racial*) distinctions marked the relations between the colonial planters, the slaves of African origin, and the indigenous ("Indian") population. Since the abolition of slavery in 1863 and the subsequent import of labor from other colonies, new ethnic groups emerged among people of Asian origins (from British India, the Dutch Indies, and China). Today, Suriname also has immigrants from Guiana (formerly known as British Guiana), Haiti, Brazil, and elsewhere, as well as "new" migrants from China.

The two largest communities in contemporary Suriname are the Hindustanis and the Afro-Surinamese, also known as Creoles. In 2004 there were 492,829 inhabitants in the entire country. The Hindustanis formed the largest ethnic group, totaling 135,117 people. With a total of 87,202 people, the Creoles came second and the Javanese third (71,879). Historically, there was a significant Jewish community in Suriname.[5] Interestingly, in 2004, 61,524 people were also registered as "mixed" and 32,579 as unknown.[6] Almost 70 percent of all Surinamese reside in the capital, Paramaribo, and its bordering district Wanica.

In terms of religion, Christians formed the largest category (40.7 percent) followed by the Hindus (19.9 percent), Muslims (13.5 percent), and others. Most Javanese in Suriname had adopted Islam, and most Creoles identified as Christians. Yet as we illustrate below in the case of Hindustanis, though important in identity and identification processes, religion did not become a marker of difference that split Hindustanis in Suriname into two antagonistic groups. Muslim Hindustanis also never permanently united with Javanese Muslims in fashioning a new and separate group exclusively based on religious similarities. In fact, at least until the early 1950s, religion was merged into one common ethnic identity as Hindustanis, or East Indian coolies.

BRITISH INDIANS IN SURINAME

The Hindustanis, who constitute the largest ethnic community in Suriname today, are the descendants of the indentured laborers who migrated from British India to Suriname between 1873 and 1916. Their arrival was closely connected to the prohibition of African slavery in 1863. In search for alternative labor on the plantations, the Dutch signed a convention with the British government in 1870 that allowed them to recruit Indian labor.[7] All in all, approximately 34,000 British Indian contract workers migrated to the Dutch colony.

These subjects from British India landed in an ethnically plural environment, stamped by Dutch colonialism (which began in the seventeenth century) and the accompanying institution of slavery to support the plantation economy.[8] Ethnic diversity increased further when the number of slaves dwindled in 1863, and the Dutch turned to China, British India, and the Dutch Indies to fill the void. Between 1893 and 1940, around 33,000 laborers came from the Dutch Indies (mostly Javanese Muslims).[9] These Javanese belonged to the Shafi'i theological school of Islam.[10]

At the outset British Indians in Suriname were marked by differences of language, religion, caste, regional background, class, and gender. They came with distinct ambitions and personal histories, and they were equipped with various physical and mental abilities in their long journey and new circumstances.[11] Men and women typically listed themselves as unmarried, and family migration was rare. Often their migration motives were a combination of poverty, personal and localized difficulties, as well as a spirit of enterprise or adventure.

Most laborers came from the regions now known as Uttar Pradesh and Bihar.[12] Initially, these contract laborers were referred to as *Calcuttyas*, coolies, or British Indians. In Suriname they were also referred to as East Indians and increasingly as "Hindustanis," especially in reference to those who were born in Suriname and acquired Dutch citizenship (after 1927). "Hindustani" referred to the region that rulers in Moghul India had labeled Hindustan and from which many had migrated, and thus not to the religious identity (Hindu) of the majority of the East Indians migrants in Suriname. After 1947, when British India ceased to exist, Hindustani became the common designation for these people of Indian descent in Suriname.[13]

The number of Muslims among the migrants was around 17.5 percent, while the number of Muslims in their home territory was around 14 percent at the time of migration.[14] Thus, the proportion of Muslims among the emigrants was relatively large. Reasons for this could have been that many recruitment agents were Muslims themselves. Besides, Muslims, unlike Hindus, faced no religious sanctions when traveling overseas. Moreover, Muslims not only were overrepresented in urban areas where recruitment was easier,[15] but also faced severe hardships and status decrease at that time in colonial India.[16] However, most British Indian migrants identified as Hindu, often from so-called lower-caste backgrounds. Brahmins (the highest caste) made up only 5 percent, even though the census of India of 1931 reported that Brahmins constituted 11 percent of the Hindu population in Bihar and Uttar Pradesh.[17]

Nevertheless, neither Hindu nor Muslim Hindustanis constituted homogeneous categories of believers. The widely heterogeneous caste background also contributed to their religious heterogeneity, and caste had affected Muslims in colonial India as well.[18] During their stay in the depots in Calcutta and the long journey that lasted for months, some "singles" became "couples," friends became "brothers,"[19] and many friendships and marriages (including interreligious ones) were long lasting.

During the 1870s and 1880s, most indentured laborers in Suriname seemed to have considered themselves "transients" rather than "settlers." In these early times, some returned home. This changed during the 1890s, when the Dutch developed a policy to encourage the plantation workers to stay and to settle in Suriname. The settlement policies proved successful, and the number of settlers increased rapidly from 1895 onward. In 1895 only 548 British Indians rented or owned a private plot of land. By 1913 their number had already gone up to 5,093.[20]

Those who decided to stay began to perceive Suriname as the country of "permanent abode," and processes of community building emerged from the soil of Suriname. By 1947, when India bifurcated into India and Pakistan, the

British Indians in Suriname had evolved as a distinct ethnic and linguistic community. Internal fragmentation among the Hindus as Muslims as well as some sense of communal (Hindu-Muslim) differences did influence their social cohesion and (sociopolitical) organization, however. Nevertheless, these contentions did not cause a definite rupture between Hindus and Muslims, as had been the case, for example, in Mauritius.[21] Their ethnic Hindustani identity continued to prevail over other identity markers such as religion.

MUSLIMS IN SURINAME

Scholars trace the history of Islam and Muslims in the Caribbean to the voyages of Columbus in the fifteenth century. For example, Chickrie argues that a small number of the African slaves such as those who belonged to the Zam-Zam and Arabi Mandinka clan had been Muslims.[22] However, with the arrival of laborers from the Dutch East Indies and from British India, the Muslim population of Suriname grew to 20 percent in the 1980s.[23] There are now more than one hundred mosques in the country. Elements of Shari'a, Islamic law, had been incorporated into Suriname's Civil Code since 1940–41, when Governor Johannes Kielstra passed the Asian Marriage Act.[24] With the consent of Muslim intelligentsia in Suriname, however, the Muslim Marriage Act of 1940 was abrogated in 2003.[25]

Muslim East Indians can also be found in British Guiana, Trinidad, Guadeloupe, Martinique, Jamaica, St. Lucia, St. Vincent, and Grenada. Centuries after enslaved African Muslims, they reintroduced Islam (or rather various Islamic syncretized traditions) in the Caribbean. Unlike Hindus (who are generally of Indian descent), Muslims in Suriname today comprise people with various (diasporic) backgrounds: the Javanese who came under a similar indenture system from the Indonesian Archipelago (between 1890 and 1940) and also a growing Afro-Surinamese Muslim community. Most Muslims in Suriname are known as ethnic Javanese. British Indian Muslims come second. In 2004 out of 66,307 Muslims, 46,156 were Javanese, and 15,636 were ethnic Hindustanis.

All sixty-four boats that brought indentured laborers to Suriname transported self-identified "Muslims." According to the personal database of these indentured laborers, the first boat, the *Lalla Rukha*, counted at least 35 Muslims among the 410 passengers.[26] These 35 people were marked as "Muslim" or "Musalman." There might have been more Muslims, such as Pathans and Afghans who were, however, not always categorized as Muslims by the Dutch administrators.[27] All in all, an estimated one-fifth of all British Indian indentured laborers were Muslim.[28] Like Hindus, Muslims were heterogeneous.

They were *saiyads*, shaykhs, Pathans, Moghals, *julahas*, fakirs, *ghosis*, and *hajams*. Most were Sunni Muslims who celebrated the Eids as well as Muharram and Milad al-Nabi, influenced by the Shi'is and Sufis of North India. Though their religious affiliation was different from other Hindustanis, they shared with Hindus similar class, ethnic, political, and even religious interests, such as preference for secular public as opposed to Christian private education, use of the Hindustani language, demand for Asian marriage acts, links with Hindustan, common festivals and professions, food culture, and dress codes.[29]

FROM SOJOURNERS TO CITIZENS

The large distance between Suriname and India certainly impacted the minds of migrants and their descendants. The entire journey from India to Suriname took approximately three to four months for sailing ships and five to eight weeks for steamers.[30] Only a few of the British Indians who settled in Suriname were able or willing to maintain contacts with India. After the first generation of migrants passed away, most connections with relatives in British India ceased. Though interest in Indian affairs remained until at least 1947, this had reduced by 1920, once organized labor migration from British India to Suriname had stopped. Pointing to the adverse situation in British India, the Surinamese Immigration Society openly dissuaded Hindustanis from returning.[31] About 2,500 Hindustanis were booked for the last boat (*Sutlej*) that took those with rights for a free return passage back to India. In the end, however, only 872 boarded.[32] By 1916, when ships stopped bringing in new migrants from India, immigrants increasingly looked upon India as the land of their ancestors and less as a homeland. Consequently, attention was devoted to adverse circumstances of Hindustanis in Suriname, among which were mentioned lack of adequate schooling for boys and girls as well as the non-recognition of Hindu and Muslim marriage rituals. Discrimination against the British Indian community was also discussed in newspapers.[33] Clearly, by 1921 Hindustanis constituted a separate ethnic community that identified neither with the Christian (and white) Dutch population nor with the Creoles or Javanese.[34] In 1927 British Indian "aliens" were formally recognized as Dutch subjects (*onderdanen*) in colonial Suriname. Substituting British India, the Netherlands became the official motherland for most among these Hindustanis. Yet this did not mean that people and happenings in British India stopped influencing Hindustanis in Suriname.

From the 1920s onward, Surinamese Muslims (and Hindus) became increasingly active religiously, politically, and economically. Muslim leaders established ties with religious bodies in not only British India but also South America, principally in British Guiana and Trinidad, which had in turn been influenced by religious leaders and organizations from British India. Kassim narrated that these ties blossomed during the 1930s and 1940s and resulted in the organization of the Inter-Colonial Muslim Conference in August 1950.[35] Delegates from Barbados, British Guiana, Dutch Guiana (Suriname), and the host territory, Trinidad, met to consider the educational, social, economic, moral, and religious problems of Muslims in the Caribbean. They intended to forge a closer relationship and cooperation through a regional Muslim organization. In Suriname itself Muslims from different ethnic backgrounds made an effort to unite under a common Islamic banner.[36] These collective actions of Muslims of distinct ethnic backgrounds in Suriname and beyond never resulted in the formation of durable alliances. Religious institutions among Muslim Hindustanis continued to be based on intra- rather than interethnic religious cooperation. However, as we will see, the transition from British Indian sojourners into Surinamese citizens went hand in hand with increasing religious institutionalization and friction. Although these dynamics did not result in a total rupture between Muslims and Hindus among Hindustanis, the 1920s until the 1940s were marked by some serious, albeit localized, communal incidents.

THE BOYCOTT: COMMUNAL CONFLICTS
IN SURINAME OF THE 1920S AND 1930S

Hindus and Muslims in Suriname looked upon British India for religious inspiration and guidance. Efforts to unite Muslims globally and endeavors to connect Surinamese Muslims to Muslims from India and Pakistan went alongside the initiatives of Hindus who tried to connect with Hindus in the diaspora and in (British) India itself.[37] In Suriname these linkages did sharpen differences within and between Hindu and Muslim Hindustanis. For instance, the regular visits of Hindu as well as Muslim religious leaders from India, from what now constitutes Pakistan, and from other regions where British Indians had settled (e.g., Trinidad and neighboring British Guiana) became intimately linked with religious fragmentation among Hindus and Muslims in Suriname and also affected internal cohesion between them. Hindustanis had always organized as one group in, for instance, the Surinamese Immigration Organization and Bharat Oeday, which had repeatedly requested that Hindu and Muslim members work together for their common cause.[38] In 1929 Javanese Muslims and Muslim Hindustanis united in the Surinamese Islamic Organization.[39] Though the group had only a few members and did not last long, the establishment of such organizations based on religion was a sign that not all Muslim and Hindu Hindustanis believed in ethnic unity above all.[40]

One of the most noteworthy confrontations between Hindu and Muslim Hindustanis in Suriname took place between the late 1920s until the early 1940s and evolved around the Islamic practice of cow sacrifice (or cow "slaughter," as labeled by Hindus at the time), also known as *kurbani*. This period of communal antagonism is generally known as "the Boycott." Even though Suriname was spared the bitter clashes between Hindus and Muslims that took place in India, many Hindustanis nevertheless recollect this period as a dark chapter in their history. The movement, however, was not widespread. It did not encompass all members of the two religious groups, and the disputes were mainly verbal. Nevertheless, our elderly informants still remembered how after 1929 until at least 1943, Hindus started boycotting Muslims in a number of places, cutting sociocultural and economic ties with them. While Muslims in Suriname had refrained from *kurbani*, since the late 1920s relations between Hindus and Muslims had become so disturbed that some people no longer cared. In a number of places, Muslims killed cows and Hindus slaughtered pigs. In the 1930s the conflicts led Hindus to boycott Muslims.[41]

Munshi Rahman Khan wrote the most extensive account about this period. For Khan, the social unrest in the country was due to the introduction of the Arya Samaj, a Hindu reformist organization from India that also started work in Suriname.[42] While their initial quest for "purification" of Hinduism caused discord between Samajees and Sanatan Hindus in Suriname,[43] tensions among Hindus were somewhat resolved at the expense of Hindu-Muslim relations. A first-generation migrant, the Hindi-speaking Rahman Khan with only lower-level formal education had particularly blamed Mehta Jaimani, a lawyer from India who had studied in Britain, spoke English, and had links with the Asiatic Society of India, Max Mueler Bhavan, and the Theosophic Society. An Aryan missionary himself from India, Jaimani had visited Suriname and other countries for religious purposes, offering lectures on the Sanskrit Vedas and Indian culture.[44] According to Khan, Jaimani had upset sixty years of brotherly relations between Hindus and Muslims in Suriname by planting "the seed of discontent and ill will amongst the communities."[45] After his departure in 1929, his followers began their preaching, and Sanatan religious followers boycotted Muslims:

> Moreover, fighting ensued if an Arya Samaji greeted a Sanatani. A number of such incidents occurred making people of both organizations feel hurt and start lawsuits against each other. Initially this friction took place between

the Arya Samajis and the Sanatanis while the Muslims befriended both these groups. Yet soon it became evident that the Arya Samajis could not conquer the Sanatanis and the two groups therefore resolved their differences and calmed down. . . . Yet, the dictum of the Arya Samaj is to criticize others during their meetings and this frequently has resulted in conflicts. The Sanatanis were the first victims while the Muslims escaped. Besides, though after some time relations between the two groups seemed to have become cordial, the cold war between them continued.[46]

In 1921 the newspaper *Suriname* still emphasized the common economic and even religious interests of the Hindu and Muslim East Indian immigrants in Suriname through the reported proceedings of the Surinamese Immigrant Organization.[47] In that year the same newspaper also witnessed cordial or even close relations between Hindu and Muslim Hindustanis during festivals such as Tadja (Tazia, also known as Muharram or Hosay).[48] By the midthirties, however, these "cordial and close relations" had been disrupted. In 1933 the two communities became further divided along confessional lines, turning into bitter enemies by 1934. By then, Hindus had united under one banner and "rallied around the cow," and this completely antagonized Muslims.[49]

While Rahman Khan's version of the Boycott was favorable to Muslim Hindustanis, other informants presented different accounts. With respect to a *kurbani* incident and the ensuing conflict between Hindus and Muslims in Livorno, the responsible district commissioner reported that he held the Muslims primarily responsible. They had, after all, not listened to him, even though he had personally tried his best to persuade the Muslims to refrain from slaughtering a cow. The Dutch commissioner also stated that the parties should not forget that they both constitute "one race."[50]

Among the number of elderly Hindustanis we interviewed regarding this phase in the communal history of Suriname, most felt that neither India's independence nor its partition had been of influence. Instead, a Hindu Hindustani, eighty-five years old at the time, held a number of local developments responsible for the communal disturbances. He elaborated:

Indeed some of us received the *Sri Venkateswara* newspaper from India whenever a ship used to come from there to Suriname. I also received *Kalyan*, a religious magazine from Gorakhpur. The Boycott [in Suriname] lasted until 1943. Pandit Ram Narain, brother of Shiv Narain, and Rozan were the reason for it. Both were very close friends and used to drink together from one glass. But Rozan cut off the head of a cow and tied it on a roadside tree. Thereafter other people started instigating fights to gain popularity.[51]

We also interviewed a pandit (priest) who used to visit Rahman Khan to study Hindi. He even referred to the latter as his "father-in-law," since his relation with one of Khan's sons was like that with a brother-in-law. At the time of our interview, this pandit was ninety-four years old. He narrated:

> In fact, *kurbani* was the reason for the boycott in the 1930s. Before that Hindus and Muslims used to have very harmonious relationships with each other. The independence of India had no effect here and was not the reason for the problems around *kurbani* here.[52]

Unlike most of our other informants but like Rahman Khan, one eighty-five-year-old Muslim, living in Livorno (Suriname), one of the centers of the Boycott, did blame India for the religious tensions in the Caribbean. He pointed, however, not to the exemplary role of communalism in India, but to the role of the Indian pandits who had come to various places in the Caribbean:

> Men from India are responsible for this situation. Guiana witnessed a massacre. Again, the responsibility lies with the men from India. That will be the case everywhere. I am against all this. Their slogan is "wherever you are, turn the place into a Hindu Hindustan, a second India."[53]

Yet while directly pointing to the harmful influences of Indian pandits on interethnic relations across the Caribbean, this Muslim informant did not speak of similar disturbances in Suriname itself. Also in his version of the Boycott, factors within Suriname, and not from British India, were the main causes.

In 1943 the Boycott was officially ended in a meeting among Hindus, Muslims, and colonial government representatives. Unlike in India, where Hindu-Muslim animosities intensified, communal harmony among the Hindustanis in Suriname was restored. When in 1947 British India became independent, Muslim and Hindu Hindustanis were content that a "free and independent Hindustan" had been established, but they regretted the "awful partition" of their Hindustan.[54] A Surinamese newspaper described how Muslims and Hindus raised three flags on the occasion: that of the Netherlands, of India, and of Pakistan.[55] They commonly prayed for the well-being of Hindus and Muslims in these three nations.

However, this harmony was temporary. Communal discord had not entirely disappeared and found its reflection in Surinamese politics during election periods. Moreover, a later text produced by Munshi Rahman Khan in the 1950s revealed that dissimilarities between Muslim and Hindu Hindustanis continued to flare up.[56] Newspaper clippings reported on political infighting in the United Hindustani Party (VHP) in 1951 for instance, when two Muslim Hindustani politicians — Mohamedradja and Jamalodin — left the VHP and joined the National Party of Suriname.[57] Reflected in an emotional debate over a slaughterhouse ordinance, the political rivalry among Hindu and Muslim Hindustanis continued to be tense in the early 1950s.[58] Nonetheless, *verbroedering* (coming together) into one ethnic community prevailed. Contemporary newspaper reports demonstrate that in the colonial and multiethnic setting of Suriname at the time, Muslims as well as Hindus in the political field preferred a common ethnic identity rather than giving primacy to religious identities, as both communities perceived that their cultural-educational, socioeconomic, and even religious interests would be better served that way.

In the next section, we argue that this outcome was also caused by the fact that alternative identities for Muslim East Indians, such as a shared Muslim identity with the Muslim Javanese or a common platform with the Creoles, did not last. Their shared Muslim identity was a less powerful unifier than class, language, customs, culinary traditions, and shared historical experiences among Hindu and Muslim Hindustanis. Such communalities also separated Hindustanis from other ethnic groups in Suriname such as the Javanese, Dutch, and Creoles.

CONTEXTUALIZING HINDU-MUSLIM
ANTAGONISM IN SURINAME

The end of the indenture system in 1916 also led to the end of colonial politics of segregation and the acceleration of "integration."[59] By 1927 Hindustanis born in Suriname officially became Dutch citizens and thereby began to reconceive their place in Dutch Suriname vis-à-vis other local ethnic groups and the Dutch colonial power.[60] Agriculture did not provide a very secure basis — being so labor intensive and little profitable — to compete with other citizens. Yet without formal education and proper knowledge of the Dutch language, social mobility became almost impossible. "The urge for a better societal position, to belong to the intellectual elite, to acquire possessions and social respect, formed the basis for a breakthrough in Hindustani attempts to emancipate in our country," wrote Ramsundersingh.[61] In Suriname of the late 1920s, education, (government) employment, religion, and development of women seemed the primary directives for the enhancement of the socioeconomic status of Hindustanis.[62]

Some scholars have argued that "the Hindustani competition with Creoles for scarce socio-economic and political resources" produced a strong tendency "within the Hindustani group to neglect the internal socio-religious differences and to stress the fact that Hindustanis were a group originating in India, having a common history and therefore a common identity."[63] Indeed, we also conclude that witnessing increased competitiveness, though we pointed to exceptions above, most Hindustanis during the first years of the 1950s agreed that separate religious identities served neither the political nor the class interests of Muslim or Hindu Hindustanis in an upcoming more autonomous Suriname.[64] Hence, in the end, Hindustanis united under the banner of a shared ethnic identity vis-à-vis other ethnic communities. Yet although we agree with the argument that animosity against Creoles possibly led to the understatement of internal differences, we also maintain that during the late 1920s, 1930s, and 1940s religion was indeed "a significant symbol system of identification, demarcation and support,"[65] which at times negatively impacted communal harmony, as illustrated above.

It is tempting to link Hindu-Muslim conflicts in Dutch Suriname to communal politics in British India and later India and Pakistan. Yet all our informants denied such a link and emphasized that local factors were responsible for the Boycott. Hindu-Muslim conflicts and subsequent reconciliation in Suriname thus call for a careful contextualization of the events, encompassing a macro but also a micro level of analysis as well as the study of their mutual interaction.

Looking at the micro level, that is, study of relations within the Hindustani community, we found that it was exactly in the process of repositioning themselves vis-à-vis other communities within Suriname that the apparent harmony within the community started to crumble. Differences between the "educated" and "uneducated" (in Dutch and Hindustani) caused great schisms, and the peaceful cohabitation between the two religious groups— also subdivided from within—started eroding. Some Hindus, who had previously hidden or changed their caste identities, now claimed upper-caste Brahman or Kshatriya caste membership. Other Hindus as well as our Munshi Rahman Khan contested this and felt that education, rather than caste, should be the criterion for a position as pandit. In this context, the so-called reformers who came from India became quite successful in their efforts to introduce new religious, sociocultural outlooks, and lifestyles among both Hindu as well as Muslim Hindustanis. Some chose religion as an important source of identification. However, our historical sources revealed that political party formation on a religious basis did not last and that indeed religious harmony was restored.

Apart from competition from without, identified above, we believe that the localized (British Indian or South Asian) culture of Islam, which marked these Muslim Hindustanis, also caused ethnic solidarity to prevail over religious similarities. This unique cultural heritage linked them, for example, to a shared place of origin, different from that of Javanese or other Muslims in Suriname.[66] Although Surina Islam, an organization that wanted to unite Javanese and Hindustani Muslims, was established in 1929,[67] the newspaper witnessed economic competition between the Javanese and Hindustani communities during that same year. Besides, Urdu, the language that Muslim Hindustanis adopted as their religious language, separated them from Javanese Muslims and from other Muslims in British Guiana, who were attracted to "arabization."[68] Together, Muslim and Hindu Hindustanis developed a common spoken language now known as Sarnami or Sarnami Hindustani. Hindustani Muslims in Suriname also preferred links with Lahore and did not seem to have much interest in "pilgrimages to Mekka."[69] This orientation toward South Asia continued after 1947, when India was partitioned and Lahore then became part of Pakistan. Rather than "de-Indianizing" their Muslim cultural practices, Hindustani Muslims in Suriname sought their preservation and invited *maulanas* (respected Muslim religious leaders) from India and Pakistan for this purpose.

ETHNIC UNITY PREVAILS OVER RELIGIOUS DISCORD

Indian indentured laborers left British India at a time when there was not much of a national identity or a "common bond of unity and fellow feeling." People might have felt Bengali, Sikh, Rajput, Maratha, or Hindustani, but certainly not Indian.[70] In Suriname most Muslim and Hindu Hindustanis, no matter how fragmented and marked by conflict and distance, chose the path of mutual collaboration along ethnic lines as a means of "integration" in new realities. In short, during the 1930s—when the Boycott reached its zenith—a strong and common ethnic identity also developed that united the Hindustanis and set them apart from other migrant groups in Suriname as well as from the Dutch colonial rulers. This ethnic unison was, however, continuously crosscut by religious forces.

When in 1947 the British left India, independence was celebrated in Suriname, but the division of British India on religious lines was not welcomed, let alone followed. On the contrary, people seemed rather disappointed with these developments in "their Hindustan." For example, in July 1947 a group of young Hindustani intellectuals wrote in their monthly newsletter, *Vikaash*, the following about India's independence and the creation of Pakistan through partition:

The moment has arrived. . . . Finally freedom, which has taken many years of furious fighting, has been regained. It already has been determined that the remaining 15,000 British troops will leave Hindustan on August 15th. Energetic men who have given everything for the good cause can now look back on what they have reached at for Hindustan. But alas! It could not be what they would have wanted so much: their ideal of a United Hindustan has been destroyed and their hopes have gone up in smoke. . . . Yet! There is hope for the future! Especially the circumstance that Hindus and Muslims are not strictly separated gives reason for hope. One expects that both states will co-operate intimately, as they share so many interests.[71]

Hence, while independence was celebrated by the people of Indian descent, partition (and the gruesome consequences of that bisection) was mourned. In Suriname peace among Hindus and Muslims returned in the course of the 1940s, and in 1949 many, though not all, Hindus and Muslims were expected to vote for the VHP.[72] In the context of different and changing local and global challenges in colonial Suriname, Hindus and Muslims of British Indian origin united on the basis of shared origin and heritage. They identified and joined with each other on the basis of historical linkages they shared with the undivided homeland called Hindustan. It was this shared identity that they emphasized and developed further when they cultivated roots in their adopted country, Suriname. Yet whereas common origin united the Hindustanis, religion also divided them into two potentially opposing groups. However, notwithstanding the described occasional friction, distrust, and interreligious tensions, ethnic identity proved stronger and more instrumental than religious affinities. What the future brings we cannot predict, however, as we have demonstrated that the chosen unison is not intrinsic but based on mutual decisions in a contextualized reality. Instead, religious (and ethnic) identities are dynamic, and communal frictions are temporal and situation dependent and should be studied as historical outcomes rather than primordial givens.

NOTES

This chapter is to a large extent based on the material collected by and on findings of the two authors between 2001 and 2005. The research, which focused on Muslim as well as Hindu East Indians in Suriname, was simultaneously carried out in Suriname, India, and the Netherlands. Part of it was supported by the Netherlands Foundation for Research in Tropical Countries under the name "A Diaspora Coming Home? Overseas Indians Reestablishing Links with India." For the purpose of this chapter, we have updated our sources and reformulated our arguments. The material used encompasses archival, autobiographical and newspaper sources, interviews, and secondary sources. See also Ellen Bal and Kathinka

Sinha-Kerkhoff, "Muslims in Surinam and the Netherlands, and the Divided Homeland," *Journal of Muslim Minority Affairs* 25, no. 2 (2005): 193–217; Ellen Bal and Kathinka Sinha-Kerkhoff, "British Indians in Colonial India and Surinam: Transnational Identification and Estrangement," *Focaal*, no. 47 (2006): 105–120.

    1. Prema A. Kurien, *Kaleidoscopic Ethnicity: International Migration and the Construction of Community Identities in India* (New Delhi: Oxford University Press, 2004), 28.

    2. Kathinka Sinha-Kerkhoff, Ellen Bal, and Anil Deo Singh, eds., *Autobiography of an Indian Indentured Labourer: Munshi Rahman Khan (1874–1972), Jeevan Prakash* (Delhi: Shripra, 2005). This concerns the English translation of the digitalized Devanagri text. The original handwritten text was translated in Dutch and published by Sandew Hira in 2003. See Sandew Hira, ed., *Het Dagboek van Munshi Rahman Khan* (Den Haag/Paramaribo: Amrit and NSHI, 2003). We herewith acknowledge our debt to Sandew Hira and Amrit Publishers and the Nationale Stichting Hindostaanse Immigratie (NSHI).

    3. Ellen Bal and Kathinka Sinha-Kerkhoff, "Separated by Partition? Muslims of British Indian Descent in Mauritius and Suriname," in *Global Indian Diasporas: Exploring Trajectories of Migration and Theory*, edited by Gijsbert Oonk, IIAS Publications Series (Amsterdam: Amsterdam University Press, 2007), 119–149.

    4. Polyethnic or plural societies are often described as deeply divided. Well-known colonial historians, such as John S. Furnivall, have generally understood these societies as constituting discrete cultural groups, integrated into one economic system, but as distinct communities, who maintain limited contact across ethnic borders. See John S. Furnivall, *Colonial Policy and Practice: A Comparative Study of Burma and Netherlands India* (Cambridge: Cambridge University Press, 1948). Not denying the existence of colonial policies of identity enforcements, in this chapter, we take a constructivist perspective and start from the premise that ethnicity emerges as a consequence of interaction and is not the (primordialist) resultant of predetermined cultural differences. In other words, people can accept or reject particular imposed identities and are therefore active players in their own identity formation, which in itself is an ongoing process. During this process persons can unite as a religious community, for instance, but also as an ethnic group, separating themselves from others considered to possess different linguistic, regional, sociocultural, and religious backgrounds. In accordance with Thomas Hylland Eriksen, we define ethnicity as "an aspect of social relationship between agents who consider themselves as essentially distinctive from members of other groups of whom they are aware and with whom they enter into a relationship." Thomas Hylland Eriksen, *Ethnicity and Nationalism: Anthropological Perspectives*, 3rd ed. (London and New York: Pluto Press, 2010), 12.

    5. Edward Dew, *The Difficult Flowering of Suriname: Ethnicity and Politics in a Plural Society* (Paramaribo: Vaco, 1996), 21–22.

    6. Chan E. S. Choenni, *Madad Sahára Sahá Saháyta: Analyse en aanpak sociale problematiek onder Hindostanen in Suriname* (The Hague: Seva Network Foundation, 2009), 34; Chan E. S. Choenni, "Integratie Hindostani Stijl: Over de migratie, geschiedenis en diaspora van Hindostanen" (unpublished paper); Chan E. S. Choenni, "Migratie naar en vestiging in Nederland," in *Hindostanen: Van Brits-Indische Emigranten via Suriname to Burgers van Nederland*, edited by Chan E. S. Choenni and Kanta Sh. Adhin (Den Haag: Sampreshan, 2003), 54–69.

    7. *Suriname*, no. 83 (October 11, 1870).

    8. Raymond S. Chickrie, "Muslims in Suriname: Facing Triumphs and Challenges in a Plural Society," *Journal of Muslim Minority Affairs* 31, no. 1 (2011): 79.

9. Ibid.

10. P. Surparlan, *The Javanese in Suriname in an Ethnically Plural Society* (Tucson: Arizona State University, 1995); Rosemarijn Hoefte, *In Place of Slavery: A Social History of British Indian and Javanese Laborers in Suriname* (Gainesville: University Press of Florida, 1998).

11. Steven Vertovec, *The Hindu Diaspora: Comparative Patterns* (London and New York: Routledge, 2000), 48–49.

12. Radjinder Bhagwanbali, *Contracten voor Suriname: Arbeidsmigratie vanuit Brits-Indië onder het indentured-labourstelsel, 1873–1916* (Den Haag: Amrit, 1996), 73.

13. C. J. M. de Klerk, *De Immigratie der Hindostanen in Suriname* (1953; reprint, Den Haag: Amrit, 1998), 43–54. It is important to note that what is now known as India is quite different from that which the contract laborers left behind. Moreover, while preindependent India was geographically larger, it did not constitute one political entity but consisted of British India, part of the larger British Empire, and some six hundred native states that were quasi dependent.

14. Ibid., 112.

15. Ibid., 112–113.

16. Francis Robinson, "The Muslims of Upper India and the Shock of the Mutiny," in *Essays in Honour of Professor E. T. Stokes*, edited by Mushirul Hasan and N. Gupta (New Delhi: Oxford University Press, 1993), 1:377–398.

17. De Klerk, *De Immigratie der Hindostanen in Suriname*, 104.

18. Peter Gottschalk, *Beyond Hindu and Muslim: Multiple Identity in Narratives from Village India* (Oxford: Oxford University Press, 2000).

19. Known as "ship brotherhood" (*jahazia bhai*) and "depot brotherhood" (*dipua bhai*). See Mohan K. Gautam, "Munshi Rahman Khan (1874–1972): An Institution of the Indian Diaspora in Surinam," unpublished paper presented at the ISER-NCIC conference "Challenge and Change: The Indian Diaspora in Its Historical and Contemporary Contexts" (University of West Indies, St. Augustine, and the National Council of Indian Culture, St. Augustine, Trinidad and Tobago, August 11–18, 1995).

20. De Klerk, *De Immigratie der Hindostanen in Suriname*, 165.

21. Amenah Jahangeer-Chojoo, *La Rose et le Henné: Une etude des musulmans de Maurice* (Moka: Mahatma Gandhi Institute, 2004), 168–207. See also Bal and Sinha-Kerkhoff, "When Muslims Leave," 75–97.

22. Chickrie, "Muslims in Suriname," 80–81.

23. ABS, Algemeen Bureau voor de Statistiek, 1980.

24. *Suriname* 91, no. 28 (1939).

25. Chickrie, "Muslims in Suriname," 87.

26. De Klerk, *De Immigratie der Hindostanen in Suriname*, 48–49.

27. See also http://www.nationaalarchief.nl/suriname/base_hindo/introductie.html and "The Lalla Rookh: Arrival of the First Hindustani Muslims to Suriname," posted on May 19, 2002, and available at http://www.Guyana.org/features/LallaRukh.pdf.

28. R. Karsten, *De Britisch-Indiers in Suriname: Een Korte Schets Benevens een Handeling voor de Beginselen van het Hindi* (Gravenhage: Martinus Nijhof, 1930); C. J. M. de Klerk, "Over de religie der Surinaamse Hindostanen," in *Van Brits-Indisch Emigrant tot Burger van Suriname*, edited by A. Manan (Gravenhage: Sticusa, 1963), 61; H. Ramsoedh and L. Bloemberg, "The Institutionalization of Hinduism in Surinam and Guyana," in *Hindu Diaspora: Global Perspectives*, edited by T. S. Rukmani (New Delhi: Munshiram Manoharlal, 2001), 123–165.

29. Raymond S. Chickrie, "The Afghan Muslims of Guyana and Suriname," *Journal of Muslim Minority Affairs* 22, no. 2 (2002): 385. See also James K. Lalmahomed, "De Invloed van de Hindostaanse Moslims" [The Influence of Hindustani Muslims], in *Hindostanen van contractarbeiders tot Surinamers, 1873–1998*, edited by B. S. Mitrasingh and M. S. Harpal (Paramaribo: Stichting Hindostaanse Immigratie, 1998), 66–72. For the special way in which Muharram was celebrated among Muslim Hindustanis, see *Suriname* 73, no. 82 (1921).

30. For example, see de Klerk, *De Immigratie der Hindostanen in Suriname*, 75.

31. *Suriname* 73, no. 16 (1921).

32. *Suriname* 73, no. 59 (1921).

33. *Suriname* 68, no. 6 (1916).

34. *Suriname* 73, no. 25 (1921); *Suriname* 81, no. 14 (1929).

35. Halima-Saʿadia Kassim, "Schisms in Caribbean Islam: Ideological Conflict in the Trinidadian Muslim Community, 1920–1950," *Journal of Social Sciences* 6, nos. 1–2 (1999): 177.

36. Chickrie, "Muslims in Suriname," 84.

37. For an example among Hindus, see the lectures of Mr. Jaimini in Suriname in 1929: *Suriname* 81, nos. 51, 55, and 61.

38. *Suriname* 73, no. 25 (1921).

39. *Suriname* 81, no. 93 (1929).

40. *Suriname* 81, no. 93 (1929).

41. C. R. Biswamitre, "Hindostaans leven," in *Cultureel mozaïek van Suriname*, edited by Albert Helman (Zutphen: De Walburg Pers, 1977), 223–224.

42. Representatives of the Arya Samaj were active in Suriname since 1912. The Arya Samaj mainly aimed at the reconstruction of the Vedic traditions and strongly protested against contemporary social practices in India such as the practice of widow burning (sati), child marriages, the hierarchical caste system, women's oppression, idol worshipping, and the social veneration of myths.

43. De Klerk, *De Immigratie der Hindostanen in Suriname*, 195–196.

44. *Suriname* 81, no. 51 (1929)

45. Ellen Bal and Kathinka Sinha-Kerkhoff, introduction to *Autobiography of an Indian Indentured Labourer*, edited by Sinha-Kerkhoff, Bal, and Singh, xxv.

46. Sinha-Kerkhoff, Bal, and Singh, *Autobiography of an Indian Indentured Labourer*, 193.

47. *Suriname* 73, no. 16 (1921).

48. *Suriname* 73, no. 82 (1921).

49. Ellen Bal and Kathinka Sinha-Kerkhoff, "No 'Holy Cows' in Surinam: Religion, Transnational Relations, Identity Politics, and the Hindostani Diaspora in Surinam," *Diaspora Studies* 1, no. 1 (2007): 31–57.

50. Report from the district commissioner of the meeting held between Hindus and Muslims in the public school in Livorno. Gouvernements-Secretaris Suriname, Immigratie en Kolonisatie, Landsarchief Suriname, no. N: 33/20.333, dated April 19, 1933.

51. Quoted in Bal and Sinha-Kerkhoff, "No 'Holy Cows' in Surinam," 41.

52. Ibid.

53. Ibid.

54. *Vikaash* 2, no. 13 (1947).

55. *West*, August 15, 1947.

56. Mohan K. Gautam, "The Relevance of Life History Writings as a Methodological Technique of Social Inquiry: The Autobiography of Munshi Rahman Khan in Under-

standing the Indian Diaspora," in *Indian Diaspora: Trends and Issues*, edited by Ajaya Kumar Sahoo and K. Laxmi Narayan (New Delhi: Serials, 2008), 12–25.

57. *Het Nieuws*, February 20, 1951.

58. Dew, *Difficult Flowering of Suriname*, 103.

59. De Klerk refers to the first decade of the twentieth century as the start of Hindustani participation in civil society. In 1910 and 1911, the first two British (competing) associations, to represent the British Indians in Suriname, were founded: in 1910 it was the Surinaamsche Immigranten-Vereeniging and in 1911 the Surinaamsche Britsch-Indiërs-Bond: Ikhtiyār aur Hak. See de Klerk, *De Immigratie der Hindostanen in Suriname*, 173–174.

60. Gautam alleged that the enactment of the new law of 1927 forced all the newly born children to be Dutch citizens as they acquired Dutch nationality and "encouraged the colonial policy for assimilation of Indians in Surinam." Gautam, "Munshi Rahman Khan," 15.

61. Karan Ramsundersingh, "Hindostanen in het Onderwijs" [Hindustanis in Education], in *Hindostanen van contractarbeiders tot Surinamers, 1873–1998*, edited by B. S. Mitrasingh and M. S. Harpal (Paramaribo: Stichting Hindostaanse Immigratie, 1998), 90–95.

62. For this section we have used, apart from material found in the National Archives in New Delhi, the West Bengal State Archives (Kolkata) and the archives in Paramaribo. We also used these sources: G. A. Grierson, *Report on Colonial Emigration from the Bengal Presidency* (Appendix to File 15–20/21, Calcutta State Archives, 1883); J. McNeill, *Report to the Government of India on the Conditions of Indian Immigrants in Four British Colonies and Surinam*, vol. 2, *Surinam, Jamaica, Fiji, and General Remarks* (London: His Majesty's Stationery's Office, London, 1915); Karsten, *De Britisch-Indiers in Suriname*; H. N. Hajary, "De Verwacht Wordende Groote Gebeurtenis onder de Britisch-Indiers in Suriname," *De West-Indische Gids* 19, no. 2 (1937): 1–3; C. J. M. de Klerk, "British-Indiers in Suriname," *De West-Indische Gids* 24, no. 25 (1942): 97–117; de Klerk, "Over de religie der Surinaamse Hindostanen"; D. Malik, "Surinam: Fascinating Experience," in *The Global Indian Diaspora: Yesterday, Today and Tomorrow*, edited by J. K. Motwani (New York: Global Organization of People of Indian Origin, 1993); de Klerk, *De Immigratie der Hindostanen*; B. S. Mitrasingh and M. S. Harpal, eds., *Hindostanen van contractarbeiders tot Surinamers, 1873–1998* (Paramaribo: Stichting Hindostaanse Immigratie, 1998); H. Orna, "A Brief History of East Indians in Suriname," in *Sojourners to Settlers: Indian Migrants in the Caribbean and the Americas*, edited by M. Gosine (Hamburg, PA: Windsor Press, 1999), 120–124; R. Ramdin, *Arising from Bondage: A History of the Indo-Caribbean People* (London: I. B. Tauris, 2000); K. Nandoe, "Suriname," in *Pioneers of Prosperity*, edited by S. Kumar (New Delhi: Antar Rashtriya Sahayog Parishad Bharat, 2000), 235–243; M. Baumann, "The Hindu Diasporas in Europe and an Analysis of Key Diasporic Patterns," in *Hindu Diaspora: Global Perspectives*, edited by T. S. Rukmani (New Delhi: Munshiram Manoharlal, 2001), 59–81; Mohan K. Gautam, "Bhojpuri Emigration to the Caribbean: The Ongoing Struggle with the Issue of the Maintenance of Cultural Identity and Link with India in Surinam" (unpublished paper); and Ramsoedh and Bloemberg, "Institutionalization of Hinduism."

63. Merlin B. Brinkerhoff and Jeffrey C. Jacob, "Racial, Ethnic and Religious Social Distance in Surinam: An Exploration of the 'Strategic Alliance Hypothesis' in a Caribbean Community," *Ethnic and Racial Studies* 17, no. 4 (1994): 636–661.

64. *Het Nieuws*, March 2, 1951.

65. Baumann, "Hindu Diasporas."

66. So-called Javanese Muslims from the Dutch East Indies (now Indonesia) in Suriname

are *kejawen*, following the syncretic practices and beliefs of Java, which incorporate old Javanese beliefs yet also Hindu-Buddhist elements.

67. *Suriname* 81, no. 93 (1929).

68. Raymond S. Chickrie, "History of My People: The Afghan Muslims of Guyana" (2001), http://www.afghan-network.net/Culture/afghan-guyana.htm; Chickrie, "Afghan Muslims of Guyana and Suriname," 381–399; Karsten, *De Britisch-Indiers in Suriname*, 20. Karsten, for example, pointed out that these Muslims were more oriented toward (British) India than toward "Cairo or Mecca" and quoted one of these Muslims as having said, "We could have written to Kairo or Mekka as well but the problem is that they publish in Arabic and never in Urdu or Persian." Besides, Urdu once was used not only by Muslims but also by Hindus in British India and part of the unique cultural heritage of the Indian subcontinent.

69. Karsten, *De Britisch-Indiers in Suriname*, 20.

70. Sajal Nag, "Nationhood and Displacement in Indian Subcontinent," *Economic and Political Weekly* 36, no. 51 (2001): 47–54.

71. Translated from the Dutch. "Liga van Hindostani's," *Vikaash (Evolutie)* 12, no. 2 (1947).

72. *Het Nieuws*, March 2, 1949.

PART II

CONTEMPORARY CARTOGRAPHIES

INSTITUTIONALIZING ISLAM IN ARGENTINA: COMPARING COMMUNITY AND IDENTITY CONFIGURATIONS

SILVIA MONTENEGRO

THE CONTEMPORARY MUSLIM PRESENCE in Argentina traces its origin to Arab migration waves in the late nineteenth and early twentieth centuries. Although most of the Syrian-Lebanese arriving in Argentina were Christians, a small minority of them were Muslims. The first Muslim associations were founded during the first three decades of the twentieth century. Given the spatial settlement patterns of immigrant flows into Argentina, many institutions were located not only in Buenos Aires, but also in various provinces, towns, and villages. In the context of a nation-building project that endeavored to homogenize linguistic and religious particularities through the secular public education system as well as a melting-pot ideology, some associations were unable to survive the founding generation. Other entities are still functioning, changing their objectives and international points of reference.

The second half of the 1980s witnessed the reconfiguration of Argentina's Islamic institutional scenario. Some new institutions were established, and others were absorbed under umbrella associations. At the same time, the institutional strength of local groups belonging to the Shiʿa branch of Islam increased under the influence of the Islamic Republic of Iran. As a result, new possibilities for the professional formation of religious specialists arose in the transnational networks between Iran and Latin America. Among Shiʿi in Argentina, Iran emerged as a new religious and symbolic frame of reference.

Subsequently, in the 1990s the local form of Islam and some of its institutional representatives gained public visibility. Shaykhs (or *shuyukh*, in Arabic) and organizations were drawn into the public arena, as the media attempted to blame Muslims for the bombings of the Israeli Embassy in 1992 and the Jewish community center in 1994, both in Buenos Aires.[1] The negative portrayal of Muslims in the Argentine press thus began long before the attacks of September 11, 2001. Discourses stigmatizing Muslims in Argentina occurred already in the 1990s. However, the impact of such media coverage was ephemeral and situational, as the media attention was moved from national news to the *Triple Frontera*, the so-called triborder area where Argentina, Brazil, and Paraguay meet. In the late 1990s and early 2000s, the dominant media narrative framed the *Triple Frontera* as a dangerous place inhabited by Muslim immigrants who were connected with terrorist cells.

In terms of Islamic identity and community formation, it is possible to notice a new trend that started in earlier times and has become more pronounced recently: in some religious centers, a generation of Argentine shaykhs with religious training and formation (with or without Arab ancestry) is replacing the foreign religious leaders who came from Arab countries or were immigrants without formal education. The Islamic Association of Argentina (Asociación Islámica Argentina), the Al-Imam Mosque, the House for the Dissemination of Islam (Casa para la difusión del Islam), José Ingenieros Alawite Mutual-Aid Association (Asociación Alauita de Beneficencia de José Ingenieros), the At-Tawhid Mosque in Buenos Aires, Ash-Shahid Mosque of Tucumán, and the Islamic Union of Rosario (Unión Islámica de Rosario) are some examples of entities with Argentine shaykhs. It is also possible to witness the ever-growing phenomenon of religious conversion to Islam among Argentines without Arab ancestry—half of the membership in some entities—who convert for different reasons.

Specific figures on the number of Muslims in Argentina are difficult to obtain because the national census does not include questions on religious affiliation. The numbers reported by different institutions vary and most often are understood as a strategy to bring visibility to the communities. The lack of verifiable data results in unreliable numbers that range from 450,000 to 700,000, according to the shaykhs, community reports, and everyday Muslims. Some institutions even affirm that there are more than 1 million Muslims in Argentina. The National Registry of Worship[2] includes eighteen Muslim institutions; however, according to my own surveys, there are more than thirty-five institutions, accounting for mosques, prayer halls, and associations and including those that belong to the Sunni, Shiʻi, Alawite, and Sufi groups.

According to the reports of the Islamic Office for Latin America (Oficina del Islam para América Latina), the number of Muslims in Argentina is more than 700,000, some 160,000 in Greater Buenos Aires alone. Other institutions, such as the Center for Islamic Studies (Centro de Estudios Islámicos), refer to 450,000 Muslims. The Islamic Center of Argentina (Centro Islámico de la República Argentina, CIRA) recognizes that it is impossible to give an exact number, but prefers to estimate between 500,000 and 700,000 Muslims in the whole country. On the other hand, the leaders of the House of Islam Dissemi-

Islamic Union of Rosario (Unión Islámica de Rosario)

nation in Argentina differentiate between those who are Muslim descendants, numbering around 700,000; those who recognize themselves as Muslims but do not practice the religion, some 300,000; and those who practice the religion, an estimated 50,000. These varying estimates suggest that open for debate are not only the numbers of Muslims but also who and what their beliefs or practices are in Argentina.

There are Shiʻi, Sunni, Alawite, Druze, and Sufi Muslims in Argentina. The immigration of Syrian Alawites led to the creation of different institutions: two in the city of Buenos Aires, two in the state of Buenos Aires, and one in the city of Tucumán. The first Druze immigrants arrived in the 1860s. In 1926 Amir Amin Arslan created the Druze Mutual-Aid Association (Asociación de Beneficencia Drusa) in Buenos Aires, and through the generations the community membership decreased. In 2009 the Druze House (Casa Drusa) sent a delegation to Argentina from Lebanon, in order to reach out to descendants and regroup them. Sufis are represented mainly by two groups: the Naqsh-bandi Haqqani Association from Argentina, with ten branches throughout the country,[3] and the Halveti Jerrahi Sufi Order in Buenos Aires. In many cases, those belonging to the Sufi community also attend mosques or Islamic centers, but their motivations and backgrounds vary. Members of Sufi groups are largely or almost entirely non–Middle Eastern and Argentine converts to Islam. In some groups, such as the Naqshbandi, we can say that they have porous borders with "new age" religiosity.[4]

Therefore, we can say that Islam in Argentina is diverse and fragmented. Muslim communities are marked by differences related to the branches mentioned above. This differentiation also takes shape through the various ways that Muslim institutions integrate religious and ethnic identities, adopt models for the transmission of religious knowledge, and carry out strategies for their own visibility. Within this heterogeneity, there coexist multiple identity constructions, types of membership, discourses, and ways to build public presence. This chapter analyzes the institutional and identity formations of one of the main institutions of Sunni Islam in Argentina, CIRA, considering its role in the attempt to become the "authorized representative" of Argentine Muslims. We compare it with some Shiʿa Islamic institutions that emerged in the mid-1980s, whose "ways of building communities" differ in many aspects from CIRA, the institution that we now turn to.

ARAB IMMIGRATION AND THE FOUNDING OF MUSLIM INSTITUTIONS

Islam arrived in Argentina as the religion of some Arab immigrants, and, as in other Latin American countries, they were locally known as "Turks" and mysterious adherents of different religions.[5] The question of inclusion, as well as the religious diversity among immigrants, has been poorly studied, and, in general, scholars paid more attention to the type of associations linked to the place of origin, such as clubs, mutual aid societies, newspapers written in Arabic, and the communities' cultural activities. These studies also focused on Arabs' patterns of language maintenance and marriage choices, from the second to the third generations. The prevailing religious groups were Maronite and Orthodox Christians, and on a smaller scale Muslim, although there are records of some other faiths among a minority of Arab immigrants.[6] The first Arab Muslims who arrived in Argentina during the most intense wave of immigration (which occurred in the period between 1918 and 1930) had a literacy rate lower than the Maronite and the Orthodox, and they also had a lower percentage of marriage outside Arabs' community and religion. However, already in the second generation of Arab Muslims, these differences with other Arab immigrants decreased, and high rates of endogamy began to drop. As an indicator of this situation, it is convenient to highlight the attenuation of the Arabic language. Although lower than in the case of the Maronites and the Orthodox, it is possible to observe that 61 percent of second-generation Muslims could not speak Arabic, 25 percent were able to speak just a few words, and only 13 percent could speak it proficiently. Marriages gradually began to extend outside the group as well. In the third generation, only 4 percent could speak Arabic, although it is still a high rate, considering it was almost zero among the Maronites and the Orthodox.[7] These data, which show a different pattern of religious cohesion, foreground how the first Muslim associations created in earlier times have been weakened or reformulated in subsequent generations.

One of the first institutions established in Buenos Aires is the Pan Islamic Association (Asociación Pan Islamismo, 1931), formed at the behest of an Egyptian immigrant and a group of Muslims who were part of the Islamic Arab Society (Sociedad Árabe Islámica), which was established in 1922. In 1940 the institution was renamed the Islamic Welfare Association (Asociación Islámica de Previsión Social), and only in 1957 did it become known as the Islamic Center of the Argentine Republic. In other provinces of the country, there already existed organizations created by Muslim immigrants: in the city of Mendoza, the Islamic Arab Society (Sociedad Árabe Islámica) was founded in 1926, in Cordoba the Muslim Arab Social Aid (Ayuda Social Árabe Musulmana) in 1928, and in Rosario the Rosario Islamic Union Association (Asociación Unión Islámica de Rosario) in 1932. In Tucumán in 1929, Sunni Muslims and Alawites created the Pan Islamic Cultural and Worship Association (Asociación Cultural y Culto Pan Islámica), and in the province of Buenos Aires, in the region of General Arenales, in the town of La Angelita in the 1920s, the Alawite Islamic Arab Society of Angelita (Sociedad Árabe Islámica Alauita de la Angelita) was established. Meanwhile, the Alawites organized institutions in Buenos Aires, the Alawite Union Association (Asociación Unión Alauita) in 1936, and the José Ingenieros's Alawite Islamic Aid Association (Asociación Islámica Alauita de Beneficencia de José Ingenieros) in 1943. These institutions brought together immigrants whose ethnic and religious identities appeared juxtaposed and who intended for the religion to be reproduced through their descendants born in Argentina.

At that time the sectarian differences were not marked, and the most notorious rift had to do with the distinction between Arab Muslims and those who were Christians. Some religious centers were shared by Shi'i and Sunni, as in the case of the Islamic Union of Rosario, the Islamic Center of Buenos Aires, and the Pan Islamic Religious and Cultural Association of Tucumán, which was shared by Sunnis and Alawites. In general, the institutions that were formed by the first wave of immigrants no longer played a unifying role, especially with regard to those that brought together the immigrants according to their regions of origin or those that had been organized as Syrian-Lebanese associations, including the Arabic-language press, which had been in decline since the 1950s. The decreasing attraction toward Arab national roots or origins made many of these associations either disappear or transform into social clubs or recreational restaurants, with little participation of actual descendants, but open to non-Arab Argentine consumers of Middle Eastern foods, Syrian-Lebanese folk dancing, and, in some cases, the Arabic language itself. Some of these institutions were crumbling, as the religious affiliation of individuals began to deepen the differences within groups. Religious entities, including Muslim ones, also had to deal with such processes and in some cases temporarily closed or brought back the descendants of the founding generation. In this period until the 1980s, community institutions faced the problems of a limited membership and perpetuating the religion among descendants.

In the 1980s new institutional spaces were created. On the one hand, in the case of Sunni Islam, the Islamic Center of Argentina inaugurated the Al-Ahmad mosque in 1986, and in 2001 the Saudi Arabian Embassy finished the construction of the Islamic Cultural Center Custodian of the Two Holy Mosques King Fahd (Centro Cultural Islámico Custodio de las dos Sagradas Mezquitas Rey Fahd). Also in the same decade, three new Shi'i mosques were created with the support of the embassy of the Islamic Republic of Iran.

REPRESENTING "ALL" MUSLIMS:
A PRIVILEGED DIALOGUE WITH THE STATE

The case of the Islamic Center of Argentina is an interesting example to analyze the building of a privileged relationship with the state. In the past decade this Sunni community institution increasingly became a partner with the state, gaining a position of public visibility in cultural, diplomatic, and political fields. Three elements have contributed to this position: a discourse that confirms the growth of Islam in Argentina and traces its roots to older immigration waves, public claims that this entity represents "all" Muslims of Argentina, and finally the opening of interreligious channels of dialogue with the Catholic Church and certain Jewish community personalities. The inclusion of some members of the CIRA directorship in political and administrative roles within the Buenos Aires city government partially enabled this institution to achieve its actual position.

Like other organizations founded by Muslim immigrants, CIRA recognizes the existence of a period when its membership decreased as a result of Muslim descendants' turning away from their cultural and religious roots. This stage

Islamic Center of Argentina (Centro Islámico de la República Argentina, CIRA)

lasted until the mid-1980s. That period is now described by CIRA as a stage of crisis that was overcome and contrasts it with the present moment of growth. This interpretation is partially sustained by the physical additions made to the mosque. These new spaces were announced along with the idea that Islam was "rapidly growing in Argentina" and that additions and alterations were necessary for such community growth. The most important festivities of the Muslim calendar were also presented, by community spokespersons, as a "record of participation" that involves thousands of Muslims. In this context, the expansion is seen as a successful achievement of the institutional policies, especially those that quadrupled the number of students in the Argentine-Arab School[8] and also increased Friday prayer attendees from twenty to about three hundred. In its own discourse, the institution prefers to ignore the fact that most of this growth is due to the conversion of Argentine people without Arab ancestry. Despite the significant presence of converted Muslims, the community emphasizes its members of Arab origin and Muslim religious figures. This fact is also evident in the administrative positions almost entirely held by Arab Muslim descendants.[9]

CIRA presents its institutional history as the creation of a space that allegedly brings together "all" Muslims in Argentina. The use of the label "mother institution" encapsulates the strategy of appealing to this raison d'être. According to this claim to represent the entire Muslim community, CIRA's shaykh is the "imam of the Muslims in Argentina."[10] In response, members of other communities claim to not feel "represented" by CIRA, either because they belong to other branches of Islam or because they do not identify with the institutional project of the entity, even though they share spaces during the festivities that involve the Islamic community. In the same way, the Al-Ahmad mosque, finished in 1986, is presented as the "first mosque in Argentina," because it was the first built in a traditional architectural style.

Another element of the construction of the entity's public image has been the increasingly important participation of CIRA in interreligious activities sponsored by the Catholic Church, the Ministry of Religious Affairs, or the Government of the City of Buenos Aires. In 2006 a then CIRA board member who also served as a Buenos Aires city administrator[11] participated in the creation of the Institute of Interreligious Dialogue (Instituto del Diálogo Interreligioso). The two other cofounders were a Catholic priest, himself in charge of the Catholic Student Center (Pastoral Universitaria), and the rabbi

Al-Ahmad mosque

Al-Ahmad mosque

of the Beth-el community, both well-known public figures, with media and public exposure. The three participated in the publication of the book *Todos bajo un mismo cielo* (All under the same sky),[12] which explores the tolerance and equality between Judaism, Christianity, and Islam as well as the challenges of the contemporary society. In this context, the relationship between the Ministry of Worship of Argentina and CIRA was strengthened. In fact, the ministry gave the institution an award in recognition of the "defense of inter-religious values." The entity maintains ties with the Catholic Church through its participation in an "Islamic-Catholic Dialogue" coordinated by the so-called Episcopal Commission for Ecumenism and Relations with Judaism, Islam, and Religions (Comisión Episcopal de Ecumenismo, Relaciones con el judaísmo, el Islam y las religiones), based in the Argentine Episcopal Conference. CIRA gained legitimacy as the Islamic community's interlocutor with the Catholic Church and the Ministry of Worship through such sustained relationships. As part of the mise-en-scène of its privileged dialogue with the state, the entity's national holidays are celebrated by inviting leading personalities across the political spectrum. The strong relationship between CIRA and the government was epitomized by the visit of the president of Argentina at a tribute luncheon proposed by the entity. This event was announced by the entity as a milestone, since no president had visited an Islamic center before.[13]

A recent controversy serves to illustrate the way in which the entity has capitalized on the relations built with the state agencies and the consequences of its policy to establish itself as a partner with the state. In the past two years CIRA initiated a series of negotiations with the national government in order to get a television program aired on the public broadcasting station. It would be the "first television program of the Muslim community in Argentina." This was accomplished in 2011, and it raised tensions between CIRA and other Arab community associations and leaders, but not between the entity and other Muslim community representatives. For eight years a sector of the Arab community aired a television show on the public television station called *Desde el aljibe*,[14] similar to a slot given to the Jewish community on the public station. This show valorized aspects of the Syrian and Lebanese cultures: art, cinema, cuisine, and the religious diversity of the community itself. At the same time, it promoted the activities of clubs, associations, and Arab entities, including the religious ones, and worked toward strengthening an "Arab" sense of belonging. CIRA's goal to obtain a Muslim community show on the public television culminated with the end of the program *Desde el aljibe*. That same slot used before by the Arab community is the one obtained by CIRA. Thus, *Desde el aljibe* was replaced by *El cálamo y su mensaje*,[15] occupying the same day and time slot. CIRA authorities explained that the replacement was not requested by them, but rather was a government decision. In response, the group responsible for *Desde el aljibe* as well as other members of different Arab institutions, including the ambassador of Lebanon in Argentina, expressed concern and discontent in the press, interviews, social networks, and blogs. Overall, they raised three questions regarding the replacement of an Arab show by an Islamic one, which basically cast doubt on the representativeness of CIRA. On the one hand, Arab community members argued that a show of that institution does not represent the multireligious Arab community in Argentina. The focus of the program *El cálamo y su mensaje* supposedly contrasted with the diversity of religious expressions among descendants. On the other hand, Arab community members also emphasized that the program did not represent the Muslim community, because the institution gathered "only a part of it." A third argument highlighted the possibility that a public television show of an Islamic center, and not of the Arab community, would lead everyday Argentines to believe that CIRA represents Arabs, which would also cause even greater confusion when issues such as the Palestinian-Israeli conflict were debated.[16]

During this controversy, another Arab cultural organization released a video comparing both shows and highlighting CIRA's lack of legitimacy to represent both the Muslim and the Arab communities.[17] In this context of conflicting expectations and controversies, CIRA issued a statement announcing that *El cálamo y su mensaje* would not be a sectarian program in the religious or institutional sense, but would be a pluralistic space for both Argentine Arab and Islamic communities. To mitigate and prevent future criticisms, the content of the program included, in addition to all activities related to CIRA and the Islamic religion, news and guests of the wider Arab community belonging to nonreligious institutions, such as social clubs or associations as well as those belonging to non-Muslim Arab religious institutions.

This struggle over television programming proves that, in order to avoid being questioned, CIRA's self-representation sought to appeal to those of Arab origin as well as those with religious affiliation to Islam. Reaching beyond the religious field, it sustained a narrative through which it would represent both the past and the present of the group: a community of Muslim Arab Argentines fully integrated into the national society. The no longer extant program of the Arab community *Desde el aljibe* devoted some time to Islam and other religions in the community, and in this way Islam had been one of many Arab religious expressions. The efforts made by CIRA for a unique space for the Muslim community on public television resulted in the substitution of the Arab program for that of CIRA. However, criticisms based on the dual argument that the center represented neither the Arab community nor all Muslims made it impossible for the new program to be exclusively dedicated to Islam. At the same time, the content of the program had to rely on the association with "Arab culture" and to preserve, in part, its predecessor show's message. Having to add cultural issues and even other religious beliefs of the Arab community, the show ended up being a Muslim and Arab cultural space, as was the original goal, considering that CIRA was not satisfied by having "space" within the Arab program. Its position changed because now it was a program directed by an Islamic center that included the dissemination of Arab culture, representing the community as plural in religious and institutional terms and Islam as one of its religious variants. Thus, the institution maintained its self-representation as part of a larger Arab community in which it was a religious minority. For Arab community representatives who publicly expressed criticism, doubts about whether CIRA represented "all" Muslims were less problematic than was CIRA's claim to represent the "Arab community" on public television.

SHIʿA MUSLIM NETWORKS AND THEIR WAYS OF BEING IN NATIONAL SPACE

In the previous section we focused on the public positioning of one of the most traditional institutions of Sunni Islam in Argentina, and now we will focus on the case of Shiʿi institutions, whose institutional origins date back to the mid-1980s. Since 1982 we observed the building of connections between local Argentine spaces and Iran, as a transnational center and reference. This construction was based on a network of interpersonal relationships and the creation of study groups and cultural activities increasingly supported by institutional spaces. Through these networks material and symbolic resources, people, and means of expansion began to flow into new areas of religious practice, which not only upheld Iran as a central node, but also implicated the relations between Argentina and the surrounding countries. Logically, after the victory of the Islamic Revolution, Iranian embassies played an important role in strengthening a network of relations with Latin America and Argentina in particular. In a mere decade, there emerged three Shiʿi-led mosques, two Shiʿi-led associations,[18] magazines and newspapers, as well as a cadre of formally trained religious specialists currently in charge of these entities.

The 1980s witnessed an important shift in the dynamics of Shiʿa Islam, based on a series of transformations that helped solidify the current cohesion between the institutions that represent this branch of the Islam in Argentina. The reconstruction of the links that constitute these networks concerns both individuals and institutions. The work of an Iranian religious specialist from Tehran, who came to Argentina in the early 1980s, was useful in the dissemination of religious and cultural activities that brought together an originally small group of followers, composed of those who were born Muslims, those who had converted, and those who were in the conversion process. The origins of this first group of students, which did not exceed a half dozen, varied, but it was formed exclusively by Argentines. It included a young man from the city of Tucumán, descendant of Syrian Alawites, who previously participated in the Youth Pan-Islamic Association and later formed part of a group of followers of a Sufi *murshid*, from whom he subsequently split. Also participating was a young man from Buenos Aires without Arab ancestry and of Catholic origin, who frequented the same Sufi group and had recently converted to Islam. Two other members were also recent converts: an Argentine of German origin and another from Mendoza. Out of this core emerged the first Argentines who later pursued religious studies at universities in Iran. They and others now run mosques and institutions created in the early 1980s. For instance, an Iranian who lived fourteen years in Argentina founded the At-Tawhid mosque in 1983 and served as its first shaykh, under the auspices of the Iranian Embassy. Located in the neighborhood of Flores, the mosque was established where there were other entities that gathered Shi'i families, including the Argentine Arab Islamic Association (Asociación Árabe Argentina Islámica), established in 1960,[19] and the Hagg Youssef Association (Asociación Hagg Youssef), founded by a Lebanese immigrant in 1935. With properties bought by the Iranian Embassy, this and other groups established the Ash-Shahid mosque in Tucumán in 1985 and the Al-Imam in Cañuelas, in the province of Buenos Aires, in 1990.

The current shaykh of the Ash-Shahid mosque was the first Argentine who, in the mid-1980s, went to study at the Imam Khomeini University of Islamic Sciences in the city of Qom. He opened a path that would be followed by others, some of whom also obtained important religious titles. Upon his return, and between 1995 and 1999, he created in Tucumán a religious training school. This school was attended by more than fifteen people from Colombia, Chile, Brazil, and Peru, some of whom went on to study in Iran or became leaders of religious institutions in their own countries. Later on, these and other shaykhs became teachers of courses designed for Latin American students at universities in Iran, spending some semesters in that country. At the same time, some of the Argentine shaykhs regularly visited institutions of neighboring countries to deal with religious issues, such as in Uruguay, and to lead other Islamic institutions, such as in Chile.

One of the outcomes of this process was the professionalization of Argentine religious specialists and the inclusion of non-Arab Argentine converts within the highest levels of this hierarchy of community associations. Studying

Ash-Shahid mosque

abroad at universities in Iran as well as earning academic-religious degrees and certificates began to be valued as a sign of professionalization and as an element of distinction when compared to ad hoc specialists in charge of traditional religious institutions founded by immigrants. Moreover, there are some institutions that rely solely on *shuyukh* who had been sent abroad for training. The leaders we interviewed had established some clear counterpoints between this specific formation in religious matters and the "old method." They clarified that in the "old method," it would be possible that someone with a trustworthy reputation who submitted himself to Islamic morals could represent an institution but, perhaps, with little knowledge of doctrine. From this point of view, we can establish a distinction between "Islamic morality" and "religious knowledge." Islamic morality appears as a recognizable way of life within early Arab immigrant communities and presumes a religious affiliation to a "cultural Islam," transmittable through education. In contrast, religious knowledge is the result of formal education and a continuous specialization. In this specific case, the tenets of Shi'a Islam could be passed universally to anyone who is interested in that knowledge. According to one of these shaykhs, who was part of the Alawite community:

In the past there was no one who had studied the Islam. People who studied the Islam started to appear only some time after the triumph of the revolution, in the beginning of the 80s. Previously, shaykhs were shaykhs by tradition, they hadn't studied anywhere. It was even a question of family heritage, and that is not the way it should be. For example, if my father is a religious person, suppose that he had studied, and if I want to be a religious person, I'll have to study. It is no longer something that is inherited. And the same happens in all professions. For instance if my father is a doctor, that doesn't mean that I will be one. But before the revolution it was like that, religious leadership was even inherited.[20]

In fact, academic degrees and titles started to figure publicly in the curriculum vitae of shaykhs. Within the Shiʿi community, these hierarchical distinctions were established according to the time one spent in formal study or the number of degrees obtained. Outside the community, the formalization of study began to function as an element that legitimates a discourse of religious specialization focused on a specific religious tradition. In these and other narratives, we find a contraposition between a cultural, inherited, and traditional Islam and "another kind" of Islam attainable through knowledge and commitment to practice. In this way, these leaders in Argentina tend to speak on behalf of a specific Islamic branch, making explicit their Shiʿi affiliation or their "Shiʿi school." In the words of another shaykh and to clarify the relation to the Islamic branches that each of them belongs to:

And that is because there has always been prejudice among the Muslims regarding the schools. It has always been attempted to hide the Sunni or Shiite faith of each Muslim, and I think it's an issue that must be overcome; there is a taboo to break. For example, while I was studying in Iran, I had Sunni classmates and we have took to the habit of talking about our differences, including our schools, and I am still doing it on an ongoing basis. . . . As an erudite Iranian once said, we must not get confused when talking about the unity among Muslims. It does not mean that I am going to leave my own school to accept the other's school, or that the others will leave their school to join mine. Each one has his school and their lessons, but we need to accept the points of coincidence between both schools.

The public acceptance and assumptions of the representation of a "school," of a certain group of Muslims from all of those existent in Argentina, are also related to the recent past in which Shiʿi institutions became socially visible in the country. These same institutions appeared when there had been already long-lasting ties established with Iran. This country appears here as an ideological and reference point to the identity of these groups.

Since the 1990s some leaders of the Shi'i organizations have played an important role in publicly refuting the accusations made against some members of the embassy and the government of Iran. These accusations were linked with the attacks perpetrated against the Israeli Embassy and the Jewish community in the same decade.[21] The discourse of some shaykhs was marked by this conflict, as well by the subsequent failures to harbor evidence against any Muslims and numerous other setbacks in the court cases.[22] The attacks against Israeli and Jewish entities generated a set of consequences in the dialogue between some institutions. These consequences could not be characterized, in any way, as a confrontation between Jews and Muslims. On the one hand, not all Jewish organizations agreed on a common position concerning conjectures regarding so-called international involvement and the local connection in planning the attacks.[23] At the beginning of the trial, it was alleged that some officials of the Iranian Embassy in Argentina, at the time of the attacks, were the "local organizers" of plots that had been somehow masterminded by Iran and Hezbollah. In this context, there were hate speeches and other hostile stances adopted between some Muslim organizations and factions of the Jewish community. But the media frenzy around local Shi'i institutions was short-lived. As stated previously, the national media spotlight would move promptly toward the Triple Border Area, contributing to the media and political imaginary statements that declared the area as a "sanctuary of Islamic terrorism." This designation comes from a supposed connection with the attacks in Buenos Aires.[24]

In the period between 1995 and 1999, Argentina's then minister of internal affairs, Carlos Corach, claimed to be investigating and dismantling the conditions that had allowed the occurrence of the attacks in 1992 and 1994. He also stated that this situation led to the need to practice the "painful trial and error method." In a section called "The Muslim Community in the Triple Border" in a book later published by the former minister, he explains the hypothesis that once moved the media's hub toward that region:

> In the late 80s, in the region of the Triple Border, the Hezbollah had already consolidated an effective organizational network. This network was ready to start producing resonant events, according to the assessments of the intelligence services of the countries historically involved in the fight against terrorism. . . . [O]ne of the characteristics of the Muslim culture is the absolute unity between religion, commercial trade, and terrorist activities which their leaders tend to identify with the idea of holy war. . . . [T]he place that was chosen to test the organization was Buenos Aires.[25]

As a community, local Shiʿi Muslims were not included in this proliferation of suspicions, despite the continuous accusations made by the minister of internal affairs during the second half of the 1990s. However, some Iranians who have lived in the country since the 1980s and contributed to the formation of the aforementioned institutions were targeted. It was alleged that they had been in contact with individuals in the Triple Border Area. Even today, two decades after the AMIA attack, sporadic statements in the media are often construed as official reports. In this coverage, some Shiʿi community representatives complain about organizations such as the DAIA, the AMIA, and the Argentine Zionist Organization (Organización Sionista Argentina), which accuse Iran of masterminding the attacks. Since then, the local representatives of these communities have obtained public visibility as Shiʿi Muslims and openly exhibited their relations with Iran as the center and role model of their religious orientation.

The other aspect that we want to mention here relates to media access and the way that Shiʿi community associations choose to make themselves visible through them. Recently, Shiʿi institutions began to search for spaces in the media, but unlike the path followed by CIRA, they took advantage of the legal transformation of the media system in Argentina, after the enactment of the 2009 media regulatory law. This new legislation made possible the emergence of television stations that were petitioned by social groups and organizations. Two of the mosques organized themselves in order to initiate the process that will legally empower them to establish their own TV channels. The At-Tawhid mosque in Buenos Aires has An-nur TV, and Al-Mahdi of the Ash-Shahid mosque has both radio and television channels. Shiʿi institutions now project themselves into a larger space of the public sphere, such as universities, nongovernmental organizations, and trade unions, which also began to take actions to obtain their own TV stations. In this way the Shiʿi institutions are moving in the common arena of diverse groups seeking access to these same resources. The TV programs are mostly locally produced and transmit various programs, including religious classes, taught by Argentine shaykhs; testimonies of converts to Islam; and presentations by students who traveled to Iran for short seminars. The material resources available to address this endeavor are undoubtedly instrumental to achieve such visibility. This has transformed the way of spreading religion: now it is specifically oriented to an Argentine audience of potentially new Muslims. This TV schedule reflects the involvement of local groups in the wider religious geography of Shiʿi Islam, showing Argentina and Argentine Shiʿi Muslims in a translocal field of practices and beliefs. This field is also constituted by horizontal networks with other spaces of Latin America and extends toward Iran with a two-way transmission of knowledge resources.

CONCLUSION

The Muslim presence in Argentina is as varied as the orientations and histories of its distinct publics. In the institutional dimension, one must take into account the differences between those entities created by Muslim Arab immigrants in the early decades of the twentieth century and those that arose, or were reconfigured, in the 1980s and subsequent decades. Among the former, some reduced their membership rosters at the same time Arab Muslim descendants decreased their participation in the religion, while others managed to reorient their activities and ways of transmitting religious knowledge, attracting and maintaining community members. However, since the 1980s, the institutions that were new or reconfigured became the most active and most able to reconcile a membership composed of both those born Muslim and converts. Geographically, one also takes notice of an institutional presence across Argentina's distinct provinces, quite consistent with those areas where there was a prominent Syrian-Lebanese immigration.

In this chapter we have referred to only two communities that allow us to think about the diversity of Islam in Argentina. On the one hand, we have focused on a Sunni institution. This institution built a privileged dialogue with the government and assumes the representation of "all" Muslims in Argentina. On the other hand, we attended to the networks of Shi'i Islam, which connects persons to religious professionalization spaces and others dedicated to knowledge transmission, material resources, and symbolic references, which also helped in the creation of institutions. The uneven social and state recognition achieved by these institutions reinforces the hierarchical stratification of the local Islamic field in which the different communities are situated. Through these two cases, which by no means exhaust all the expressions of Islam in Argentina, we want to emphasize that they represent two different models in the construction and reproduction of religious communities. The first one, represented by CIRA, involves religious adhesion as part of one's migrant origins, though the community includes Muslim converts and new immigrants, such as Africans. Here Islam appears as the legacy of the migrant generation who came to Argentina and enjoyed success. This corporate strategy is clearly aimed at supporting and sustaining such a message, exhibiting and staging the relations with influential government officials, and building its legitimacy as "mother institution." This arrangement shows that this institution relates itself toward others from a privileged position. In so doing, its relations with the government's secretary of worship, the Catholic Church, as well as other powers have become fundamental. As was shown, the struggle to find a place in public television symbolized the public recognition of that institution, not without criticism from other sectors. Subsequent controversies within different parts of the Arab community over whether a television show of an Islamic center can represent the Arab community, or a similar show of the Arab community would be a better representation of the diversity of the religious expressions, including Islam, illustrate the delicate balance negotiated and, to some extent, maintained by CIRA. The identity of this institution seems to follow the model of a "cultural choice,"[26] where Islam appears to be conflated with a culture of origin or ethnic roots, and it is preserved in the context of the forms of sociability cultivated by a community of Argentine Arab Muslims. In this sense, the institutional focus is not only based on an apparent Arabness but also based on legitimizing the representation of the community through Argentine national networks.

From a distinct position, Shi'i communities dialogue with and belong to the national space. The transnational relations cultivated with Iran as a central point of reference provide the community autonomy in the national panorama, and that autonomy promotes a "mode of being" in the local religious field. This pattern results in a dissemination and presentation of the religion, targeting an audience primarily in Argentina as well as attracting new members through their conversion to Islam. In fact, the national leadership of communities is in the hands of converted Argentine shaykhs, who operate nowadays in a transnational network with the surrounding countries throughout Latin America itself. An accumulation of resources from the Shi'i community affords them a position that does not depend on local political and religious power. These resources are both material and symbolic. Among the first are the mosques whose property was purchased by the Iranian Embassy, as well as resources for publications, translations made by Argentine members, as well as other ways of spreading the religion. The symbolic or human resources include the formation of a group of Argentine citizens with formal education and religious specialization at universities in Iran, as well as study-abroad programs that enable these and other members to travel and undertake short periods of formalized study in Iran. Inextricably fusing national and transnational places, Shi'i institutions construct themselves in Argentina through a trilogy of mosques that appeared after the 1980s as well as farther-flung networks. The resultant Shi'i institutional discourses give shape to a specific and particularized version of Islam as universally affordable.

NOTES

This chapter summarizes the general findings of more detailed studies about Muslim communities in Argentina, which I have developed since 2005 as a researcher at Argentina's

National Council of Technical and Scientific Research (CONICET), specifically in the field of individual and collective projects.

1. The Embassy of Israel in Buenos Aires on March 17, 1992, and the Jewish Community Centre (AMIA) on July 18, 1994. The attacks against both entities remain officially unresolved.

2. The governmental agency under the Ministry of Foreign Affairs, International Trade and Worship (Ministerio de Relaciones Exteriores, Comercio Internacional y Culto) keeps track of non-Catholic religions officially recognized by the Argentine government. Such entities must meet certain mandatory and organizational requirements to be registered, and their authorities must be legally recognized.

3. El Bolsón (Río Negro), La Consulta (Mendoza), San Lorenzo (Santa Fe), Mar del Plata (province of Buenos Aires), Rosario (Santa Fe), Chascomús (province of Buenos Aires), Capilla del Monte (Córdoba), Glew (province of Buenos Aires), La Plata (province of Buenos Aires), and the city of Buenos Aires.

4. Silvia Montenegro, "Contextos locales y expresiones contemporáneas del Islam," in *Modernidad, religión y memoria*, edited by Fortunato Mallimaci (Buenos Aires: Ediciones Colihue, 2007), 93–101.

5. For a chronology of the stages and reasons for migration, see Jorge Bestene, "La inmigración sirio-libanesa en la Argentina: Una aproximación," *Estudios Migratorios Latinoamericanos* 12, no. 9 (1998): 239–267. For Arab communities in Argentina and an overview of studies on the subject, see Silvia Montenegro, "Panorama sobre la inmigración árabe en Argentina," in *Los árabes en América Latina: Historia de una emigración*, edited by Abdeluahed Akmir (Madrid: Siglo XXI, 2009), 61–98. For Arab immigration in Argentina, see Abdeluahed Akmir, *Los árabes en Argentina* (Rosario: Editorial de la Universidad Nacional de Rosario, 2011); as well as Abdeluahed Akmir, "La Inmigración árabe en Argentina, 1880–1980" (PhD diss., Universidad Complutense de Madrid, 1990).

6. On immigrant registry forms, there is a lack of data on the religiosity of immigrants. In some cases, the classification criteria use categories such as "Ottoman," "Turkish," "Persian," and "Arab" as if they were religious affiliations. For a record of the religion of the Arabic-speaking immigrants that covers the period from 1882 to 1925, see Gladys Jozami, "Identidad religiosa e integración cultural en cristianos sirios y libaneses en Argentina, 1890–1990," *Estudios Migratorios Latinoamericanos* 9, no. 26 (1994): 118–130.

7. Akmir, *La Inmigración árabe en Argentina*, 272–326.

8. The Argentine-Arab school Omar bin al-Khattab belongs to CIRA and was founded in 1991. It covers preschool, elementary, and high school levels. In 2009 it became confessional, including the study of Islam.

9. According to one interviewee, the Egyptian shaykh in the institution between 2005 and 2009 oversaw 215 conversions. A small group of African immigrants, Senegalese, and other sub-Saharan African countries also attend the center.

10. CIRA's religious specialists hail from University of Al-Azhar in Egypt. Some historical research suggests that contacts between Argentine Muslim community circles or members and religious leaders trained in Al-Azhar began in the early decades of the twentieth century. On this topic, see, among others, Steven Hyland, "'Arisen from Deep Slumber': Transnational Politics and Competing Nationalisms among Syrian Immigrants in Argentina, 1900–1922," *Journal of Latin American Studies* 43, no. 3 (2011): 567.

11. The then CIRA secretary-general was also secretary of social and community management of the government of the Autonomous City of Buenos Aires and, in 2007, minister of human and social rights of the city government.

12. Edited by a journalist, the book brings together the dialogue between a priest, Guillermo Marcó; a rabbi, Daniel Goldman; and Omar Abboud. See Ricardo López Dusil, *Todos bajo un mismo cielo: Diálogos entre la cultura católica, judía y musulmana* (Buenos Aires: Edhasa, 2005).

13. The visit took place in 2009 during a luncheon among leaders of Arab and Islamic community, ambassadors, and politicians.

14. "From the *aljibe*." An *aljibe* is an underground water cistern.

15. "The pen and its message."

16. In a letter to the general secretary of CIRA read during the launch of the TV show, and reproduced in different media, the Lebanese ambassador congratulated the Islamic center but also announced that he would work so that the program *Desde el Aljibe* could again be on public television. Among other arguments, he mentioned: "I fear that the establishment of an Islamic Centre program, *Desde el aljibe*, is interpreted as that a center that represents the Arab community and, therefore, to transform the image of the Israeli-Arab conflict into a religious conflict, thereby giving Israel what it always sought: to oppress the claims of rights in addition to civil lawsuits, historic and human, of the Arabs, and giving the erroneous impression that the conflict is a Muslim-Jewish conflict."

17. The video was released by Fertile Crescent Entertainment (Cine Creciente Fértil). This civil society association is dedicated to the dissemination of Arab cinema and documentary. It aired the same music used by the program *Desde el aljibe* to frame different national, religious, social, and political affiliations (Muslim, Lebanese, Syrians, Jews, Iraqis, Christians, Palestinians, Kuwaitis, atheists, progressives, conservatives, agnostics, reactionaries, leftists, radicals, poor, rich, *peronistas*, and professionals). It concluded that the program that featured all these groups would be taken off the air. CIRA is mentioned as a monopolistic institution that seeks to erode Argentine Arabness, because it was allegedly an "entity that is only part of the Islamic community" and an "entity that does not represent most." The final slogan asked: "Do not censor 4 million Argentine Arabs."

18. We refer to the Islamic Argentine Organization (Organización Islámica Argentina), founded in 1985 as a legal entity to support Shi'i mosques and societies in Argentina, which are linked to each other and to the Argentine-Islamic Society (Sociedad Argentino Islámica), located in Cañuelas.

19. The entity was created from the merger of three institutions: the Asociación Cultural y Social Solidaridad Islámica Argentina of 1925, the Sociedad Cultural y Social Alianza Árabe Argentina of 1931, and the Club Social y Cultural Juventud Arabe Argentina of 1943.

20. Interviews conducted during 2012 for my research project: "Biographical Trajectories and Institutional Contexts among Argentine Shaykhs" (supported by the National Scientific and Technical Research Council, CONICET, Argentina).

21. We are not referring, in any possible way, to the legal evolution of the ongoing trial, but referring only to its social and media translation as the discursive field of some communities and organizations.

22. The most emblematic case is the one regarding the shaykh of the Al-Imam Mosque in Cañuelas who is also president of the Islamic Argentine Society (Sociedad Islámica Argentina), even though all shaykhs, at different times, made or have made public pronouncements.

23. We could not explain here the complexity of the debates about it, but rather point out that some groups from within the Jewish community emerged that were not in agreement with the position of the leading organizations of the community. Formed by family members and some friends of the victims, Active Memory (Memoria Activa) denounced the

Argentine government as responsible for covering it up and inaction. It considered the hypothesis of a local connection and international authorship. The Association for the Clarification of the Unpunished AMIA Massacre (Asociación para el Esclarecimiento de la Masacre Impune de la AMIA, also known as APEMIA) was formed eight years later, at the urging of some participants in Active Memory. It also accused the Argentine government of a cover-up, framing the AMIA case as the continuity of state terrorism and declaring that the erroneous hypothesis of the international leadership of the attacks as a way to avert responsibility and practice concealment. Both Active Memory and APEMIA disagreed with the leaders of the Delegación de Asociaciones Israelitas Argentinas, also known as DAIA, and the Asociación de Mutuales Israelistas Argentinas, or AMIA. Active Memory argued that there was complicity between these entities in the nonclarification of the cause, and APEMIA added that this injustice was facilitated by the accusations against Iran and the Hezbollah party.

24. For a detailed analysis of the national and transnational media coverage on the Triple Border from the late 1990s to 2005, see Silvia Montenegro and Veronica Giménez Béliveau, *La Triple Frontera: Globalización y construcción social del espacio* (Buenos Aires: Miño y Dávila, 2006).

25. Carlos Corach, *Triple Frontera* (Buenos Aires: Fundación de estudios políticos del tercer milenio, 2003).

26. Steven Vertovec, "Diaspora, Transnationalism and Islam: Sites of Change and Modes of Research," in *Muslim Networks and Transnational Communities in and across Europe*, edited by Stefan Allievi and Jørgen Nielsen (Boston: Brill Leiden, 2003), 323.

CHAPTER 5

CONVERSION, REVIVALISM, AND TRADITION: THE RELIGIOUS DYNAMICS OF MUSLIM COMMUNITIES IN BRAZIL

PAULO G. PINTO

BRAZIL HAS A LARGE Muslim population,[1] which was formed after the late nineteenth century by successive waves of migration from the Middle East (Syria, Lebanon, Palestine) and by the conversion of Brazilians. Muslim communities are mostly urban, and, according to the 2010 national census, the largest are located in São Paulo, Foz de Iguaçu, Curitiba, São Bernardo do Campo, Brasília, and Rio de Janeiro. There are important sociological differences between them. For example, the Muslim community in Rio de Janeiro has not received a significant influx of recent immigrants, a fact that makes the processes of the construction and transmission of Muslim identities more dependent on local and national cultural dynamics. In contrast, in the other aforementioned Muslim communities, the production of Islamic identities is strongly influenced by transnational Islamic movements and by the constant contact with Islam as practiced in the Middle East.[2]

As most Muslim immigrants to Brazil came from the Arab Middle East, mainly Lebanon, Syria, and Palestine, they were identified with the large Arab community in the country.[3] In the first half of the twentieth century, the majority of Arab immigrants were Christian (Maronite, Melkite, Orthodox), with Muslims constituting around 15 percent of the total.[4] The number of Muslim immigrants arriving from the Middle East increased considerably after the 1970s, outnumbering their Christian counterparts. Among Muslim themselves, there was a great diversity of interpretations and forms of living Islam, as they comprised Sunnis, Druze, 'Alawis, and Shi'is.

The first Islamic institutions in Brazil were charitable societies, created in the 1920s and 1930s. The oldest was the Muslim Charitable Society (Sociedade Beneficente Muçulmana) of São Paulo, founded in 1929. While this institution was clearly Sunni, it aimed to be a reference for all Muslims in Brazil. However, Druze and 'Alawis created their own institutions in other parts of Brazil. Already in 1929 the Druze Charitable Society (Sociedade Beneficente

Druziense) was created in Oliveira, Minas Gerais, and in 1956 it was transferred to Belo Horizonte, the capital city of the province. In 1931 the ʿAlawi community in Rio de Janeiro created the ʿAlawi Muslim Charitable Society (Sociedade Beneficente Muçulmana Alauíta), which remained an institutional reference for all Muslims in the city until the 1950s.

During the 1950s and 1960s, other such societies were founded by Muslim communities elsewhere. Sunni Muslims in Rio de Janeiro created the Muslim Charitable Society of Rio de Janeiro (Sociedade Beneficente Muçulmana do Rio de Janeiro) in 1951. In 1957 the Muslim community in Curitiba, constituted by both Sunnis and Shiʿis, created the Muslim Charitable Society of Paraná (Sociedade Beneficente Muçulmana do Paraná). In 1969 the Druze Brazilian House (Lar Druzo Brasileiro) was created in São Paulo. These institutions functioned as spaces where the community gathered for both religious and social activities. More than ritual spaces, they served as arenas of socialization of the younger generations born in Brazil into both Middle Eastern cultural traditions and the Arabic language through the social interaction between families. They also provided a space for forging friendships and matrimonial arrangements within Muslim communities.

Their religious life was also centered in these Muslim charitable societies, where the Friday prayers were performed and where took place the celebrations of the ʿEid al-Fitr, which marks the end of the fasting during Ramadan, and ʿEid al-Adha, the feast of the sacrifice that marks the end of the pilgrimage of the hajj. The ritual practices of Islam gained importance and visibility in the life of the community only after the construction of mosques in some Brazilian cities. With funding from Egypt, the Muslim Charitable Society of São Paulo built the first mosque in Brazil, named Brazil Mosque (Mesquita Brasil), between 1946 and 1960. The religious activities of the Muslim community of São Paulo started to be held in the still unfinished mosque in 1950. For more than a decade after its inauguration, the Brazil Mosque remained the sole mosque in the whole country.

In 1972 the Muslim Charitable Society of Paraná built the Ali Ibn Abi Talib Mosque in Curitiba. During the 1980s and 1990s the availability of funding from Saudi Arabia and Iran, as well as from Jordan and the Gulf countries, allowed Muslim communities and institutions to build mosques in Rio de Janeiro, Belo Horizonte, Campo Grande, Cuiabá, Brasília, and other cities in Paraná and São Paulo. While the majority of these mosques were Sunni, the increasing number of Shiʿi immigrants that arrived in Brazil after the 1970s and the establishment of transnational links with Iran led to the creation of Shiʿi religious institutions and the construction of Shiʿi mosques and *husayniyyas*. The main Shiʿi religious institutions in Brazil are the Mesquita do Brás in São Paulo and the Husayniyya al-Imam Khomeini in Foz do Iguaçu.[5] The mosque in Curitiba, which is used by a community that is composed of both Sunnis and Shi'is, had Sunni shaykhs until 1983, when it started to be led by Shi'i shaykhs.

Cemeteries were also an important element in the organization and consolidation of an Islamic religious landscape in Brazil, for they produced a sense of continuity between the various generations and inscribed a sense of territorial belonging into Muslim identity. The first Islamic cemeteries were created in the 1980s, and nowadays there are three of them, in Guarulhos (São Paulo), Foz do Iguaçu, and Curitiba. The creation of these cemeteries brought some changes in the burial practices of Muslims in Brazil. Before, the dead were brought to the mosque, where it was said the *salat aljanaza* was performed, after which they were buried in Christian cemeteries in family tombs or mausoleums very much like those of non-Muslims, with marble or granite slabs that showed the wealth of the family of the deceased.

With the Islamic cemeteries came a certain homogenization and individualization of the tombs, emphasizing the equality among the members of the community and their religious difference in comparison to traditional Catholic burial practices in Brazil. The Islamic cemetery of Curitiba, which was created in 1983, shows this process of production of shared Islamic burial practices in the Muslim communities in Brazil. The lavish architecture and materials used in older family tombs that were brought from other cemeteries by the families who owned them stand in contrast to the simplicity of the more recent ones, which are individual graves marked only with small black granite plaques inscribed with the *bismillah* and the Qur'anic sentence "Every soul shall taste death" (Kul nafs dha'iqa al-mawt) in Arabic and the name and the dates of birth and death of the deceased in Portuguese. A small picture of the deceased is present on almost all tombs, evoking the funerary traditions of the larger Brazilian society, which are also present in the fact that people usually visit the graves of their dear ones on November 2, the Catholic day for remembering the dead and a national holiday in Brazil.

The construction of mosques gave more visibility and prominence to the religious aspect of Muslim institutions, especially in relation to their function as spaces of sociability for the community. This process gave a new impetus for Brazilians without Muslim ancestry to convert to Islam. Conversion started to become a visible, albeit very discreet, phenomenon during the 1990s, although there was almost no systematic effort to attract converts among the Muslim communities in Brazil. Many converts were attracted to Sufism, and most Sufi communities were organized during this period. The largest and oldest Sufi community is the one of the *tariqa*[6] Shadhiliyya Yashrutiyya (Cha-

zulia Yashrutia), which was created in São Paulo by Lebanese and Syrian immigrants in the 1960s. This community gathers three to four hundred participants, all of them Arabic-speaking immigrants and their descendants, in its
weekly *dhikr* (mystical evocation of God). There are two other Sufi communities with a significant number of members, a *zawiya* (Sufi lodge in Arabic)
of the Naqshbandiyya Haqqaniyya in Rio de Janeiro, which was created in
1996, and a *tekke* (Sufi lodge in Turkish) of the Khalveti Jerrahi order in São
Paulo, which was created in 1992. The ritual gatherings of these communities
assemble around twenty to thirty people, all of them Brazilian converts to
Islam. There are other Sufi *tariqas* in Brazil—such as the Tijaniyya, Gandu-
ziyya, Naqshbandiyya Khalidiyya, Mariamiyya, Shadhiliyya, and Shadhiliyya
ʿAlawiyya—in Rio de Janeiro, São Paulo, and the Northeast, but they have
very few followers. With the exception of the Tijaniyya, which has a community made up mostly of African immigrants, all these *tariqas* have Brazilian
converts as followers. However, they have fewer followers than those mentioned above, ranging from ten to twenty adepts.[7]

With the exception of the Shadhiliyya Yashrutiyya, the Muridiyya, and the
Tijaniyya, which are linked to Arab and African immigrants, the Sufi *tariqas*
were brought to Brazil by converts who entered into contact with them
abroad—in the United States, Turkey, Algeria, and Syria. Brazilian converts to
Sufism are from middle-class extraction and were first attracted to it as part of
a "spiritual quest," which was usually lived in the circuit of New Age religions
in Brazil or abroad. Interestingly, the Sufi communities that were constituted
in Brazil emphasize the moral and ritual obligations of Islam as a fundamental
part of their religious life. This allows them to avoid criticism from the Salafi-
inspired Islam that is dominant in the mosques and Islamic institutions in
Brazil, as well as to distance themselves from the New Age appropriations of
Sufi spirituality that circulate in the Brazilian religious landscape.

In addition, Brazilian converts who create Sufi communities envision
their religious mission as spreading Islam throughout Brazilian society and
attracting new converts as well. Nevertheless, they have a very small role in the
phenomenon of conversion to Islam in contemporary Brazil. The number of
converts to Islam through Sufism is very small if compared to the universe of
conversions in non-Sufi environments, such as mosques and Islamic centers.
Furthermore, after conversion in non-Sufi Islamic institutions, most people
tend to follow Salafi versions of Islam, with the flux of these converts toward
Sufism being practically nil.

The dynamics of conversion to Islam changed after September 11, 2001,
when globalized discourses about Islam enhanced the visibility of the Muslims
in Brazil and the interest of non-Muslim Brazilians. Although most media

discourses about Islam and Muslims were stigmatizing, there were some counterdiscourses that presented them in a positive light, such as the soap opera *O Clone* that was screened on Brazilian TV just after the terrorist attacks of 2001.[8] The intensification of the processes of globalization of Brazilian society through the media, migration, and the increasing affirmation of the country as a player in international arenas also enhanced the interest in Islam as an element of the contemporary political and cultural debate.

Conversion to Islam also creates new opportunities of globalizing oneself, as converts often engage in the study of Arabic and undertake the pilgrimage to Mecca, to the holy cities of Iraq and Iran in the case of the Shiʿis, or to Turkey and Algeria in the case of some Sufis. A few others even go to live some years in the Middle East, usually studying Arabic and Islam in the centers of religious learning of Egypt, Syria, Saudi Arabia, and Iran. Therefore, as I have argued elsewhere, conversion to Islam in contemporary Brazil can also be understood as a form of "conversion to globalization."[9]

While conversion to Islam is connected to processes of globalization of Brazilian selves, with the converts often adopting Arabic names and Middle Eastern or North African attire, and incorporating words and sentences in Arabic in their everyday interactions with Muslims and, sometimes, non-Muslims, it also includes processes of "creolization"[10] of Islam in local cultural and biographical contexts. One convert, a man in his thirties who worked as a journalist at a local newspaper, commented on these processes by telling me during a conversation after the Friday prayer at the mosque of Porto Alegre, "Many people think that they became Arabs after converting to Islam. They change their names, their way of dressing, even give up habits that are not forbidden in Islam. I didn't do any of that. I am a Muslim, but my name is Luís and here is my bowl of mate (*chimarrão*)." This convert had been to the Middle East a few times and had some knowledge of Arabic, but he claimed his belonging to the Muslim community and indexed his participation in its globalizing aspects from an identity that was not only Brazilian but distinctly local, as his reference to the bowl of mate, a major symbol of the gaucho[11] identity, implied.

These processes led to a dramatic increase in both the number of converts and their symbolic importance for Muslim communities in Brazil. Nevertheless, the increasing numbers of Brazilians converting to Islam did not uniformly develop across Brazil. For example, while the proportion of converts in the Sunni Muslim community of Rio de Janeiro rose from 50 percent in 2000 to 85 percent in 2009, it remained practically nil in the Sunni and the Shiʿi Muslim communities in Foz do Iguaçu, which are among the largest in Brazil. The appearance of conversion to Islam as a significant phenomenon happened in the communities that created arenas of interaction and channels of dialogue with non-Muslim Brazilians, such as courses about Islam, Arabic language, or "Muslim culture"[12] that were open to the general public. The conversion of Brazilians did not happen in Muslim communities that continued to consider themselves as spaces solely devoted to the maintenance of the religious cultural tradition of Middle Eastern immigrants and its transmission to their descendants.

Neither was the phenomenon of conversion to Islam evenly distributed across social class divisions. As the attraction of Islam was linked to the expansion of the cultural imagination of the prospective converts beyond the national borders of Brazil and their connection to globalizing trends in the Brazilian society, it is not surprising that almost all the converts come from the mid- to lower echelons of the urban middle class of teachers, students, public servants, and small businessmen. In smaller numbers some members of the upper middle class—physicians, lawyers, dentists, and engineers—also converted to Islam after the 1990s. The few cases of lower-class Brazilians converting to Islam were usually people with strong personal connections to Muslims through work, friendship, or kinship or with high cultural capital. This was the case of a group of people who converted to Islam in one of São Paulo's slums, who were either activists of the Black Movement or linked to hip-hop music. While they could be considered as part of the popular social strata because of their economic situation, in terms of cultural horizons they were more akin to the members of the lower middle class than to their neighbors in the periphery of São Paulo.[13]

By the middle of the first decade of the 2000s, Brazilians' conversion to Islam became an established part of the religious life of the Muslim communities of Rio de Janeiro, Salvador, Recife, Fortaleza, Porto Alegre, and, on a smaller scale, Curitiba. In São Paulo and its metropolitan area, due to the presence of a great number of Muslim communities organized around mosques and *musallas* (prayer halls), there are a variety of situations, with some communities being oriented to the conversion of Brazilians, while others remain ethnically marked as "Arab" communities. Despite the fact that converts constitute the majority of the members of some communities—such as Rio, Salvador, and Recife—converts are still a small minority in the general context of Muslim communities in Brazil.[14]

The incorporation of new converts has not been without tension and conflict. In Muslim communities where Middle Eastern immigrants and their descendants constitute the majority of members, converts are confronted with a religious universe in which Arabic is the main linguistic context of both ritual practices and informal social interactions and where cultural proficiency in

Middle Eastern traditions is as valued as the knowledge of canonical religious rules. The contrast of linguistic and cultural competences marks the boundaries[15] between ethnic categories, such as "Arab" and "Brazilian,"[16] which organize the interaction between converts and Muslim-born members in the Muslim communities in Brazil.

These ethnic distinctions also inform religious hierarchies, as Muslims of Middle Eastern descent usually consider themselves to be "better Muslims" than converts, for they already have a "Muslim culture" as well as some degree of understanding of Arabic. Converts respond by rejecting the idea that inherited Middle Eastern cultural traditions give a better understanding of Islam, which they usually define as the set of beliefs, ritual, and rules established in the holy texts of the Qur'an and the hadith. Many converts in Rio and São Paulo told me that they consider their religious knowledge to be superior to that of "the Arabs," as they refer to Muslims of Middle Eastern descent, saying that they study Islam to become Muslim, while the latter only repeat inherited customs that sometimes are not grounded on the sacred texts.

In this context, it is not by coincidence that the Brazilian converts feel attracted by some trends of the Salafiyya, in particular those influenced by the Wahhabi emphasis on the Qur'an and the hadith as the only sources of religious legitimacy. Salafi Islam is dominant in the religiosity of the converts. The codification of Islam done by Salafi preachers as a clearly bounded set of beliefs, rituals, and moral rules is easily adaptable to the pedagogic apprehension of Islam that marks the religious experience of the Brazilian converts. An analogous phenomenon that became visible during the 2000s is the success of Tablighi missionaries, usually South Africans of Indian or Pakistani descent, in recruiting adepts among Brazilian converts in São Paulo. The emphasis of the Tablighis on the emulation of the biographic example of the Prophet allows the Brazilian converts to bypass the doctrinal debates and the cultural variation of religious practices among Muslims of Middle Eastern origin, while unambiguously constructing themselves as "good Muslims."

In Muslim communities in which the converts have a significant demographic or symbolic presence, the issue of the access of converts to religious knowledge was resolved or minimized through the adoption of Portuguese as a language for religious communication together with Arabic. Thus, in the Mosque of Light (Mesquita da Luz) in Rio de Janeiro, the Friday sermon is done in Portuguese, with only passages from the Qur'an being said in Arabic, and in the Mosque of Pari (Mesquita do Pari), which belongs to the Muslim Youth League (Liga da Juventude Islâmica) in São Paulo, the sermon is said in Arabic with simultaneous translation to Portuguese available through earphones provided for non-Arabic speakers.

Nevertheless, in many other communities, Brazilian converts still face religious contexts marked by ethnic hierarchies. As a result, a new trend emerged during the past decade with the creation of *musallas* by groups that are discontent with the ethnic hierarchies of the communities dominated by Muslims of Middle Eastern origin. This phenomenon is particularly visible in São Paulo, home to the largest Muslim population in Brazil. A group of Muslims from various countries of sub-Saharan Africa created in 2005 a *musalla* in a commercial building in downtown São Paulo, which is named Bilal al-Habashi, the name of the Ethiopian ex-slave who became a companion of the Prophet and the first muezzin. At the time of my visit in 2006, this *musalla* was led by a Ghanaian imam (prayer leader). Also, a group of Brazilian converts created in 2007 the *musalla al-firdaus* (Musalla of Paradise) in the neighborhood of Paraíso (Paradise) in São Paulo. Interestingly, despite stating that their decision to break with the communities to which they belonged was due to difficulties in finding their place in a religious universe dominated by "the Arabs," they chose a Muslim-born Brazilian of Lebanese origin as imam because of his proficiency in Arabic. This shows that the Brazilian converts do not reject the religious use of Arab cultural diacritics, such as the Arabic language, but rather reject their use to create hierarchies within the Muslim community.

The conversion of Brazilians was not the only possible path taken by Muslim communities in order to ensure their continuity in the Brazilian society. Since the 1980s there has been a religious revival among the descendants of Muslim Middle East immigrants. While the 1960s and 1970s were marked by a steady decline in the religious practice and the involvement with community affairs by the generations born in Brazil, the 1980s marked a slow process of religious revival among Brazilian Muslims of Middle Eastern descent. The causes can be linked to the revival of ethnicity in Brazil, as the form of Islam cultivated by descendants of Muslim immigrants is connected to Arab identity, as well as Islam as a public religious practice on a global scale. By 2000 some Muslim communities in Brazil, like that of Curitiba, started to create conditions for new generations to articulate their Muslim, Arab, and Brazilian identities in the local social and cultural context. In order to show this diversity, I will analyze here the religious dynamics of Muslim communities in Rio de Janeiro, Curitiba, and Foz do Iguaçu.

THE REALM OF THE CONVERTS: THE MUSLIM COMMUNITY IN RIO DE JANEIRO

The Sunni Muslim community in Rio is rather small in comparison to those in São Paulo or Paraná. The leaders of the community estimate that there are five thousand Muslims in the whole province of Rio de Janeiro, with more or less a thousand of them being directly or indirectly connected with the Muslim Charitable Society of Rio de Janeiro (Sociedade Beneficente Muçulmana do Rio de Janeiro, SBMRJ), which constitutes the religious and institutional center of the community.[17] Until 2007 the religious activities of the Sunni Muslim community took place in a prayer hall in a commercial building in downtown Rio. After that date the religious activities moved to a new mosque that is being built in the Tijuca neighborhood. This is the only mosque currently operating in Rio de Janeiro, for the mosque built in the neighborhood of Jacarepaguá in 1983 has been closed since the mid-1990s. There is one *musalla* downtown and another in Copacabana. There is also the 'Alawi Muslim Charitable Society in Tijuca, which serves as a space for sociability and for the celebration of 'Alawi rituals, such as 'Ashura and the Mawlid al-Nabawi (Birth of the Prophet).[18]

Despite the small size, the Sunni Muslim community in Rio is particularly interesting because it is the largest one in Brazil in which members are not predominantly of Arab origin. The history of this community is marked by a series of cultural reorientations that allowed it to create a form of insertion in the local society based on the incorporation of new members through the conversion of Brazilians. The result is a multicultural and multiethnic community that includes Arabs and their descendants, Africans (many of whom are foreign students or immigrants), and non-Arab Brazilians who have converted to Islam from other religious traditions. The non-Arab Brazilians are, in fact, the majority in the community, while Arabs and their descendants make up only 10 percent of the membership. The number of non-Arab Brazilian converts increased dramatically after 2000, when they constituted about half of the members of the community,[19] reaching the level of 85 percent of the membership in 2007.

The first Muslim institution in Rio de Janeiro was the 'Alawi Muslim Charitable Society of Rio de Janeiro (Sociedade Beneficente Muçulmana Alauíta do Rio de Janeiro), created in 1931 by 'Alawi immigrants from Syria. While the society was linked to the 'Alawi community, its founding charter states that it is devoted to taking care of "everything related to the interests of those affiliated to the 'Alawi Muslim rite in particular, and of the Muslims in general."[20] This pan-Islamic horizon allowed the 'Alawi society to serve as a religious institution to the Sunni Muslims and its shaykh to be their religious leader for decades, despite the religious differences between the two branches of Islam.[21]

The Sunni Muslims created the Muslim Charitable Society of Rio de Janeiro only in 1951.[22] Though an institutional reference for the Sunni Muslim community, it held no religious activities. Therefore, Muslim religious life in Rio de Janeiro continued to be centered in the ʿAlawi society. The SBMRJ functioned as a social club, in which Sunni Muslims could meet and establish social networks based on religious identity. The activities of the society in the 1950s were described by Khalil Ayubi,[23] who later became responsible for its transformation, as "having nothing to do with religious practice. . . . The president and the secretary would say 'In the name of the Muslim Society this session is open' and then would chat about Freemasonry [for they were Freemasons], the Arab movies that they had seen at the ABI,[24] work, life, etc."

This situation changed when Khalil Ayubi—a Lebanese immigrant who was returning to a second, and definitive, stay in Brazil—became the president of the SBMRJ in 1968. He transformed the office of the society into a *musalla*, covering the floor with carpets and removing the furniture. In 1970, with funding from Saudi Arabia, an Egyptian shaykh trained in Al-Azhar became the imam of the Sunni community, and all its religious rituals, such as the daily prayers, started to be performed in the *musalla* of the SBMRJ. This move created in practice two Muslim communities in Rio de Janeiro, a Sunni and an ʿAlawi one that, while remaining connected for some time, would eventually develop divergent paths.

The emphasis on the religious aspects of the SBMRJ was accompanied by other efforts to mobilize the Sunni Muslims in Rio de Janeiro—which by 1970 were almost all immigrants from Lebanon, Syria, and Palestine and their descendants—around their religious identity. Besides the daily prayers held at the *musalla* of the SBMRJ, the efforts were directed to transmit a Muslim identity and Islamic religious knowledge to the descendants of the Muslim immigrants who were born in Rio. Therefore, during the 1970s the Sunni Muslim community in Rio de Janeiro saw its religious identity as part of a cultural heritage brought to Rio by immigrants from the Middle East, one that should be transmitted to the new generations.

The greatest symbol of the investment of the leadership of the community in the religious education of the new generations as a form of ensuring the continuity of the community was the creation of an Islamic school in 1976. The school was an initiative of Khalil Ayubi who, as director of the SBMRJ, bought a preexisting primary school in the working-class suburb of Parada de Lucas and transformed it into the Islamic-Brazilian Cultural and Educational Center (Centro Educacional Cultural Islâmico Brasileiro). The Islamic school had the regular Brazilian curriculum with classes in Arabic and "Islamic religion" (*religião islâmica*). The Arabic teacher was a Syrian Christian sent by the Syrian Embassy, and the teacher of Islamic religion was a member of the Sunni community in Rio.

While the school was created to provide an institutional framework for the transmission of religious knowledge and revival of Muslim identity among the descendants of Middle Eastern immigrants, which included a system of grants to those who could not pay, not a single student came from the Muslim community. All seventy-five students were non-Muslim Brazilians. The majority of them received a Muslim religious education with the agreement of their families.

The absence of Muslim students was not a result of the lack of Middle Eastern families in the surrounding areas, for as Khalil Ayubi recalled:

> There were many Palestinian Muslim families nearby, but they never sent their sons and daughters to the school, they were not rich at all but they preferred to put their kids in other private schools, despite the fact that we offered grants to those who could not pay.

The reluctance of Muslim families of Middle Eastern origins in sending their offspring to the Islamic school and their opting for private schools show how their efforts in the schooling of the generations born in Brazil were directed toward the acquisition of cultural competencies that could be converted into social capital in the Brazilian society instead of the transmission of a religious and cultural heritage.[25] Despite success in attracting non-Muslim Brazilian students and giving them a Muslim religious education, which would possibly be a source of converts, after Khalil Ayubi left the presidency of the SBMRJ, the community lost interest in the school, and it closed in 1984.

The construction of the first mosque in Rio also showed the limitations of the project of maintaining the community through the transmission and constant affirmation of a Muslim identity closely linked to the cultural heritage of Middle East immigration. A mosque was built in 1983 in the neighborhood of Jacarepaguá with funding from Jordan and Saudi Arabia. The construction of the mosque aimed to give a common religious reference to the Muslims in Rio de Janeiro.[26] The building of the mosque created a new religious arena in the community, and inscribed Islam in the religious landscape of Rio de Janeiro, inducing greater intensity in the religious practice of a generation of Muslims of immigrant descent who were born in Rio. During the celebrations of 'Eid in the 1980s, hundreds of people went to the mosque.[27]

However, the large distance that separated the mosque from the neighborhoods where most Muslims lived and worked led to a continuous decline in its attendance, to the point that it had to be closed. Khalil Ayubi remembered the difficulties the community faced due to the location of the mosque:

> We tried to minimize the problem of the distance by providing buses that departed from the headquarters of the SBMRJ at Lapa [downtown Rio] to the mosque in Jacarepaguá, but still it took a long time to get there. In the

beginning the mosque was full; later on you could count in your fingers the number of people there. . . . We had no other choice than go back to performing the prayers at the *musalla*.[28]

The failure of community to support projects based exclusively on the transmission and revival of the codification of Islam as cultural heritage led to a decade of decline in the number of members in the Muslim community of Rio de Janeiro. This decline culminated in the actual lack of a shaykh for the community by the mid-1990s. This situation was resolved only after 1997, when a group of Muslims born or raised in Rio introduced reforms that changed completely the cultural orientation of the SBMRJ and, therefore, of the community itself.

At that time the SBMRJ was directed by a Sudanese, Abdelbagi Osman, also known as Abdu, who had incomplete religious studies in Libya and served as the imam of the community. Abdu, together with some members of the community, in particular two brothers born in Rio of Syrian descent— Munzer and Sami Isbelle—who had studied Arabic and one year of Islamic jurisprudence at the Islamic University of Medina, started to change the codification of Islam officially fostered by the community. They emphasized the universalistic aspect of Islam and, adopting a Salafi framework, tried to present it as a religious system "free" of Middle Eastern cultural references. This approach contrasted with the one previously dominant in the community, which strongly connected Muslim identity to Arab cultural diacritics.

This change in the codification of Islam was accompanied by a series of transformations that aimed to widen the audience of the religious discourses produced by the leaders of the community. Thus, Portuguese gradually replaced Arabic as the main language of the Friday sermons, which allowed both Muslims of Arab descent born in Brazil and Brazilian converts to participate in one of the main arenas of transmission of religious knowledge of the community. Also, courses on the Arabic language, the history of Islam, and "Islamic culture" started to be offered to Muslims and non-Muslims, creating an important arena of socialization for Muslims born in Brazil and converts to Islam, as well as a channel of dialogue with the larger Brazilian society.

These courses allowed the leaders of the community to give a larger visibility to their codification of Islam as well as to their criticism of the negative representations of Muslims and Islam that circulated in the Brazilian society and media. Furthermore, the courses also created an instance of cultural mediation between various representations, expectations, and doubts that the students had in relation to Islam and the religious codification fostered by the leaders of the SBMRJ. This cultivated the intellectual curiosity of some of the non-Muslim students, who gradually became more personally involved with the form of Islam practiced by the Muslim community in Rio de Janeiro. In addition to the universalistic codification of Islam and the adoption of Portuguese as the main linguistic context of the religious discourses, this discursive arena provided an important channel to attract prospective converts to the community.

The number of converts increased steadily, gaining momentum after 2001, when the greater visibility that Islam attained in the cultural imaginary of the Brazilian society enhanced the dynamics of conversion. After a few years, converts constituted the absolute majority of the Muslims in Rio, changing the cultural and religious character of the community. As the process of conversion to Islam in the Muslim community in Rio is centered on the acquisition of a Muslim identity through individual commitment to the beliefs, practices, rules, and norms of Islam as they are defined and codified by the community, the increase in the number of converts led to an individualization of Muslim religiosity.

Indeed, the individual is the target of the official religious discourses that circulate in the community. The sermons emphasize individual responsibility, rational choice, and conscious intention as the bases of faith. All collective rituals—such as daily prayers, fasting during Ramadan, or the pilgrimage of the hajj—are the object, at the appropriate period of the religious calendar, of sermons that emphasize that their religious merits are valid only if they are performed with the full rational and emotional engagement of the individual. It is a recurrent theme in the discourse of the leadership of the community that Muslim identity is not inherited, but rather something that is achieved through the acquisition of religious knowledge and the conscious shaping of one's behavior according to the moral rules of Islam.

This kind of religiosity that connects religious knowledge and faith is based on the codification of Islam that is fostered by the leadership of the SBMRJ. The leaders of the Muslim community in Rio define their understanding and practice of Islam as deriving from the Salafiyya. According to them, Islam is a definite and bounded set of beliefs, rules, and moral norms that are inscribed in the Qur'an and the hadith. Sami summarized this position during a course that he was teaching at the SBMRJ in 2008:

Islam is what is stated in the Qur'an and in the traditions of the Prophet, peace be upon him. That is the Islam of the revelation. After that, because of historical reasons and influence of culture and other religions, people started to interpret and add things, creating variation and deviation from the original message. Here in the SBMRJ we think that these other practices and beliefs might seem correct to those who follow them, but we don't accept them for us.

Other religious traditions of Islam, such as Shi'ism and Sufism, are often criticized and pointed out as examples of "deviations" from the prophetic message. Also, Sunni religious traditions that do not have explicit references in the sacred texts—such as the celebration of the Mawlid al-Nabawi (the Birth of the Prophet)—are also rejected as innovations that deviated the Muslim community from its mythical unity.

Nevertheless, the religious authorities of the Sunni community in Rio de Janeiro have a very particular interpretation of the Salafiyya, which for them is mainly the idea that all aspects of Muslim religiosity should be grounded in the Qur'an and the hadith. They do not follow the literalist or political trends of the Salafiyya,[29] framing their interpretation of Islamic doctrines as a moral discourse centered on the individual who aims to insert him- or herself into the larger society as a pious Muslim. This orientation toward creating a Muslim religious life in a non-Muslim society leads the leaders of the community to adopt positions that could be better classified as "modernist" rather than "Salafi," usually drawing inspiration from European or North American Muslim sources.

One example is the official position of the SBMRJ on female converts who were already married to non-Muslim husbands before their conversion. According to Munzer, who does the Friday sermon (khutba), as there is no consensus among the Islamic scholars on the issue of whether the marriage would still be valid, it is up to each individual female convert to decide if she will remain married to her non-Muslim husband. This opinion is inspired by a similar decision by the European Council of Fatwas. Similar issues of whether it is licit to work in a bar, to celebrate one's birthday, or to eat in non-Muslim houses where pork is served with other food are also left up to the individual consciousness of each member of the community.

This "Salafi minimalism" had been possible because the community has traditionally refused to receive shaykhs appointed by other religious institutions, in particular those from Saudi Arabia.[30] However, since 2012 there has been a process of integration of the community with the Islamic institutions based in São Paulo and, through them, with the globalized networks of patronage that spring from Saudi Arabia and the Gulf countries. In 2014 a new imam, a Brazilian who studied in Sudan, was appointed to the mosque, and a more assertive form of the Salafiyya became the normative reference in the community.

The SBMRJ also offers spaces and forms of sociability alternative to the Brazilian cultural traditions that are seen as "un-Islamic," such as Carnival, which is particularly present in the everyday life of the Muslims in Rio. During Carnival there are activities of "Islamic camping" or "spiritual retreat" that are usually held at farms or hotels in the countryside. On these occasions those

Friday sermon at the Mosque of Light (Mesquita de Luz), Rio de Janeiro

who want can retreat to an "Islamic" environment where leisure activities, such as sports or hiking, are mixed with praying and the study of Islam.[31] Other traditions linked to the urban middle-class culture such as Mother's Day or Children's Day sometimes also receive an "Islamic" version in the SBMRJ or are the object of commentaries in the sermon about how a Muslim should behave during their celebration.

On the other hand, the SBMRJ is very conscious of its position in Rio's religious field, in which the Muslim community tries to inscribe itself as part of the local "religious diversity" with a discourse of tolerance and coexistence. Since 2008 a delegation from the Muslim community has participated in the annual March against Religious Intolerance,[32] where it shares with other religious traditions, such as Catholicism, Judaism, and African-Brazilian religions (Candomblé and Umbanda), a space of belonging to Rio's religious imaginary. This performative affirmation of the Muslim community as part of the local religious landscape is an important way of presenting Islam as a legitimate alternative for conversion in Rio's "religious market." The construction of a new mosque, the Mesquita da Luz (Mosque of Light), in 2007, can also be seen as a way of inscribing Muslim religiosity in Rio's urban landscape.

Representatives of the Sunni Muslim community of Rio de Janeiro at the March against Religious Intolerance at Copacabana Beach

The importance of the efforts to create a religious codification of Islam, as well as mechanisms for its transmission (sermons and texts in Portuguese as well as courses) that were adapted to the local social and cultural conditions of the Muslim community in Rio, must not prevent us from seeing that they are also connected to processes that point to transnational religious horizons. The processes of localizing Islam in Rio are usually coupled with others that globalize the religious imagination of the *carioca* Muslims.[33] This is particularly true with the converts, whose socialization in the doctrines, practices, and values of Islam goes together with the construction of a transnational religious imagination centered on the Middle East and its holy sites. Several Friday sermons talk about the past and present religious and political situation of the Middle Eastern societies. Examples about Muslims living in Europe, China, or the United States are also used frequently as moralizing stories in the sermons.

Many converts take the course on Arabic language, aiming to read the Qur'anic text in its original version, but also to acquire enough linguistic competence to be able to interact with Middle Eastern cultural and religious realities. Others spend some time living in Syria, Egypt, or Saudi Arabia in order to study Arabic and "learn how life is in a Muslim society," as summarized by one convert who had lived in Syria. The hajj (pilgrimage to Mecca) is another occasion for the converts to add an experiential dimension to the transnational religious imagination that connects them to the sacred site in the Middle East. All these experiences of direct contact and acquisition of first-hand knowledge of the Arab Muslim societies of the Middle East provide the Sunni converts in Rio de Janeiro with a form of cultural and religious capital that allows them to affirm their Muslim identity and their belonging to the *umma* on equal terms with those born Muslim.

Therefore, the disciplinary practices developed by the SBMRJ's religious authorities (sermons, courses, normative texts, and so forth) have produced a process of "objectification" of Islamic tradition, generating a religious system of cultural and social practices that serves as a conscious normative point of reference in the life of the faithful.[34] This "objectified" Islam presented as a local form of the Salafiyya facilitates the integration of the converts in the community, downplaying the cultural differences between individuals and allowing the construction of an inclusive Muslim identity that connects the local realities of the Muslims of Rio de Janeiro with the transnational horizons of their religious imagination.

RITUALS OF REVIVALISM:
THE MUSLIM COMMUNITY IN CURITIBA

The Muslim community in Curitiba, a prosperous city of around 1.7 million inhabitants and capital of the state of Paraná in southern Brazil, has about 5,000 members.[35] In 1957 the Muslim Charitable Society of Paraná (Sociedade Beneficente Muçulmana do Paraná) was created as a space where the members of the community could meet and socialize. Shaykh Muhammad, who served as shaykh of the community between 2002 and 2006, stressed the importance of the space of sociability created in the Muslim Charitable Society:

> The community in Curitiba was very smart to create first a club [the space of sociability in the Muslim Society] and then worry about building a mosque, since the club allows for the integration of families, and particularly, keeps the youth together and interested in Islam. If young Muslims do not do things together and feel that Islam is just about praying at the mosque or following the rules of the religion, they will eventually lose interest in becoming good Muslims.

This community has always gathered Sunni and Shi'i members. While the Shi'i were always active in the organization of the community, as can be seen in the fact that the first president of the Muslim Charitable Society was a Shiʿi, the Sunnis were more important demographically. This situation changed in the 1970s, when the civil war in Lebanon and the Israeli invasion of South Lebanon intensified the influx of immigrants from southern Lebanon and the number of Shiʿis grew to represent half of the community membership. While there were differences between Sunnis and Shiʿis, they were minimized in the early years of the society by the fact that religious identities were transmitted as part of a cultural heritage connected to Arab identity. The sectarian tensions in the community erupted only after the construction of the mosque, when debates about Islamic identities, practices, and transnational imaginaries divided Sunni and Shiʿis.

Thus, it is not surprising that the first project to keep the new generations born in Brazil committed to their Muslim identities was centered in the transmission of Arabic language with the creation of an Islamic school. The Escola Islâmica do Paraná (Paraná Islamic School) was founded in 1969 with sixty students, all from Muslim families.[36] The school followed the Brazilian national curriculum with classes on Islam and the Arabic language. While many Muslim families did send their children to study in the school, the number of students was not enough to supply the financial needs of the institution, which depended on donations from other members of the community to maintain its activities. The financial difficulties and conflicts between the shaykh and other members of the community led to the closing of the Islamic school in 1972.[37]

The end of the Paraná Islamic School also reflected a shift in the mechanisms of transmission of the religious identity and maintenance of the community among the Muslims in Curitiba, for it coincided with the construction of the Imam Ali Ibn Abi Talib Mosque in 1972.[38] This mosque, which was built in "international Islamic" style, with minarets, horseshoe arches, and a dome, pointed to a greater importance of religious practices as an arena of affirmation and transmission of the Muslim identity. While the Muslim community had at least two major religious traditions, Sunnism and Shiʿism, informing the religious beliefs and practices of its members, during the 1970s the mosque was led by Egyptian Sunni shaykhs who graduated from the University of Al-Azhar.[39]

This arrangement lasted until 1983, when it was unsettled by changes internal and external to the community. The growing immigration from South Lebanon made the number of Shiʿis in the community increase to the point of constituting half of its members. In the international arena the Iranian Revolution of 1979 created new models of Shiʿi identity, providing many Shiʿis with more assertive ways of expressing their religious identity. Likewise, the Islamic Republic installed in Iran started to make available funding for Islamic institutions and communities in order to export its interpretation of Islam and to dispute with Saudi Arabia religious and political influence in international Islamic arenas. In this context the Shiʿi members of the community secured funding from Iran for the shaykh's salary, as well as the maintenance and decoration of the mosque. Indeed, until 2012—when both the interior and the exterior of the mosque were covered with mosaic tiles in Persian style—the Persian carpets covering the floor of the mosque, the framed verses from the Qurʾan in Persian calligraphy, and the *mihrab* made of neo-Safavid styled tiles, with a bilingual inscription in Arabic and Portuguese stating "Gift from the Islamic Republic of Iran, 1996," expressed the connections between the community and Iran.

The rise in influence of the Shiʿi members of the community led to the appointment of a Qom-educated Lebanese Shiʿi shaykh, Abbas Baghdadi, as the imam of the mosque in 1983. Since then, all shaykhs of the mosque have been Shiʿi. The shaykhs were mostly Lebanese, but there were also Iraqis and Iranians among them. Many members of the community still remember how the first Shiʿi shaykhs were committed to the revolutionary ideology fostered by the Islamic Republic of Iran, praising it in their sermons and even putting a picture of Ayatollah Khomeini in the prayer hall of the mosque. This explicit affirmation of Ayatollah Khomeini's interpretation of Shiʿi identity as the official codification of Islam in the mosque did not please many Sunnis in the community. These tensions were deepened by the ongoing Iran-Iraq War (1980–1988), which provided a transnational political framework to the internal disputes within the community for the right to define the local interpretation of Islam and its symbolic and practical connections to normative horizons in the Middle East. Thus, Shiʿi members of the community would assert their newly found position of power by expressing support for the Islamic Republic of Iran, while Sunnis would try to restore their symbolic capital by claiming to defend Arab identity and culture through their identification with the Iraqi side of the conflict. According to a senior member of the community:

> It was a very difficult time. Accusations and disputes over the "right" way of being Muslim and Arab divided the community.[40] Even praying together became impossible. The community was on the verge of breaking apart.[41]

According to Shaykh Muhammad Khalil, who led the community in Curitiba from 2002 to 2006, this situation started to revert only by the mid-1990s, when a Lebanese Shiʿi shaykh, also educated at Qom, decided to tone down the politico-religious militancy that prevailed in the mosque until he took charge of it. He withdrew from the mosque all political or sectarian symbols,

such as the portrait of Ayatollah Khomeini and the images of the holy figures of Shi'ism. This shaykh and some other leading figures of the community started to reconcile quarreling factions by constructing a supra-sectarian
Muslim identity based on doctrinal and ritual elements that were shared by
both Sunnis and Shi'is. One of the pillars of this process of reintegration of
local Sunni and Shi'i Muslims into a moral community, which was grounded
on the religious space of the mosque of Curitiba while also keeping strong
symbolic and practical transnational links to the Middle East, was the tendency to minimize the ritual and doctrinal boundaries between Sunnism and
Shi'ism in tandem with an emphasis on the shared cultural references that
shaped the religious practices of the adepts of both traditions.

Therefore, Arabic was consecrated as the main linguistic context of both
official (discourses, sermons, ritual formulae, and so on) and informal (ordi-
nary conversations) interactions within the community; concrete signs of
sectarian differences between Sunni and Shi'i Muslims, such as the pieces of
stone and wood or clay tablets made of the sacred soil of Karbala that the
Shi'is use for touching their heads while praying, were removed to discrete
locations in the back of the prayer hall of the mosque; and Sunnis and Shi'is
were encouraged to freely mingle without any particular order during prayers,
so as to resignify their differences as individual idiosyncrasies in a shared performance of a collective ritual tradition. The leaders of the community developed discourses that stress the supra-sectarian pan-Islamic inclusiveness of
the community. In 2010 the vice president of the Muslim Charitable Society
of Paraná explained to a group of visitors that "the mosque of Curitiba is the
only religious place besides the Haram in Mecca where Sunni and Shi'is pray
as equal members of the community."[42] This same sentence was repeated on
several other occasions by other members of the community, showing how
successful were the efforts to overcome sectarian tensions and integrate the
opposing groups into a moral community. This was done through the emphasis on shared ritual practices as well as the incorporation of values and
practices from Middle Eastern culture in the everyday life of the community.
The result was a stable but inward-looking religious community, which was
resistant to the incorporation of new members who were not Arabic-speaking
immigrants or their descendants.

However, despite its success in overcoming its internal conflicts, the Muslim community in Curitiba had to face, during the 1970s and 1980s, the decline in religious practice among the generations born in Brazil. While the
emphasis on Middle Eastern cultural patterns of religious practice that were
expressed in Arabic worked well to create shared religious understandings
and experiences among those who had the cultural and linguistic proficiency
to fully participate in this process, it alienated many young Brazilian Muslims

Friday prayer at the Imam Ali Ibn Abi Talib Mosque in Curitiba. Note the tiles in Persian style covering the *mihrab* and the large picture of the Haram and the Kaaba in Mecca on the wall.

who, albeit being of Middle Eastern descent, had very limited knowledge of Arabic and Middle Eastern cultural traditions or who were exposed to other forms of living Islam, some of them coming from the Middle East itself.

The challenge posed by the decline in religious practice among the Brazilians of Muslim descent was dealt with in other communities, such as the one in Rio de Janeiro, through creating mechanisms to promote Islam in the larger Brazilian society and incorporate the eventual converts into the community. However, there was a strong resistance within the Muslim community in Curitiba toward any efforts to attract converts from the non-Muslim Brazilian population. One reason was that a convert would bring to public debate the divisions of the community, for there would have to be a consensus on what doctrines and rituals he or she had to learn in order to become a proper Muslim, risking a revival of the sectarian tensions that were so painfully contained. Indeed, in 2003 Shaykh Muhammad Khalil told me that the community had no plans of doing *daʿwa* (spreading Islam) or any scheme to integrate possible converts in its milieu.

Nevertheless, among some members of the community, there was the feeling that something should be done in order to guarantee the continuity of the Muslim community, which was among the largest ones in Brazil. In 2005 the president of the Muslim Charitable Society of Paraná, Jamil Iskandar,[43] made a speech in the mosque after the Friday prayer, in which he said:

> We must do something to attract the new generations back to Islam, back to our community. We need to invest in the education of the children as well as to create an environment that interests the youth. Otherwise, in a few years people will pass in front of this building, which will become a museum or a ruin, and say: Here is where the Muslims used to pray.

In this context, some changes were implemented in the community. The main promoter of these changes was Gamal Oumairi, who is the son of the first president of the Muslim Charitable Society of Paraná and is currently its vice president. Gamal, who was born in Curitiba from Lebanese Shi'i parents, had done incomplete religious studies in Qom, Iran. After returning to Curitiba, he decided to dedicate his time to reviving the religious life of the Muslim community. His efforts have the support of both the president of the Muslim Charitable Society and the current shaykh of the mosque, Muhammad Radawi, a Qom-educated Iranian of Iraqi descent.

Since 2005 the sermon in the Friday prayer has been accompanied by a summarized translation in Portuguese, in order to allow those who cannot understand Arabic to get its message. Since 2011 the participants in the Friday prayer have also received a printed translation of the sermon in Portuguese, which is also available on the web page of the mosque.[44] Also in 2005, the mosque started to regularly be open on Sunday mornings to visitors and tourists,[45] who would receive a tour of the building, the newsletter edited by the community, and basic explanations about Islam given by Gamal or any other member of the community who happened to be present. This opening of the mosque to visitation aimed to inscribe the Muslim community into the cultural landscape of Curitiba[46] in order to raise the interest in Islam among non-Muslim Brazilians and, maybe more important, among people of Muslim descent who became uninterested in religious practice or in the activities of the community. Gamal explained to me in 2005 that, despite facing resistance from some members of the community, he insisted on keeping the tours of the mosque on Sunday mornings because, in his words:

> It's important to show people how the Muslim community lives and how it built such a beautiful landmark as this mosque. This will make the younger generations proud of their Muslim heritage and more interested in getting

involved in the community life. We have to show that Islam is part of Curitiba's heritage in order to make the Muslims who were born here eager to live
their religious heritage.

The investment in the new generation of Muslims intensified in 2007 with
the reopening of the Islamic school Escola Brasileira-Árabe (Brazilian-Arab
School), with twenty students in the elementary level. Also, in the same year
courses in Arabic, Islamic culture, and Islam for adults started to be minis-
tered at the mosque by the shaykh or by Gamal. The content of the courses is
also available in Portuguese on the community's web page. As most of these
changes were conceived and executed by Shi'i members of the community,
Shi'ism became a more visible influence in the religious life of the community.

Even the mosque is gradually acquiring a more clear Shi'i identity—which
is aesthetically expressed by the tiles in neo-Safavid style donated by the Iranian
government that decorate its *mihrab*, arches, and cupola—notwithstanding
the fact that there are still mechanisms to ensure the visibility and integration
of the Sunnis in the community. So when the shaykh is traveling, the Friday
sermon is delivered by a Sunni member of the community, who also leads the
prayers.

While most of the changes in the religious life of the community were
made to keep the interest of the younger generations of Muslims in Islam,
they also created a cultural environment more accommodating to the conversion to Islam of Brazilians without any Muslim ancestry. The rise of the
Shi'i influence in the community also eased the ambiguity about the normative models to be presented to the prospective converts, diminishing their
potential threat to the stability of the community. Thus, the small, but rising,
number of converts to Islam[47] who are members of the Muslim community
in Curitiba benefit from the structure of courses and bilingual speeches that
were created in the past few years for the members of the community who
were born in Brazil.

The need to transmit religious meanings, values, and practices to a Muslim
youth that does not have proficiency in the cultural traditions of the older
generations of immigrants from the Middle East transformed even the religious practices of the community. The sermons became more pedagogical,
explaining in detail all their moral points and making references to precise
passages in the Qur'an or the hadith where the listeners could find further information. Informal ways of testing and inducing religious knowledge among
the members of the community were developed, such as regular "quiz con-
tests" about the suras (chapters) of the Qur'an. Those who scored highest in
the number of correct answers to forty-one questions would get a Qur'an or a

book with Ali's sermons, as well as the general recognition of the community of their religious knowledge.

In 2011 a quiz about the sura Al-Fatiha asked: "What does sura mean?"; "When is it allowed to not recite the sura Al-Fatiha?"; "How is Al-Fatiha different from the other suras?"; "Why do all Muslims start their activities with Bismillah?"; "Which sura does not begin with Bismillah?"; and so on. These quizzes produce a process of objectification of the religious tradition by bringing to scrutiny not only the religious knowledge as learned from the reading of the Qur'an, but also general habits and practices constructed as Islamic and their relation to the content of the sacred text. In this sense, they shift the basis of Muslim identity from an inherited cultural tradition to an acquired religious knowledge that has both doctrinal-discursive and ritual-practical dimensions.

This attribution of knowledge to habits is extended to rituals, which are also submitted to pedagogic performances for and by the children. Therefore, the rituals of 'Ashura now include a moment in which both the sons and the daughters of the members of the community[48] recite poems to Husayn, Fatima, and Ali to all those present. Afterward, they join the adults in a short performance of *latmiya* (chest beating), before leaving the *husayniyya* that exists under the mosque. According to the current shaykh:

> It is important that the kids not only learn about Husayn and the 'Ashura, but also join in the remembrance of him. Islam is not just learning, it is feeling. How can you believe if you do not feel it in your heart?

Therefore, the project of religious revivalism fostered in the Muslim community in Curitiba is centered on the construction of a tradition of knowledge to be learned and enacted in relation to a series of habits and practices understood as Islamic, as well as the emotional education of the believer, through the induction of a series of religious experiences in the ritual contexts of the community.

TRANSNATIONAL TRADITIONS:
THE MUSLIM COMMUNITY IN FOZ DO IGUAÇU

The Muslim Community in Foz do Iguaçu, in the state of Paraná, is almost totally composed of Lebanese and Palestinian immigrants and their descendants. The Lebanese constitute a large majority within the community. Although there are no reliable statistics for the number of Muslims in Foz do Iguaçu, the religious leaders of the community advance numbers that range

'Ashura at the *husayniyya* in the Imam Ali Ibn Abi Talib Mosque in Curitiba. Note the children performing the ritual on the right.

from 18,000 to 22,000 Muslims[49] in the area of the "Triple Border" (*Tríplice Fronteira/Triple Frontera*). This area is the intersection of the national borders of Brazil, Argentina, and Paraguay and has three cities, one in each country, that have different levels of integration with each other. The economy of this region is oriented toward transborder commerce and tourism, for it harbors the Iguazú Falls at the border between Brazil and Argentina, which is a major tourist attraction of both countries.

Paraguay has no major touristic attraction in its city Ciudad del Este. This city of around 170,000 inhabitants developed as a major commercial hub that feeds the Brazilian market with both certified and counterfeit imported electronics and luxury goods from Asia, Europe, and the United States. The commerce in Ciudad del Este is mainly controlled by Arab and Chinese immigrants and their descendants. Many Brazilians also work in Ciudad del Este. Foz de Iguaçu, on the Brazilian side, is the largest city of the region with around 256,000 inhabitants and is fully integrated with Ciudad del Este, with a constant flux of people and goods flowing between both cities. The Arab Muslim community is spread between both cities, with those who are better off economically tending to live in Brazil and those recently arrived living in

Paraguay. Puerto Iguazú on the Argentinian side, with 32,000 inhabitants, is the smallest and the least integrated in the transborder economy of the three cities, with no Arab or Muslim community. The Muslim community in the Triple Border gained great visibility after September 11, 2001, as it was targeted by the discourses on international terrorism fostered by the Argentinian and American governments, which tried to link it with the bombing attacks against the Israeli Embassy and the AMIA (Jewish Mutual-Aid Society of Argentina) in Buenos Aires in 1992 and 1994 as well as with militant groups in the Middle East.[50]

There are Islamic institutions in both Foz do Iguaçu and Ciudad del Este. In Foz do Iguaçu there is the Mesquita Omar Ibn al-Khatab, which belongs to the Sunni community, and a *husayniyya* in the Sociedade Islamica de Foz do Iguaçu, which belongs to the Shi'i community. In Ciudad del Este the Shi'i community has the Mesquita del Profeta Mohammed, and the Sunni community has a prayer hall in a commercial building, both in the commercial center of the city. In 2012 the Centro Arabe Islámico Paraguayo (Paraguayan Arab Islamic Center) started the works to build a large Sunni mosque in Ciudad del Este, giving more visibility to the Sunni community in the religious landscape of this city. While there is a great circulation of people between the institutions belonging to the same sectarian group, with the mosque and *musalla* in Paraguay functioning more during the working hours and the mosque and the *husayniyya* functioning for celebrations and collective prayers at night or during the weekends, there is almost no circulation of Sunnis to Shi'i religious institutions and vice versa.

The existence of separate institutions reveals the importance of the sectarian boundaries for the Muslims in Foz do Iguaçu. While both communities present a discourse of Islamic universalism, stressing the unity of Islam and the irrelevance of sectarian divisions, there is a great awareness of the existence of two Muslim communities with discrete understandings and practices of the religion. Despite their differences and rivalries, the Sunni and the Shi'i communities agree on their Muslim and Arab identity. The leaders of both communities see their role as the maintenance of the Arab Muslim identity of their community and its transmission to the new generations.

This was summarized by Shaykh Ahmad, who was one of the shaykhs of the Sunni mosque of Foz do Iguaçu when I asked him if his community had any plans to spread Islam in the Brazilian society. He said:

No, we have no plans for *da'wa* [preaching and spreading Islam] among the non-Muslims. Actually our main concern is to create conditions for the Muslims to remain Muslims, and for the new generations to not go away from Islam. If we manage to do that, we can say that we were very successful.

Indeed, neither the Sunni nor the Shiʿi community has any plan for attracting new converts to Islam, thus showing a complete identification of Islam and Arab ethnicity in their definition of the Muslim identity. The transnational connections with the Middle East are very active, with an intense circulation of people, goods, and ideas from Brazil to Lebanon and back. Many marriages are done with grooms and brides from Lebanon, to the point that some of the wealthier families send their sons and daughters in order to learn Arabic and the cultural traditions of their region of origin. These transnational ties are important symbolically and economically, as many families have properties and businesses both in Lebanon and in Brazil. Although there are some cases of marriage with non-Muslim Brazilian and Paraguayan women, I did not come across any case of a mixed Sunni-Shiʿi couple, showing again the strength of the sectarian divide.

However, the very construction of Islam as a cultural heritage that, in principle, is shared by all Middle Eastern immigrants and should be transmitted to their descendants enhanced the awareness about the sectarian differences between Sunni and Shiʿi Muslims. In order to be able to transmit a general "Muslim identity" that is defined as a specific cultural content, the community had to reach a consensus about the doctrinal and ritual elements that constitute it. Therefore, the various doctrinal and ritual references that marked the boundaries between Sunni and Shiʿi constructions of the Islamic tradition were linked to the cultural traditions that circulated in the community, which in the end led to a division along sectarian lines.

Shaykh Muhammad Khalil, who became the leader of the Shiʿi community in Foz do Iguaçu in 2006 after leaving his position in the mosque of Curitiba, considered the division between Sunnis and Shiʿis to be the effect of the introduction of Wahhabi-influenced understandings of Islam into the Sunni community, forcing the Shiʿi to create their own religious institutions. According to him, the religious consensus that existed in the community due to the fact that they all shared cultural understandings of Islam as it was practiced in the Middle East was broken by the introduction of what he saw as an intolerant religious ideology by non-Lebanese shaykhs.

On the other hand, Shaykh Ahmad, who was born in Brazil and did his religious studies in Saudi Arabia, blamed the Shiʿis for the division of the Muslim community:

We were all together in this mosque until the Shiʿis built their Husayniyya. Then it was impossible to keep the community together, because they would perform rituals [of the ʿAshura] there that are not acceptable for us. They preferred to maintain these rituals than to continue with us. It is better this way, they have their religion and we have ours.

There were nonreligious institutions, such as the Clube da Unidade Árabe (Nadi al-Ittihad al-Arabi/Arab Unity Club), which managed to gather the Sunni and Shi'is on an ethnic basis as Arabs. However, the club closed a few years ago due to financial problems. The narratives about the end of the club also entice mutual accusations from the Sunni and the Shi'i communities, with the Sunnis saying that the Shi'is were responsible for the club bankruptcy and the Shi'is accusing the Sunnis of closing the only institution where members from both communities could interact as Arabs.

The strong identification of Islam with cultural diacritics of the Middle Eastern societies can be seen in the investment that these communities make in their transmission to the new generations. Thus, the Sunni community has the Escola Árabe Brasileira (Arab Brazilian School), which functions in a building near the mosque, and the Shi'i community has the Escola Libanesa Brasileira (Lebanese Brazilian School). There is also a Shi'i Lebanese school in Paraguay. The main purpose of these private schools is to teach Arabic to the descendants of the Muslim immigrants, in order to allow them to keep their linguistic and cultural ties with the Middle East.

However, despite the obvious purpose of maintaining the transnational character of the Muslim community, the schools also serve as an instrument of cultural localization in the Brazilian (and Paraguayan) society. Both schools teach the regular national curriculum common to all Brazilian schools, public or private, together with a large number of hours for Arabic (and English) as a foreign language. Therefore, while the Arab school enables the new generations of Muslims to maintain transnational cultural connections, it also gives them a clear insertion in the Brazilian educational and economic context.

This complex interaction between transnational and local elements in the constitution of the Arab Muslim identities is even more apparent in the Lebanese-Brazilian Scout Group (Grupo de Escoteiros Líbano-Brasileiro), founded in 2005 by the Shi'i community in a building next door to the *husayniyya*. The president of the group, a member of the Shi'i community, stressed that the Lebanese-Brazilian Scout Group was very much part of the scene of youth associations in Foz do Iguaçu, having intense relations with the other two boy scout groups in the city and participating in the activities of the União dos Escoteiros do Brasil (Brazilian Scouting Union). In this sense, the scout group is an instrument of insertion of the Muslim community in the local social context and even in the Brazilian nation-state.

However, this affirmation of belonging to the local society is articulated with the affirmation of cultural diacritics that delimit the boundaries of the Arab Muslim community as a particular group with the Brazilian nation-state. The president of the Lebanese-Brazilian Scout Group expressed this double process when he explained the purposes that informed the creation of the group:

> The idea to create the scout group was to provide to our youth a space for healthy entertainment, where they could meet and know each other, as well as other kids who are not from the [Muslim] community. It is very important to teach them [the young ones] social responsibilities and the respect for nature and the environment. In this sense the scout group can be seen as part of the education of our sons and daughters as Muslims and as citizens. Of course, the idea to create a group for the Lebanese and the rest of the Arab community comes from the necessity to allow the young generations to live a normal life while teaching them to respect the customs that define us as Muslims and Arabs. We have boys and girls in all the activities, but we make sure that everything goes within the boundaries of the Islamic morality, in particular in our camping activities. But, of course, it just reinforces a healthy and respectful atmosphere that is the essence of scouting.

In this statement we can see that Arab and Muslim identities are treated as having equivalent or, at least, overlapping cultural meanings, as both are referred to as a set of "customs" and moral values related to the Middle East societies. The activities of the group use both Portuguese and Arabic as their linguistic contexts. This identification between ethnic and religious identities was stressed by the president of the group, who pointed out that while most members are Shiʿis, the group also gathers Sunni, Druze, and Christian descendants of Arab immigrants who see in it a space where Arab identities can be reinforced among the new generations born in Brazil. Therefore, we can say that the scout group fosters identities and creates cultural competences that allow its members to negotiate their insertion in the local society, in the Brazilian nation-state, as well as in the transnational social networks and symbolic systems that connect them to the Middle Eastern societies.

These multiple layers of local, national, and transnational social imaginaries that are fostered by the Lebanese-Brazilian Scout Group are condensed and expressed in their honorary patron, Akil Merhei. Merhei was the president of the Lebanese-Brazilian Scout Group until he was killed together with his wife and two kids in the indiscriminate bombing of South Lebanon by the Israeli army in the 2006 war. The figure of Akil Merhei condenses several layers of meaning in the symbolic rendering of his life and death.

In what interests this analysis, he represented at the same time a local public figure, known and loved by many, who fostered the insertion of the

Arab Muslim community in the society of Foz do Iguaçu; a transnational Arab Brazilian who lived and worked in Brazil as well as maintained his cultural and personal ties with Lebanon, where he took his family for vacations and visiting relatives; and a "martyr" (*shahid*) who became a victim of the regional and global conflicts that involved the Middle East. In this sense, the figure of Akil Merhei works as a dominant symbol[51] in the context of the Lebanese-Brazilian Scout Group, allowing the condensation and articulation of the gamut of identities (Brazilian, Lebanese, Arab, Muslim, and so on) that organize the various spheres of belonging through which the group's members circulate.

Similarly, while the religious imagination of the Muslim community is oriented toward the Middle East, there is a sharp consciousness of its belonging to the local religious field, which means the possibility of exposure of its members to the religious proselytism and transit of identities that characterize a dominant model of religiosity in Brazil. Thus, the creation in Foz do Iguaçu of the Brazilian Christian Church for the Arabs (Igreja Cristã Brasileira para os Árabes) and of the Arab Evangelical Church (Igreja Evangélica Árabe/Kinissa Injiliyya Braziliyya), both of which aimed at converting Muslims to Evangelical Christianity, is perceived as a threat to the community by some Mus-

Banner depicting Akil Merhei at the Lebanese-Brazilian Scout Group (Grupo de Escoteiros Líbano-Brasileiro) in Foz do Iguaçu

Banner of the Arab Evangelical Church (Igreja Evangélica Árabe/Kinissa Injiliyya Braziliyya), saying "Smile, Jesus Loves You" in Arabic, on a street in Foz do Iguaçu

lims, while it is accepted as part of the local reality by others.[52] The shaykhs of both the Sunni and the Shi'i communities said that the Evangelical were free to preach to Muslims, but they dismissed the vision of this as a threat. "A true Muslim would not renounce his faith," said Shaykh Ahmad.

Shaykh Muhammad, the leader of the Shi'i community, elaborated more on this point:

Well, we cannot do anything about that. Here is not Lebanon, where missionary work is forbidden. Here it is part of our reality. I saw the banners in Arabic [that the members of the Arab Evangelical Church carry on the streets of Foz do Iguaçu] saying "Smile, Jesus loves you" [*Ibitsam Yasu' yuhibbak*]. Well all I can say is that when I see the banner I smile and agree that the sentence is true, Jesus loves us as Muslims because we accept him as a prophet. The Evangelicals managed to put a teacher of sports in the [Sunni] Arab school and people in the [Sunni] mosque were very upset and ended up by firing him. I would let him stay, because I believe that the teachings of Islam are stronger than their [the Evangelicals'] arguments and I bet that after sometime he [the teacher] would become a Muslim.

From this statement we can say that the Arab Muslims in Foz do Iguaçu have a sharp consciousness of belonging to the local religious field and having to play by its rules, while their religious identity articulates them with transnational religious and ethnic contexts in the constitution of the Arab Muslim communities in the Triple Border region. The religious identities that are constructed and mobilized in these communities articulate local, national, and transnational spheres of belonging. Islam is objectified by the members of both the Sunni and the Shiʿi communities as the religious context of a cultural heritage that connects them to the Middle East as well as gives them a framework for belonging and positioning themselves in Brazilian society.

CONCLUSION

The comparison between Muslim communities in Rio de Janeiro, Curitiba, and Foz do Iguaçu shows the diversity of the religious dynamics of Muslim communities in Brazil. Although they face similar challenges, basically how to maintain the community and to transmit Muslim identity to the generations born in Brazil, they have developed very different mechanisms and religious orientations to cope with them. The Muslim community in Rio de Janeiro reoriented itself toward the conversion of non-Muslim Brazilians, the one in Curitiba developed a project of religious revivalism, and the one in Foz do Iguaçu successfully established mechanisms of adaptation and reinvention of the religious tradition brought by the Middle Eastern immigrants. These differences are the result of divergent histories of immigration and insertion in the local society. In the cases in which profound cultural transformations were also present, as in the fostering of conversion or revivalism, changes in religious dynamics were also linked to the actions of certain individuals who acted as Fredrik Barth's "cultural entrepreneurs,"[53] identifying cultural processes and shaping their outcome by mobilizing the members of the community around their leadership.

A common characteristic of these cultural entrepreneurs that helped to diversify the religious configuration of Islam in Brazil, such as the Isbelle brothers in Rio or Gamal Oumeiri in Curitiba, is their proficiency on all levels of the continuum between local and transnational cultural references. Born in Brazil from Middle Eastern immigrant families, bilingual in Arabic and Portuguese, and with direct experience of living in the Middle East, they could act as cultural mediators in the process of reconfiguration of the connections between local, national, and transnational religious trends that shape the cultural imaginary of the Muslim communities in Brazil. An important aspect in their biography is the incomplete religious studies in Saudi Arabia and Iran, which gave them both the cultural capital to legitimize the changes that they implemented in the religious lives of their communities, as well as freedom in relation to the constraints imposed on the shaykhs. In the community in Foz do Iguaçu, the role of cultural entrepreneurs is more diffuse, as the ruptures with the model of transmission of a Middle Eastern cultural heritage are less sharp. Nevertheless, there is no doubt that Akil Merhei also acted as such in several aspects. Therefore, the general picture of the Muslim communities in Brazil is one of constant differentiation and reconfiguration of the various symbolic and practical realms that constitute their religious life.

NOTES

1. The demographic census of 2010 gives the number of 35,167 Muslims in Brazil (http:// www.ib.gov.br/home/estatistica/populacao/censo2010/caracteristicas_religiao_deficiencia /default_caracteristicas_religiao_deficiencia.shtm). Muslim religious authorities speak of 1 to 2 million Muslims in the country. Raymond Delval estimated the number of Muslims in Brazil to be 200,000 in 1983. See Raymond Delval, *Les Musulmans en Amérique Latine et aux Caraibes* (Paris: L'Harmattan, 1992), 201. In 2010 the Pew Forum estimated the Muslim population of Brazil as being 204,000 (http://features.pewforum.org/muslim-population -graphic/#/Brazil). I consider, based on my ethnographic knowledge, that plausible estimates for 2014 could range between 100,000 and 200,000 Muslims in Brazil.

2. The data analyzed here were gathered in several periods of ethnographic fieldwork that I did in the Muslim communities in Rio de Janeiro, São Paulo, Curitiba, and Foz do Iguaçu, as well as shorter visits to the communities of Recife and Porto Alegre, since 2003. These ethnographies were made possible by research grants given by CNPq and Faperj.

3. There are no reliable estimates of the number of Arabs (meaning those who claim Arab, Syrian, Lebanese, Palestinian, and/or Syrian-Lebanese identities) in Brazil, which, of course, would still vary according to the definition of "Arab" used in them. The Arab institutions and some scholars advance numbers that range between 2 and 6 million Arabs and their descendants in a population of 190 million Brazilians. The larger figures are less likely to correspond to any demographic reality but reflect the greater recognition and visibility that the Arab immigrants and their descendants have achieved in Brazilian society. See John Tofik Karam, *Another Arabesque: Syrian-Lebanese Ethnicity in Neoliberal Brazil* (Philadelphia: Temple University Press, 2007), 10–13; Oswaldo Truzzi, *Patrícios: Sírios e Libaneses em São Paulo* (São Paulo: Hucitec, 1997).

4. Jeffrey Lesser, *Negotiating National Identity: Immigrants, Minorities and the Struggle for Ethnicity in Brazil* (Durham, NC: Duke University Press, 1999).

5. There is also a small Shi'i mosque in Ponta Grossa, in the province of Paraná.

6. The Arabic word *tariqa*, which means "path" and is usually translated as "Sufi Order," refers to two distinct, albeit complementary, religious realities: the rituals, doctrines, and models of mystical experience of a particular Sufi tradition and the social organization of this tradition into patterns of power relations and community life.

7. For an overview of the Sufi *tariqas* in Brazil, see Mario Alves da Silva Filho, "A Mística Islâmica em Terræ Brasilis: O Sufismo e as Ordens Sufis em São Paulo" (master's thesis, Pontifícia Universidade Católica de São Paulo, São Paulo, 2012), 111–162.

8. Silvia Montenegro, "Discursos e Contradiscursos: O Olhar da Mídia sobre o Islã no Brasil," *Mana* 8, no. 1 (2004).

9. Paulo G. H. R. Pinto, *Islã: Religião e Civilização, Uma Abordagem Antropológica* (Aparecida: Ed. Santuário, 2010), 219.

10. On creolization as the constant production of local-global hybrids, see Ulf Hannerz, *Transnational Connections: Culture, People, Places* (London: Routledge, 1996).

11. The inhabitants of the state of Rio Grande do Sul, in Brazil's extreme South, are known as *gaúchos* and have a strong regional identity that they construct in a relation of both belonging to and distinct from the Brazilian national identity.

12. In the Muslim communities of Rio de Janeiro, São Paulo, and Curitiba, it is common to have courses on Muslim culture, Muslim society, or Muslim civilization offered to the general public. The content of these courses usually includes canonic explanations, according to the codification of Islam that is officially adopted by each community, on the use of the veil by Muslim women, Muslim gender ideals, halal food, Islamic moral rules in everyday social contexts, critique of media discourses on Islam, and the presentation of general—and often idealized—aspects of social life in Muslim-majority societies, the examples of which are usually Saudi Arabia for Sunnis and Iran for Shi'is.

13. This phenomenon attracted a lot of interest from the European media, which announced a new era of conversion to Islam among Brazil's poor despite the fact that the whole group of converts in the slum was very small (it had around twenty members) and had not had a significant effect of spreading Islam in the neighborhood. See http://www.courrier international.com/article/2009/04/01/islam-hip-hop-dans-les-favelas.

14. There is no reliable data on the proportion of converts in the total Muslim population of Brazil. Some Muslim leaders in Rio and São Paulo gave me estimates ranging between 5 and 10 percent. For ethnographic accounts of female converts in Muslim communities in Rio de Janeiro and São Paulo, see Gisele Chagas, "Preaching for Converts: Knowledge and Power in the Sunni Community in Rio de Janeiro," in *Ethnographies of Islam: Ritual Performances and Everyday Practices*, edited by Baudoin Dupret, Thomas Pierret, Paulo G. Pinto, and Kathryn Spellman-Poots (Edinburgh: Edinburgh University Press, 2013); and Cristina Maria de Castro, *The Construction of Muslim Identities in Contemporary Brazil* (Lanham, MD: Lexington Books, 2013).

15. For the construction of ethnic boundaries through cultural contrasts emerging from social interaction, see Fredrik Barth, introduction to *Ethnic Groups and Boundaries*, edited by Fredrik Barth (1969; reprint, Prospect Heights, IL: Waveland Press, 1998).

16. In the use of these categories in the Muslim communities in which I did my fieldwork, "Brazilian" refers to any convert without Arab ancestry, while "Arab" has a more complex meaning. Those who were born Muslims and have Middle Eastern origins are classified as "Arabs." However, a Brazilian convert of Middle Eastern descent would be also classified as "Arab," and not as "Brazilian," showing the importance of ethnicity in the internal hierarchies of the Muslim communities in Brazil. In the communities where there is a significant presence of African Muslims, as in the cases of Rio de Janeiro, Salvador, and Recife, "African" appears as another ethnic category that is used to classify and organize discrete cultural competences and forms of understanding and living Islam.

17. The incertitude of the numbers is reproduced at the local level, as the Muslim institutions do not keep systematic records of their members or of the families that constitute the community. Raymond Delval recorded that he was told in 1983 that there were 12,000 Muslims in the state of Rio de Janeiro, of whom 5,000 lived in the city of Rio, while there were

only 60 members registered in the Muslim Charitable Society of Rio de Janeiro (Delval, *Les Musulmans*, 233–239). The difference between Delval's numbers and those that were given to me by the Muslim Charitable Society of Rio de Janeiro reflects the decline in the number of members that the Muslim community of Rio suffered during the 1980s and 1990s, as well as other factors such as the tendency of the current leadership of the society to define as a Muslim only those who effectively have some religious practice and to focus only on the Sunni community, excluding the 'Alawis from their estimation. The 2010 demographic census registered only 964 Muslims in Rio de Janeiro, which is Brazil's second-largest city, with some 6.3 million inhabitants.

18. 'Alawis are an esoteric Shi'i sect that exists in Syria, Lebanon, and southern Turkey. The 'Alawi community in Rio performs the Friday prayers in the prayer hall at their society and celebrates some holy dates, such as 'Ashura and the Mawlid al-Nabawi. The 'Alawis are considered to be heterodox Muslims by many currents in Sunni Islam, such as the Salafiyya. The 'Alawis in Rio de Janeiro usually do not attend the religious activities at the (Sunni) Muslim Charitable Society of Rio de Janeiro. Some 'Alawis told me that the Salafi tendencies of the Sunni community discourage them to attend the mosque or to engage in the activities of the SBMRJ.

19. Silvia Montenegro, "Dilemas Identitários do Islã no Brasil" (PhD diss., Universidade Federal do Rio de Janeiro, 2000).

20. Estatutos da Sociedade Beneficente Muçulmana Alauíta do Rio de Janeiro (Rio de Janeiro: SBMA, n.d.), 3–4.

21. Paulo G. H. R. Pinto, *Árabes no Rio de Janeiro: Uma identidade plural* (Rio de Janeiro: Ed. Cidade Viva, 2010), 119–121.

22. I found no evidence to support Raymond Delval's reference of 1930 as the year of creation of the (Sunni) Muslim Charitable Society (Delval, *Les Musulmans*, 234). He has probably mistaken the Sunni Society for the 'Alawi one, which was created in 1931.

23. Interview with the author, 2009.

24. The building of the Associação Brasileira da Imprensa (Brazilian Press Association) in downtown Rio had an auditorium that was rented by the Arab community to screen Arab movies from the 1950s to the 1970s.

25. In Brazil private schools are believed to provide a better education than public schools, which suffer from years of underfunding and neglect by the state.

26. At that time the 'Alawi community was without a shaykh of its own. Therefore, many 'Alawis did the Friday prayer at the mosque of Jacarepaguá, where the shaykh, as most 'Alawis, was a Syrian (Delval, *Les Musulmans*, 239).

27. Ibid., 136.

28. Interview with the author, 2009.

29. Bernard Rougier, introduction to *Qu'est-ce que le Salafisme?*, edited by (Paris: Presses Universitaires de France, 2008), 15–19.

30. Silvia Montenegro, "Identidades Muçulmanas no Brasil: Entre o Arabismo e a Islamização," *Lusotopie* 2 (2002): 59–79.

31. This creation of alternative spaces of religious sociability is not exclusive to Muslims, as devout Catholics and Evangelical Christians also have their own "spiritual retreats" in order to avoid the festivities of Carnival.

32. This march was created in 2008 after episodes of violence between members of Evangelical churches and adepts of the African-Brazilian cults. Almost all religious groups, including the Catholic Church and the Jewish community, participate in this march, which

takes place on Copacabana Seaside Avenue, but many Evangelical churches refuse to participate, for they say that they are the real victims of the intolerance of the other religious groups.

33. The word *carioca* means "someone who was born in Rio."

34. For a definition of the process of "objectification" in contemporary Muslim contexts, see Dale Eickelman and James Piscatori, *Muslim Politics* (Princeton, NJ: Princeton University Press, 1996), 38.

35. This number was given to me by the vice president of the Muslim Charitable Society of Paraná during an interview in January 2012. Until 2008 the leadership of the society talked about 5,000 families. The 2010 demographic census registered 1,307 Muslims in Curitiba.

36. Wanessa M. R. Storti, "Educação árabe em Curitiba: A escola islâmica do Paraná (1969–1972)" (master's thesis, Universidade Federal do Paraná, Curitiba, 2011), 44.

37. Storti, *Educação Árabe em Curitiba*, 73.

38. The Imam Ali Ibn Abi Talib mosque in Curitiba is the second-oldest mosque in Brazil, having been built twelve years after the Mesquita Brasil in São Paulo.

39. The first shaykh arrived in 1967, before the construction of the mosque, in order to organize the religious life of the community. From 1957 and 1967 the religious rituals were informally officiated by a member of the community. Omar Nasser Filho, "O Crescente e a Estrela na Terra dos Pinheirais: Os Árabes Muçulmanos em Curitiba (1945–1984)" (master's thesis, Universidade Federal do Paraná, Curitiba, 2006), 118.

40. Besides a few Palestinians and Syrians, almost all members of the community are of Lebanese descent.

41. This crisis marked the collective memory of the community as a turning point in its existence. This is expressed by the attribution of all failures and difficulties faced by the community to the heightening of sectarian tensions between Sunnis and Shi'is during the Iran-Iraq War. Therefore, Shaykh Muhammad Khalil and other members of the community told me in interviews that I did with them in 2005 that the Islamic school was closed because the tensions between Sunnis and Shi'is within the community made it impossible to reach a consensus on the curriculum to be taught to the students. Of course, the school had been closed for more than a decade when these divisions became relevant in the internal dynamics of the community.

42. In the prayer hall of the mosque, there is a large picture of the Haram and the Ka'ba, giving a visual dimension of the symbolic link that the members of the community try to establish between the two mosques.

43. Jamil Iskandar was a professor of Arab and Islamic philosophy at the Catholic University of Paraná, in Curitiba, and nowadays teaches the same discipline at the Federal University of São Paulo (UNIFESP), while retaining his position as president of the Muslim Charitable Society of Paraná.

44. http://www.ibeipr.com.br.

45. The mosque is located in the historical district of downtown Curitiba, and every Sunday there is an antique fair on the street in front of it that attracts a large crowd of visitors.

46. Curitiba has a strong urban identity as a cultured and Europeanized "model city" in Brazil. This claim is performatively expressed, negotiated, and lived by its inhabitants in Curitiba's planned urbanism, strong public expression of ethnic identities linked to the waves of European immigration in the nineteenth and twentieth centuries, and lively theater, music, and museum scene.

47. Conversion to Shi'ism is not as widespread as to Sunni Islam, being still a very low-

key phenomenons that is more important in São Paulo, where there is a Shiʿi institution created by converts and led by an Iranian shaykh, the Imam ʿAli Cultural Center (Centro Cultural Imam ʿAli), which has around 50 members. In Curitiba there are fewer converts who are integrated into the mosque. The other Shiʿi communities, such as the one in Foz do Iguaçu, have a small number of women who converted through marriage.

48. The kids who participated in the rituals ranged from six to eleven years old. They were wearing black T-shirts with "Ya Husayn" written in black, and all the girls were unveiled.

49. The 2010 demographic census registered 5,599 in Foz do Iguaçu (not counting those residing on the Paraguayan side of the border).

50. Silvia Montenegro and Veronica Giménez Béliveau, *La Triple Frontera: Globalización y construcción social del espacio* (Buenos Aires: Miño y Dávila, 2006).

51. Victor Turner defines the properties of the dominant symbols as condensation, unification of disparate meanings in a single symbolic formation, and polarization of meaning. See Victor Turner, *The Forest of Symbols: Aspects of Ndembu Ritual* (Ithaca, NY: Cornell University Press, 1967).

52. The Brazilian Christian Church for the Arabs is a branch of the God's Assembly and was present in Foz do Iguaçu from 2001 to 2006. This church closed that year after failing to convert any Muslim Arabs. The Arab Evangelical Church, which is a branch of the Baptist Church, continues its missionary work and succeeded in converting a few Shiʿis and Druze to Evangelical Christianity. See Silvia Montenegro, "Proyectos misionales y representaciones sobre la diversidad cultural: El Evangelio transcultural para Árabes en la Triple Frontera," in *La Triple Frontera: Dinámicas culturales y procesos transnacionales*, edited by Verónica Gimenez Béliveau and Silvia Montenegro (Buenos Aires: Espacio Editorial, 2010).

53. Fredrik Barth, *Models of Social Organization* (London: Royal Anthropological Institute, 1966), 18–21.

CHAPTER 6

GUESTS OF ISLAM: CONVERSION AND THE
INSTITUTIONALIZATION OF ISLAM IN MEXICO

CAMILA PASTOR DE MARIA Y CAMPOS

Islam, like Judaism in a predominantly Christian culture,
can offer a sense of attachment elsewhere,
to a different temporality and vision,
a discrepant modernity.[1]

IN THINKING OF ISLAM in Latin America, it is useful to note two processes that are parallel yet distinct: one, the presence of Islam as a religious tradition in the region and, the other, its visibility in the public sphere. This text will attend to the latter, situating it in a web of global phenomena: the transregional entanglement of postcolonial histories and hierarchies, new mobilizations of *daʿwa*—invitation to the faith—afforded by late-twentieth-century accumulations, and the reconfiguration of religious horizons through unprecedented mediations. Early cartographies of Islam in the Americas are relevant to this analysis insofar as they are recovered by agents claiming historical depth for present practices.

I will claim that in a postcolonial setting, where hierarchies of race, class, and "civilization" index and constitute each other in complex ways, conversion allows new Muslims in Mexico to step outside of local ideologies of dominance and difference.[2] It offers the opportunity to sidestep, to circumnavigate discourses that define them as subaltern, by establishing direct access to faraway regions and the privileges of foreignness and cosmopolitanism through faith. Public performances of devotion, narratives surrounding the choice to convert, and debates raging in a number of Internet forums established by converts suggest that conversion can be pursued as a gendered strategy of resistance to Mexican and global postcolonial class formations.

Islam as a religious tradition arrived in the Americas hand in hand with Christianity, in the shadow of the Spanish Reconquista that was extended in the conquest of the New Spain.[3] It was not until 1543 that a royal decree banned the "passing of Moorish converts" to the American territories.[4] Muslims were also among the African populations brought to the Americas through the Atlantic slave trade; slaves and freedmen from Islamicized regions of Africa practiced orthodox and heterodox variations of the tradition, some of them syncretic with West African social practices.[5]

Islam surfaced again among the French imperial troops that backed the second French intervention in Mexico (1862–1867). The French colonial army included an Egyptian division and a number of Algerian soldiers, some of whom stayed behind after the fall of the Second Empire. A decade later in the 1870s, hundreds of thousands of migrants from the eastern Mediterranean began to trickle toward the Americas, many of them Muslim.[6]

Given the late abolition of the Holy Inquisition in 1820 and the controversial institutionalization of religious freedom in Mexico in 1860, it is perhaps not surprising that these early Muslim populations did not generate institutional spaces or a visible presence in the Mexican public sphere.[7] The history of Islam's irruption in the Mexican public sphere is much more recent. It is linked to new circuits and logics of circulation that have brought a small number of new Muslim migrants but, more important, resulted in growing numbers of converts to Islam in Mexico.

Islam in Mexico acquired unprecedented visibility in 1995, when a Sufi community emerged among indigenous populations on the outskirts of San Cristóbal de las Casas, Chiapas. The mission's leader, Spaniard Aureliano Pérez Yruela, also known as Emir Naifa, describes himself as a Marxist before embracing Islam.[8] A missionary of the Movimiento Mundial Murabitun, he is said to have attempted communication with Marcos—the speaker for the Zapatista movement—in the hopes of convincing him of carrying on the Zapatista struggle in the name of Islam.[9] His mission of da'wa in San Cristobal— the Centro de Desarrollo Social para Musulmanes—is a utopian community of sorts in which several Spanish, *tzotzil*, *tzeltal*, and mestizo families participate. It provides converts and missionaries with sources of employment, food, and education.[10] According to Fox and other press reports, there were about three hundred local converts as of 2005, who participated in productive projects—a carpentry workshop, a bakery, a restaurant, and a school established by the Murabitun movement to support the community.

The current Murabitun World Movement unfolds around the Darqawi Shadhili Qadiri *tariqa*, or Sufi brotherhood, founded by Scottish-born Shaykh Abdalqadir as-Sufi. Shaykh Abdalqadir embraced Islam in Morocco in the late sixties and has devoted years of traveling, lecturing, and publishing to bringing together new Muslims, initially in London and later also in Berkeley, California. Though Abdalqadir is currently based in Cape Town,

South Africa, his brotherhood has developed a global reach and inspired communities in Denmark, Malaysia, South Africa, and a particularly vibrant community in Granada, Spain. *Tariqa* members are mostly middle-class converts who approach Islam from a European cultural tradition.

According to Hernández González,[11] Pérez Yruela and another Andalusian, Esteban López Moreno, along with Mexican Luis García Miquel first founded the Unión Islámica de México, also known as Misión para el Da'wa AC, or Comunidad Islámica en México. Though these institutions were conceived as part of the Murabitun World Movement, missionary families circulate in a circuit that links the community in Chiapas with the community in Granada quite specifically. The association has been accused by the Mexican press of being a terrorist mission and of cultivating links to global terrorist networks.[12] While such accusations are unfounded, they provide clues to local perceptions of Islam and thus to the logic of conversion in the contemporary Mexican context. Most male converts to Islam in Mexico are youths from urban lower-middle-class backgrounds. Women who convert tend to be a bit older and to have professional education and employment, though they often share the men's modest background.[13]

MIGRANTS AND CONVERTS

Muslim communities in the Americas are made up of migrants—people from regions such as the Middle East and South Asia—and a growing number of converts. Eastern Mediterranean migrants constitute the most numerous from the late nineteenth century through the present. Lebanese diplomatic personnel in Mexico estimate that about 5 percent of a total of 400,000 migrants and people of Mashriqi descent currently residing in Mexico are Muslim, some 20,000 souls.[14] Lindley-Highfield cites an estimate of 39,000 Muslims in Mexico, 1,000–2,000 of whom he claims are converts who embraced Islam over the past decade.[15] According to Mexican national census (INEGI) data, there were 1,421 Muslims in Mexico in 2000, 929 men and 492 women. By 2010 the census reported 3,760 Muslims.[16]

Tracing Muslim paths has been complicated by the fact that they did not establish sites of worship in the early decades of the twentieth century. Such institutional anchors played important roles as sites of participation where networks and beliefs could be cultivated by successive generations of migrant origin in the case of Christian and Jewish populations. In the case of the Christian traditions of the Mashriqi migration—Maronite, Melkite, and Greek Orthodox—it was through the synergy of local migrant efforts and transnational church bureaucracies that funding and staff were provided to establish local sites of worship.

Most mosques and *musallas* (prayer halls) in Latin America have been built since the 1990s, even in areas that host considerable Muslim populations.[17] The absence of early community organization could derive in part from Mashriqi Muslim practice, which privileges a direct relationship between the believer and his creator.[18] The demographics of the migrations could also be evoked to explain this absence. The relatively small numbers of believers, their geographic dispersion, and the diversity of migrant Muslims—including Druze, Sunni, and Shi'a—probably discouraged the early formation of Muslim institutions in Mexico. Another factor that might explain the institutional bifurcation could be the tradition of *millet* autonomy that Christian and Jewish populations enjoyed within the Ottoman order. Autonomy required a tradition of community organization that these populations reproduced in diaspora, as we can observe in the rich institutional landscape they generated.[19]

Migrant Muslims in Mexico have historically concentrated in two regions. Much of the early-twentieth-century Shi'i migration settled in the northern region of La Laguna and the growing city of Torreon. Sunni and Druze have largely settled in Mexico City, where the majority of migrants of all traditions clustered in the second half of the twentieth century. According to oral history, many Mashriqi families of diverse religious traditions, especially those who settled in rural areas, eventually began participating in Catholic institutions. Muslim men who married local women, as many did, were often absorbed by their commercial projects and delegated the spiritual instruction of children to their Catholic mothers and their kin. These children were often baptized and went on to complete Catholic ritual life cycles.

This process of religious localization is narrated in an interview by Omar Weston, a Mexican convert leader of one of the new convert communities, with Augusto Hugo Peña Delgadillo. When asked how many Muslim families there are in the Laguna region today, Delgadillo responded:

> Between 35 and 40, with 170–220 individuals. Those are the ones who practice Islam, because if you count the children and grandchildren of the first Muslims that came here, there are at least 200 families. . . . The religious aspect took a back seat, since a lot of them married Christian Mexican women and did not do much to preserve Islam in their family. Some came from Syria [and Lebanon], and one at least from Palestine. Most Muslims, maybe all of the ones that came, are Shiites, the Palestinian Muslim was Sunni, and his children and grandchildren are Catholic today.[20]

Some descendants of these families have turned back to Islam in recent generations, with the establishment of centers of Muslim education and worship in many Latin American cities.[21] The Torreon community built its first mosque only in 1986. In 2001 the community in the Laguna region could still imagine itself as the greatest concentration of Muslims in Mexico. Barely a decade later, however, convert communities in various Mexican urban centers are much more numerous.[22]

In Mexico the convert population has grown substantially in the past decade. Practically nonexistent a scant twenty years ago, converts now constitute the vast majority of Muslims participating in spaces of worship, more than 80 percent according to local Muslim authorities. Migrants and converts interact with each other and with global institutions of Islamic *da'wa* in diverse dynamics of devotion. As was also the case with other religious traditions in the late twentieth century, Islam's expansion as a global faith in recent decades has afforded the increasing standardization and disciplining of boundaries between Muslims and unbelievers as well as of belief itself.[23]

This growing unification of orthodoxy established and propagated by global Islamic missions contrasts with the regional diversity of Muslim practice even as it reflects the historical diversity of Islam. In Mexico City the more strictly observant and orthodox communities at the Centro Educativo de la Comunidad Musulmana and Dar al Hikma, led by a migrant board of directors and Isa Rojas, a young Mexican shaykh with eight years of religious training in Saudi Arabia, respectively, coexist with several Sufi orders and Shi'i establishments. Sometimes describing their practice as Sufi "excess," Shaykh Rojas is collegial toward the female leadership of the Jerrahi order and the transnational leadership of the Naqshbandis.

MOSQUES, *MUSALLAS*, AND OTHER PLACES OF WORSHIP

Various Muslim places of worship have sprung up in and around Mexico City since the mid-1980s.[24] The first, a gathering space for Friday prayer known as the Club Egipcio, was initially located on Masaryk Avenue, in the upperclass Polanco neighborhood. It was established in 1984 by an Egyptian migrant, Mr. Ibrahim, in close collaboration with the Egyptian Embassy, which provided funds to rent a locale as well as funding to bring an Egyptian imam (prayer leader) trained in the prestigious Al-Azhar University in Cairo between 1984 and 1987. The club operated as a space to celebrate Muslim holidays, as well as a site for religious teaching and Arabic-language lessons.[25] Given the financial support of the Saudi ambassador at the time—offered not in an official capacity but as a personal pious donation—the community, which initially clustered around the Egyptian Club, moved in the 1990s. It first rented space on Musset Street, also in Polanco, and then relocated to a small space in back of the Pakistani Embassy, which quickly became too small for the growing convert population.

In 1987 a mosque for a convert community that follows the Istanbuli Nur Ashki Jerrahi Sufi order was established with financial and spiritual support of *tariqa* authorities in New York and the authorization of the spiritual leader in Istanbul. Located on Sinaloa Street in the upper-middle-class Condesa neighborhood, this community is led by Shaykha Amina Jerrahi, of Puerto Rican origin, who embraced Islam in New York while working there as a journalist. Other Sufi groups are also present in Mexico City, among them the Murabitun, which we encountered in Chiapas, who have the Centro Ibn Khaldun in Coyoacán, and a growing Naqshbandi population with strong ties to the leadership of Abdul Rauf Felpete in Argentina.

Currently, there are two main Muslim spaces that uphold a fairly orthodox Sunni tradition. One of them is the most recent avatar of the migrant and diplomatic community of the Club Egipcio, the Centro Educativo de la Comunidad Musulmana, which was established as a civic association in 2001 by Muslim migrants from Morocco, Pakistan, and Lebanon, most of whom are no longer in Mexico. The CECM operates with funds collected among the faithful and the generous support of the Sadiqi family, a family of prosperous Pakistani migrants who lend and rent spaces in which the community gathers habitually and additional spaces where Muslim holidays are celebrated.

Niaz Sadiqi is the eldest brother of the Sadiqi family and was the first family member to migrate to Mexico in 1979. He traveled to work as an accountant for the Pakistani Embassy. He describes his support of the community as stemming from his late father's wish that his son make a pious contribution by establishing a "house for God" in Mexico. He himself is not particularly pious. Married to a Mexican woman according to Catholic rites, he describes most of his friends as non-Muslims. "I pray, but I don't agree with fanaticism. I pray because it gives my soul peace. We should serve humanity—we should love the earth. . . . [I]n Islam it is said that the place that feeds you is your country. I believe in humanity and human evolution, that we see that where there is a lack of education there is abuse—in the Muslim religion this is forbidden. Abusing ignorance. [In Mexico] there are fanaticisms, religious people. But there is openness, people listen to you."[26]

The other large Sunni center is the Centro Cultural Islámico de México (CCIM), the product of collaboration between migrants and converts. It was initially housed in Mexico City in the middle-class Narvarte neighborhood in 1994 and is now based in Tequesquitengo, Morelos.[27] The leader of the CCIM, who also maintained a space of *da'wa* in the middle-class Coyoacán in Mexico City for a few years, is Omar Weston, a Mexican convert of British ancestry who embraced Islam in the United States and later studied in Saudi Arabia. The CCIM has been very active in *da'wa*, staging public performances of prayer in nodal urban sites such as Mexico City's Zócalo, lecturing in cultural centers, and organizing Internet forums and local publications such as *Islam en tu Idioma*, a short-lived periodical by and for Mexican converts.

Though the CECM attracts much of the personnel of Muslim majority embassies temporarily living in Mexico City and migrants in various branches of established and itinerant commerce, it currently brings together a female population composed almost entirely of Mexican converts. Said Louahaby, a professional translator in his midforties, one of the founders and leaders of the CECM as a civic association, Moroccan by birth but living in Mexico since 1980 and married to a Mexican convert to Islam, characterized participants' socioeconomic backgrounds and interactions as follows:

> There are two types—I am free, but there are people with set incomes—with salaries, like the diplomats. Foreigners here work independently or in business, they work in embassies. . . . Very few work in Mexican companies. A very small minority, very well defined—they make much more money. In the embassies there are ambassadors, consular and business agents, accountants and translators. They earn in dollars and euros. They come to pray [with us]. Then there is another type of people—businessmen, merchants—[their earnings] fluctuate a lot. There are also others who are very poor. Most of them are Mexican. They don't have the possibility of being independent. Sometimes they form a majority, as converts. These people sometimes we have to give them support not only spiritually but materially in order for them to be strong [in Islam].[28]

Several smaller groups have resulted from ideological and practical fractures within the larger Sunni communities. One of these is a Salafi group, an offshoot of Weston's leadership, briefly based in a rented space in the working-class Colonia Balbuena for some time under Muhammad Ruiz's leadership but now joining the Dar al-Hikma community for Friday prayer. A Sunni group with Sufi leaning, led initially by a onetime CECM imam, Syrian Muddar Abdulghani of Latakkia, and currently by a South African, meets in the working-class Colonia Normal. This group separated from the CECM in 2007.

Muddar now heads a community in San Cristobal de las Casas, Chiapas, where two new mosques have been built recently, one by the Murabitun, architecturally imitating the Friday mosque of Granada, the other by a Sunni community funded by various US-based associations, among them Why Islam. Finally, a Mexican convert with eight years of jurisprudence training in the University of Medina of Saudi Arabia, Isa Rojas brings CECM converts together at his Institute of Language and Arabic Culture Al-Hikmah, in the working-class neighborhood of Aragon. This practice began during the process of remodeling the CECM headquarters in 2010. Given Isa's leadership and his popularity, converts visit this space from neighboring towns and cities: Atlacomulco, Toluca, Texcoco, Monterrey. The Murabitun movement in Chiapas has also fragmented.[29]

Some of the most prosperous migrants and higher-echelon diplomats find current places of worship small and below their status, and there have been efforts under way for a couple of decades to build a large and luxurious Sunni mosque that are complicated by the diversity of current conversion. It is not unheard of, however, for the same converts to participate in several of the currently available spaces. Since 2013 the Association of Mexican Islamic Women (Asociación de Mujeres Musulmanas Islámicas, AMMI), led by Lizbeth Marquez, a Mexican convert and former directive board member at the CECM, has established a Shiʿi prayer space in the middle-class Roma neighborhood. Lizbeth, who cultivates close ties to Iran, initially encountered Islam while traveling as a Mexican tae kwon do champion. Hizmet, the global education and interfaith dialogue network founded by Turkish Fetullah Güllen, has operated a cultural center in Polanco and a school in Valle Dorado in Mexico City since 2003.

DAʿWA: AN INVITATION TO FAITH

Choices staged by agents engaged in circulating Muslim discursive traditions are crucial mediations through which people encounter and eventually embrace Islam. Such mediations involve selecting which aspects of the tradition to present to populations embedded in historically non-Muslim social formations, the particular institutional and textual forms presented by the invitation to the faith, and the local contexts that mediators navigate. In Mexico we find diverse *daʿwa* efforts. Some have emerged from local initiatives, while many institutions based elsewhere contribute literature and spiritual guidance to Mexican converts. Many such efforts imply synergies and collaborations.

The recent institutionalization of Islam in Mexico derives from and feeds off of and into three important dynamics. First is the role played by the expansion of Islam in the United States, a social space through which Mexicans and other Latin Americans frequently transit as laborers. Second is the growth of global *daʿwa* since the 1970s, particularly the multiplication of orthodoxies in the re-Islamization of historically Muslim regions and fresh global missionary efforts funded through petroleum profits. This new *daʿwa* involves new rivalries, in particular between a Saudi project for the expansion of their Sunni Islam and an Iranian project envisioning the growth of a Shiʿi orthodoxy. Third, the intensely transregional production of *daʿwa* efforts in Mexico today becomes visible through circulating *daʿwa* literature.

The Islamic missionary presence in the United States is relevant to the

Mexican process given that the majority of current convert leaders who have established institutions in Mexico have discovered Islam as labor sojourners in the United States. This is the case of Weston's leadership of the CCIM, the Jerrahi community led by Amina, and the congregations in Guadalajara and Tijuana. As the large numbers of Latino converts reported in urban centers such as Los Angeles also suggest, what we observe over the past decades is the circulation of Islam in North America as a region entangled through economic and social ties rather than as a space divided by national boundaries.[30]

As Haddad has underscored, in order to understand the dynamics of conversion to Islam, it is important to observe the particular configurations and history of the various Islamic missions present in a given context. The term *da'wa* emerged in the United States during the twentieth century "as the preferred term to refer to the message and propagation of Islam."[31] Among the institutions that were established in the United States for the purpose of inciting locals to join the faith are the Islamic Society of North America, the Islamic Circle of North America, and the Tableeghi Jama'at.

The earliest one, the Ahmadiyya Movement in Islam, was set up to counter Christian missionary efforts in India and came to the United States with the Centennial Exhibition of 1876 in Philadelphia.[32] Though it initially sought to establish a propitious environment for Muslim migrants and to convert white North Americans, the Ahmadiyya soon turned to preaching Islam among African Americans, presenting it as an egalitarian faith that does not racially discriminate among its faithful. These missionary efforts resulted in the propagation of an orthodox Islam and various heterodox ones, such as the Moorish Science Temple, the Nation of Islam, and Ansaru Allah, among others.

Among the most important ideologues to have formulated strategies for *da'wa* in "the West," Haddad mentions Khurram Murad of the Pakistani Jamaati Islami, author of *Islamic Movements in the West* (1983) and *Da'wa among Non-Muslims* (1986). Ismail al-Faruqui was particularly influential with the Muslim Student Association and the Islamic Society of North America through Hammudah Abd al-Ati's text *Islam in Focus* (1978).

As I have noted, in recent decades global *da'wa* and Islamic movements originating in historically Muslim regions and among Muslim diasporas have become increasingly present and important in Mexico, indexing the global reach of competing visions of Islamic orthodoxy. Among institutions with a global presence today we find the Muslim World League, the Saudi Dar al-Iftah, the Iranian World Organization of Islamic Services, the Kuwaiti Islamic Heritage Society, the World Assembly of Muslim Youth, Why Islam, Helping Hand for Relief and Development, and Turkish Hizmet.[33] Such organizations offer a wide array of ideologies and philosophies of *da'wa*, some offering funding for the construction of places of worship and the training of religious specialists.

A quick overview of publications distributed free of charge in Mexican *da'wa* centers reveals an important diversity of transnational links not only in the circulation but also in the production of *da'wa* literature. The publishing house Ediciones Tikal of Girona, Spain, publishes *El Jardín de los Justos: La tradición oral del Islam, los hadices, recopilada en el siglo XIII* by Iman Nawawi. The Understanding Islam Foundation of Culver City, California, publishes the *Breve Guía Ilustrada para Entender el Islam*. Amana Publications in Beltsville, Maryland, produces, with the support of Al Huda Books Company of New Orleans, *El Corán Sagrado y la traducción de su sentido en Lengua Española*, translated by Shaykh Kamel Mustafa Hallak, who lives in Damascus, with a prologue by Dr. Abdulkhabeer Muhammad, director of the Centro Internacional de Estudios e Investigaciones Islámicas in Panamá. Amana also publishes translations of the Qur'an into English, French, and Portuguese.

Islamic proselytism in Mexico is inserted in a global process that has intensified as of the 1980s in the Anglophone world and entangled with these movements' publishing industry, as well as with the publishing industry of the Spanish-speaking world. In 1986, for example, a Spanish interpretation of the Qur'an commissioned by former Pakistani ambassador to Mexico Abdullah Said was published in Mexico. The Spanish-language text was approved by the Ahmadiyya Anjuman of Lahore, and the Mexican publishing house Tierra Firme came out with ten thousand copies of the edition.[34] A Mexican convert based in the state of Veracruz mentions books supplied by "our brothers in Argentina—I think it's called the Organización Islámica para América Latina— books which have been sent to us from Houston, TX, from Dar as Salaam and some books from Alexandria, Egypt from Islamic Messagement."[35] Among institutions contributing books to Mexican Muslims we also find WAMY (the World Assembly of Muslim Youth); the Islamic Center in Washington, DC; and various others.

In recent decades, Sufism has acquired a central role in the expansion of Islam through conversion, particularly in Euro-America, as van Nieuwkerk and Jawad have noted.[36] It has also been important to this process in Latin America. In Mexico it was the vehicle for the establishment of the first publicly visible congregations, the Jerrahi *tariqa* in 1987 and the Murabitun in Chiapas in 1995.[37] Sufism as it has developed in the West, authors have argued, is particularly appealing to women, considering the valorization of women's ritual roles in conversion.

In Mexico converts sometimes invoke the scientific truth value of Qur'anic narratives or the Muslim recognition of a common prophetic tradition with

Christianity extending from Abraham to Jesus. It is crucial to note that both arguments were developed in discourses recommending Islam to non-Muslims. Such tropes speak to a variety of social actors whose common experience of subalternization shapes their vision of a radical equality offered by Islam.

SITUATING CONVERSION

The Chiapas community with which this text opens helps us begin to situate conversion to Islam in Mexico. The Murabitun Center and other Muslim communities are located in marginal areas of the city of San Cristóbal de las Casas, neighborhoods mostly populated by indigenous migrants expelled from rural regions, who present a range of conversion trajectories. Given what we could call the political economy of conversion in Mexico, conversion to Islam shares some similarities with conversion to Protestantism in rural areas. It is not only the neighborhoods of Nueva Esperanza, La Hormiga, and La Nueva Maravilla and El Peje de Oro in San Cristóbal where new Muslims concentrate that present great religious diversity. Only 64 percent of the population in the state of Chiapas is Catholic these days, the lowest percentage in all of Mexico.[38]

Community fractures and expulsions in various regions of Chiapas have for several decades been associated with demographic growth and land-redistribution disputes. Such tensions become visible in practices that cultivate or question client networks that channel state resources—for example, through affiliation to official political parties or opposition movements. Like the Zapatista movement itself, which we could identify as yet another of these series of conflicts, these disputes have often acquired a religious dimension and resulted in conversion to various American Protestant churches active in the region since the 1940s.

The motivations and logics for conversion are multiple. Conversion, however, habitually entails changes in personal and kinship networks as well as the socialization of converts into orthodox religious practices. It is important to note that in Mexico, as in other Latin American cases, conversion often occurs through kinship ties. Converts who encounter Islam independently frequently facilitate the conversion of parents, siblings, grandparents, and others. Global media are often at work as well. Community leaders have pointed out in interviews the importance of the avalanche of media coverage since September 11, which set Islam in a central if deeply problematic role in the global public sphere. They joke about how no patron could have ever achieved the visibility for Islam that the xenophobic campaign of the North American media did. "First men began converting, then women," they remarked. A similar conversion peak occurred in the wake of the Arab revolts and revolutions of 2011–2014, which mesmerized global media.

Many converts' narratives express a particular interest in the egalitarian message of Islam; some have even argued that it provides an opportunity to build a Latin American Nation that appears to echo the Nation of Islam proposed by the African American movement of the 1960s:

> The mission which the Latin American Nation itself imposes . . . must be dignified and sovereign, fulfilling in this way a historical mandate which will allow it access to privilege, may Allah—the Only God—allow it thus. Latin America aspires to define its own modernization and rules for commercial treaties, with a different rationality than the one which we live today, without materialism, without consumerism and without wasting resources. To continue its civilizational emergence, the people of Latin America should begin by not assimilating the foreign as their own.[39]

The role that conversion to Islam plays in different contexts enables converts to mark a critical distance vis-à-vis their own society and articulates the conflictive relationship they have with its norms, as highlighted in analyses of conversion of African Americans in the United States[40] and of Euro-American women in the United States and Germany.[41] In these cases, scholars have argued that it is the perception of one's own exclusion that leads those marginalized to seek conversion.

The idea that Islam can operate as a theology of liberation that offers a language of protest accessible to different marginal groups has been proposed by Winter.[42] I argue that the possibilities that Islam offers go beyond a rhetoric that matches the anti-imperialism of many Latin American nationalist discourses. This vision of a collective on an ascending trajectory has its counterpart in individual aspirations.

CONVERTS AND COSMOPOLITANS

In the Mexican case, converts are in fact populations subject to various marginalizations. Before encountering and embracing Islam within the local logic of subalternization, conversion marks a distance or a distinction that confers tangible advantages. Friends and family who have not converted sometimes interpret conversions as the pursuit of class distinction, especially among those who come from modest backgrounds. Being Muslim is *different*, offering a marker of cosmopolitan distinction that becomes a strategy for exiting consumer society's mass-produced identities and local taxonomies of class. That is, more than a resistance that implies a refusal, conversion operates as a subversion that confers desirable attributes on converts. Using *hijab* is chic, some female converts have said. "In a country in which genealogies are everything, someone who is nobody—who is not of French, or Spanish origin or anything, well through Islam he is someone, it gives you distinction, you are different," a young male convert told me in conversation.

To be Muslim in Mexico is to be cosmopolitan. Such cosmopolitanism indexes affluence, such as the prosperity associated in the popular imaginary with the Mashriqi migrant communities—the "Lebanese" one mingles with in spaces of worship. It indexes sophistication, given converts' familiarity with Arabic calligraphy, prayers, and conversational formulas performed in Arabic—beginning with the *shahada* and followed by frequent interjections that inhabit everyday conversation and are spoken in Arabic: "Asalamu alaikum wa rahmatu Allah wa barakatu," "Alhamdulillah," "Mash'allah," and so on.

If you are young and male, it may even provide the opportunity of an Islamic education overseas, through a system of scholarships that fund young men who will return to lead converts and missions in their places of origin. Nagib Pérez, a Mexican student of Arabic in Medina, interviewed six young men from Latin America who were students at the Islamic University of Medina, all men between nineteen and twenty-five years old. All of them emphasize as their favorite aspect of the experience the companionship of people from all over the world and the most difficult being away from their families. Although no institutional or official provisions are made to facilitate employment once they are back in their home countries, the brightest and most committed among these young Islamic scholars join a transnational proselytizing intelligentsia. Ethnography suggests that they are well placed to cultivate client relationships with Saudi charities, which fund the building of mosques, translation and charity initiatives, and constant worldwide travel to Muslim conferences.

Though access to mosques and *musallas* is increasingly available to converts living in urban centers, cyberspace resources and communities represent important parallel habitations. In Mexico and Central America the Internet is a fundamental tool of discovery and socialization into the new faith. It is also, crucially, a labyrinth that provides autonomy to the convert subject vis-à-vis Muslim authorities by providing direct access to textual foundations and a variety of interpretations. Finally, the centrality of the Internet to constituting convert communities and subjects marks them generationally and professionally as a young population with privileged access to expensive technology.

The Internet is where many converts initially encounter Islam, either through chats with Muslims or through Islamic websites. After conversion it is also a space of socialization—both in the sense of simply spending time with other Muslims, hanging out, and in the sense of learning about appropriate behavior and ritual practice. It affords opportunities for Muslims in rural areas with very scattered Muslim populations to stay in touch with communities of coreligionists that change quickly, in tandem with technology. Initially taking the form of Yahoo! groups, chats, and scheduled forums, most activity now centers on social networks like Facebook. As correspondence within the Islam en tu idioma Internet group confirms, the new Muslims who interact through this medium are scattered throughout Mexico and beyond: in rural areas of Veracruz, as well as the cities of Cardel and Xalapa; in Coahuila, Cancun, Guadalajara, Mexico City, Monterrey, Chetumal, Abasolo, Guanajuato; Morelia, Michoacán . . . ; and they interact with other mostly Spanish-speaking Muslims in Spain, Saudi Arabia, Uruguay, Argentina, and Cataluña, among other places.[43] New Muslims discuss theological and personal dilemmas and locate fellow converts and migrants in neighboring or distant regions and countries for the purposes of consultation, recreation, and debate through these forums.

Many converts rely on the Internet as an authoritative source of Islamic texts and social prescriptions. Though some consultations are fairly trivial and involve standardized answers—for example, the quick identification of ritual dates such as the beginning and end of Ramadan in any given calendar year—other queries suggest a profound questioning of authority. The Internet affords young converts a "third way" so that they do not need to rely on local authorities who are sometimes perceived as tied to particular "foreign" political projects. For those seeking personal autonomy of interpretation and those on the quest to shape a "Mexican" Islam for themselves and their growing convert communities, the Internet is foundational. A young convert who participates in both an orthodox Sunni and the Sufi Jerrahi communities answered my questions regarding how he solved doubts about his practice and Islam in general with a subversive grin and two words—"Shaykh Google!"

The everyday functioning of cyberspaces as spatiotemporal bridges that afford community building and the socialization of new Muslims into cosmopolitan orthodoxy is exemplified by a long debate initiated by someone calling himself a "rural Muslim." His repeated queries regarding proper Muslim practice, which he described as difficult given his isolation in a rural region with no Muslim neighbors or institutions, resulted in the following advice in the *Islam en tu Idioma* forum:

Assalam alaikom wa rahmatulah wa barakatuh
For our dear brother Omar Cruz of Veracruz.
Receive our salam and a brotherly hug from my husband.
Tasnim e Ibrahim
The supplication which should be done to seek counsel from ALÁH, before making an important decision (Salat Al-Istijarah):
When one wants to do something permissible and is unsure about which is the best path to take, one makes use of a special prayer to perceive divine illumination, prays two voluntary Rak'a at any time of day or night, recites what one wishes of the Corán after the opening (Al-Fátiha), praises ALÁH and asks for blessing on his messenger; then one invokes ALÁH with the following supplication transmitted by Al Bujari, in the Hadiz which says:
"ALÁHumma inni astajíruka bi'ilmíka, wa astaqdíruka biqudrátika taqdiru wala aqdir, wa ta'lamu wala a'lamu wa anta a'lamul-guiub.
ALÁHumma in kunta ta'lamu ana hadal-amra (at this point mention the matter on which you are consulting) *jairun li fi dini, wa ma'ashí wa'áquibat amri wa a'yilih, i wa ayilihi, faqdirhu wa iasirhu li, zumma bárik li fih wa in kunta ta'lamu ana hadal-amra* (at this point mention the matter on which you are consulting) *sharun li fidíní, wa m'ashi wa 'aquíbati amri, wa a'yilihi wa ayílihi, fasrifhu a'nni wasrifni a'nhu waqdir li'aljaíra haizucan, zumma ardini bihi."*[44] [sic]

Based in Mexico City and an assiduous participant in CECM spaces when I met her in 2006, Tasnim is a professional lawyer in her early forties. Married to a Muslim Lebanese immigrant, she wore severe *hijab* and was a particularly observant and informed Mexican convert who periodically posted Arabic-laden advice, Qur'anic excerpts, and exegesis for the benefit of fellow converts. She also invested considerable effort in disciplining Muslim migrant women, extending her *da'wa* efforts in the sense of vigilant cultivation of the pious self by born Muslims that Mahmood describes as the primary purpose of *da'wa* in the contemporary Egyptian mosque movement.[45]

Given the central role of modern technologies such as the Internet in the process of socialization into the new religious community, conversion and participation in Muslim spaces also index modernity and high levels of education, probably even a professional status. According to the former imam's wife at the Mexico City *musalla*, a Mexican convert herself, most women who embrace Islam in Mexico are professionals in their late twenties and thirties, from urban, lower-class backgrounds. Omar Weston, another Mexican convert and the leader of the Tequesquitengo community, corroborated this portrayal, adding that most converts are young and come from humble backgrounds. A convert in Veracruz states, "Most of us are young and we don't have tangible property, we have to look for work wherever it can be found."[46]

CONVERSION EXPERIENCES

The following conversion experiences were published in the magazine *Islam en tu Idioma* (Islam in your language), edited by Omar Weston. As van Nieuwkerk has noted, conversion narratives produced outside of the ethnographic encounter are an important source since they evidence the convert's effort to present himself or herself before an audience other than the ethnographer, in this case the convert community that the publication interpellates.[47] In contrast to the homogeneity that van Nieuwkerk finds in the narratives of Dutch women converts online, though the texts we are dealing with here are also intended as "exemplary narratives" that show other converts and potential converts a virtuous trajectory that has taken the narrative's protagonist toward a new faith, the trajectories exemplified are quite diverse.

Certain trends are important, however. As I noted earlier, the Internet offers a global space that affords long-distance encounters with Islam and Muslims. The global public sphere is by no means a neutral one—it is heavily colored by mass-media discourses on Islam—yet it also affords personal encounters that are notable precisely because of such a polarized backdrop, one that can shift individual perspectives. Ayesha Umm Kareem narrates the following:

I came to know Islam through the internet in November 2001, I remember it well because I was at my new job, that computer had a chat system installed called ICQ which I was not at all familiar with. An Algerian Muslim started talking to me in French but I never answered, one day he said in Spanish "hola" and I spoke with him, he told me his name "Mohammed," the delicateness of his manners was very striking for me. So I picked up an Atlas and looked up Algeria located in North Africa, 98% Muslims and 2% Jewish and Christian minorities and I assumed that someone so kind would be part of those minorities but I was greatly surprised when he said he was Muslim, it was fear, surprise and also an enormous curiosity. The film "Not without my daughter" had etched itself deeply in my mind in my adolescence; the image of bad Muslims, aggressive, abusive of women did not fit with Mohammed, especially when he spoke to me of his great love for his mother and his family. . . . Later I read an extensive article on Algeria, France, the Muslim women's veil, I understood for the first time that the veil is given a political use, it was when I began to understand that imperialists-colonialists use it as a weapon before the mass media to say that Muslim women are oppressed and my out-look started to clear up.[48]

Convert biographies, especially those of women, frequently reflect a spiritual pilgrimage that includes various previous conversions.[49] Ayesha continues her narrative as follows:

> Then it occurred to me to type in islam.com.mx in the internet finder to know if there was some webpage in Mexico. To my surprise I found that there were Muslims in Monterrey, I wrote to the email address indicated and the next day they answered, I met them, they gave me books, they answered my questions. . . . I was born in a Catholic family and had been a practicing Catholic but when I turned seventeen I left the idea that Jesus is God. Later I had been sympathetic to Hinduism and I was even vegetarian for two years, married a Hindu and had a son but my marriage didn't last long, in fact the divorce was a relief in the sense that I didn't have to follow my husband's religion anymore which made me feel that everything I did was a sin.[50]

Despite her initial media-inspired misgivings about Islam, Ayesha's trajectory reflects an eagerness to engage with different religious traditions as a personal practice that should result from a personal quest and personal choice.

Encounters leading to conversion also happen in person, but even in those cases the Internet allows access to other converts, facilitating interaction and the cultivation of the new faith. Ana narrates her encounter with Islam:

> I came to know Islam thanks to a brother from Brazil who is of Lebanese origin and lives in my city; I am originally from Mérida, Yucatan but I have been living in the City of Chetumal, Quintana Roo for a few years now. The brother I mentioned one day spoke about giving me a gift, which would be very useful to me. . . . He took the "present" out of his bag, a book, which he kissed before putting it in my hands, and he said to me: this one will be very useful in your life and the life of your children, to lead it in a good path. He explained that before opening it, an ablution was necessary, and he showed me how to do it. Without being able to stop, I read and read and the more I did it I realized that my heart felt peace, since there is nothing better than reading our holy Qu'ran and receiving from it the serenity of our anxieties. After that I was lucky to join the Islam en tu Idioma forum and had the joy of taking lessons with Brother Issa García, that's where I met my little sister Malak. . . . After being Muslim my intentions were to see a mosque, which is what led me to implement the plan of visiting the nearest one. Belize is

three hours from where I live, so I decided to visit it in the company of sister Malak. . . . [T]ogether we traversed many kilometers in which I never ceased to learn something new, since sister Malak read aloud to me on the road while I drove. . . . [S]ome lady teachers from the musalla received us and guided us to Imam Karim. . . . The community in Belize is very poor, economically speaking, they don't have all the necessary resources but even then, alhamdulilah, with a lot of effort they have set up the school which they have right there, in which they teach the children about Islam and basic education. . . . The community though small Alhamdulilah is very close knit, the sisters who participate there are very nice, I have had the opportunity to go a few more times and get to know them and take my children with me to Juma'a.[51]

Conversions frequently occur among people who have had an intense spiritual commitment to other religious traditions. Some of the women I have interviewed have been Evangelical preachers, have wanted to be nuns, or operated as missionaries. Many women, like Ayesha, narrate conversion as a result of or a precursor to marriage. Noor says the following:

My name is Noor Isabel Triaki, I live in Morelia, Michoacán, México. . . . I'm going to tell you the story of how I came to Islam; I was a Catholic missionary, then I worked in the bishopric of Michoacán, but that was exactly where I realized that God was not there. Later continuing my search for God I followed Buddhism for three years, and I realized that God was not there either. Afterwards I finished my undergraduate degree in graphic design, and I received a scholarship to study for a masters' degree in Aberdeen in Scotland. During my stay in Scotland I got sick with bronchitis. I had a classmate and my best friend in class, an Iranian girl, who invited me to her house to get better, because being on my own I wasn't getting better. Through this rapprochement I had the opportunity to interact more closely with them, I really liked how they prayed, how they lived among themselves and with other Muslims. When I finished the masters' program I went to England and had another friend of Pakistani origin. . . . Sometime later I applied for an internship in Michigan, USA and I got it. When I arrived in Ann Arbor I looked for the mosque, Dearborn is not so far away, where there are so many Muslims, mashallah! It took me some months to do *shahada* (testifying of faith). . . . [A] year later I met my husband and we got married.[52]

My analysis is based on a contrapuntal reading of convert texts with conversion narratives that I have elicited in interviews since 2006 as well as my participant observation in community spaces and diplomatic settings.

CONCLUSION

Islam in Mexico, as it emerged in the past few decades, is a diverse phenomenon. While the conversion process is clearly entangled with global networks and dynamics, especially the expansion of Islam in the United States and proselytizing efforts launched from the Middle East, it also responds to local logics and individual aspirations to spiritual satisfaction and social distinction. The contrasting profiles of women and male converts as well as their common subaltern position within Mexican class formations suggest that conversion to Islam in contemporary Mexico is, for many of them, a gendered strategy of resistance.[53]

ANNEX 1. AHLUL BAYT ISLAMIC CENTER, MEXICO CITY (2013)

I. SOCIOECONOMIC PROFILE

Table 6.1. Respondent's gender

Gender	Freq.	Percentage
Masculine	3	25
Feminine	9	75
Total	12	100

Table 6.2. Respondent's age

Age	Freq.	Percentage
20 to 30 years	5	42
30 to 40 years	4	33
40 to 50 years	2	17
More than 60 years	1	8
Total	12	100

Table 6.3. Respondent's marital
status

Marital status	Freq.	Percentage
Single	6	50
Married	6	50
Divorced	0	0
Other	0	0
Total	12	100

Table 6.4. Respondent's schooling

Degree	Freq.	Percentage
Elementary	0	0
Jr. High school	0	0
High school	2	16.67
Undergraduate	7	58.33
Graduate	3	25
Total	12	100

Table 6.5. Respondent's state of
residence

State	Freq.	Percentage
D.F.	7	70
Durango	1	10
Estado de Méx.	1	10
Puebla	1	10
Total	10	100

II. CONVERSION PROCESS

Table 6.6. Respondent's
previous religious affiliation

Religion	Freq.	Percentage
Catholic	9	90
Others	1	10
Total	10	100

Table 6.7. Year the
respondent embraced Islam

Year	Freq.	Percentage
2002	3	27.27
2004	1	9.09
2006	1	9.09
2008	1	9.09
2011	4	36.36
2013	1	9.09
Total	11	100

Table 6.8. Respondent's
motivation for embracing Islam

Reason	Freq.	Percentage
Ideological	0	0.00
Affective	6	54.55
Intellectual	3	27.27
Marital	2	18.18
Total	11	100

III. RELATIONSHIP WITH MUSLIM INSTITUTIONS

Table 6.9. Respondent's
participation in activities
at Muslim institutions

Participates?	Freq.	Percentage
Yes	10	83.33
No	2	16.67
Total	12	100

Table 6.10. Respondent's
frequency of participation in
activities at Muslim institutions

How much?	Freq.	Percentage
Little	3	27.27
A lot	5	45.45
Always	3	27.27
Total	11	100

Table 6.11. Respondent's frequency of
contact with other Muslims

When?	Freq.	Percentage
Occasional	1	10
Once a week	2	20
2 or more times a week	3	30
Daily	4	40
Total	10	100

Table 6.12. Respondent's
frequency of prayer

How many?	Freq.	Percentage
5 daily prayers	7	87.5
Friday	0	0
Occasional	1	12.5
Total	8	100

Table 6.13. Respondent's extent
of Qur'an reading

How much?	Freq.	Percentage
Some	7	63.64
A lot	2	18.18
All	2	18.18
Total	11	100

ANNEX 2. CENTRO EDUCATIVO DE LA COMUNIDAD MUSULMANA, MEXICO CITY (2012)

I. SOCIOECONOMIC PROFILE

Table 6.14. Respondent's
gender

Gender	Freq.	Percentage
Masculine	21	55.26
Feminine	17	44.74
Total	38	100

Table 6.15. Respondent's age

Age	Freq.	Percentage
Less than 20 years	1	2.63
20 to 30 years	12	31.58
30 to 40 years	19	50.00
40 to 50 years	4	10.53
50 to 60 years	2	5.26
Total	38	100

Table 6.16. Respondent's marital status

Marital status	Freq.	Percentage
Single	20	54.05
Married	15	40.54
Divorced	1	2.7
Other	1	2.7
Total	37	100

Table 6.17. Respondent's schooling

Degree	Freq.	Percentage
Elementary	1	2.7
Jr. High school	2	5.41
High school	13	35.14
Undergraduate	20	54.05
Graduate	1	2.7
Total	37	100

Table 6.18. Respondent's monthly income

Income (MXN*)	Freq.	Percentage
No indep. income	3	10
Less than $1,500	2	6.67
$1,500 to $3,000	2	6.67
$3,000 to $6,000	6	20
$6,000 to $12,000	11	36.67
$12,000 to $24,000	2	6.67
$24,000 to $50,000	3	10
More than $50,000	1	3.33
Total	30	100

*Mexican peso

Table 6.19. Respondent's state of residence

State	Freq.	Percentage
D.F.	26	68.42
Jalisco	4	10.53
Estado de México	7	18.42
Foreigner	1	2.63
Total	38	100

II. CONVERSION PROCESS

Table 6.20. Respondent's previous religious affiliation

Religion	Freq.	Percentage
Catholic	28	90.32
Buddhist	2	6.45
Other	1	3.23
Total	31	100

Table 6.21. Year the
respondent embraced
Islam

Year	Freq.	Percentage
1987	1	3.23
1988	1	3.23
1999	1	3.23
2001	1	3.23
2002	1	3.23
2005	1	3.23
2006	2	6.45
2007	3	9.68
2008	1	3.23
2009	5	16.13
2010	10	32.26
2011	4	12.9
Total	31	100

Table 6.22. Respondent's
motivation for embracing Islam

Reason	Freq.	Percentage
Ideological	2	7.14
Affective	13	46.43
Intellectual	12	42.86
Marital	1	3.57
Total	28	100

III. RELATIONSHIP WITH MUSLIM INSTITUTIONS

Table 6.23. Respondent's participation in activities at Muslim institutions

Participates?	Freq.	Percentage
Yes	21	65.62
No	11	34.38
Total	32	100

Table 6.24. Respondent's frequency of participation in activities at Muslim institutions

How much?	Freq.	Percentage
None	2	6.9
Little	11	37.93
A lot	9	31.03
Always	7	24.14
Total	29	100

Table 6.25. Respondent's frequency of contact with other Muslims

When?	Freq.	Percentage
Occasional	7	20
Once a week	16	45.71
2 or more times a week	7	20
Daily	5	14.29
Total	35	100

Table 6.26. Respondent's
frequency of prayer

How many?	Freq.	Percentage
5 daily prayers	26	72.22
Friday	6	16.67
Occasional	4	11.11
Total	36	100

Table 6.27. Respondent's extent
of Qur'an reading

How much?	Freq.	Percentage
Occasional	13	44.83
Frequent	10	34.48
All the time	6	20.69
Total	29	100

ANNEX 3. TARIQA NUR ASHKI AL-YERRÁHI, MEXICO CITY (2011)

I. SOCIOECONOMIC PROFILE

Table 6.28. Respondent's
gender

Gender	Freq.	Percentage
Masculine	12	48
Feminine	13	52
Total	25	100

Table 6.29. Respondent's age

Age	Freq.	Percentage
Less than 20 years	1	4
20 to 30 years	9	36
30 to 40 years	10	40
40 to 50 years	2	8
50 to 60 years	3	12
Total	25	100

Table 6.30. Respondent's marital status

Marital status	Freq.	Percentage
Single	15	60
Married	6	24
Divorced	1	4
Other	3	12
Total	25	100

Table 6.31. Respondent's schooling

Degree	Freq.	Percentage
Jr. High school	3	12.5
High school	12	50
Undergraduate	7	29.17
Graduate	2	8.33
Total	24	100

Table 6.32. Respondent's monthly income

Income (MXN*)	Freq.	Percentage
$1,500 to $3,000	1	5.56
$3,000 to $6,000	3	16.67
$6,000 to $12,000	7	38.89
$12,000 to $24,000	4	22.22
$24,000 to $50,000	1	5.56
More than $50,000	2	11.11
Total	18	100

*Mexican peso

Table 6.33. Respondent's state of residence

State	Freq.	Percentage
D. F.	24	100
Total	24	100

II. CONVERSION PROCESS

Table 6.34. Respondent's previous religious affiliation

Religion	Freq.	Percentage
Catholic	14	66.67
Buddhism	5	23.81
Others	2	9.52
Total	21	100

Table 6.35. Year the
respondent embraced
Islam

Year	Freq.	Percentage
1991	1	5.56
1994	1	5.56
2000	2	11.11
2001	3	16.67
2004	1	5.56
2005	1	5.56
2006	1	5.56
2009	3	16.67
2010	1	5.56
2011	4	22.22
Total	18	100

Table 6.36. Respondent's
motivation for embracing Islam

Reason	Freq.	Percentage
Ideological	0	0
Affective	1	6.25
Intellectual	15	93.75
Marital	0	0
Total	16	100

III. RELATIONSHIP WITH MUSLIM INSTITUTIONS

Table 6.37. Respondent's
participation in activities
at Muslim institutions

Participates?	Freq.	Percentage
Yes	22	100
Total	22	100

Table 6.38. Respondent's
frequency of participation in
activities at Muslim institutions

How much?	Freq.	Percentage
Little	3	15
A lot	16	80
Always	1	5
Total	20	100

Table 6.39. Respondent's frequency of
contact with other Muslims

When?	Freq.	Percentage
Occasional	1	4.17
Once a week	1	4.17
2 or more times a week	17	70.83
Daily	5	20.83
Total	24	100

Table 6.40. Respondent's
frequency of prayer

How many?	Freq.	Percentage
5 daily prayers	8	40
Friday	3	15
Occasional	9	45
Total	20	100

Table 6.41. Respondent's extent
of Qur'an reading

How much?	Freq.	Percentage
None	1	7.14
Occasional	12	85.71
Frequent	1	7.14
Total	14	100

ANNEX 4. INSTITUTE OF LANGUAGE AND ARAB CULTURE DAR AL-HIKMAH, IN MEXICO CITY (2014)

I. SOCIOECONOMIC PROFILE

Table 6.42. Respondent's
gender

Gender	Freq.	Percentage
Masculine	12	63.16
Feminine	7	36.84
Total	19	100.00

Table 6.43. Respondent's age

Age	Freq.	Percentage
Less than 20 years	3	15.00
20 to 30 years	7	35.00
30 to 40 years	7	35.00
40 to 50 years	2	10.00
50 to 60 years	1	5.00
Total	20	100.00

Table 6.44. Respondent's marital status

Marital status	Freq.	Percentage
Single	12	60.00
Married	6	30.00
Divorced	1	5.00
Widowed	1	5.00
Total	20	100.00

Table 6.45. Respondent's schooling

Degree	Freq.	Percentage
No formal studies	1	5.00
High school	7	35.00
Undergraduate	11	55.00
Graduate	1	5.00
Total	20	100.00

Table 6.46. Respondent's state of residence

State	Freq.	Percentage
D. F.	9	45.00
Estado de México	11	55.00
Total	20	100.00

II. CONVERSION PROCESS

Table 6.47. Respondent's previous religious affiliation

Religion	Freq.	Percentage
Catholic	12	85.71
Jew	1	7.14
Others	1	7.14
Total	14	100.00

Table 6.48. Year the respondent embraced Islam

Year	Freq.	Percentage
1993	1	7.14
2003	1	7.14
2009	1	7.14
2011	1	7.14
2012	3	21.43
2013	3	21.43
2014	4	28.57
Total	14	100.00

Table 6.49. Respondent's motivation for embracing Islam

Reason	Freq.	Percentage
Ideological	1	6.25
Affective	4	25
Intellectual	11	68.75
Marital	0	0
Total	16	100

III. RELATIONSHIP WITH MUSLIM INSTITUTIONS

Table 6.50. Respondent's
participation in activities
at Muslim institutions

Participates?	Freq.	Percentage
Yes	18	90.00
No	2	10.00
Total	20	100.00

Table 6.51. Respondent's
frequency of participation in
activities at Muslim institutions

How much?	Freq.	Percentage
Little	9	45.00
A lot	7	35.00
Always	4	20.00
Total	20	100.00

Table 6.52. Respondent's frequency of
contact with other Muslims

When?	Freq.	Percentage
Occasional	1	5.26
Once a week	4	21.05
2 or more times a week	7	36.84
Daily	7	36.84
Total	19	100.00

Table 6.53. Respondent's
frequency of prayer

How many?	Freq.	Percentage
Doesn't pray	2	11.76
5 daily prayers	14	82.35
Friday	1	5.88
Total	17	100.00

Table 6.54. Respondent's extent
of Qur'an reading

How much?	Freq.	Percentage
Occasional	9	47.37
Frequent	6	31.58
All the time	4	21.05
Total	19	100.00

ANNEX 5. ISLAM GUADALAJARA, IN GUADALAJARA CITY, JALISCO (2014)

I. SOCIOECONOMIC PROFILE

Table 6.55. Respondent's
gender

Gender	Freq.	Percentage
Masculine	5	50.00
Feminine	5	50.00
Total	10	100.00

Table 6.56. Respondent's age

Age	Freq.	Percentage
20 to 30 years	4	36.36
30 to 40 years	3	27.27
More than 60 years	4	36.36
Total	11	100.00

Table 6.57. Respondent's marital status

Marital status	Freq.	Percentage
Single	5	50.00
Married	3	30.00
Divorced	1	10.00
Other	1	10.00
Total	10	100.00

Table 6.58. Respondent's schooling

Degree	Freq.	Percentage
Elementary	1	12.50
High school	1	12.50
Undergraduate	4	50.00
Graduate	2	25.00
Total	8	100.00

Table 6.59. Respondent's state of residence

State	Freq.	Percentage
Jalisco	9	100.00
Total	9	100.00

II. CONVERSION PROCESS

Table 6.60. Respondent's previous religious affiliation

Religion	Freq.	Percentage
Catholic	6	85.71
Others	1	14.29
Total	7	100.00

Table 6.61. Year the respondent embraced Islam

Year	Freq.	Percentage
2006	1	14.29
2010	2	28.57
2012	1	14.29
2013	2	28.57
2014	1	14.29
Total	7	100.00

Table 6.62. Respondent's motivation for embracing Islam

Reason	Freq.	Percentage
Ideological	0	0
Affective	3	42.85
Intellectual	4	57.14
Marital	0	0
Total	7	100

III. RELATIONSHIP WITH MUSLIM INSTITUTIONS

Table 6.63. Respondent's
participation in activities
at Muslim institutions

Participates?	Freq.	Percentage
Yes	5	55.56
No	4	44.44
Total	9	100.00

Table 6.64. Respondent's
frequency of participation in
activities at Muslim institutions

How much?	Freq.	Percentage
Little	3	42.86
A lot	3	42.86
Always	1	14.29
Total	7	100.00

Table 6.65. Respondent's frequency of
contact with other Muslims

When?	Freq.	Percentage
Occasional	1	11.11
Once a week	2	22.22
2 or more times a week	4	44.44
Daily	2	22.22
Total	9	100.00

Table 6.66. Respondent's
frequency of prayer

How many?	Freq.	Percentage
5 daily prayers	8	100.00
Total	8	100.00

Table 6.67. Respondent's extent
of Qur'an reading

How much?	Freq.	Percentage
Occasional	2	22.22
Frequent	1	11.11
All the time	6	66.67
Total	9	100.00

NOTES

1. James Clifford, *Routes: Travel and Translation in the Late Twentieth Century* (Cambridge, MA: Harvard University Press, 1997), 257.

2. On Mexico and the postcolonial condition, see Camila Pastor de Maria y Campos, "The Mashreq in Mexico: Patronage, Property and Class in the Postcolonial Global" (PhD diss., University of California, Los Angeles, 2009). Though formal independence from colonial formations occurred earlier in Latin America than in the regions associated with the birth of postcolonial scholarship, Mexican formations of class and their racializations bear heavy marks of the colonial process. As I have argued elsewhere, I sustain that they can be productively analyzed through the lens of postcolonial and subaltern studies, understood here as theoretical tools. In fact, one could speak of a postcolonial global. Scholars making similar arguments are Ileana Rodriguez, Claudio Lomnitz, Michael Herzfeld, John Beverly, José Rabasa, Florencia Mallon, and the Latin American Subaltern Studies group at large.

3. On the sixteenth-century Iberian imagination of the American Indian other as Muslim, see ibid. The Reconquista was the medieval Christian reconquest of Iberian territories conquered and settled by Muslims in the eighth century. The progressive southward expansion of Christian kingdoms and principalities lasted many centuries and culminated in the expulsion of the last Muslim rulers from Granada in 1492. For a historical reconstruction of the presence of Muslims in New Spain and newly independent Mexico, see Raymond Delval, *Les Musulmans en Amerique Latine et aux Caraibes* (Paris: L'Harmattan, 1992); and Roberto Marín Guzmán and Zidane Zeraoui, *Arab Immigration in Mexico in the Nineteenth and Twentieth Centuries: Assimilation and Arab Heritage* (Mexico City and Austin, Texas: Instituto Tecnológico de Monterrey, 2003).

4. Archival sources report on scarce but sustained arrivals of "Moors" as trade specialists in New Spain, such as members of the servant retinue of a bishop who refused to travel without two dozen Moorish tailors, for example. Teresa Castelló Yturbide, personal communication, on material housed at the Archivo General de la Nación, Mexico. Toussaint has remarked that the peak of *mudejar* art in Mexico coincides with the final expulsion of *moriscos* from Granada in 1612. Manuel Toussaint, *Arte mudéjar en América* (Mexico City: Editorial Porrúa, 1946). *Mudéjares* is the term used in Christian sources for Muslims left behind in newly Christian territories as political frontiers receded and Muslim-ruled Iberian regions shrank toward North Africa. *Moriscos* is the term used for Muslims of Al-Andalus who were forcefully converted when Muslim territories in the South of the Iberian Peninsula came under Christian rule, especially after 1507. *Mudejar* art is the Islamicate aesthetic that continued to be popular in newly Christian Spain.

5. For a portrait of the variations in African Islam present in the Americas, see Abdurrahman bin Abdullah al-Baghdadi al-Dimachqui, *El deleite del extranjero en todo lo que es asombroso y maravilloso*, translated from Arabic by Paulo Farah (São Paulo: BibliASPA, 2007). For a scholarly overview, see Sylviane Diouf, *Servants of Allah: African Muslims Enslaved in the Americas* (New York: New York University Press, 1998).

6. On the eastern Mediterranean migrations to Mexico, see Theresa Alfaro-Velcamp, *So Far from Allah, So Close to Mexico: Middle Eastern Immigrants in Modern Mexico* (Austin: University of Texas Press, 2007); Pastor de Maria y Campos, "Mashreq in Mexico"; and Zidane Zeraoui, "Los árabes en México: El perfil de la migración," in *Destino México: Un estudio de migraciones Asiáticas a México, siglos XIX y XX* (Mexico City: M. E. Otta Mishima, El Colegio de México, Centro de Estudios de Asia y Africa, 1997).

7. Though rooted in a longer European history of wars of religion, the mid-nineteenth-century controversy surrounding official religious freedom in Mexico was centrally tied to anxieties regarding Protestantism and American Protestant expansion into Mexican territories. It was linked to conservative elite efforts to control trade and defend industry, especially in northern Mexico, and was aggravated by the Mexican-American War of 1846–1848 and US annexation of vast Mexican territories. Islam was present in the debates as a foil to Christian civilization and religious freedom that was equated by its detractors with the dangers of an immoral society and threats to women's liberties.

8. Conrad Fox, "La Meca Chiapaneca," *Gatopardo* (May 2005). The Murabitun World Movement's project of Islamic restoration considers the return to political and economic forms of early Islam a moral imperative. The Murabitun argue that Muslims owe political loyalty to a prince or emir rather than to a nation-state. Aureliano therefore takes on the title of emir rather than that of imam, as spiritual leaders in Muslim contexts today more often call themselves.

9. Morquecho cited in Fox, "La Meca Chiapaneca."

10. It is a utopian community in a literal sense, insofar as it seeks to implement in the world an ideal society according to the Murabitun model.

11. Cynthia Hernández González, "El Islam en la Ciudad de México: La orden Halveti Yerrahi y su ritual de iniciacion a partir de los años 80 del siglo XX" (bachelor thesis, ENAH, México DF, 2004).

12. On the late-twentieth-century popular production of an imaginary on Islam in the Mexican context through the press and other media, see Pastor de Maria y Campos, "Mashreq in Mexico."

13. My own observations coincide with those of Muslim converts and leaders in this

convert profile, according to interviews and conversations conducted during fieldwork in Mexico City in 2006 and 2010–2014.

14. Interview by the author with His Excellency Ambassador Nouhad Mahmud, México DF, 2006.

15. Mark Lindley-Highfield, "Muslimization, Mission and Modernity in Morelos: The Problem of a Combined Hotel and Prayer Hall for the Muslims of Mexico," *Tourism, Culture & Communication* 8 (2008): 85–96. A note on numbers: all numbers presented in this chapter are to be understood as social gestures produced by agents. It is impossible to "ground" statistics or to offer a statistical map, since all census figures currently available are estimates produced by informed individuals who operate within political projects. I direct an ongoing research project attempting a census of the Muslim population in Mexico, and after eight months of systematic fieldwork with a research team in various spaces of worship in Mexico City, the very small numbers of respondents do not coincide with much larger estimates by community leaders. The large proportion of converts in spaces of worship, however, is an observable constant.

16. http://www.inegi.org.mx/prod_serv/contenidos/espanol/bvinegi/productos/integra cion/sociodemografico/religion/Div_rel.pdf and http://www.inegi.org.mx/prod_serv/con tenidos/espanol/bvinegi/productos/censos/poblacion/2010/panora_religion/religiones _2010.pdf.

17. Announcement on the new *musalla* opening in Leon, Guanajuato and the Mezquita Al-Daʿwa Islamica and the Centro Islámico in Guatemala, active since 1995 and 1980, respectively, in *Islam en tu Idioma: Revista Bimestral* 1 (September–October 2005).

18. In contrast to Christianity, which operates through centralized ecclesiastical hierarchies, Islam is often defined through a direct relationship between the believer and his creator. Though there is a body of legal and theological experts—the ulama—and the institutions in which they are trained have played an important historical role in shaping Islamic interpretation, in everyday contexts a group of Muslims designates whoever is most versed in religious knowledge among those present to lead prayer. There is no ritual need for a specialist as intermediary.

19. On the institutional landscape of the Mashriqi migrations in Mexico, see Pastor de Maria y Campos, "Mashreq in Mexico"; Camila Pastor de Maria y Campos, "Lo Árabe y su Doble: Imaginarios de fin de siglo en México y Honduras," in *Contribuciones árabes a las identidades Latinoamericanas*, edited by Karim Hauser (Madrid: Casa Árabe, 2009); and Camila Pastor de Maria y Campos, "Inscribing Difference: Maronites, Jews and Arabs in Mexican Public Culture and French Imperial Practice," *Latin American and Caribbean Ethnic Studies* 6, no. 2 (2011): 169–187.

20. *"En la actualidad, cuantas familias musulmanas hay en la Laguna?*, 35–40, con 170–220 individuos. Estos son los practicantes del Islam, porque los hijos y nietos de los primeros musulmanes que llegaron por acá, hay por lo menos 200 familias. . . . La cuestión religiosa se relego debido a que muchos de ellos se casaron con Mexicana Cristiana y no hicieron mucho para preservar el Islam dentro de su familia. . . . Algunos llegaron de Siria [y Líbano] y uno cuando menos de Palestina. La mayoría de musulmanes, quizás todos los que llegaron son chiítas y el palestino musulmán era sunni y sus hijos y nietos son católicos hoy." Published in *Islam en tu Idioma: Revista Bimestral* (January–February 2006).

21. My interview with Karim Nuñez and his family, Mexico City, 2005.

22. Serhan in Fernando Lopez Pérez, "Suraya, la Única mezquita en Mexico," http://www.jornada.unam.mx/2001/10/16/052n1con.html.

23. Robert Hefner, "Multiple Modernities: Christianity, Islam, and Hinduism in a Globalizing Age," *Annual Review of Anthropology* 27 (1998): 83–10; Saba Mahmood, *Politics of Piety: The Islamic Revival and the Feminist Subject* (Princeton, NJ: Princeton University Press, 2005).

24. This section is informed by various interviews by the author with community leaders and committed converts, among them Said Louahaby, Amina Jerrahi, Julio Mello, Isa Rojas, Said Al-Ajdar, and Pavel Ulrich, Mexico City, 2011. I also thank Sherine Hamdy for initial guidance on Muslim spaces of worship in Mexico City in the 1980s.

25. Delval, *Les Musulmans en Amerique Latine*, 274.

26. "Yo rezo, pero no comulgo con el fanatismo. Rezo porque si me hace tranquilizar mi alma. Hay que servir la humanidad—hay que amar la tierra . . . en Islam dice el lugar que te da de comer es tu patria. Yo creo en la humanidad y la evolución humana, verlo que donde hay falta de educación hay abuso—en la religión musulmana es prohibido. Abuso de ignorancia. [En Mexico] si hay fanatismos, gente religiosa. Hay una apertura, te escuchan." Interview by the author with Niaz Sadiqi, Mexico City, 2011.

27. The CCIM is headed by Omar Weston, a Mexican convert of British ancestry. Various interviews by the author in Mexico City, 2005.

28. "Hay dos tipos—yo soy libre, pero hay gente con ingresos fijos—con salarios, como los diplomáticos. Los extranjeros aquí trabajan de manera independiente o negocios, trabajan en embajadas . . . muy pocos trabajan en compañías mexicanas. Una minoría muy pequeña, definida—ellos ganan mucho más dinero. En las embajadas hay embajadores, agentes consulares y de negocios, y contadores y traductores. Ganan en dólares o en euros. Ellos vienen a rezar. Luego hay otro tipo de gente—de negocios, comerciantes—están fluctuando mucho. Existen también otros que son muy pobres. La mayoría de ellos son mexicanos. No tienen posibilidad de ser independientes. A veces forman una mayoría, como convertidos. Estos a veces tenemos que apoyarlos no solo espiritualmente sino materialmente para que sean fuertes." Interview by the author, Mexico City, 2011.

29. Sandra Cañas Cuevas, *Koliyal Allah Tsotsunkotik, "Gracias a Allah somos más Fuertes": Identidades étnicas y relaciones de género entre los indígenas suníes en San Cristóbal de las Casas, Chiapas* (Mexico City: Tesis de Maestría en Antropología Social, CIESAS, 2006), 7.

30. By North America I mean Mexico, the United States, and Canada. See Jonathan Friedlander's work on Latino converts in Los Angeles; and press coverage of the phenomenon, for example: http://www.nytimes.com/2011/01/09/nyregion/09muslims.html?scp =2&sq=latino%20islam&st=cse.

31. Haddad in Karin van Nieuwkerk, *Women Embracing Islam: Gender and Conversion in the West* (Austin: University of Texas Press, 2006), 22.

32. Ibid., 21.

33. Ibid., 23.

34. Delval, *Les Musulmans en Amerique Latine*, 275.

35. Omar Abdullah, "La Comunidad de Musulmanes Veracruzanos," in *Islam en tu Idioma: Revista Bimestral* 2 (November–December 2005).

36. Van Nieuwkerk, introduction to *Women Embracing Islam*; Haifaa Jawad, "Female Conversion to Islam: The Sufi Paradigm," in ibid.

37. Sufism refers to diverse practices and textual traditions associated with mystical forms of Islam that peaked in the medieval period, when great mystical figures established such traditions throughout the width and breadth of the Muslim world. Sufism privileges the relationship between an initiate and his or her spiritual teacher, a charismatic figure who

has often encountered conflict with religious orthodoxy and its institutions as it establishes brotherhoods of initiates who cultivate their teacher's tradition. In various historical contexts, Sufi brotherhoods have also been recruited by state agents for state-building projects.

38. Cañas Cuevas, *Koliyal Allah Tsotsunkotik*, 7.

39. Shaykh Yahya Susquillo, "Principios Islámicos para América Latina," *Islam en tu Idioma: Revista Bimestral* 1 (September–October 2005).

40. Gwendolyn Simmons, "African American Islam as an Expression of Converts' Religious Faith and Nationalist Dreams and Ambitions," in *Women Embracing Islam*, edited by van Nieuwkerk.

41. Monika Wohlrab-Sahr, "Symbolizing Distance: Conversion to Islam in Germany and the United States," in *Women Embracing Islam*, edited by van Nieuwkerk.

42. T. Winter, "Conversion as Nostalgia: Some Experiences of Islam," in *Previous Convictions: Conversion in the Present Day*, edited by M. Percy (London: Society for Promoting Christian Knowledge, 2000).

43. These are the geographic categories through which migrants situate themselves; note the fact that they territorialize on different scales.

44. Posted in the *Islam en tu Idioma* Yahoo! group, March 2006. I have translated the Spanish text and preserved the original transliterated Arabic where it appears.

45. Mahmood, *Politics of Piety*.

46. Omar Abdullah, "La Comunidad de Musulmanes Veracruzanos," *Islam en tu Idioma: Revista Bimestral* 2 (November-December 2005).

47. Van Nieuwkerk, *Women Embracing Islam*.

48. "Conocí el Islam por Internet en noviembre del 2001, lo recuerdo bien porque estaba en mi nuevo trabajo, esa computadora tenía instalado el sistema de chat llamado ICQ que yo desconocía por completo. Un musulmán de Argelia comenzó a hablarme en francés pero nunca le conteste, un día me dijo en español 'hola' y hable con el, me dijo su nombre, 'Mohamed,' la delicadeza de sus modales llamaron mucho mi atención. Entonces tome el Atlas y busque Argelia ubicada en el norte de África, 98% musulmanes y 2% minorías de judíos y cristianos y supuse que alguien tan amable seria de esa minoría pero mi sorpresa fue grande cuando me dijo que era musulmán, fue miedo, sorpresa y también una enorme curiosidad. La película 'La Huida, no sin mi hija' se había quedado profundamente grabada en mi mente en mi adolescencia, la imagen de musulmanes malos, agresivos, maltratadores de mujeres no concordaba con Mohamed, sobre todo cuando me hablaba del gran amor por su madre y por su familia. . . . Posteriormente leí un extenso artículo sobre Argelia, Francia y el velo de las musulmanas, entendí por primera vez que al velo se le da un uso político, fue cuando comencé a comprender que los imperialistas-colonialistas lo usan como arma ante los medios de comunicación para decir que las musulmanas están oprimidas y mi panorama se fue aclarando." Ayesha Umm Kareem, "Mi encuentro con el Islam," *Islam en tu Idioma: Revista Bimestral* 2 (November–December 2005).

49. Van Nieuwkerk finds a similar phenomenon among Dutch women converts. See van Nieuwkerk, *Women Embracing Islam*.

50. "Entonces en el explorador se me ocurrió para saber si habría alguna página en Mexico. Para mi sorpresa encontré que en Monterrey había musulmancs, escribí al correo que indicaba y al día siguiente me contestaron, los conocí, me dieron libros, contestaron mis preguntas. . . . Yo nací en una familia Católica y había sido practicante, pero a los 17 años deje la idea de que Jesus es Dios. Después había simpatizado con el hinduismo e incluso fui vegetariana por años, me case con un hinduista y tuve un hijo pero mi matrimonio no duro

mucho, en efecto el divorcio fue un alivio en el sentido de que ya no tenía que seguir la religión de mi marido que me hacía sentir que cada cosa que yo hacía era un pecado." Ayesha Umm Kareem, "Mi encuentro con el Islam."

51. "Conocí el Islam gracias a un hermano de Brasil de origen Libanés que radica en mi ciudad; yo soy originaria de Mérida, Yucatán pero radico desde hace algunos años en la Ciudad de Chetumal, Quintana Roo. El hermano antes mencionado un día me hablo de hacerme un regalo, el cual me serviría. . . . Saco de una bolsa el 'regalo,' un libro, el cual beso antes de ponerlo en mis manos, y me dijo: este te servirá mucho en tu vida y en la de tus hijos, para llevarla por un buen camino. Me explico que antes de abrirlo, era necesario hacer una ablución, y me enseñó cómo hacerla. Sin poder parar leía y leía y mientras más lo hacía me daba cuenta que mi corazón sentía paz, ya que no hay nada mejor que leer nuestro sagrado Qur'an y recibir de el la tranquilidad a nuestras angustias. Después de eso tuve la fortuna de entrar al foro Islam en tu Idioma y tener la dicha de tomar clases con el hermano Issa García, ahí conocí a mi hermanita Malak. . . . Después de ser musulmana mis intenciones eran conocer una mezquita, cuestión que me hizo llevar a cabo el plan de visitar la más cercana. Belice se encuentra a tres horas de donde yo vivo, por lo tanto decidí visitarla acompañada de la hermana Malak . . . juntas recorrimos largos kilómetros en los que no deje ni un instante de aprender algo Nuevo, ya que la hermana Malak me leía en el camino mientras yo manejaba. . . . Nos recibieron unas maestras de la musalah, las cuales nos guiaron con el Imam Karim. . . . La comunidad de Belice es muy pobre, económicamente hablando, no cuenta con todos los recursos necesarios pero aun así, alhamdulilah con mucho esfuerzo han sacado adelante la escuela que ahí mismo tienen, en la cual enseñan a los niños acerca del Islam y la educación básica. . . . La comunidad aunque pequeña Alhamdulilah es muy unida, las hermanas que la frecuentan son muy agradables, he tenido la oportunidad de ir un par de veces y seguirlas frecuentando y llevar a mis hijos conmigo al Juma'a." Ana Mónica Mena Canto, "El Islam en Chetumal," *Islam en tu Idioma: Revista Bimestral* 2 (November–December 2005).

52. "Me llamo Noor Isabel Triaki, vivo en Morelia, Michoacán, México. . . . Les voy a contar mi historia de cómo llegué al Islam; yo fui misionera Católica, después trabaje en la curia con el Arzobispado Michoacano, pero justamente fue donde me di cuenta de que Dios no estaba ahí. Más tarde continuando con mi búsqueda de Dios seguí el budismo por unos tres años, y me di cuenta de que tampoco estaba Dios. Posteriormente terminé mis estudios de Licenciatura en Diseño Gráfico, y me otorgaron una beca para estudiar la maestría en la Universidad de Aberdeen en Escocia. Durante mi estancia en Escocia enferme de bronquitis. Yo tenía una compañera y mi mejor amiga de la clase, una chica Iraní, quien me invito a su casa a recuperarme, pues estando sola no me recuperaba. Mediante este acercamiento tuve la oportunidad de convivir más de cerca con ellos, me gustaba mucho como oraban, como convivían entre ellos y otros musulmanes. Cuando termine la maestría me fui a Inglaterra y tuve otra amiga de origen Pakistaní. . . . Tiempo después apliqué a un interinato en Michigan, USA y me lo dieron. Legando a Ann Arbor busque la mezquita, cerca esta Dearborn, donde hay tantos musulmanes, mashallah! Tardé unos meses más en hacer shejada (testificación de fe). . . . Un año después conocí a mi esposo y nos casamos." *Islam en tu Idioma: Revista Bimestral* 2 (November–December 2005).

53. Tables prepared by Miguel Fuentes and Belem Barrera based on the questionnaire applied during the Ethnographic Census of the Muslim Population in Mexico (2011–2014). The project was directed by Camila Pastor and received generous funding from CIDE.

CHAPTER 7

CUBANS SEARCHING FOR A NEW
FAITH IN A NEW CONTEXT

LUIS MESA DELMONTE

ARE THERE MUSLIMS IN CUBA?[1] For many people, Islam and Cuba are fundamentally remote from one another, incompatible, or even mutually exclusive. This view derives from a stereotyped vision of the island, which mixes old images of a very open culture flavored with music, dances, cigars, and rum alongside some distorted, quixotic, or devilish perceptions of its five decades of revolutionary process. This facile vision obscures a fuller understanding of the diverse religious elements that develop in light of the current sociocultural realities being reconfigured in the country.

This chapter explores the intersection between Islam and Cuba. Historicizing the presence of Islam in the Caribbean and more specifically in Cuba, this study shows that Islamic conversions in Cuba are new phenomena lacking continuity with the first Muslims who arrived on the island centuries ago. Today, Muslim community formation in Cuba should be understood in relation to the general liberalization of religious practice, the so-called special period or socioeconomic crisis in the 1990s, as well as the diplomatic and geopolitical links developed by Cuba's foreign policy toward the Islamic world. It is this relatively recent time frame in which this community has constituted itself.

BACKGROUND ELEMENTS

Islamic faith in Cuba, as in many other parts of Latin America, is commonly characterized as dating back to the Spanish conquest. Most likely, some sailors who traveled with Christopher Columbus in 1492 were crypto-Muslims or converts from Islam (see Cook's chapter in this volume). During centuries of colonization by the Spanish, moreover, Moorish slaves, *imazigen* slaves (Berbers), as well as Muslim African slaves (Mandingos, Fulani) were not able to practice their faith and suffered forced conversions, in accordance with

Spanish laws of the sixteenth century. These laws prohibited "the entrance in the New World of Berber slaves or free persons converted from Moorish parentage and their descendants," because "in this new land where we are planting the new faith it is good to avoid the presence of the sect of Mohammed, or any other offense to God our lord, that could damage our Holy Catholic faith."[2]

Although Catholicism was the official religion and Muslim practices were banned, other religious practices of African origin persisted in Cuba through a process of transculturation, according to well-known anthropologist Fernando Ortiz. In his *Contrapunteo Cubano del Tabaco y del Azúcar*, Ortiz states:

> I am of the opinion that the word *transculturation* better expresses the different phases of the process of transition from one culture to another because this does not consist merely in acquiring another culture, which is what the English word *acculturation* really implies, but the process also necessarily involves the loss or uprooting of a previous culture, which could be defined as a deculturation. In addition it carries the idea of the consequent creation of new cultural phenomena, which could be called neoculturation.[3]

Generally speaking, the abolition of slavery in the nineteenth century favored new influxes of Asian labor to the Caribbean region. These migrants came from India (including Hindus and Muslims) as well as from the island of Java in Indonesia. The case of Cuba, however, was somewhat different, due to the constant migration of labor forces that arrived from Spain. Instead of receiving groups from India or Indonesia, Cuba took advantage of farm laborers from Jamaica and Haiti as well as Chinese coolies in order to provide the necessary labor on the island.

The weakening of the Ottoman Empire also favored other migration flows at the end of the nineteenth and the beginning of the twentieth centuries. In general, these population movements consisted of Christians and Muslims from the Middle East to Latin America. Cuba served mainly as a transit point for migrants interested in reaching the United States, Mexico, and other countries, but many of the newcomers decided to stay on the island.

In general, two main patterns of Muslim migration can be detected in the Caribbean region. In many cases, Muslim migrants were isolated and inserted in small communities with a weak religious life; the group dispersed; there was no *masjid*, no imam, no madrasa; they lost their basic practices (*salat*, *zakat*, *sawm*, hajj); and the religion was not transmitted in the family context. There was a process of assimilation and conversion, so Islam became commonly seen as a "religion of the elders." In other words, there were Muslims but no Muslim institution building. In other cases (mainly in Guyana, Suriname, and Trinidad and Tobago), Muslim migrants built mosques, the Islamic community associated and grew, they kept their practices and identity, they developed strong contacts with the *umma*, and they even, according to Raymond Delval, created "focuses of Islamization."[4]

The Cuban case is more in line with the first type. In fact, there was no development of any form of Islamic community in Cuba during the first decades of the twentieth century. There was neither group cohesion nor self-identification, although the presence of Muslims is reported, for example, in some old registration acts of the Lebanese consulate in Havana.[5] There were individual or domestic practices, but not a single mosque was built. Additionally, there is no news regarding the formation of any Muslim associations, so it seems that a process of conversion to other religions and assimilation within the larger Cuban culture prevailed.

It is not easy to find very strong data about the migrants from the Middle East to Cuba. In many cases, their names and regions of origin were changed or distorted, and they were not asked about their religious beliefs. In his excellent book *Los Árabes en Cuba*, Rigoberto Menéndez deals with the history of Arab migration to the island, the institutionalization of the community life, and their connections to the Middle East, but he also points out that there were Muslim observances but not Muslim institutions.

Those first Middle Eastern migrants to Latin America and the Caribbean were followed by other waves during critical periods in Middle East history (1948, 1967, 1973, and continuing today), but the process stopped in the Cuban case due to the Cuban Revolution of 1959 and the more stringent immigration policy that was subsequently adopted by the government.

While the restricted immigration policy was a clear obstacle to new potential immigrants from any part of the world, including the Middle East, Cuban foreign policy developed close relations with many Arab and Islamic countries as part of its global projection, including landmark events such as the severing of relations with Israel in 1973 and the organization of the Sixth Non-Aligned Movement Summit in Havana in 1979.

In that same year, the Arab Union of Cuba was founded through a process involving the combination of various associations. Although some members of the Arab community migrated to the United States following the revolution in 1959, the group had great potential to consolidate its inner linkages. The Arab Union also developed strong relations with Cuban political spheres such as the Ministry of Foreign Affairs and the Department of International Relations of the Cuban Communist Party.

It is well known that Cuba has granted scholarships to students from

Africa, Asia, and Latin America,[6] explaining the presence of some Muslim students on Cuban soil since the start of this educational program. However, these students maintained their faith in the private sphere in order not to interfere with the materialist-dialectic Marxist-Leninist education they were receiving. In later periods, Muslim students developed their practices in a more open manner as a result of the reevaluation and amendments on religiosity that came to be promoted by the Cuban political leadership.

One of the first signs of these reevaluative processes can be found in the interview of the Brazilian Dominican friar Frei Betto with Fidel Castro in 1985, published in a book entitled *Fidel y la religión.*[7] There the Cuban president said that in no way should socialism and communism interfere with a person's internal life or deny the right of every human being to his or her own thoughts or religious beliefs.

This process was later reinforced in 1991 when the Fourth Congress of the Cuban Communist Party said that religious persons could be full members and militants of the party. A year later, two important constitutional amendments were approved. Article 8 clarifies: "The state recognizes respects and guarantees freedom of religion. In the Republic of Cuba, religious institutions are separate from the state. The different beliefs and religions enjoy the same consideration."[8] Previously, Article 54, Section 1, of the 1976 Constitution expressed the following notion: "The Socialist state, that bases all its activities and educates the people on the scientific materialist conception of the universe, recognizes and guarantees freedom of consciousness, the right of everyone to profess and practice, within the framework of respect for the law, the religious belief of his preference."[9] This reference to religion was strengthened and replaced by Article 55 in the 1992 Constitution: "The state, which recognizes, respects and guarantees freedom of conscience and of religion, also recognizes, respects and guarantees every citizen's freedom to change religious beliefs or to not have any, and to profess, within the framework of respect for the law, the religious belief of his preference."[10]

These new political and juridical approaches made possible the public emergence of Islam in Cuba at the beginning of the 1990s. This took place in the context of moments of deep uncertainty and disappointment, precipitated in large part by the ending of the Soviet Union and the collapse of European socialist countries. Those large-scale and sudden changes in international relations strongly affected the Cuban economy. The severe economic crisis that resulted was named the "Special Period in Time of Peace" and was officially explained as a result of the "dual blockade" imposed by the United States and former socialist partners.

This new situation strengthened an unprecedented kind of spiritual searching and encouraged religious practice. In a parallel way, there was also a process of recovering other kinds of communal identities. These new developments were intertwined with economic motivations. The reconstruction of communities of Spanish origin, the revitalization of the Jewish community, as well as the interest in demonstrating juridical links with ancient European relatives were similarly connected to the interest in migration or receiving the economic support that some members of different diasporas began to access.

THE NEW CUBAN ISLAMIC COMMUNITY

At this particular juncture, Pedro Lazo Torres (Yahya), a common citizen who was working as a thermoenergy technician and a Spanish-French translator, made the following discovery: "I found a Qur'an, I started to study it, and, as I was searching for a spiritual space, I understood Islam and accepted it as a revealed faith."[11] Pedro Lazo continued to provide a more profound analysis:

> I was personally motivated by the fact that Islam demands a daily and total dedication from the believer, a total devotion. For example, I came from a Christian church, but I felt it didn't satisfy my spiritual needs as Islam does. For me and others, embracing Islam meant a change in our lives. I relate my adoption of Islam at the starting of the '90s with the openness decided during the Fourth Congress of the Cuban Communist Party, and the new level of confidence this induced in the people, in order to practice any religion in a free manner. Today there are more motives [for embracing Islam] because there are more sources of information, and we have an Islamic religious organization in Cuba.[12]

Since that early moment, this pioneering convert began to gather others in order to form the new Cuban Islamic community.

At the beginning of the 1990s, the group mainly consisted of Afro-Cubans from urban areas with serious economic problems in Havana. This pattern, however, has been changing in recent years, and the Islamic community has taken on a wider socioeconomic and racial diversity. Today the main groups in Havana are located in Marianao, el Cerro, la Víbora, and Alamar. There are also, however, new small groups in other cities, such as Camagüey, Las Tunas, and Holguín,[13] that are members of Cuba's Islamic League (Liga Islámica de Cuba), the paramount Muslim organization on the island. Other groups, though they are not very active, can be found in Matanzas, Isla de la Juventud, Villa Clara, Ciego de Ávila, Santiago de Cuba, and Cienfuegos.[14]

Since its inception, the new community has been supported by some diplomatic missions in Havana, particularly those of Nigeria, Algeria, and Iran. In recent years, the Iranian Embassy in Havana seems to have been the most active in this regard. Islamic missions coming from countries such as Qatar, the United Arab Emirates, and Saudi Arabia were also active in promoting contacts, offering support, organizing gatherings for commemorating national days and Islamic festivities, and extending invitations for participation in hajj (though until 2011 these attempts were unsuccessful due to bureaucratic obstacles).

It is not difficult to find many opinions expressing doubts about the original legitimacy of the community. These skeptics point out that it is quite difficult to determine how many of the members of the Muslim community are sincere believers and have found a new answer in Islam. Expressions of faith are usually combined with pragmatic interests, such as experiencing new social recognition, participating in different activities sponsored by embassies in Havana, being in contact with foreign Islamic delegations, receiving some economic support, leaving the country, and so on. Some members of the Cuban Islamic community have developed high expectations toward the Muslim countries that promote the spreading of Islam, considering them to be very wealthy nations with institutions that will support Muslim communities all over the world, including in Cuba. Some other members mix spiritual needs and pragmatic interests in their religious lives.[15] In any case, the new Islamic community in Cuba has developed in the middle of a long social and economic crisis.

Pedro Lazo is considered the leader of the whole Muslim community. However, since its beginning a division between Shiʿis and Sunnis has existed. In the case of Sunnis, in reference to the four schools of jurisprudence, they say that "Cuban Islam does not adopt one particular school of thought (Hanafi, Maliki, Shafi'i and Hanbali); it is a mixing of Maliki and Shafi'i. . . . [W]e search for a global learning, that is, to take from the four philosophical schools the best parts that could be adapted for Cubans."[16] This trend of mixing, rejecting, or ignoring the differences between the Islamic schools is also present in many places in the Muslim diaspora, being also a feature of the followers of Salafism and Wahhabism.

It is also very important to bear in mind the flexible interpretations that many Cuban Muslims have argued for since the beginnings of the community, favoring the need to develop a specific "Cuban Islamic faith." This formation of Islam should take into account some particularities of the Cuban social and cultural reality, such as the possibility of eating pork and drinking alcohol, avoiding fasting (*sawm*), not carrying out circumcision, and understanding the Qur'an only through translations in Spanish, because "Allah knows all languages."

Hassan Félix Ávila, a member of the Cuban Islamic community, has pointed out, "This is a gradual process, and [adopting new habits] cannot be reached in just a few months or a year."[17] Along the same lines, Lazo and other Cuban Muslims wrote, years ago:

> In reference to food regulations, not only is pork forbidden for a Muslim, but also other foods containing animal blood. In Cuba the population receives products as mincemeat with soy, goose mince, and others, that have animal blood in them. These foods should not be eaten, but if there is no other choice, we can do it invoking the name of Allah (*bismillah*).
> . . . [W]e recognize that there is a tendency in Cuba to consume alcoholic beverages, but this is something that diverts the believer from his obligations, and we explain to them that you cannot pray if you have drunk alcohol. In general, drinking alcohol is under the consideration of the believer and his consciousness in front of God, although we emphasize that it is not correct for a Muslim to drink alcohol. We consider this as a process; it must be internalized.[18]

At least in public manifestations, the community is acting more in line with the basic precepts of the Islamic faith, but such arguments in favor of a "flexible and pragmatic Islam" are regularly expressed.

During the first years of these new Islamic initiatives, Cuban Muslims occasionally prayed in the House of the Arabs (Casa de los Árabes), a cultural institution that is part of the City Museum (especially the *salat al juma'a*).[19] But afterward they developed their ceremonies in their own houses, mainly in Pedro Lazo's house, where the Mezquita de la Piedad (Mercy Mosque) is located and where they pray with the few *surahs* they have memorized. Different ceremonies such as marriages and funerals were initially headed by Muslim diplomats, but this situation is also changing, given the increase in knowledge about Islam itself on the part of the Cuban Muslim community.

The Shi'i community has its own Center for Islamic Thought and Studies (Centro de Reflexión y Estudios Islámicos), called Al-Ma'asumin.[20] The Shi'a followers are members of Cuba's Islamic League. One of the most prominent Cuban Shi'a Muslims, Hassan Félix Ávila, is a member of the league's board. Hassan Félix was one of the Cuban Muslims who had the opportunity of studying abroad and is recognized by other believers and by Cuban academics for the dedication and seriousness of his study of Islam; he carried out his religious studies in the Jaamaatul Mustafa University, linked to the Hauza Imam Khomeini in the city of Qom, in Iran.[21]

In addition to these two main groups of Sunnis and Shi'is, there is also a group of Sufis who are developing their activities in a separate manner and who are not members of Cuba's Islamic League.

The number of Cuban Muslims is estimated by different sources and with divergent figures. The official website of the Cuban Foreign Affairs Ministry[22] (MINREX) recognizes 200, but Pedro Lazo maintained that, in 2011, there were 250 Cuban Muslims who were formal members of Cuba's Islamic League[23] and that the Mercy Mosque was regularly visited by 37 or 38 members, although sometimes they had received up to 70 Cuban Muslims.[24]

The total figure estimated is on many occasions much higher when Cuban Muslims talk about all the Muslims living on the island on a permanent or temporary basis. For example, they estimate a total of 2,100 Muslims, reaching that figure after including the approximately 1,000 medical students from Pakistan, some other foreign Muslims working in embassies or companies, as well as foreign students and many other Cubans who have recited the Confession of Faith, or *shahada* (although it is not known if they are regular practitioners). In reference to this last group, Hassan Félix has said, "It is very difficult to detect who is practicing Islam on a personal basis, and who has abandoned the faith."[25]

The Islamic community has recognized that they have lost members. In the words of Hassan Félix, "As it happens in every religious group, there are conversions and desertions. And it is like this due to the fact that individuals search answers for their internal questions. The Islamic Cuban community keeps its friendly relation with them [Muslims who keep their distance] because it is conscious that in religious matters there shouldn't [be] impositions."[26]

Cuba's Islamic League has a wide socioeconomic and educational profile. Among its members are doctors, architects, engineers, artists, workers, and students. The community is relatively young. In terms of gender, it was predominantly male in its initial stages, but in 2014 there appears to be more equality in terms of gender composition. According to Eloísa Valdés Pérez, an official in charge of the Muslim community at the Office of Religious Affairs of the Central Committee of the Cuban Communist Party, "There are no gender problems between the Cuban Muslims. Sunnis have a larger proportion of men, but Shi'is are balanced."[27] Yahya Pedro Lazo Torres goes into more detail:

The Cuban Islamic community is *not* predominantly masculine. Women represent 42% of the total of Muslims in our country, and even in some provinces they are a majority. We have had more than a hundred marriages of women with Muslim males according with the Law of Allah and the Sunna of the prophet Mohammed (PBUH). Many of the women were Christians and others had no religion at all. Some Cuban men have also reached Islam through marriage with Muslim women from Algeria (3), Malaysia (5), Jordan (3), Syria (1), Venezuela (1), Canada (3), Egypt (3) and Guyana (3). During many years, a permanent disinformation campaign about women and their rights in Islam has developed. . . . The topic of gender is widely debated by our sisters inside our community and it is an object of serious consideration. We, as men, are invited to these exchanges, and we contribute to the correct understanding of these matters by non-Muslims.[28]

The various activities of the Islamic community have never been prohibited, and it has even been able to maintain periodic contact with the Department of Religious Affairs of the Central Committee of the Cuban Communist Party. However, there was a strong refusal on the part of the Cuban government and party officials to formally recognize the Islamic community. In February 2007, this was resolved when the community was officially included in the Registro de Asociaciones, as Liga Islámica de Cuba (Cuba's Islamic League), with Pedro Lazo as its head.

It is likely that warmer relations with Islamic countries such as Iran, Qatar, and, more recently, Saudi Arabia could have helped with the official recognition and support for the national community of Muslims. It seems that the topic was, in fact, discussed during visits of high-ranking religious persons and delegations from Islamic countries, particularly during the visit in May 2001 of Shaykh Mohammed ibn Nasser Al-Aboudy, undersecretary-general of the Muslim World League (MWL).

The Islamic League has received some food support from the MWL and since 2007 has also established contacts with Turkey's Humanitarian Relief Foundation (IHH). This organization has offered food aid during the holy month of Ramadan to Cuban Muslims and to some foreign Muslim students in Cuba who also received cash donations.[29] These and other Islamic organizations, as well as some embassies of Islamic countries in Havana, have supported Cuban Muslims with books, general literature, and other instructive materials related to Islam. The members of the community gather frequently in their different groups in order to read and study the Qur'an, meditate about the *tawhid* and the sunna of the Prophet Muhammad, and exchange views about books written by Islamic experts; some of them are even studying

Arabic and Farsi. Guyanese Muslims who are studying in Havana have also been important for Cuban Muslims.

One of the main aspirations of the Cuban Muslims is to have a mosque. They carry out their religious practices in an individual manner or in small groups, as described earlier, and only on very special occasions (such as the Eid al Fitr) do they gather the whole community in a place owned by the state: the workers' social club El Náutico. The Cuban government has received some foreign proposals to build a mosque and has discussed the topic occasionally with donors, envoys, and delegations, but has not accepted the offers. The web page of the Foreign Affairs Ministry states that "the building of a mosque has been approved, so the first steps have been undertaken,"[30] and it is said that it is going to be built with Cuban financial sources only, which could be a suitable option in order to avoid favoring the political and religious preferences of any one particular Islamic country.

Cuban Muslims who were interviewed emphasized their very good relations with the Cuban Communist Party, with governmental authorities, as well as with other religious groups in Cuba. There are even some members of the Islamic League who are militants of the party and the Young Communist League.

PERCEPTIONS, PROBLEMS, AND GEOPOLITICAL IMPLICATIONS

I can personally attest to this intersection between Islam and Cuba, having worked for twenty years in the Center for African and Middle Eastern Studies (Centro de Estudios de África y Medio Oriente, or CEAMO, a wing of the Department of International Relations of the Cuban Communist Party), as well as with officials from the party, the Foreign Affairs Ministry, and experts coming from military and security institutions. They regularly made a clear differentiation between developing relations with Islamic states and forging links with Islamist movements from the Middle East and other parts of the world. They were reluctant with regard to the latter, but the former fits into the permanent purpose of Cuban foreign policy, which is to build official relations with the highest possible number of countries.

CEAMO wanted to organize international seminars in order to exchange ideas on the evolution and impact of Islam in these societies with international experts, academics, and even members of some of the major Islamic political organizations. However, it never received the necessary approval to convene such academic events. CEAMO was able to organize only limited workshops with professors and researchers from different institutions in Havana such as the Higher Pedagogical Institute and the Department of Contemporary

History at the University of Havana as well as other local professionals interested in these topics. The few seminars held were convened by CEAMO in coordination with the Center of Studies on Asia and Oceania (Centro de Estudios de Asia y Oceania, or CEAO), the Arab Union of Cuba (Union Árabe de Cuba), and the House of the Arabs of the City Museum (Casa de los Árabes). CEAMO and CEAO obtained approval to constitute the Group for Studying Islam (Grupo de Estudios sobre Islam), which had a very short life and limited experience. Its only publication was *El Islam en la contemporaneidad* (Contemporary Islam), a short booklet published in 1993.

Cuban authorities were reluctant to develop any kind of relation with Islamic opposition movements based on the perception that they were a very complicated matter and that they would not contribute to Cuban national interests or its foreign policy. It was believed that such activities might exacerbate tensions with the United States' political spheres, adding undesirable, troubling elements to the already highly complex Washington-Havana agenda. At the same time, Cuba has been historically committed to developing diplomatic and commercial relations with all possible states of the world, including Islamic states, in order to counteract the U.S. policy of economic sanctions and its historic attempts to isolate the island politically. It was also important to avoid contact with Islamic organizations dubbed "problematic," which in many cases were opposed to the established governments where they were based. This could be interpreted as an act of interference in the internal affairs of those countries, always a sensitive topic for Cuban authorities.

Taking all these things into consideration, it is useful to investigate the sudden and short-lived scandal that took place in Spain during September 2011, when a Cuban national with permanent Spanish residence was arrested for alleged ties to al-Qaeda. The twenty-four-year-old suspect, José Ernesto Feliú Mora (Khalid Siyf Allahu Almaslul), was accused of inciting terrorism. According to Spain's Interior Ministry, he had been a suspect of investigation since 2010. He was an alleged member of al-Qaeda and purportedly posted 1,120 radical, mostly self-made, videos on the Internet. He was also taken into custody for having used the Internet for radical indoctrination and recruitment, as well as distributing public messages aimed at provoking terrorist attacks.

Civil Guards (Guardia Civil) detained him, but he was immediately released on provisional liberty after an arraignment before Judge Fernando Andreu at the National Court (Audiencia Nacional), which handles terrorism cases. The court-appointed defense lawyer, Francisco Fernandez Castan, argued for all charges to be dropped, saying that police allegations against the Cuban violated his "freedom of expression." The judge, however, upheld the charges of alleged links to al-Qaeda, while police further probed the suspect's belongings, which were seized at the time of his arrest in Mallorca, Spain.[31]

It is obvious that a case such as this could be interpreted more as an individual acting on his own will or a matter of psychological instability rather than fabricating systemic linkages between the Cuban government and an Islamic terrorist organization such as al-Qaeda. In fact, Feliú Mora converted to Islam while living in Spain, he was never a member of the Cuban Muslim community, and his extremist position was not dangerous enough to merit the sustained attention of Spanish authorities, as he was immediately released.

Instead of being dismissed, the case of Félix Mora was seized upon by the famous Cuban American congresswoman and head of the House of Representatives' Committee on Foreign Affairs, Ileana Ros-Lehtinen (R-FL). Motivated by her active anti-Castro position, Ros-Lehtinen declared that the case of Feliú Mora raises concerns about the Cuban government and its links with terrorists rings, concluding, "I cannot say that it is a fact that al-Qaeda has linkages with the Cuban tyranny, but that would not surprise me. . . . The Cuban dictatorship would be delighted with rolling out the red carpet to al-Qaeda."[32]

In fact, instead of having "delightful" experiences with Islamic factors, one might reasonably emphasize the fact that, in reference to nonstate Islamic movements, the position of the Cuban government has been remarkably distant. Toward its own Cuban Muslims, the Havana authorities have opted to maintain a respectful stance.

Around this time, however, the political power of the island has had to face an even more complicated matter regarding Pakistani Muslim medical students. In the aftermath of the October 8, 2005, earthquake, the government of Cuba sent direct medical assistance to Pakistan and offered one thousand medical scholarships for talented students from the affected areas. These Cuban scholarships include tuition, lodging, books, food, and all other matters pertaining to their medical studies. Additionally, the government of Pakistan promised to give one hundred dollars for each student as a monthly spending allowance.

However, this cooperative agreement began to fall apart in September 2010. Pakistani medical students on the outskirts of Jagüey Grande, a small town in the middle of Matanzas Province, went on strike and presented different demands, arguing that the education they were receiving did not measure up to the requirements they need to pass the Pakistan Medical and Dental Council examination. They pointed to unsatisfactory living conditions and said that their campus lacked basic facilities, such as a library, a proper laboratory, specimens for dissection, and so on. In addition, they demanded more access to and practice in hospital facilities and stated that their stipend from the Pakistani government was insufficient.[33] In response, Cuban special forces, armed with assault rifles, trained dogs, and full riot gear, stopped the demonstration.

At the first stages of the crisis, Cuba's Islamic League expressed to the Pakistani students its willingness to help in developing a dialogue with state officials, but according to Pedro Lazo it was not possible due to the fact that "some of [the students] adopted extreme positions."[34] In any case, the goodwill shown by the Cuban Muslim community should have been welcomed by Cuban authorities; instead, it was ignored and dismissed.

This incident ended with the deportation of seventeen Pakistani students for various reasons, including "disciplinary grounds." It came to the attention of some observers outside Cuba because of the strong show of force by the Cuban special troops unit.[35] Although the motives that provoked the protests were evidently valid, the manifestations of discontent were obviously wrapped up in political and religious components. Elements such as generalized protests, strikes, violent acts, and the interrelated Islamic factor may have concerned Cuban authorities and perhaps explains their overreaction. This episode showed that Cuba is far from having a "delightful" experience with Islamic elements or making any attempt to "roll out the red carpet."

These interactions are also useful to reject the accusations made by Republican presidential candidate Michele Bachmann in September 2011. The Minnesota congresswoman cited "reports" that "Cuba has been working with another terrorist organization called Hezbollah,"[36] the predominantly Shi'i political party and social movement in Lebanon. Apparently through the reproduction of this speculation, which was originally published in the Italian newspaper *Corriere della Sera*,[37] Bachmann, a prominent member of the conservative Tea Party movement, wanted to strengthen her low popularity by resorting to old strategic equations from the 1960s and the Cuban missile crisis, but now adding a scary Islamic ingredient. She said, "Hezbollah has been potentially looking at wanting a part of missile sites in Iran. . . . So of course, when you are 90 miles offshore from Florida, you don't want to entertain the prospect of hosting bases or sites where Hezbollah can have training camps or perhaps have missile sites or weapons sites in Cuba. This would be foolish."[38]

Havana's authorities have had relations with Hezbollah, as one of the officially recognized political parties present in Lebanon, a country with good diplomatic links with Cuba. High officials of the Cuban Communist Party have met leaders of many different political organizations (including Hezbollah) during their visits to Lebanon,[39] and the organization sent a greeting during the celebration of the Sixth Congress of the Cuban Communist Party in April 2011.[40] The Cuban Embassy in Beirut also participates in many different diplomatic activities that include contacts with Hezbollah representatives.[41] Cuba does not designate this political organization as terrorist, but one that contributed decisively to the withdrawal of the Israeli military forces from South Lebanon. But that positive view, shared by many, can hardly substantiate a strategic relationship between Cuba and Hezbollah. Havana's authorities know perfectly well that such an action could be strategically suicidal.

CONCLUSION

In summary, the presence of a small Islamic community in Cuba today is mainly the result of conversions generated in a very particular context of the recent political, social, and economic period of Cuban history and has neither connection nor continuity with the previous Muslim presence in Cuba. Despite the existence of doubts that can be found in different sectors of Cuban society and political structures about the original legitimacy of this phenomenon and its evolution, it seems that Cuban Muslims will remain as one of the newest elements of the Cuban religious and political field for the foreseeable future.

From the geopolitical point of view, it is predictable that the Cuban authorities will maintain their traditional policy of developing relations with the largest possible number of Arab and Islamic countries as part of its global projection. Its new Muslim community is just beginning to gain a modest presence in that agenda. Cuba will also avoid any kind of identification with Islamist movements that could generate ambiguities in their posture concerning terrorism or inducing new frictions in the long Cuba-U.S. confrontation.

NOTES

1. The author wants to deeply thank Dr. Rigoberto Menénde Paredes, director of the House of the Arabs (Casa de los Árabes) in the Museum of the City, Havana, Cuba, for his full and crucial support of this research project.

2. Quoted by Miguel Rodríguez Ferrer, *Naturaleza y civilización de la grandiosa Isla de Cuba* (Madrid, 1876), 2:485–486.

3. Fernando Ortiz, *Contrapunteo cubano del tabaco y del azúcar* (1940; reprint, Havana: Consejo Nacional de Cultura, 1963), 103.

4. Raymond Delval, *Les musulmans en Amérique Latine et aux Caraibes* (Paris: Editions L'Harmattan, 1992).

5. Rigoberto Menéndez, *Los Árabes en Cuba* (Havana: Ediciones Boloña, 2007), 233–252.

6. More than fifty thousand had graduated by 2008.

7. *Fidel y la religión: Conversaciones con Frei Betto* (Havana: Oficina de Publicaciones del Consejo de Estado, 1985).

8. Constitution of the Republic of Cuba, 1992, Cubanet Documents, http://www.cuba net.org/ref/dis/const_92_e.htm.

9. Republic of Cuba, Political Constitution of 1976, Political Database of the Americas, http://pdba.georgetown.edu/Constitutions/Cuba/cuba1976.html.

10. Constitution of the Republic of Cuba, 1992.

11. Quoted in Organización Latinoamericana para la Defensa de la Democracia, "Inicio del Islam en Cuba," April 2008, http://ciempre.com/bin/content.cgi?article=42.

12. Interview with Pedro Lazo Torres, Havana, Cuba, October 28, 2011 (translation by the author).

13. Ibid.

14. Online interview with Hassan Félix Ávila, October 25, 2011 (translation by the author).

15. All these topics require further and deeper study. In spite of the slow pace of general reforms in Cuba, they nonetheless are creating new situations and challenges, so it will be imperative to study the Cuban Muslim community in light of these new circumstances. One key aspect could be the repercussions of the new migration law of January 2013 and its impact on a wide variety of activities. Among these are traveling to undertake hajj and *umrah*, carrying out Islamic studies abroad and coming back to the country, and experimenting with different levels of insertion of Cuban Muslims in the global *umma*, both for Muslims living on the island and for those who could have traveled and established themselves abroad.

16. Quoted in http://ciempre.com/bin/content.cgi?article=46.

17. Hassan Félix interview.

18. See El Islam en Latinoamérica, Cuba, "Inicio del Islam en Cuba" and "Cómo vive y practica su fe el musulmán cubano," http://www.islamhoy.org/.

19. The weekly *salat al juma'a*, held on Fridays, is the only prayer practiced and allowed nowadays in the House of the Arabs.

20. The Fourteen Infallibles (Ma'asumin) are religious figures from between the sixth and ninth centuries, who Twelver Shi'i Muslims believe are infallible, that is, "divinely bestowed [with] freedom from error and sin." This quality of infallibility is known as *Ismah* or *Esmat*. The Fourteen Infallibles are Muhammad, his daughter Fatima Zahra, and the twelve imams.

21. There are three other Cubans who studied in Qom and will also be interviewed in the future: Gerardo Reza M. Felipe, Wilfredo Muhammad Cot Burgos, and Raizman Zayd Barzaga.

22. MINREX, "La religión en Cuba," http://america.cubaminrex.cu/Actualidad/2008 /Religion_Cuba.html.

23. A very small number compared with a population of eleven million Cubans.

24. Pedro Lazo interview.

25. Hassan Félix interview.

26. Ibid.

27. E-mail interview, January 23, 2014 (translation by the author).

28. E-mail interview, April 14, 2014 (translation by the author).

29. See IHH Insani Yardim Vakfi, "Cuban Muslims Offered Fast Breaking Dinner," http://www.ihh.org.tr/12983/en/; and IHH Insani Yardim Vakfi, "IHH Holds Mass Iftar in Cuba," http://www.ihh.org.tr/ihh-kuba-da-toplu-iftar-verdi/en/.

30. MINREX, "La religión en Cuba."

31. Al Goodman, "Suspected al Qaeda Operative Is Released, but Must Check In," CNN, September 23, 2011, http://www.cnn.com/2011/09/23/world/europe/spain-al-qaeda-arrest /index.html.

32. Quoted by Juan Carlos Chávez in "Joven cubano buscó entrenarse con Al Qaida," *El Nuevo Herald* (Miami), September 22, 2011, http://www.elnuevoherald.com/2011/09/22 /1029525/joven-cubano-busco-entrenarse.html.

33. See Overseas Pakistani Friends, "The Plight of Pakistani Medical Students in Cuba," https://www.opfblog.com/9267/the-plight-of-pakistani-medical-students-in-cuba/.

34. Pedro Lazo interview.

35. See http://www.youtube.com/watch?v=kaBLj40Ydb4.

36. Quoted in Dana Khraiche, "U.S. Presidential Candidate Says Cuba Sponsoring Hezbollah," *Daily Star* (Beirut), September 28, 2011, http://www.dailystar.com.lb/News /Politics/2011/Sep-28/149924-us-presidential-candidate-says-cuba-is-sponsoring-hezbollah .ashx#axzz1dt5VLhtX.

37. Olimpio Guido, "L'Hezbollah sbarca a Cuba 'Prepara nuove azioni,'" *Corriere della Sera* (Milan), August 31, 2011, http://archiviostorico.corriere.it/2011/agosto/31/Hezbollah _sbarca_Cuba_Prepara_nuove_co_9_110831020.shtml.

38. Quoted in Neil King Jr., "Bachmann Warns of Hezbollah Training Camps, Weapons in Cuba," *Wall Street Journal* Blogs, September 26, 2011, http://blogs.wsj.com/washwire /2011/09/26/bachmann-warns-of-hezbollah-training-camps-weapons-in-cuba/.

39. For example, during his visit to Lebanon in March 2001, José Ramón Balaguer, at the time head of the International Relations Department of the Central Committee of the Cuban Communist Party, met with leaders of different Lebanese organizations, including Hezbollah. See Actividades del Partido, "Compendio Informativo para coberturas periodísticas," http://congresopcc.cip.cu/referencias/cronologia-2/actividades-del partido-iv-congreso.

40. See "Mensajes de saludo al Sexto Congreso de nuestro Partido," *Granma* (Havana), April 22, 2011, http://www.granma.cubaweb.cu/secciones/6to-congreso-pcc/artic-034.html.

41. Hezbollah members, together with other representatives of many Lebanese political organizations, also assist with different commemorative activities organized by the Cuban embassy in Beirut. See, for example, Embajada de Cuba en Líbano, "Celebran en Líbano la Victoria de Girón y los resultados del VI Congreso del Partido," http://www.cubadiplomatica .cu/libano/ES/Inicio/tabid/19717/ctl/Details/mid/30423/ItemID/3037/Default.aspx. See also Sitio del Ministerio de Relaciones Exteriores de Cuba, "Participa embajador de Cuba en Líbano a conmemoración de Hezbollah por aniversario de la liberación," June 1, 2009, http:// www.cubaminrex.cu/Actualidad/2009/Mayo/Participa7.html.

CHAPTER 8

MUSLIMS IN MARTINIQUE

LILIANE KUCZYNSKI

IN A SURVEY ENTITLED "Contacts de civilisations en Martinique et en Guadeloupe" published by UNESCO in 1955, anthropologist and poet Michel Leiris noted the existence of several religious currents.[1] Aside from Catholicism, in which he detected influences of African religions such as can be seen in the Day of the Dead, he remarked upon the presence of Hindu cults that concerned more than simply immigrants from India. He also underlined the continuing success of the North American Protestant missions, especially the Seventh-Day Adventists, who had considerable financial means at their disposal and could recruit adepts in all strata of society.

Martinique's built space today reveals this religious diversity: next to the Catholic churches and a few Hindu temples, many Adventist or Evangelical churches can be seen, not to mention other buildings for various persuasions, including three Orthodox churches and a synagogue, among others. However, there is no mention of Islam before Raymond Delval's 1981 research for his book *Les musulmans en Amérique Latine et aux Caraïbes*, in which he devoted ten pages to Martinique. Yet Muslims do not appear in more recent studies on the religious phenomenon in the Caribbean such as the book published in 2000 by Laënnec Hurbon.[2] Indeed, it is only toward the end of the 1970s that Muslims on the island started to form a collectivity, though it remained almost totally ignored by other inhabitants. The aim of this chapter is to illustrate the diverse origins of Muslims in Martinique and the way Islam has entered into the island's social, cultural, and political history. We will analyze the frictions and negotiations that took place between the various constituents of the group—and with the global society—that have marked its construction and its surfacing in the public sphere. We conclude by assessing how this small religious minority can guarantee its continuity in Martinique.[3]

A COMPOSITE AND MOBILE *UMMA*

Martinique's recent history has been marked by repeated waves of migrants, and Muslims are very much part of such movements onto the island. In the twentieth century, the first Muslims to arrive in Martinique were Palestinians who almost all came from Ramallah. According to their own narratives, they stopped by chance on their way to South America in the 1920s to 1930s. These Muslims are part of a migratory current that began toward the end of the nineteenth century, when primarily for economic and political reasons Arabic-speaking people of the eastern Mediterranean, mostly Christian, left territories under Ottoman rule.[4] The Palestinians were peddlers at first, then settled in the towns, mainly in the center of Fort-de-France, and specialized in commerce, especially the garment trade.[5] For a long time called "Syrians," a broad category that included all merchants from the eastern Mediterranean, regardless of their land of birth or religion,[6] they are well-known figures of contemporary life in Martinique. They make appearances in novels set in Fort-de-France during the 1950s and '60s,[7] and they are considered by the authors of *In Praise of Creoleness* an integral part of Creole culture.[8] When discussing Muslims, therefore, it is necessary to note that some of their families have been on the island for three or even four generations, the youngest being born there, possessing French citizenship and speaking Creole as well as Arabic.[9]

It must be pointed out, however, that these "Syrians" of Muslim descent for a long time did not claim to be Muslim at all—and were not identified as such. The first generation did not really practice their religion, both because they had not been very religious in their homeland in the first place and because they wanted to fit into the local population. In the long term, some families definitively distanced themselves from Islam. At the same time, they chose to identify themselves as Arab. Until the end of the 1990s, a good number of "Syrians," Christian and Muslim, met in an "Arab club," a place of family leisure. Beginning in the 1980s, however, several "Syrians" turned to Islam, because they visited the homeland, received newcomers[10] on the island, or were influenced by concurrent Muslim institution building in Martinique, discussed later.

Muslims from the Maghreb also live in Martinique. They work as itinerant merchants, businessmen, technicians, professionals, and in particular as doctors, often temporarily employed in the various medical services and hospitals of the island. It should be noted that there are many Maghrebis who, though originally Muslim, never say they are and do not frequent the islands' mosques. This, however, does not prevent some of them from contributing financially, particularly to the construction of the new mosque. Palestinians and

North Africans are usually cast in the same frame and called "Arabs," which today tends to replace "Syrians." However, Palestinians are still less likely to be identified as Muslims than their Maghrebi counterparts.

West Africans from Senegal, Mali, and Guinea have lived on the island since the late 1960s. Among them, the number of *marabouts* and traveling salesmen is not insignificant, but there are also a few technicians, teachers, and professionals. Most attended Qur'anic school in their homeland when they were small. Some belong to Sufi brotherhoods (*qadriyya, tijaniyya, muridiyya*) but do not necessarily publicize the fact. The followers of the same brotherhood organize meetings outside of the mosques. A certain blurring of these religious particularisms is noticeable, due to the small number of followers. The island also hosts Muslims from Reunion Island, the Comoros (especially military personnel), and converts from mainland France; the latter often survive on temporary jobs.

To this *umma*—the result of several different migrant waves—must be added Martinicans who converted to Islam either on the island, in mainland France, or more seldom in Africa. Aside from infrequent and circumstantial conversions,[11] it is above all close contact with other Muslims that has attracted people from Martinique to Islam. In mainland France, Martinicans, Maghrebis, and Africans have long been made to live together in immigrant worker hostels as well as in voluntary associations for workers and students. Martinican conversion is often the result of having met a particular Maghrebi or African in such circumstances.[12] More recently, it is under the influence of the *tabligh* movement,[13] then of Salafist inspired groups, very active in large French cities and poorer suburbs, which young Maghrebis, Africans, as well as Martinicans living in those environments have turned toward Islam. In Martinique interactions with Africans, and one specific charismatic *marabout* to whom we will return later, played an important part in the conversion of Martinicans on the island. Some of them even traveled to West Africa. In the mid-1980s, a handful of Martinicans, enlisted by Islamic organizations, enrolled in Saudi universities for several years.

The diversity of Muslims on the territory of Martinique sets Islam apart from all the other religious groups present on the island. The vast majority of fundamentalist churches have been very largely accepted by the inhabitants of Martinique;[14] conversely, the small Jewish population of the island is basically made up of foreigners and includes practically no Martinican converts.[15] With its large proportion of migrants and its Martinicans converted in so many different places, Islam on the island bears the obvious mark of globalized exchanges and worldwide migratory flows, much like Martinique itself.

In this contemporary situation, the presently very hackneyed term "creolization," which has several meanings,[16] is hardly appropriate to designate what is rather the coexistence of Muslims endowed with distinct cultural and ethnic identities.

However, the balance among Muslims of different cultural and ethnic backgrounds varies. Until the mid-2000s, it included western Africans who played an important part in social life and festive moments. Members of the Mouride brotherhood would meet to recite *khassaïds*[17] and would set up a solidarity fund in order to pay for the repatriation to Senegal of those Mourides who had died in Martinique. But many of them went back home or elsewhere. As for Martinican Muslims, there are presently a few young managers who converted in France and now returned to the island and a few retirees.

That fluctuation can be explained by the fact that the Muslim population is very mobile. It must first be noted that Muslim migrants, even if they have been present on the island for a long time, have remained closely attached to their region of origin. Merchants that originally arrived from Palestine, for example, shuttle back and forth between Martinique and the Palestinian territories, where some own businesses, as well as in Jordan, France, and other places where there is a Palestinian diaspora. Some aspire to retire in their country of origin. Their endogamous behavior is also revealing of their attachment: the young men go to look for a wife in the Middle East, not in Martinique.[18]

Though temporalities and motivations vary, such mobility is proper to the island itself: migrants from varied backgrounds remain for the time it takes to work on a site, to fill a temporary position; some come to try their luck; others leave to study, to find a job, or for better living conditions. Beyond the Muslim case, these centrifugal and centripetal movements affect the island's entire population to a certain extent, particularly because the job market is limited, and rising unemployment forces more and more young people to leave.[19] Martinique's Muslim population is thus in constant flux and continuously regenerated.

The fact that Islam in Martinique is part of a contemporary transnational framework is not the only factor that explains its emergence. Analyzing the conversion to Islam of Caribbean subjects whose forebears were caught up in the transatlantic slave trade shows how, for them, the phenomenon resonates with both ancient and modern Caribbean history.

THE CONVERSION OF MARTINICANS

I have analyzed the complex itineraries and reasons that have drawn Martinicans into Islam elsewhere in greater detail.[20] It should first of all be noted that converts previously experienced other religions among Adventists, Evangelists, Jehovah's Witnesses, or other fundamentalist churches, not to mention the more esoteric sects such as the Roses-Croix. Joining these religions has been interpreted by some analysts of Martinican society as seeking protection against "Creole distress": it is portrayed as a "refuge against uncertainty, social isolation, doubts about one's identity, and, above all, against the threat of the *quimbois*."[21] When their search for relief is not satisfied, it is not infrequent that the new believers (including new Muslims) pursue their quest in another direction.[22] However, on the one hand, that multiplicity does not necessarily denote aimlessness or distress but can also be interpreted as "a reticular configuration with [a] non dominant pole identifiable as having a monopoly on the tools of symbolic representation";[23] on the other hand, one also encounters on the island Martinican Muslims firmly established in their faith, who have been leading an Islamic way of life for dozens of years and are also very interested in the spiritual debates on religion. They show that belonging to Islam depends on many other elements aside from "distress."

It is well known that the processes involving self-identification are a sensitive issue for Caribbean subjects. Avoiding any exclusive classification by origin and all racial pigeonholing in their self-definitions, most of the inhabitants of Martinique who have the transatlantic slave trade in their background call themselves "Martinicans" above all (or, more largely, "Caribbeans").[24] Only secondarily do some of them also identify themselves as Afro-descendants, Afro-Caribbeans, Caribbeans, Creoles, even Europeans, and so on, according to their personal orientations and depending on the circumstances or the particular moment in their own lives. Behind an apparently simple consensus—the fact of calling oneself Martinican—that way of oscillating between different cardinal points of belonging, that multiplicity of references, which are still always a subject of debate,[25] can also be found among Martinicans converted to Islam.

Though the idea of *umma* runs against all distinctions based on color and ethnicity, it would seem that for some Martinican Muslims, Islam is associated with Africa. It should be noted, however, that the connection between Islam and Africa is very often overlooked. Also, as noted above, it is through Africa or contact with Africans in various settings that some Martinicans discovered Islam. The return to Africa, particularly to Sahelian Africa, may lead to Islam. However, we must not forget how ambivalent that reference to Africa in the Caribbean is. I will not review here the complex feelings of attraction and repulsion that Martinicans entertain for that continent: deliberate efforts to forget the more remote part of their history have long existed side by side with passionate revivals of African cultures and trips to the continent.[26] One must also not forget the pivotal and pioneering role of Rastafarianism in reimagining Africa, a movement to which several Muslims rallied before converting to Islam. That movement did as much to give rise to the idea of black pride in Martinique as the theory of Negritude developed by Césaire and Senghor in the 1930s, who postulated that Africa was the Mother. As to black nationalism and the Pan-Africanist movement, they developed particularly in the United States and have had little impact in the French Caribbean.

Conversion sometimes also leads to reworking West Indian history as well. Following US African Americans, some Muslim Martinicans are certain that the vast majority of slaves were Muslims. Scholars disagree over the percentage of enslaved African Muslims who arrived in the Americas. Sylviane Diouf, for example, suggests 15 percent,[27] while Lovejoy considers it to be less than 10 percent.[28] Aminah McCloud, on the other hand, claims a "large portion."[29] Therefore, concerning the French Caribbean, evidence of a Muslim presence previous to the abolition of slavery is tenuous. But the near absence of historical traces in no way discourages Martinican Muslims from claiming an Islamic past in the Caribbean, an allegation that claims that some heroes of the slave revolt in Haiti were Muslim.[30] In the same way, redesigning a Muslim memory attributes the discovery of the West Indies not to Christopher Columbus but, much earlier, that is, prior to the onset of the slave trade, to African or Moorish Muslims.[31] In locating Islam on the islands before Columbus, Martinican Muslims see themselves as reverting to the very origins of the "New World." Pride and resistance are the values that these reconstructions of memory associate with Islam.

But there is a more fundamental argument that attracts Martinicans to Islam, an argument that for some coexists with the notion of returning to Africa and to Negritude, whereas for others it represents a later stage in their personal itinerary. It is mainly the conception of man in Islam that appeals to Martinican Muslims. The idea of a universal man (*al-insân*) created by Allah and the idea that every individual is nothing more or less than the son of Adam are for them quite potent: they allow one to subversively declare that all men are equal despite the slave trade and its subsequent violent inequalities. Declaring membership in the *umma*, which postulates the brotherhood of all its members, points in the same direction. Doing away with color distinctions and transcending a painful history, Islam allows for a new identity in which the West Indian Muslim can take his place the same as any man, in the continuity of a unique ancestry. It is therefore clearly a sense of freedom, equality, and universality that converted Martinicans derive from Islam.

One might go even further: clearly, for some Martinican Muslims who did not find that equality or that liberty in the Christian world or in the French Republic, Islam as a social imaginary represents a possible alternative to the contemporary place of Martinique, as part of France but subjugated to the mainland. As stressed by Beriss, "For many Antilleans, the ideals of freedom and equality have long been associated with the French Republic."[32] But in a social context where unemployment and violence threaten the structure of collective existence, in a political context where many note the failure of French departmentalization and feel they have been granted only an ambivalent and imperfect citizenship,[33] Islam represents a reservoir of countervalues. As a Martinican Muslim told us, Islam is "the only untamed religion," while for another it is the "only way out to avoid being fooled by the system." More than a reaction of "distress" or even than the expression of the need for recognition in the sense developed by Honneth,[34] Islam for converted Martinicans represents a force to combat social degradation and the colonial powers. However, in Martinique, contrary to what took place in the United States, aside from one or two activists, Muslim objections to this postcolonial order are rarely expressed in explicit political terms. Indeed, political matters are never discussed in the two mosques, motivated as much by a desire to limit thought and action to the strict religious sphere as by a determination to avoid tensions within the group. The airing of political views is also considered to be out of place in a context in which Muslims are in a minority and prone to abuse.[35] Thus, people are content to use the alternative values associated with Islam in order to transform their personal lives.

Finally, the last aspect to which Martinican Muslims are sensitive is the fact that Islam calls itself the last of the prophecies, the one that "perfected all the rest," to quote one of our interviewees. That synthetic and global vision of Islam can be seen as echoing "Creoleness," which integrates different elements.

Thus, the conversion to Islam of a minority of Martinicans is one of the phenomena that reveal the tensions and expectations of Martinican society today, of its gnawing search for respect and equality, and of the importance that society lends to questions of power and leadership.

As Muslims in Martinique gradually organize, these issues crop up both in their relations with the island's administration and society and within the group itself, which, as we have stressed, is very mixed, very versatile, and made up of subgroups with strong ethnic identities.

SOME STAGES IN THE DEVELOPMENT OF ISLAM IN MARTINIQUE

Since they presently account for less than 1 percent of the population of Martinique,[36] Muslims remain largely unfamiliar. Most Martinicans still identify them with "Syrian" merchants and do not know there are Muslims of other origins, too. Islam is frequently perceived through Western media, which has little to do with the real life of Muslims on the island.

It is true they have always been discreet. The two prayer rooms, located in working-class neighborhoods in the middle of Fort-de-France, are located in residential or office buildings and are hardly noticeable if one doesn't know they exist. Only the mosque now being built in a somewhat out-of-the-way part of town explicitly draws attention to the Muslim presence. This institution-building presence goes back to the 1970s.

Before then, the few Muslims on the island, mainly of West African origin, were isolated, unaware of others of the same faith. They first came together as a group thanks to the enthusiasm of a *marabout* from Mali. He came to Martinique mainly as a healer and strongly impressed people in Fort-de-France because of his activity, great presence, and energy. Negritude was then on the upsurge, and the fact that he was of African origin certainly counted for the Martinicans who met him. Several Martinicans converted. He was also set on developing Islam on the island and opened the first collective prayer room in his own home. He did his utmost to unite the Muslims scattered throughout the island, exhorting particularly the merchants of Palestinian descent to practice Islam. He became the imam of the budding group and gained the support of the Grande mosque of Paris in 1978. In Martinique a whole Muslim way of life grew up around his charismatic personality: prayers, initiation to Islam, building a *halal* slaughterhouse, doing the first burial according to Muslim ritual, struggling to have Muslim first names accepted by the French administration, striving to familiarize Martinicans with Islam, and projecting an Islamic cultural center on the island by applying for funding from Saudi Arabia and other countries.

That first period of effervescence, when everybody regardless of origin (West African Muslims, Muslims from Palestine or the Maghreb, converted Martinicans) seemed to bond with the *marabout* imam, was short-lived. He quickly lost his official support in France. Power struggles and opposition from those who had been his followers ensued. At the heart of the dispute lay what some saw as the limits of his wisdom, but even more his activity as a healer and *marabout*, presented by his detractors as the wrong road to follow by an up-and-coming Muslim community.[37] This Muslim Sahelian founder was thus displaced in 1983 by the arrival of a young man from Senegal who had been educated in the universities of Saudi Arabia and appointed by the Muslim World League (Ligue islamique mondiale), and who became the new imam and professor of Arabic.[38] The charismatic model was done away with and replaced by an authority representing an institution: the Muslim World League. The choice of a Senegalese[39] was of utmost importance: in the context of Martinique, it was crucial to avoid an Arab imam, that is, a white man, for fear of offending the island's Martinican and African Muslims. Nevertheless, his appointment was badly received by the *marabout* imam's entourage and by some of his Martinican students, who were sickened by the aspersions cast on their master's religious legitimacy and felt robbed of their collective project to develop Islam in Martinique. The conflict led to a division in 1984, still felt today: the more modest prayer room used by few worshippers is an offshoot of the larger one, being composed of followers of the *marabout* and having as imam one of his former Martinican students. The second prayer room assembles all those who followed the new Senegalese imam. It has become much larger than the older prayer room, and Muslims of all origins attend it. Some of them are in control of the new mosque being built.

Behind the religious controversy that opposed a certain Sahelian Islam (which has a strong *maraboutic* character) to an Islam presented as more "orthodox"—controversy that led to the original group breaking up—other divisions become visible. Those who were primarily responsible for the Malian *marabout*-imam being ousted, as well as the converted Martinican who was his close disciple, were Muslims of Palestinian origin, who by doing so were posing as the defenders of the legitimate faith even if they did not directly claim it for themselves. The fact that they picked up the project to build a mosque was felt to be a fraud by some Martinican Muslims who had been at the inception of this project without being able to follow through with it for lack of funding.[40] What the Martinicans resented deeply was that they, alongside the Malian *marabout*-imam, were having their Muslim identities devalued by the "Arabs." Some of them even went so far as denouncing that devaluation as a form of colonialism, which the strategic appointment of a new Senegalese imam (black) only masked—although he was respected by many Martinicans for his competence as a religious leader. Clearly, the coexistence of Muslims of diverse origins in the same territory is far from being free of tensions caused by questions of power.

However, the project of the mosque also had to contend with the French administration. Though the project to build a Muslim cultural center existed early on, Muslims remained invisible for a long time, and only little by little and cautiously did some of them wish to make their presence felt in the public sphere. Therefore, during the 1990s when the erection of the mosque became a reality, "we walked on tip-toes," to quote the master builder. Several things can explain their discretion. First of all, some felt the fear of being stigmatized in a context where, as we have said, Islam is unfamiliar. Despite the diversity proclaimed by the champions of Creoleness, Muslims were weary that particular features of their group were coming out into the open.[41] In the words of a Muslim Martinican woman, having long resided in a large city in the East of France: "Over there you can go to the mosque in your *djellaba*, here [in Fort-de-France], it's impossible." Besides, though the secular French context defends the freedom to believe and the equality between religions and proclaims the neutrality of the state, building mosques has nevertheless provoked much debate. The same situation exists in Martinique, though, it must be said, the presence of Muslims was never turned into a "problem" there as it was in mainland France. The Fort-de-France city council, legally obliged to give its consent, refused to grant the building permit for a long time, in spite of the concessions made by the project's promoters, especially concerning the height of the minaret, which had to be reduced. Technical demands masked the city council's and neighbors' questionable reservations. In the end, a request addressed to the mayor of the time, writer Aimé Césaire, managed to unlock the situation.

In seeking a positive minority status on the island, Muslims have also petitioned authorities for space in the cemeteries to allow burying the dead according to Islamic ritual. That initiative, considered by some Muslims more important than building the mosque, has also been vehemently expressed in mainland France. On the island, it was countered by the "Jacobinism" of the French Republic, that is, by a certain degree of ignorance of the rules and regulations on the part of the administration and their extreme reluctance to make what they consider any exceptions to state neutrality by granting public space to a specific religious practice.[42] The only solution available up to now[43] has been to privately buy an unmarked vault in a cemetery, but the general alignment of the place does not allow turning the bodies toward Mecca, and, in accordance with French law, the dead person is buried in a coffin. It clearly appears that this interpretation of the secularism of French law is exclusionary in itself.

The visibility of Islam in Martinique has thus created some friction with the administration, which is only now beginning to accept—with difficulty—the fact that cultural and religious diversity can be freely expressed. But on the whole, while seeking to further their demands, Muslims themselves are convinced of the need to compromise with Martinique's social and cultural environment. Thus, the very rare attempts to *da'wa* in the streets of Fort-de-France rapidly disappeared by the Muslims' own choice, who preferred to keep a low profile. Similarly, up to now no full veil (*niqab*) has appeared on the island.[44] Women who want to cover their heads wear a simple scarf attached around their necks or behind the nape of the neck. It should be mentioned that having one's "head attached" (according to local terminology) corresponds to an ancient custom in Martinique that older women have always respected. Because of that, Muslim women easily blend into the general female milieu.

Though the desire to coexist is shared by the vast majority of Muslims, it is largely due to the fact that they are aware of belonging to a small religious minority under the scrutiny of others. The result is that the Islam taught in Martinique is theoretically tolerant and not exclusive. The imam of the largest prayer room likes to recall the first period of Islam before an independent Muslim community grew up, when sharing food and space with non-Muslims was the rule, aside from what is formally forbidden by the religion. As for the leader of the smaller prayer room, he says, somewhat more anxiously, "Allah pardons when you act by constraint," that is, in an environment as yet not very propitious for Muslims.

The general attitude of avoiding ostentation is accompanied by an attempt to strengthen Islam in harmony with the context of the island. For example, considering that Islam accepts having one's "head attached," a Martinican Muslim declared that "the veil is not part of Martinican culture; we're not Arabs." In the same way, he would not be favorable to applying Shari'a law on the island: "We're not here to adopt the extremist side of things. Islam adapts to people's cultures."

The attempt to fit into the local context also marked the various phases of the new mosque's construction. Objections were equally forthcoming from the Muslim group itself, concerning the size and the style of the mosque's architecture. The mosque was financed mainly by donations from Saudi Arabia, as well as gifts from Martinican Muslims, and the master builder is a merchant of Palestinian origin, the same man whose family has been in Martinique for several generations and who was largely responsible for both the departure of the *marabout*-imam and the opening of the new prayer room. He drew up the blueprints, reinterpreting one of the mosques in Ramallah, his own family's hometown, and has overseen every step of its construction. Its architecture, influenced by Middle Eastern models, was contested by some Martinican Muslims who would have preferred a "Creole" architecture. The same goes for the imposing size of the edifice planned by the Palestinian master builder, judged by some as pretentious for such a small religious minority. However, as during the episode of the eviction of the *marabout*-imam, it is more generally the feeling of being excluded from what concerns Islam on their island that upsets Martinican Muslims. What they see as "Arab" domination has led some of these Martinican Muslims to want to make their own way in Islam as a group. But that attempt did not receive universal approval, never materializing into a new schism in the community.[45]

Once again, this illustrates how sensitive an issue the question of power is in Martinique. The denunciation of the master builder of the mosque, who is considered by some to be the group's benefactor and by others to be an autocrat, allows the expression of ethnic tensions in the community. Through him the "Arabs" as a group are criticized by the others. The debate over this figure shows how ethnic elements become embedded in the religious community and how variable are both the limits of the ethnic groups and the Muslims' representations of them. The "Arabs" are sometimes considered to be an integral part of the Martinican *umma* and society, while in many contexts they are designated as the symbol of the dominant other. But aside from that way of relating to power, focalizing on the "Arabs" translates Martinican Muslims' specific desire to anchor Islam in a Caribbean way of life or at least to disengage it from the "Arab" grip, felt to be too absolute in the Muslim world generally. Martinican Muslims are particularly concerned with melding Islamic and Martinican ways of being, because their cultural identity is complex and they are caught in a double bind (not to mention a double consciousness, were we to paraphrase Du Bois): on the one hand, they aspire to live Islam in the *umma* as an alternative way of life, and, on the other hand, they are deeply rooted in a culture and history as well as attached to a particular language, Creole.

More than in other contexts where Islam is in a minority position, striking the difficult balance between self affirmation, membership in Martinican society, and negotiation within the Muslim public itself is therefore the crux of the debates among Muslims of the island.

MUSLIM INSECURITY IN MARTINIQUE

A few patterns mark the thirty years of the organized Muslim presence in Martinique and the perspectives at hand. Both groups' regular activity is based on prayer, especially the Friday prayer, which, as might be expected, draws the largest number of participants and still constitutes a fairly small crowd, especially in the smaller prayer hall. However, Muslim engagement increases considerably during the Muslim holidays in which those who usually stay away from places of prayer also participate. Collective outings are organized from time to time, such as picnics on the beach, an activity that Martinicans love to engage in.

In the larger prayer room, lessons in Arabic and reading the Qur'an are arranged by the imam and Arab-speaking women who teach beginners. But these lessons attract few pupils, and attendance is patchy. At different times some Muslims have tried to organize lectures or show films on specific points of doctrine[46] or offered a cultural introduction to different Muslim countries.

However, these events are generally not very popular. The relative indifference to everything beyond prayer can be explained by the makeup of the group itself. It includes many merchants, caught up in their work, who, according to one Muslim's remark, only come to the mosque "in a rush" and have no time for other activities. In the larger prayer room, the questions put to the imam before the Friday sermon reveal a drastic need for basic information on religious practices and a serious concern with orthopraxy: few Muslims have a more extended knowledge of the religion. There are few intellectuals among them who show any curiosity for Muslim history, arts, and sciences.

Meanwhile, a more urgent question regards how to organize young people, who are seen to represent the future. Given that very few entire families convert to Islam, younger converts stem from families whose members belong to different religious groups. In these and related contexts, tensions arise between Muslim and non-Muslim relatives and friends over matters concerning daily life and Muslim or non-Muslim observances and circumvention. Children and teenagers are particularly exposed: it is not always easy to resist wearing a miniskirt or avoid Carnival or Christmas parties—where the traditional dish is pork. Confronted by a perceived threatening situation, some Muslims have begun supporting families in their efforts to give their children a Muslim education, trying to offer young adults a stimulating place for an alternative sociability within the framework of the mosque. In this regard, a women's association[47] has organized small parties with brochures and entertainment based on Muslim themes and offered gifts to the children at the end of Ramadan.

All these efforts depend, of course, on the goodwill of a handful of volunteers who risk burnout for lack of assistants and who are limited by the available resources. On this point, a comparison with Jews who opened a kindergarten, or Adventist groups who have many schools and training centers,[48] highlights the precarious nature of Islam in Martinique. It is true that the group is too small to promote institution building as efficient as those of Adventists, who are strong in numbers and particularly dynamic on the island.

Beyond the fragile links that bring parents and children together for a few events, or other small groups of friends, Muslims rarely organize community events. Of course, one might stop for a while in a merchant's bazaar or drink a fruit juice in a stand run by a young Muslim. But it is mainly in the mosques, after the Friday prayer, that people greet each other, exchange news, and occasionally suggest organizing a collective outing. Thus, aside from the consciousness of belonging to the *umma*, organized public collective life among Muslims on the island can be qualified as limited. Some of them even appear isolated, either because they are geographically distant from the center of Fort-de-France (where the mosques are) or by choice. It would seem that most Muslims are not willing to form a group at any price. One Muslim reflected, "We see each other at the mosque but aside from that everyone practices the Islam he wants at home." Indeed, solidarity and assistance are expected to come from one's family, not from one's Muslim "brothers," and this reliance on kin is widespread in Martinique. Islam is not, or still not, conducive to creating social links in Martinique because being Muslim is only one of the many facets of a plural identity that draw together persons of varied backgrounds, each belonging to many different networks themselves.

Thus, it is the Friday prayer, more than wider solidarity networks or collective, pan-Islamic mobilization, that unites the groups in the two prayer rooms that exist on the island. However, the main explanation for such interrelations is the mobility of Muslims, mentioned at the outset of this chapter, which, it should be remembered, also concerns Martinican Muslims, in particular the youth, the very ones who are supposed to be educated as Muslims. The nature and amplitude of migrant waves typical of Martinique point to structural rather than temporary causes. Migrants enable the constant renewal of the Muslim public in Martinique, and this fluctuation ironically ensures the continuity of Islam on the island. Of course, there is a small core of Muslims established on the island: mainly Martinicans and a few families of "Syrians" who have lived there for generations. They make the commitment over the long term and bear the responsibility for keeping up the mosques and their initiatives, sometimes in the hardly propitious conditions analyzed above. These old "Syrian" families become somehow conflated with all the Muslims on the island. However, sometimes they are stigmatized as the "Arab" other. The ethnic lines of differentiation within the community are evident especially in relation to Muslims of African origin, who often feel that they are just passing through Martinique and engage very little in the processes of institution building on the island. One man of Senegalese origin, who is married to a Muslim Martinican woman and has lived on the island for a long time, complained: "Africans invest in their own mosques." Thus, the diversity in origin of the Muslim public of Martinique, which is one of its defining features, explains why a significant number of them are only marginally involved at the local level, a fact that is made even more sensitive in that the group is numerically small. This has constituted a barrier to its cohesion.

What is more, the sense of belonging to the *umma* does not replace but rather accentuates more particular ethnic ties in Martinique. For instance, a Muslim man from Guinea notes that for him, one of the attractions of the mosque on Fridays is that he will meet other Africans there. Similar affinities exist among Muslims from the Middle East. In other words, the Muslims in Martinique relate to one another through linguistic and cultural ties rather than solely religious ones. As noted by John Voll, "the Caribbean experiences of Muslims" indicate that "immigrant and diasporic identities are based more on language and culture than they are on religion."[49] This visibility of ethnic difference among Muslims tells us as much about the plurality of Islam as about the centrality of ethnic boundaries to Creole nationalisms in the Caribbean.

Though the Muslim public is made up of migrants moving about various continents, it is striking to note that Martinican Muslims maintain almost no official contacts with Muslims on other islands of the Caribbean. At the time of the first period of institution building on Martinique, mentioned above, the *marabout*-imam tried to establish contacts with the Muslims of Trinidad. In 1982 he had taken part in the Congress of the Islamic Mission for the Caribbean and South America (Conférence de la mission islamique de la Caraïbe et de l'Amérique du Sud). These contacts ended in the 2000s, due to not only the costs of transportation, but also the linguistic differences between the French-, English-, and Spanish-speaking islands of the Caribbean.[50] Yet relations are no closer with the mosques in Guadeloupe or other French-speaking islands or with Muslim institutions of France.

This does not prevent individual contacts from being made with other Muslims around the world, buttressed by the travels already mentioned in this chapter. In addition, contacts with the *umma* are facilitated by the Internet. Through the World Wide Web, Muslims in Martinique glean all sorts of information and buy books, clothing, and other Muslim accessories. Some also have access to Saudi television. Only time will tell if exposure to a globalized Islam will result in homogenizing practices or further distinguish the Islamic history of the Caribbean itself.

CONCLUSION

Created by diverse and mobile currents, the Muslim population in Martinique is clearly connected to the wider trends that shape Martinican society. Due to its complex makeup and the gradual affirmation of its presence, the Martinican *umma* stretches beyond national borders and participates in challenging the official French reticence to allow the expression of cultural, ethnic, or religious pluralism. However, the Muslim minority in Martinique expresses itself much less vehemently than is the case on mainland France.

Several factors go toward explaining this: the relatively small number of Muslims, the context of a small island where coexistence with other cultures and religions appears inevitable, and the very nature of the Muslim group, whose members are diversely involved in collective Muslim life. But the explanation for that modest sort of mobilization also lies in the complex identity of Martinican Muslims, who must cope with both being attached, albeit very critically, to French citizenship and being strongly and diversely anchored in the history, cultures, and social issues of the Caribbean. Therefore, the adoption of Islamic values represents only one element among others in the process of construction of the self among the Muslims in Martinique.[51]

As a consequence of migration, the identity of the Muslims in Martinique is often expressed in ethnic terms. Sometimes the ethnic categories are claimed by the agents themselves, as we have seen with the "Arabs" who, though being Martinican, also express and communicate this ethnic identity. In other contexts, the ethnic categories are used as an emblem of otherness in order to express conflicts around power and authority, as was the case of the criticism expressed against the "Arabs" by the other members of the Muslim community. Therefore, the traditionally emphasized capacity of Islam to reach across languages, cultures, and peoples does not yet seem sufficient to bring unity to this group, which is in the process of creating an identity of its own.

NOTES

This essay was translated by Gabrielle Varro.

1. Michel Leiris, *Contacts de civilisations en Martinique et en Guadeloupe* (Paris: Gallimard/UNESCO, 1955).

2. Raymond Delval, *Les musulmans en Amérique latine et aux Caraïbes* (Paris: L'Harmattan, 1992); Laënnec Hurbon, ed., *Le phénomène religieux dans la Caraïbe* (Paris: Karthala, 2000).

3. This article is based on field research carried out among the Muslims of Martinique during seven visits to the island from 2000 to 2011 and two brief visits to Guadeloupe. This study has received financial support from the research group Laboratoire d'Anthropologie Urbaine (IIAC/CNRS/EHESS).

4. For an analysis of the reasons for Levantine emigration toward South America, see Denis Cuche, "Un siècle d'immigration palestinienne au Pérou: La construction d'une identité spécifique," *Revue Européenne des Migrations Internationales* 17, no. 3 (2001): 87–118. The author notes that the migrants saw America as an "imprecise destination" (91).

5. Some are still traveling salesmen, though.

6. They were similarly called *turcos* in Latin America, because they harked from the Ottoman Empire. See Cuche, "Un siècle d'immigration palestinienne au Pérou," 99; and Paulo Pinto, "Arab Ethnicity and Diasporic Islam: A Comparative Approach to Processes of Identity Formation and Religious Codification in the Muslim Communities in Brazil," *Comparative Studies of South Asia, Africa and the Middle East* 31, no. 2 (2011): 314.

7. Especially in Raphael Confiant's novels.

8. According to Bernabe, Chamoiseau, and Confiant, "Creoleness is the interactional or

222 CONTEMPORARY CARTOGRAPHIES

transactional aggregate of Caribbean, European, African, and levantine cultural elements, united on the same soil by the yoke of history." See Jean Bernabe, Patrick Chamoiseau, and Raphael Confiant, *Eloge de la créolité/In Praise of Creoleness* (Paris: Gallimard, 1989–1993), 87.

9. They speak the Middle Eastern variety of Arabic.

10. Immigration from Palestine never really ceased and was more or less spurred on by the economic and political events affecting the Near East.

11. Generally the case of a future spouse who converts in order to be able to marry a Muslim woman.

12. Between 1963 and 1982, many young people from a French Overseas Department were transferred to mainland France via a specialized organization, BUMIDOM. They became a workforce for industry and the public services (hospitals, the mail). Due to the significant number of migrants from the West Indies in the Paris region, some have dubbed them the "third island" to add to Martinique and Guadeloupe. See Alain Anselin, *L'émigration antillaise en France: La troisième île* (Paris: Karthala, 2000).

13. This international movement for the promotion of Islam, born in India in 1927, spread to France at the end of the 1960s.

14. This does not mean that there are no foreign believers among them; there also exist in Martinique some specifically Haitian fundamentalist churches.

15. William F. S. Miles, "Caribbean Hybridity and the Jews of Martinique," in *The Jewish Diaspora in Latin America and the Caribbean: Fragments of Memory*, edited by Kristin Ruggiero (Portland, OR: Sussex Academic Press, 2005), 139–162.

16. A recent critical evaluation of this notion can be found in Jean Luc Bonniol, "Au prisme de la créolisation: Tentative d'épuisement d'un concept," *L'Homme* 207–208 (2013): 237–288; and Christine Chivallon, "Créolisation universelle ou singulière? Perspectives depuis le Nouveau Monde," *L'Homme* 207–208 (2013): 37–74.

17. Religious poems written by Cheikh Amadou Bamba, founder of the brotherhood.

18. It must nevertheless be noted that men of the first generations who came to the island lived with Martinican women, a fact that today has become exceptional.

19. During the second quarter of 2010, overall unemployment reached 21 percent and 48 percent for the younger age brackets (Institut National de la Statistique et des Études Économiques).

20. Liliane Kuczynski, "L'islam en Martinique: Entre universalisme et élaboration d'une mémoire antillaise," in *Expériences et mémoires*, edited by Bogumil Jewsiewicki and Erika Nimis (Paris: L'Harmattan, 2008), 171–187.

21. The *quimbois* is the West Indian form of witchcraft. See Raymond Masse, *Détresse créole: Ethnoépidémiologie de la détresse psychique à la Martinique* (Quebec: Presses de l'Université Laval, 2008), 234.

22. The more religious, the imams in particular, think those unstable Muslims, considered unenlightened, are sinning by *shirk*, because they connect Allah and prayer directly to the acquisition of worldly goods. The injunction to dissociate prayer from other objectives has become a recurrent theme in Friday sermons.

23. Christine Chivallon, "Beyond Gilroy's *Black Atlantic*: The Experience of the African Diaspora," *Diaspora* 11, no. 3 (2002): 369.

24. In what follows we keep to this usage and employ the term "Martinican" for that part of the island's population descended from the slave trade, among whom certain individuals converted to Islam.

25. This multiplicity of references also motivates many academic debates; see, for example, those stirred up by Paul Gilroy's book *The Black Atlantic: Modernity and Double Consciousness* (London: Verso, 1993) and the article by Christine Chivallon quoted in note 23.

26. A recent example of the fascination with Africa is when, in December 2011, at the instigation of a new association, Kwanzaa was celebrated for the first time in Martinique; the fete symbolizes the Pan-Africanism created in 1966 by African Americans in the United States, whose aim is to tie up with all those who, all over the world, acknowledge their African roots.

27. Sylviane A. Diouf, *Servants of Allah: African Muslims Enslaved in the Americas* (New York: New York University Press, 1998), 48.

28. Paul Lovejoy, *Slavery on the Frontiers of Islam* (Princeton, NJ: Markus Wiener, 2004), 237.

29. Aminah Beverly McCloud, *African American Islam* (New York: Routledge, 1995), 1.

30. The liberation of Saint-Domingo (1803) took place in 1804.

31. This opinion can also be found amid the Muslim circles of the United States and is reproduced in several books, such as the following, written by a convert from Trinidad: A. B. Omowale, *L'islam, âme de l'humanité* (Lyon: Tawhid, 1991).

32. David Beriss, *Black Skins, French Voices: Caribbean Ethnicity and Activism in Urban France* (Boulder, CO: Westview Press, 2004), 128.

33. It should be remembered that Martinique is a French Overseas Department. Voting in January 2010, the majority of Martinicans refused the institutional evolution of the island toward greater autonomy. Nevertheless, many strongly resent their economic and cultural subjection to France: "It is unacceptable that other people should think in our place," one of them declared.

34. Axel Honneth, *The Struggle for Recognition: The Moral Grammar of Social Conflicts* (Cambridge: Polity Press, 1995).

35. To my knowledge they have expressed themselves in this way only once, during a demonstration against the Sabra and Shatila massacres (1982), a demonstration at which only a handful of Muslims, led by their then imam, were present.

36. In 2010 the island had around four hundred thousand inhabitants. The complete absence of statistics means that one can estimate only very vaguely the number of Muslims concerned, around five hundred. This number is approximately the same in Guadeloupe. It is much larger in the other Caribbean islands such as Trinidad and Tobago and Barbados. In Haiti the number of Muslims seems to be rapidly increasing.

37. One should remember that Marabouts have long been accused of *shirk* by the strictest Muslims. That does not prevent their way of doing things, in particular using the Qur'an as a talisman, from being quite widespread in the Muslim world. See Constant Hames, ed., *Coran et talismans: Textes et pratiques magiques en milieu musulman* (Paris: Karthala, 2007).

38. Details on these troubled times can be found in Liliane Kuczynski, "Une mosquée en Martinique," *Archives de sciences sociales des religions* 151 (July–September 2010): 25–46.

39. For lack, no doubt, of a Martinican considered competent.

40. For details of this conflict, see ibid.

41. On this topic, see Liliane Kuczynski, "Négociations et affirmations d'une religion minoritaire: L'Islam en Martinique," in *La religion de l'autre: La pluralité religieuse entre concurrence et reconnaissance*, edited by A.-S. Lamine, F. Lautman, and S. Mathieu (Paris: L'Harmattan, 2008), 163–174.

42. Let us recall that cemeteries in France are under municipal administration and that creating private cemeteries is prohibited.

43. This was an emergency solution when a Martinican Muslim died in 2002.

44. In France a controversial law passed in 2011 forbids wearing the *niqab* in places governed by state law.

45. This is contrary to what took place in Guadeloupe where, in the 1990s, young Guadeloupeans came together to found a new mosque in opposition to the one that existed, judged too marked by African Muslim ways of doing things. Here again, religious opposition covers up other divisions.

46. Such as death in Islam or its stand on organ donations.

47. This association was created in 2006.

48. Adventists share with Muslims the same dietary prohibitions, the refusal of fetes, and the requirement of modest dress.

49. John Voll, "Muslims in the Caribbean: Ethnic Sojourners and Citizens," in *Muslim Minorities in the West: Visible and Invisible*, edited by Yvonne Haddad (New York: Altamira, 2002), 265.

50. We should note that on a much more general level, the political and economic integration of Martinique in the Caribbean is a work in progress.

51. For an analysis of the complexity of that Caribbean identity construction in mainland France, see Audrey Célestine, "French Caribbean Organizations and the 'Black Question' in France," *African and Black Diaspora: An International Journal* 4, no. 2 (2011): 131–144.

CHAPTER 9

FORMING ISLAMIC RELIGIOUS IDENTITY AMONG
TRINIDADIANS IN THE AGE OF SOCIAL NETWORKS

HALIMA-SA'ADIA KASSIM

MUSLIM IDENTITY IS SHAPED by and connected to the social institutions of family, *masjid* (mosque), and *maktab* (religious classes) in complex
and multiple ways by means of time and space. The extent to which religious
consciousness is fostered by these social institutions to create a Muslim identity reconfirms the existence of group norms and values that in turn work to
develop and affirm clear faith-based self-sentiments. This would likely influence their participation and functioning in the everyday life as well as within
the existing social institutions. Youth have been conceived as a phase in the life
cycle charged with social and cultural change and agency. They are constantly
subject to new influences, the most recent being new media that contributes to the negotiation, contestation, affirmation, reiteration, and celebration
of identities. Muslim youth in Western societies are also influenced by new
media, including social networking sites (SNS). This chapter seeks to provide
an exploratory assessment of young Muslim adults' use of SNS in the construction of their identity in Trinidad. Rather than argue that SNS is a medium
that necessarily competes with or substitutes for "traditional" Muslim spaces,
this chapter demonstrates that SNS provides an additional arena to continue
to build on debates or conversations that are part of this wider Islamic public
sphere.

Over the years research into the East Indian and Muslim community sometimes converged, and broad themes were interrogated based particularly on
communal identity and religious commitment. To that end, there have been
studies of migration and settlement, identity consciousness explored through
the development of civil society and faith-based organizations, governance
of those organizations, gender and sexuality, as well as festivals. We are now
living in a world where information and ideas are (in)formed by media and
new media. Both media and new media therefore have the potential to be

transformative vis-à-vis ideas and attitudes. SNS is an important part of contemporary youth culture.

Despite the pervasiveness and influence of new media on youth cultures, there has been limited research on the use of SNS and its impact on Caribbean youth. There has not been much investigation into the significance of religion or the representation of religious faith and practice in the lives of young people. This chapter seeks to understand the place of religion in the lives of young Muslim adults through their use of SNS. It contributes to understanding young Muslim adults' presence on the Internet and their participation in the production of online content through extended conversations about religion and religiosity.

MUSLIMS IN THE CARIBBEAN

In 2010 a demographic study by the Pew Research Center's Forum on Religion and Public Life estimated that 78,000 Muslims resided in Trinidad and Tobago. At 5.8 percent of the total population, the estimated Muslim population in 2030, the study noted, would increase to 80,000, though the percentage would remain at 5.8 percent as the rest of the population grows as well. The presence of the Muslim population in the Caribbean is a result of migration, forced and voluntary. As is generally posited in the recounting of historical circumstances on the presence of Islam in the Caribbean and particularly Trinidad, there were three main streams: the African slaves, the Indian indentured immigrants, and the Arabic-speaking immigrants from the eastern Mediterranean and Levant region referred to locally as Syrian-Lebanese.[1]

While the enslaved African peoples[2] were the first to bring Islam to the Caribbean, by the time of emancipation there was no continuous African Muslim presence. However, from the 1960s the global outgrowth sparked a level of consciousness about black roots and identity in which conversion or reversion to Islam was one of the outcomes.[3] This quest for identity was also informed by the realization that their forefathers were Muslims.[4]

In Trinidad most Muslims are descendants of South Asian immigrants who arrived in Trinidad from India in 1845 to 1917 as part of indentured-labor schemes for the sugar plantations. During that period some 143,939 indentured laborers arrived in the colony, of which it is estimated that 80 percent of the migrants were Hindus, 15 percent were Muslims, and the rest were tribal, Christians, Sikhs, and others.[5] The majority of Muslims who arrived were Sunni Muslims, believed to be of the Hanafi school of thought, along with some Shi'is. By the late nineteenth century, this group of immigrants, sufficient in numbers, earnestly and visibly began (re)constructing a community.[6]

They prescribed the tenets of Islam as identified in the Qur'an (Holy Book) and the hadith (reports of statements or actions of Muhammad or of his tacit approval or criticism of something said or done in his presence) and heroes such as the Prophet Muhammad (u.w.b.p.) who served as a model of behavior and rituals manifested through the Islamic greeting of salaams and social and religious ceremonies.[7] They planned the construction of a *masjid*, the development of *maktabs*, and the founding of denominational schools.[8] The socialization within the extended family networks and the *maktabs* provided the means for the passage of the transmission of knowledge. Religious classes continue to be offered by imams (priests) or other Islamic scholars at the *masjid* or the Islamic institutes, thus facilitating the creation of *iman* (faith), *taqwa* (God consciousness),[9] and the training of Islamic scholars.

The "Syrian-Lebanese" who migrated to the Americas between 1860 and 1914 constitute the third wave of Muslims arriving in the Americas, including Trinidad. Similar to the percentage of Muslims from South Asia, it is estimated that Muslims constituted 15 to 20 percent of the total arriving population. Although numerically small and generally a closed ethnic group, the influence of the Syrian-Lebanese (Muslims and Christians) on the society of Trinidad and Tobago is quite large.[10]

Despite the somewhat discrete grouping of the Muslim community, they have over the years made a mark on the landscape of Trinidad and Tobago. These distinct groups have contributed to the survival of Islam in Trinidad through symbols, rituals, heroes, and values mentioned earlier. Today, there are more than one hundred mosques in the country generally affiliated with the major Islamic organizations in Trinidad and Tobago. There is some variation in the interpretation of Islam among the local Muslim community, with the Sunni Muslims dominating. Ahmadiyyas and Shi'is are also present in the minority. There are several Muslim primary and secondary schools and two institutions, the Darul-Uloom and Haji Ruknudeen Institute of Islamic Studies, that produce locally trained scholars and imams as well as teach the Arabic language and Islamic law. In 2005 an Islamic television channel, Islamic Broadcasting Network (IBN Channel 8), was born. In the next year, the TriniMuslims.com website was created. Since then, Muslims of Trinidad and Tobago, through organizations, youth movements, and *masjids*, are establishing a presence on the World Wide Web and social networking media.

As the twentieth century shifted from an emphasis solely on economic and political justice for oppressed groups to a focus on (multi-) cultural citizenship,[11] there was the introduction of culturally and religious specific legislation such as the Muslim Marriage and Divorce Act of 1935 that was last amended in 1980, burial rites, and the introduction of Eid-ul-Fitr (festivity after completing the fasting month of Ramadan) as a public holiday in 1967. Muslims have also played a significant role in the economic development of the country, as enslaved and indentured laborers on the plantations to peddlers and merchants to now being among the professional class and owners of businesses employing many individuals as well as holding important political positions. All of this suggests that in spite of their heterogeneity, Muslims have been a critical mass and have been able to participate and influence the development of their homeland and attain critical citizen rights.

These discrete streams or movements and historical experiences as immigrants and settlers have influenced the distinctive character of Islam in Trinidad. As a minority within a larger ethnic community, Muslims traditionally defined themselves by their communal ethnic identity and then religious identity (e.g., Indo-Muslims), though this is changing as Muslims become more confident of themselves. It may be further asserted that the younger generation, freed from the limitations of historical circumstances and as a result of time combined with the globalizing influences of media and new media, is less likely to see its identity through the narrow confines of ethnicity or geographic origin. Ethnic identity is giving way to a definition by way of faith: religious commitment to Islam. Ethnicity, therefore, remains a convenient nomenclature to reference the different groups of Muslims within the society.

CONCEPTUALIZING THE MUSLIM DIASPORA IN THE INTERNET ERA

The corpus of scholarly interest and research on the Internet is growing as much as inquiry into the new media in local, global, and transnational contexts. To that end, there is a growing corpus of work that interrogates trends in the use and impact of SNS on lived realities, sociality, and the culture of the community and the wider society. SNS provides a bounded space where users construct a semipublic or public profile by creating a list of other users with whom they share a connection or interest and, typically, share content. Ellison and boyd (2013) argue that while SNS has "evolved . . . their foundational activities—sharing content with a bounded group of users—are fundamentally the same."[12] To that end, presentation of self and targeted content distribution among an articulated group of connected users may likely "support more productive exchanges"[13] where accountability and motivation are more likely to be questioned.

As noted earlier, there is limited research on the Internet and, in particular, Facebook (FB) within the Caribbean. This is surprising given that in May 2012, there were 455,540 users of FB in Trinidad and Tobago, according to

Socialbakers.com, a global social media and digital analytics company. Daniel Miller's *Tales from Facebook* examines the use of FB through portraits of twelve FB users in Trinidad and is particularly welcome as it reiterates the importance of localization, communality, and solidarity as well as the role of FB in building and mediating forms of sociality within Trinidad culture.[14] *Tales from Facebook* shows that Trinidadians use Facebook to supplement and indeed to deepen personal relationships.[15]

Scholarly examinations of religion and its presence on the Internet are also increasing, attentive to the tension and complexity of the new media and Islam in local, global, and transnational contexts.[16] Muslims from a large variety of ethnic, linguistic, religious, and political backgrounds are using the Internet for discussing Islam and Muslim affairs and for apologetic or polemical reasons. Skovgaard-Petersen explored the use of new media by Egyptian theologian Yusuf al-Qaradawi.[17] Given the presence of the Muslim diaspora in the Americas, Europe, and the Pacific, the *'ulama* (religious scholars) have recognized the importance of the reach of their messages to those Muslims. No longer as in the nineteenth century do they have to visit and engage Muslims face-to-face; they now have virtual reach and contact with the Muslim diaspora through the Internet. Muslims' use of the Internet and social media to find and communicate religious information is also a growing subject of interest, as evidenced by an ongoing research project led by the Institute of Strategic Dialogue in the United Kingdom.[18]

Bobkowski in "Self-disclosure of Religious Identity on Facebook" investigated whether Christian young adults accurately self-disclosed their religious identities in their Facebook profiles and the extent to which social desirability might shape such self-disclosures.[19] He relied on interviews with five undergraduate FB users who were members of a religious campus group affiliated with an Evangelical Christian denomination. The results suggested that religious young people tend not to label themselves as "Christians" in their profiles, but they self-disclose their religious identities in the context of their offline activities and relationships. Furthermore, their religious self-disclosures or concealments are guided by social desirability and a concern to present themselves as moderate Christians.

SNS provides a space in which one can create a masked, blended, or exaggerated identity in a public sphere. At the same time, it provides a place for the production and consumption of information that is no different from information flows within physical spaces like the *masjid*. The Internet and SNS can be powerful tools for emphasizing "Muslimness" and a clearly articulated space to provide different and nuanced interpretations of Islam, thus creating additional opportunities for youth to explore and find alternative interpretations of Islam or to ask questions about Islam, offer an Islamic perspective on global affairs, and rationalize happenings in the Muslim world. These new forums operate in tandem with other forms of socialization and knowledge transfer—family, *masjids*, *maktabs*, lectures by Islamic scholars, among others—which can facilitate the extension of the Muslim self.

CULTURE, MEDIA, AND CONSCIOUSNESS

The increasing popularity of the Internet coincided with a new breed of believers who were being fashioned through the decade of the 2000s—Generations Y and Z.[20] The Internet provides an opportunity to alter and transform knowledge, perspectives, and behaviors using a multiplicity of approaches and may be increasingly seen as a social authority by the youth on issues and ideas relating to modernity. The creation of Web 2.0, which allowed for the creation and exchange of user-generated content, altered the relational top-down power. It provided a new ethos. As Best notes, "Because the world that we know is one that increasingly belongs to us, to others, and to our machines, our continued survival requires explorers."[21] For Generations Y and Z, this is the world in which they live and interact and which provides validation of ideas, opinions, and perspectives and through which they seek information on "taboo" issues. In fact, for boyd and Ellison, social network sites are Web-based services that enable their users to perform three activities: "construct a public or semi-public profile within a bounded system, articulate a list of other users with whom they share a connection, and view and traverse their list of connections and those made by others within the system."[22]

As active consumers and participants, youth are using new media as a means for agency and knowledge and to meet their needs for constructing a sense of self. Online interactive media further complicate the question of boundaries between inner self and the social world. Cyberculture and, in particular, Web 2.0 are major sites of activity used to construct and reinforce identity, knowledge, and beliefs as well as provide a mediated sphere of socialization. New media becomes a key factor in the lives of youth mediating socialization, knowledge, relationships, and identity. While individuals are free to create any variety of possible selves, the pool of possible selves derives from the categories made salient by the individual's particular sociocultural and historical context as well as from the models, images, and symbols provided by the media and by the individual's immediate social experiences.[23] Youth, argues Dolby and Rizvi,[24] are surrounded by a "dizzying array of signs and symbolic resources dislodged from traditional moorings that forces a (re)-thinking of their identity, [their] place within the Muslim community and the wider society."[25] In this regard, one is forced to acknowledge that youth have a multiplicity of identities that they juggle and jostle but ultimately unite to make a subject or person—female, daughter, sister, friend, student, Muslim, Trinidadian, and so on. Nevertheless, one cannot be reduced to a series of types of identities. The concept of possible selves is therefore multifaceted and malleable in space and time but with aspects that are continuous and stable.

Identities are often reproduced and influenced by a myriad of factors, sometimes in response to but often as a way of making a statement about perception of self, perception of self within peer groups and their various communities, including the local and global *umma* ([Islamic] community). It may be posited then that through cyberspace, young people become observers, consumers, and engagers in (re)defining and understanding the wider world that fuels and validates identities. This is similar to Kenway and Bullen's concept of "youthful cyberflaneurs," who see the object of the young cyberflaneur's inquiry as the global cultural economy and who uses the new technologies as tools to support that inquiry.[26]

The individual may be drawn to mediated experiences that interlace with his or her experience, lived reality, and choice of construction and projection of the self. The recontextualized experience via new media, while providing for socially shared meanings, is also about making sense of self, Islam, and the wider environment. Thus, it may be that the perceived absorption of media provides opportunities for youth to understand the self as embedded in Islamic communities while querying and seeking answers to difficult questions, challenging commonly held attitudes and stereotypes about Islam, and discussing "taboo" topics, thus creating virtual communities in their own right.

As cyberspace expanded and online forums were established by the *'ulama*, a mediated, if somewhat strategic, space was created where there were distribution and consumption of knowledge. But the relational power between producers and consumers remained. The engagement between the *'ulama* and the believers concerning ideas of modernity, particularly those that may be of interest to youth, remained somewhat conservative. And further, Muslim youth, particularly Trinidad's Muslim youth, are generally socialized not to question the tenets of Islam or contest the pervading status quo and ideology. At present, the new media facilitates small and gradual institutional change, thereby reinforcing the status of the *'ulama*, particularly in small and conservative countries like Trinidad and Tobago. The opportunity for what Coyne and Lesson call "punctuated change," that is, the media catalyzing rapid institutional overhaul, is somewhat delayed.[27] Thus, within the new media landscape there needs to be some catalyst or tipping point that can activate en-

Table 9.1. Facebook User Trends in Trinidad and Tobago

	Total number of Facebook users	Penetration (population) (%)	Penetration (Internet users) (%)
December 2011	442,520	35.89	90.91
May 2012	455,540	37.08	93.93
Change	13,020 (2.8%)	1.19	3.02

Source: Trinidad and Tobago Facebook Statistics, Socialbakers.com, December 2011 and May 2012.

gagement on issues of relevance to the youth. This will require consumers to alter their mental models and create pressure for the producers (in this case the *'ulama*) to make the corresponding change in the supply of knowledge, while the consumers continue to engage in dialogue by leveraging the tools of social media to build a common knowledge and reciprocal interest. As opinion providers and consumers shift in response to technological developments, the essence of long-held traditions of religious authority and interpretation will also shift to the consumer—the Muslim youth. In the meantime, there is likely to be measured but isolated dynamism from the youth through SNS contributing to marginal changes in engagement and conversations with the *'ulama* on issues of relevance to them as related to their faith and the practice of such in a fast-changing world.

Social networking is a popular medium of communication for young people today where people interact with pages, groups, events, and community pages and upload photos as well. Facebook is rapidly growing internationally and in Trinidad and Tobago. Globally, according to Facebook's statistics, there were more than 800 million active users, with more than 50 percent logging into FB on any given day at the end of November 2011, and by the end of March 2012 there were 901 million monthly active users with an average of 58 percent logging into FB daily. Based upon data from Socialbakers.com, the total number of FB users in Trinidad and Tobago increased by 2.8 percent of the population from December 2011 to May 2012 (table 9.1). Facebook penetration in Trinidad and Tobago relative to the country's population and Internet users also increased during the period and was 37.08 percent and 93.93 percent, respectively, by March 2012 (table 9.1). While cell-phone penetration rate is high, mobile Internet subscription remains low,[28] and users are dependent on hot spots and free public Wifi access points.

Figure 9.1 shows that between December 2011 and May 2012, those aged

Figure 9.1

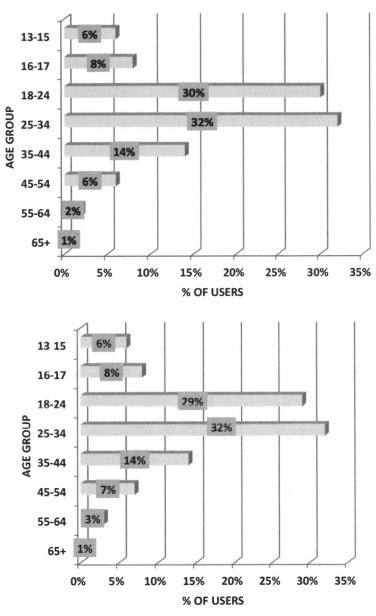

Source: Trinidad and Tobago Facebook Statistics, Penetration, Demography—Socialbakers. *Socialbakers Social Media (Facebook, Twitter . . .) Marketing, Statistics, & Monitoring—Socialbakers*. http://socialbakers.com/facebook-statistics/trinidad-and-tobago, December 2011.

twenty-five to thirty-four accounted for the largest group of users, followed by users aged eighteen to twenty-four. The biggest gain in the last three months (March–May 2012) was recorded by the age group of thirty-five to forty-four, which differs from the period October to December 2011, where the biggest gain in users was in the age group of eighteen to twenty-four. The study targeted persons eighteen to twenty-four, as discussed below, and falls within the fastest-growing group. It can plausibly be assumed that this age group will have at least a secondary-level education and will quite likely be pursuing or have completed a tertiary-level education. Age, Internet access, and "the level of mobile literacy (i.e., the ability to perform a variety of tasks on a mobile phone using a variety of mobile applications) among the general population"[29] will more likely impact the use of SNS. The number of male and female users remained constant from December 2011 to May 2012. There are currently 47 percent male users and 53 percent female users in Trinidad and Tobago.

However, data on Muslim users, particularly those of the diaspora, seem to be scarce, though it is probable that Muslims regardless of geography, ethnicity, linguistic, political, and religious backgrounds are using SNS to deepen personal relationships; interact with pages, groups, events, and community pages; upload photos; and possibly discuss Islam and Muslim affairs. In November 2011, specifically, Socialbakers.com showed that five Islamic applications featured in the top-fifteen ranking of "Lifestyle > Religion Apps" among active FB users. By April 2012 three Islamic applications featured in the top-fifteen ranking of "Lifestyle > Religion Apps" among active FB users (table 9.2). Although Qur'an Verse and Random Ayat remained in the top five, there was a decline in the number of users between November 2011 and April 2012. To that end, are fewer Muslims now accessing and using FB in Trinidad and Tobago, or are they masking religious self-disclosure through limiting access and use of daily applications?

METHODOLOGY

This study relied on sixty-two surveys administered randomly to Muslim students following *salat al-jum'a* (Friday prayers) at the University of the West Indies (UWI) in Trinidad and Tobago in November 2011. The timing of the administration of the survey is important. While it provided the best possible space to access the Muslim student population, it was distributed in a space and at a point when piety was likely to be high, thus influencing the responses. It, therefore, allowed the respondents to stress their "good Muslim" selves.

During the Friday prayers men are in the front rows, and women make up the last few. These prayers are incumbent for adult males, and, as such, males dominate in numbers. As a result, the returns on the survey were tilted toward them, with 69 percent male respondents and 31 percent female respondents. In terms of age, 76 percent were eighteen to twenty-two years old and 18 percent between twenty-three and twenty-seven, while 6 percent were from twenty-eight to thirty-five years old. In regard to ethnic and national origin, these respondents self-identified as 81 percent Indian, 6 percent African, 6 percent mixed, 2 percent Syrian-Lebanese, and 5 percent other. An estimated 90 percent of the respondents were single, while 7 percent were married. Of those surveyed, 85 percent were undergraduate students, and 11 percent were registered in postgraduate programs. Eighty-six percent considered themselves religious, and 14 percent saw themselves as not religious. Further, 41 percent identified themselves as very active in Islam, while 45 percent considered themselves somewhat active in the practice of Islam.

The focus group was highly suitable for the objectives of the survey. Eighty-five percent of those surveyed indicated that they were very comfortable using a computer, and 94 percent stated they accessed the Internet one or more times a day. Eighty-nine percent of the survey respondents indicated they had a social media account, with 90 percent of these indicating they had a FB account. Among those surveyed, 10 percent and 21 percent indicated they also held a MySpace and Twitter account, respectively. Among this group, 68 percent indicated that they accessed their account once or more a day, while 11 percent indicated they accessed their account a few times a week. Interestingly, 15 percent also had a Muslim-specific social media account with sites such as Naseeb, Muslimsocial.com, Salam, and AlWahy.

This survey was followed up by five interviews with undergraduate students to build on the views from the survey in November 2011. The panel of respondents was assembled through contact with the president of the University of West Indies Islamic Society (UWIIS)[30] and was drawn from its membership roster. Two males and three females were interviewed, ranging in age from nineteen to twenty-one. They are referred to here as Ibrahim (male, twenty-one, computer science and mathematics), 'Umar (male, nineteen, mechanical engineering), Yasmin (female, twenty-one, linguistics and humanities), Sarah (female, twenty-one, geography), and Maryam (female, twenty-one, chemistry and mathematics). Each interview was conducted face-to-face. Ibrahim and 'Umar were interviewed together, as were Sarah and Yasmin; Maryam was interviewed individually. All of the respondents knew each other through the Islamic society. Sarah and Yasmin, however, knew each other from high school as well. Interview lengths ranged from forty minutes to one hour.

The five interviewees used FB as their primary SNS, and all of them regularly logged onto their FB accounts. In the case of Ibrahim, he logged on

Table 9.2. Users of Facebook Applications—Lifestyle > Religion Apps (November 2011 and April 2012)

NOVEMBER 2011				APRIL 2012			
FB Applications (Lifestyle > Religion)	Religion	Daily Active Users	Monthly Active Users	FB Applications (Lifestyle > Religion)	Religion	Daily Active Users	Monthly Active Users
Qurʾan Verses	Islam	6,000	190,000	Dios Te Habla Hoy (God Speaks to you today)	Catholic/Christianity	10,000	100,000
Dios Te Habla Hoy (God speaks to you today)	Catholic/Christianity	20,000	130,000	Qurʾan Verse	Islam	2,000	40,000
Daily Tarot Cards	Occult/New Agers	3,000	40,000	Random Ayat	Islam	10,000	20,000
Random Ayat	Islam	20,000	30,000	Bíblia Diária (Daily Bible)	Catholic/Christianity	3,000	20,000
Bíblia Diária (Daily Bible)	Catholic/Christianity	3,000	20,000	Daily Tarot Cards	Occult/New Ager	2,000	20,000
Daily Bible Scripture	Catholic/Christianity	2,000	9,000	Biblia Na Każdy Dzień (Bible Every Day)	Catholic/Christianity	5,000	7,000
Daily Bible Scripture	Catholic/Christianity	2,000	9,000	Daily Bible Scripture	Catholic/Christianity	2,000	6,000
Madrid11	Catholic/Christianity	200	8,000	Dua	Islam	200	5,000
Biblia na każdy dzień statistics (Bible Every Day)	Catholic/Christianity	5,000	7,000	Yo Oro Por Ti (I pray for you)	Catholic/Christianity	60	3,000

Application	Religion			Application	Religion		
Dua	Islam	200	5,000	Tiempo Con Dios (Time with God)	Catholic/Christianity	200	2,000
Free Qur'an	Islam	200	5,000	Holy Synaxarium Bible	Catholic/Christianity	100	2,000
Synaxarium Bible	Catholic/Christianity	200	4,000	Életcseppek (Drops of Life)	Catholic/Christianity	100	1,000
Alkitab Hari Ini (the Bible Today)	Catholic/Christianity	300	3,000	Napi bibliai ige (Prisoners bibliai IgE)	Catholic/Christianity	200	1,000
Al-Qur'an Online	Islam	100	3,000				
Tiempo con Dios (Time with God)	Catholic/Christianity	400	3,000				

Note: The list provided here includes some examples of Facebook applications — lifestyle and religious applications.

Source: Religion Applications: Facebook Statistics, Socialbakers.com, December 2011 and May 2012.

"multiple times a day, once by the computer," while ʿUmar accessed his account "once a day." Yasmin logged onto her account "sometimes once a week, sometimes once a month . . . because of time and because of lack of access to internet at home," while Sarah accessed her account "every day—more than once, including weekends." Maryam indicated that she accessed her account "three times a week."

LIMITATIONS OF THE STUDY

The survey was administered following the Friday prayers at a point when piety was high. Thus, the responses may have captured an exaggerated level of piety. Further, the *salat al-jumʿa* is incumbent on adult males, and, as such, it was not surprising that there were more male respondents, reflective of the nature of the congregation and space. Due to the nature of the group, this survey captured mostly males aged eighteen to twenty-two, hence gender or age differential analysis was not undertaken, although from a cursory look no apparent gender differences were revealed. The small sample of this research, and the fact that most interviewees were members of the same Muslim student association, are the most obvious drawbacks. The interviews and surveys provided some insight into the lives of the respondents. Further research should draw upon larger samples to generate richer accounts of how young people's religious identity is being (in)formed or aided by SNS, taking into consideration socioeconomic variables such as parental educational background and religiosity as well as the religious socialization of the respondents.

DISCLOSURE OF RELIGIOUS IDENTITY

Seventy-six percent of the respondents indicated that they disclosed their religious affiliation on SNS. When further interrogated about why they disclosed this information, the respondents indicated it was related to identity and *daʿwa* (denotes the preaching of Islam). For the respondents who identified *daʿwa* as their main objective for disclosure, they wanted to "shar[e] my Islamic views with others" and "spread the teaching of Islam." For those who disclosed they were Muslims because it is an intrinsic part of their identity, they indicated that "they were proud to be Muslim"; "because I am a proud Muslim and not afraid to show it"; "I love my religion. Islam is the best!"; "being part of who I am"; and "I am honoured to receive the gift of islaam [*sic*]." For others, it was more a question of identity as it relates to association and beliefs. As such, the respondents indicated "because I let people know the real me"; "don't want people to see me trying to be false to myself"; "so the persons associated within my account know my beliefs"; and "would like to let people know who I am and what I am upon." Some respondents were more explicit in the responses, saying that they "like to let people know about my religion beliefs so that they would respect my decision and also so that neither they nor myself would be influenced by any other religion or otherwise"; "I am not ashamed or shy about being Muslim so I like people to know that I am Muslim so that I can portray Islam in a good way as I know it to be"; and "I am not afraid to show my religious views" and "will not compromise Islam for anything for respect."

The interviewees also disclosed their religious views, indicating that on their FB profile pages they indicated "Muslim or Islam." They further indicated that they did not identify sect because they hold the view that "Muslim[s] should be about an entire unit and not about sects; Muslims are not about following a certain sect of the religion—they should be one"; "it is the religion of the Prophet Muhammad (u.w.b.p.)"; "the right way for any Muslim is to follow Qur'an and the Hadith, the main sources of information"; and there is "too much controversy saying one Sunni or Shi'i—a kind of tension [develops] if it is found out you are a different sect—so I stay away from that."

Of those surveyed, 73 percent indicated that they use their sns account to post religious messages. This can be interpreted as an articulation of portraying themselves as true and real to the public. Respondents were asked to identify the types of Islamic messages they would post on their profiles. Of the responses, 52 percent indicated hadith, 47 percent *ayah* from the Qur'an, and 53 percent Islamic greeting or wishes. Ibrahim also noted that he would post quotations from Islamic poets such as Boonaa Mohammed or Islamic video clips from YouTube.

ENGAGEMENT AND AGENCY IN THE USE OF SNS

Muslim youths use sns like many others—to communicate, to connect, and to organize. Generally, they connected and reconnected with friends; communicated with family and friends; shared stories, photos, images, and music; built consciousness about a particular cause; discussed religious issues; played games; organized events (e.g., mosque events); connected with classmates for study projects; and discussed Islam. The uses of sns reflect the real-life activities within and across various locales.

Thirty percent of respondents indicated they use sns to discuss Islam. Though open to exchanging ideas about their religion, they also recognized that other users were less than likely to engage them. 'Umar, for instance, indicated that "people come with their own perception and so listening and openness to new ideas do not really happen. . . . [I]t's just a focus on the problem, the solution is forgotten or not taken into consideration. Those who used Facebook to discuss Islam acknowledged that others might avoid engaging them.

By and large, SNS has provided a platform for people to share more information and different kinds of information more openly and with more people. SNS, according to Maryam,

> give[s a] certain amount of freedom; it allows you to post anonymously—so, yes, it gives you that freedom. It is a little tight because you cannot say certain things, it brings up a whole new discussion . . . and say you say something [bad] about something and someone can then post something bad about you because it's a view they don't share . . . so a certain amount of freedom.

Consequently, one has to be cautious about what and how something is said. Ibrahim notes that in discussing aspects of Islam, "some issues cannot stand alone it has to be substantiated so it not smart to put up things that require additional explanation." The extent to which Yasmin and Sarah felt that SNS allowed them to discuss and comment on ideas on Islam was mediated by a sense of group security and trust. As such, ideas on Islam were discussed among Muslim friends or within certain Muslim groups that the users traversed based upon shared notions about Islam. That said, Yasmin and Sarah felt there was a space on SNS to challenge the negative ideas on and about Islam. Emerging from this narrative is the notion that SNS is providing not so much an open competitive or alternative space but one that coexists along with the traditional socializing spaces—homes, *masjids*, *maktabs*—and both challenges and complies with already well-established norms and hierarchies.

When asked specifically about what they discuss on Islam, the results were interesting. As indicated, the *maktabs* focus on building Islamic knowledge. There are limited spaces for discussion of contemporary issues or those impacting the community, particularly the youth or the practice of the faith. Sixty percent of the respondents from the University Islamic Society indicated they used SNS to discuss misperceptions about Islam. Given the public perception of the *hijab* (head covering worn by Muslim females) as a symbol of female oppression, absence of freedom, and its association with cultural and political beliefs, it is not surprising that the subject of veiling was discussed on SNS by 40 percent of the respondents. The respondents also used SNS to discuss misconceptions about women in Islam (35 percent) as well as gender equality and Islamic feminism (26 percent). These issues also stir the public imagination and spur debates on the role and status of Muslim women and the influence of Islam as religion and as culture on the lives and lived realities of women. Nineteen percent indicated that they discussed issues of marriage, and 6 percent discussed divorce.

Yasmin indicated that while she does not really use SNS to post information about Islam, she would comment on statements posted. Her point of view is informed by the Qur'an. However, in responding to the misperceptions of women in Islam, she noted:

> [As] much as [people] want to make women's rights in everything—patriarchy will always be there. With the advent of Islam women were allowed a batch of rights, it was always something present in the Islamic world, but it is new to Western world. So, there are issues . . . in context of countries baby girls are killed, women are denied inheritance, issues with polygamy and so on but Islam gives women rights. . . . People do not know how to interpret Qur'an and Hadith.

Maryam indicated that she would discuss misperceptions about Islam, particularly regarding a general aspect about Islam. She noted there are often misunderstandings and fascination relating to topics such as women in Islam, polygamy, and *hijab*, so she has "done a lot of research so I can answer questions or make comments" on SNS that would be in line with Islamic perspectives. Some issues such as sexuality, dating, marriage, and divorce Maryam indicated she would discuss but only with selected people on SNS.

Thirteen percent indicated they discussed taboo Islamic topics, such as sexuality. The issue of homosexuality did not emerge in the interviews. When asked, there were hesitancy and discomfort among interviewees. At the same time that homosexuality in Islam is considered a sin as well as a crime under Islamic law, there are also gay Muslims. Interviewees acknowledged their presence. In fact, there was a reference to Daayiee Abdullah, the first openly gay imam in the American Muslim community ("First Openly Gay Imam to Launch a Website"). Though there was no indication that women leading prayers would be discussed via SNS, there was a corollary in a conversation that noted women leading *salat* is acceptable only insofar it is a women-only group. Reference was made to all-female mosques with female imams in China.

Twenty-one and 10 percent of the respondents indicated they used their SNS to discuss human rights and poverty, respectively. These lower numbers belie the solutions and measures provided for Islam to alleviate poverty and the understanding of human rights.[31] Maryam noted that she would discuss the issue of poverty through the Islamic lens of *zakat* (obligatory form of charity) and *sadaqa* (voluntary act of giving alms).

Many young people globally, as in Trinidad and Tobago, use SNS as a form of activism and engagement and an expression of consciousness. The aspect of political Islam and political movements seems to be of lesser interest to members of the society. For instance, only 8 percent indicated they discussed the Arab Spring on their profile, while 13 percent discussed jihad (struggle). On issues such as these, Maryam indicated she would stay away, as she would where debates need to be informed by Shari'a (Islamic law) and *fiqh* (Islamic jurisprudence). There is a growing body of academic and market research that suggests individuals who are in their midtwenties and younger are civic minded and are creating their own brand of social consciousness, influenced by several global events (such as terrorist attacks, large-scale natural disasters, and so on), informed by media and new media. The extent to which the interest in global affairs is knowledge driven is a given, but that in turn relates to access to information informed by knowledge and social connectivity. Perhaps, more important, it relates to the confidence of young Muslims to openly discuss these issues. One must also consider that the Muslim youths interviewed from the UWIIS came of age in a world in which Islamophobia was present, and this may act as a constraint to their voice. Trinbagonians (citizens of Trinidad and Tobago) have clear notions of self that are constructed and deployed in private or public domains and even clearer ideas that opinions on religion and politics should be cautiously discussed, if at all, in the public sphere. This message, in particular, may likely permeate discussions relating to political Islam and political movements by young Muslim youths on SNS.

As noted earlier, the spiritual manifestations of Islam form the core of knowledge transmission at *maktabs*. SNS opens space, albeit limited space, based upon the views of respondents for discussion and commentary on Islamic practices, contemporary issues, and political Islam. Ibrahim noted that he is generally "careful of what information I take from people. I read Islamic articles to benefit myself [but] from trusted and authentic sites." The interviewees acknowledged they would engage in self-directed seeking of information through trusted scholars' websites and the Qur'an and hadith. However, they preferred to seek the opinion of *'ulama* and imams directly as it relates to *fiqh*. Once again, SNS simply provides an additional space and medium for the continuation of dialogues that already exist in the Islamic public sphere.

RELIGIOUS MODERATION

My research also focused on the social desirability of presenting oneself to the public as it relates to religion. I therefore sought to answer questions regarding the kind of persona that is presented to the public, one's negotiation of self within the public sphere, and one's positioning of self and persona vis-à-vis others. In a world where young men and women are more educated and increasingly incorporating ideas about modernity into their lives, it is likely that notions of modesty may become more fluid as it is subject to market logic. Female public presence will be refashioned by their ideas of modernity as well as their participation in the labor force and social consciousness and activism. To that end, there will be a continuing mix of responses ranging from reactionary to liberal with regard to modesty and virtual modesty as the understanding of these issues changes to meet new demands and challenges. Hence, modesty will be shaped by an individual's sense of personhood and self. The gender dichotomy about modesty and virtual modesty among Muslims will persist as it is influenced by faith. In fact, several hadith stress the connection between faith and modesty; "Modesty and faith are interlinked: if either of them is lacking, the other is lacking too." In this case, modesty is shaped by Islamic principles or the great tradition, as documented by Celia E. Rothenburg.

As noted earlier, there are varying positions regarding whether the use of sns is *halal* (permitted) or *haram* (not permitted). Such perspectives provide rich fodder for asking Muslim youth about their views on the use of sns. In this instance, 82 percent felt that the use of sns was *halal*. Ultimately, respondents felt that the purpose for which sns is used determines whether it is *halal* or *haram*. For instance, one person indicated that sns "is good for *da'wa* but not very Islamic in terms of close adherence to Islamic etiquette." For Maryam, "it is acceptable, in my opinion; we are living in the twenty-first century. It [sns] is a means of spreading and getting information on Islam, accessing certain information—know what we are about and use it for the right purpose—what we suppose to do." Yasmin said, for instance:

> [I] do not see why it's not [*halal*] if you're using in a positive way—once adhering to rules of Islam—post up things about Islam. But if not . . . example putting up haram photos, loose speech, a girl not talking to too many boys. Another problem is time wasting and time wasting is haram when one could be reading salat.

Of the options given regarding what contributed to making sns *halal*, the respondents surveyed indicated the following factors made sns permissible: sharing messages, opening up topics for discussion, posting video clips on Islam (55 percent); learning more about Islam (55 percent); connecting with the *umma* (50 percent); refuting misinformation about Islam (50 percent); engaging in *da'wa* (48 percent); and strengthening *iman* or faith (27 percent). Conversely, individuals who considered sns *haram* said that it distracts one from being productive (31 percent) and that it is filled with *fitna*, which connotes temptation of events and activities (31 percent) and distracts one from spending time for the sake of Allah (29 percent). Respondents also indicated that SNS causes one to devote energy to an activity that promotes self to the outside world, that it makes *iman* weak, and that it endangers the Muslim family.

Ibrahim and ʿUmar adamantly felt their real and virtual personae match and that Islam defines their character and their activities. In that regard, ʿUmar said he is selective of the places he goes, so he would not "go anywhere that is compromising to Islam." Ibrahim noted that "a lot of photos are posted on FB," and, as such, he tries "to be careful with the crowd I hang with; I assume photos are taken and will be posted therefore I am careful." He also noted that he has Muslim and non-Muslim friends on FB, and if and when non-Muslim friends tag him in photos that are not Islamic he would untag himself. When asked how that has affected friendships, he indicated he would explain his reasons for untagging and his friends understand. Maryam, for instance, noted that she exercises discretion both in real and in virtual life, and, further, "Islam guides my choices on what I put or do not put on my profile." This distinction by FB users regarding their participation in *halal* activities and activities they were photographed in as participants reflects an appreciation of Islamic standards of modesty.

Seventy-nine percent of the respondents felt there should be a level of self-determined virtual modesty, as it relates to photographs and images of self and friends on FB. Modesty, or *haya*, is an intrinsic part of Islam and relates to behavior, speech, and appearance as well as being mindful of God at all times, as articulated in several hadith. As Ibrahim noted, Islam emphasizes modesty for everyone. Some females, he said, wear the *hijab* and put up compromising photos of themselves; modesty is for everyone, but it weighs less on males than on females. Modesty should exist in the real and virtual worlds. Sarah, on the other hand, noted:

> Modesty is personal and is related to socialization and is dependent on choice. So, someone may post nude or half naked photos of themselves or at parties. [One] can tell them but it's a choice, you can't force them to do it. You associate with people—their positive aspects. You remember that your way is your way and their way is their way.

Maryam believed that virtual modesty is "very important. . . . [I]t is defeating the purpose of modesty in regular life and then posting non-modest things in your profile. Having *hijab* in your regular and daily life and not on FB does not make sense—it conflicts—makes you a hypocrite."

Modesty is seen as nonnegotiable in the Islamic ethos that has been internalized by the respondents. Modesty thus becomes intimately connected with notions of the self, the body, and community, as well as with the cultural construction of identity, privacy, and space.[32]

Young Muslims are quite active on social media in nuanced ways. They reflect the complexity of negotiating multiple identities of age, sex, and religion, which are already mediated by living in a multiethnic and multireligious society. On FB they were likely to have both Muslim and non-Muslim friends, participate in multiple and different groups, as well as engage to varying degrees in dialogue and commentary. This included "liking" (a button where a user can express that he or she likes, enjoys, or supports certain content) Islamic (79 percent) and non-Islamic pages (60 percent). Their online presence is as rich as it is diverse. For instance, 63 percent indicated they were a member of non-Islamic groups on FB, while 61 percent indicated they were members of Islamic groups on FB.

Membership in the UWIIS student group was common among the respondents, given that they were at the university and the Islamic society was the *umma* in that particular spatial context. They were also members of various local Islamic organizations that had a FB or Twitter presence in which it can be assumed they and their families were affiliated. Additionally, they were members of Islamic educational groups such as AlBaseerah, Ahlusunnahtt, and Markaz al Ihsaan, among others. Applications such as Arabic Word of the Day and Daily Qur'an/Hadith were used by the young Muslims on campus, none of which featured on the top fifteen "Lifestyle > Religion Apps" used by Trinidadians on Socialbakers.com. Not surprisingly, then, based upon usage and engagement, 81 percent of respondents believe that SNS is and can be a powerful tool for *da'wa*.

Interestingly, those who did not join a Muslim-specific group on SNS indicated that there was "too much conflict in local Islamic groups: both real and virtual [as well as the] lack of mature people to manage," and "the groups are generally negative. . . . They do not provide an avenue for me to learn about my religion." Another respondent noted that "I choose not to because I don't want other members of the group [to] add me and then criticize me about not being a good Muslim because of FB activities." Among the more pedestrian responses were there was no opportunity, hard to find interesting ones, never got invites, or never stumbled across one. Yet 85 percent indicated that SNS can motivate individuals to be closer to the *deen* (religion), and 85 percent also indicated that it can aid in *taqwa*.

SNS can build bridges of understanding and assist in building and enhancing knowledge and consciousness of causes, but it is providing additional means of engagement and social connectivity. Inasmuch as SNS influences social connectivity and engagement, it can also shape faith consciousness and religiosity. Fifty-five percent of respondents indicated that SNS positively influenced their interpretation of Islam because of the social connectivity that can be established through SNS and the wide array of knowledge zones available to build and enhance their understanding and knowledge of Islam. Some 16 percent indicated that SNS negatively influenced their interpretation of Islam. This is because of extremism, the bombardment of negative images of Islam, and the presence of Islamophobia that lends itself to many prejudices against Muslims. Among the views articulated was that there are "many wars going on in Muslim countries [and that is] affecting [people's] views of the *umma*." Some people, it was remarked, "don't care all that much for Islam and are more keen to the modern way of life." Additionally, SNS influences one to believe things that are not Islamic. These contribute to the escalation of "*fitna* which causes problems between people or create chaotic situations that tests one's faith." It was also felt that "a lot of rubbish is being done and said on it—blasphemying [*sic*] of Islam."

At the same time, 56 percent affirmed that SNS positively influenced their view of the *umma*. Respondents noted that the "Muslim *umma* can be very productive and hence can show the rest of the world what Islam is about," and there were "many good reports of Muslims doing good things for people around the world [that] shows how many Muslims truly care about Islam." They also suggested that Islam is growing, with "many people taking Shahada [declaration of faith]." Some also spoke less of the deeds of Muslims and more of the sense of connectedness: one respondent reflected, "I now know how many of us there are and no longer feel alone in my faith," and another felt "connect[ed] with a mass number of Muslims." This sense of connectivity and seeing Muslims through a mediated lens led to a strengthening of "their *iman*."

CONCLUSION

As a bounded user, the focus is on self-presentation and targeted content distribution within a profile or within a closed or open group, and thus the Muslim user may more than likely seek to present herself or himself in an "Islamic way," living Islam, but mediated by living in a modern society. The research group participants were all members of the secular University Islamic Society, and thus they were negotiating and contextualizing Islam within that milieu. SNS also includes sites of secularization and, as such, may not embody Islamic values. Gen Y and Gen Z users are likely to see SNS as value laden but, nevertheless, access and use it for information seeking and exchange and interpersonal connections—deepening existing connections or extending connections. Young faith-conscious people are likely to integrate SNS into the practice and exploration of their faith. In this regard, SNS can function as both bridging and bonding mechanisms within a social networking system.[33] Within the bounded space, participants see themselves as part of a broader community that diffuses information and provides opportunity for debate and discussion that may not otherwise be deliberated.

This research asked, "To what extent is religious identity among Trinidadian Muslims formed or informed by SNS?" The survey questionnaire and interviews focused on self-disclosure and self-identification, religious moderation, and religious engagement in the use of SNS to extrapolate how religious identity and *taqwa* were shaped or molded by SNS.

The Internet allows users to be in control of their public personae. At the same time, one has to filter these disclosures through the lens of social and religious desirability—the audience to which the young Muslims are playing on their SNS profiles. Since SNS is young people's means of communication and connection with friends, it is not unrealistic that religious identification and references would appear in their online profiles.

They were proud to be Muslims. Group debate was present on issues relating to religious identity, religious moderation, and engagement on and with SNS. Despite the global perception of Islam as it relates to a political Islam, the young Muslims contacted in this study were not ashamed to be Muslims. They did not mute or hide their religion or religious views. Their virtual lives were reflective of or an extension of their real lives by their very social connections and connectivity as well as activities. As such, the respondents in this study portrayed themselves as both real and authentic. It must not be forgotten that adherents tend to perceive Islam as a way of life, and, consequently, the norms, values, and mores of being Muslim were reflected in their virtual lives as they negotiated the virtual environment. In fact, it was an actualization of their Muslim identity. Muslim youth demonstrated that among their possible selves, the Muslim self remained continuous, constant, and stable. As such, there was no contestation of controversial or taboo issues that would remotely contradict existing *fiqh*. Bobkowski, in a similar study among Evangelical Christians, found that youth were unlikely to disclose that they were "Christian" in their profiles and presented their religion in an effort to present themselves as moderate Christians.[34] In stark contrast, my study found that Muslim youth used SNS to further define and refine their politics or codes through Islam as a way of life. The marking of religious identity on SNS may be seen as a public and political action by these young Muslim adults.

Consistent with online personae, it is possible that the respondents may be indicating an exaggerated online religious identity, a carefully controlled performance of the presentation of self before an audience. Consideration needs to be given to the continuum of religious identity from nominal to practicing that would inform religious engagement. This would also influence and mediate religious conversations with their peers. Further, the national and local environment including the socializing institutions (family, *masjids*, and *maktabs*) would also inform their online identities. Given the multicultural and multireligious nature of Trinidad, citizens give expression to their religious identity in various ways. The Muslim presence is neither muted nor contested, and as such youths may feel more empowered to express their religious identity rather than negotiate it. Social desirability may play a role, but it is more likely that it is the consciousness and awareness of the omnipresence of Allah (God) that ensure the congruence between their public and private selves and their real and virtual lives.

In general, these individuals carefully posted scripts and photos that gave validation to their Muslim identity. It was these cues that served to define them in the public eye, and they also served as indicators for the public to engage them. It should be recalled that some would delete or untag themselves if they felt the content was *haram*. Arguably, they took advantage of the asynchronous nature of online communication to adjust their profiles to better reflect what they considered to be their real selves, informed and mediated by Islam.

This chapter served as an exploratory assessment of how young Muslims' religious consciousness is (in)formed, aided, and mediated by sns. As young people, digital natives, incorporate new media into their daily lives, the amplifying of religious socialization may become more relevant and meaningful. In the meantime, they are somber and selective "youthful cyberflaneurs," defining the parameters of the use and engagement with sns. They balance what they perceive as inauthentic to Islam in a nonconforming environment to their ideals and ideas. The findings presented here suggest a group of young people who are highly religious and desire their personae and profiles to accurately reflect the role that religion plays in their lives. They strive to present themselves as authentically religious, an affirmation, reiteration, and celebration of their identity as Muslim. In actualizing the Muslim self, they sustain their *deen* and *taqwa*. Despite being surrounded by a "dizzying array of signs and symbolic resources," they were not "dislodged from traditional moorings."[35] They constructed public profiles of self that portrayed them as "good Muslims" and within a space that allowed them to traverse connections defined by the faith and their politics. For the most part, they saw sns as playing only a small part in their religious formation and identity and consciousness.

It was seen as a positive influence on their perception of Islam and the *umma*. While sns has the potential to reconfigure religious socialization, faith, and consciousness, it is still in the formative stage. In the meantime, the family, *masjids*, *maktabs*, and lectures by Islamic scholars will remain an intrinsic contributor to the development and sustaining of the *deen*, and thus sns, at this point in time, adds another medium to the formation of an Islamic identity.

NOTES

I would like to express my appreciation to Afeef Ali-Mohammed of the University of the West Indies Islamic Society for arranging the administering of the surveys and the interviews. To those who participated, I would also like to express my appreciation. To Andrew Nakawaza, who compiled the data for me, and Dr. Perry Polar, who assisted with the data verification and editing, I would like to say thank you.

1. John Voll, "Muslims in the Caribbean: Ethnic Sojourners and Citizens," in *Muslim Minorities in the West: Visible and Invisible*, edited by Yvonne Haddad (New York: Altamira, 2002).

2. With regard to the presence of African Muslims in Trinidad, see Brinsley Samaroo, "Early African and East Indian Muslims in Trinidad and Tobago," in *Across the Dark Waters: Ethnicity and Indian Identity in the Caribbean*, edited by David Dabydeen and Brinsley Samaroo, Warwick University Caribbean Studies (London: Macmillan, 1996).

3. Halima-Saʿadia Kassim, "The Crescent in Trinidad and Tobago: Building Community" (unpublished manuscript); Halima-Saʿadia Kassim, "Institutionalising Islam: Community Building and Conflict in the Caribbean," paper presented at "The Global South Asian Diaspora in the 21st Century: Antecedents and Prospects" (University of the West Indies, St. Augustine, Trinidad and Tobago, 2011).

4. Voll, "Muslims in the Caribbean."

5. Halima-Saʿadia Kassim, "Rings, Gifts and Shekels: Marriage and Dowry within the Indo Muslim Community in Trinidad, 1930 to the Globalized Present," in *Bindi: The Multifaceted Lives of Indo-Caribbean Women* (Kingston: uwi Press, 2011), 52–97.

6. The four distinct phases of reconstruction are as follows. First, the late nineteenth and early twentieth centuries were besieged with fluidity, as the local Muslim community struggled to assert itself through community building characterized by the building of mosques and the growth of member-driven community-specific organizations and associations under the Friendly Societies Ordinance (e.g., the Islamic Guardian Association, East Indian National Association, and East Indian National Congress). Second, the period of the world wars (1914–1945) witnessed the creation of separate communal organizations, articulation and advocacy of local Muslim concerns, and development of transnational links through the visits of missionaries. Third, the mid-twentieth century saw the growth in the attractiveness of modernization and Westernization, which were difficult to resist, and by the 1960s many younger Muslims, especially those with a secular education, became assimilated into the wider society. There was also the continued development of transnational links through the visits of missionaries and revitalization of Islam and the Muslim community in general. The establishment of Muslim denominational schools continued. There was continued formation of the organizations aimed at showcasing Islam as compatible with

modern-day life. Finally, the period commencing from around the 1970s onward witnessed a new dispensation. It was one that was service oriented, modernistic, yet faith driven, and the development of organizations reflected that ethos. In the early twenty-first century, the thrust was to engage and appeal to Muslims via media and new media. This period also saw the continued development of transnational links through the visits of missionaries and study abroad.

7. This is based on the onion model, as posited by Clifford Hofstede, a cultural anthropologist.

8. The passage of the Education Ordinance no. 10 of 1948 allowed non-Christian incorporated bodies recognized by the state to establish schools and receive state aid. To this end, the Muslim community embarked on school-building exercises throughout the country.

9. *Taqwa* literally means to protect and could be that one protects oneself from the wrath of Allah by protecting oneself from indulging in things that Allah forbids. It signifies the obedience to the rules of Islam while avoiding *haram* and additionally abstaining from unsuitable things in life. Muslims are to be guided by the love of Allah (God) and the willingness to obey what Allah has mandated in the Qur'an. In the Qur'an the idea of *taqwa* is mentioned extensively as the way Muslims should live their lives in order to please God and attain success in this world and the hereafter. Several verses in the Qur'an state that the path to happiness and fulfillment in this world is letting *taqwa* guide daily decisions. *Taqwa*, thus, is often used in the context of God consciousness.

10. The Joshua Project Progress Scale is an estimate of the progress of church planting among a people, group, or country. The project indicates that the estimated population of the Syrian-Lebanese community is twenty-seven hundred; the primary religion is Islam, in particular Sunni Islam; and the percentage of Christian adherents is more than 5 percent. See People-in-a-Country Profile, Joshua Project, http://www.joshuaproject.net/people-profile .php?rop3=109662&rog3=TD.

11. Kassim, "Rings, Gifts and Shekels."

12. N. B. Ellison and danah boyd, "Sociality through Social Network Sites," in *The Oxford Handbook of Internet Studies*, edited by W. H. Dutton (Oxford: Oxford University Press, 2013), 159.

13. Ibid.

14. Daniel Miller, *Tales from Facebook* (Cambridge: Polity Press, 2011); Rhianne Jones, "Book Review: Daniel Miller, *Tales from Facebook*," *Cultural Sociology* 6, no. 1 (2012): 129–137.

15. Brian Alleyne, "Review of Daniel Miller's *Tales from Facebook*," Academic.edu, http:// goldsmiths.academia.edu/BrianAlleyne/Papers/1552462/Review_of_Daniel_Millers_Tales _From_Facebook_Polity_2011_.

16. Göran Larsson, "Oxford Bibliographies—Islam and the Internet," http://oxford bibliographies.com/view/document/obo-9780195390155/obo-9780195390155-0116.xml.

17. J. Skovgaard-Petersen, "Profetens Jihad," *Carsten Niebuhr Biblioteket* 6 (n.d.): 9–12.

18. The "Muslims in the European Mediascape" Research Project (2010) is conducted in partnership with the Vodafone Foundation Germany and the British Council and explores the complexity of media used and produced by Muslims and non-Muslims in France, the United Kingdom, and Germany. The project also investigated the diversity of media production and programming and its relationship to intercommunity attitudes. The research will take an in-depth look at identifying the relationships between social cohesion and trends in the use and production of media in view of key variables, including socioeconomic background, education, gender, ethnicity, religion, generation, personal and private intercul-

tural relationships, and age. See Monika Metykova, "Muslims in the European Mediascape Research Project," http://www.strategicdialogue.org/islam-diversity-social-cohesion/muslim -media-research/.

19. Piotr S. Bobkowski, "Self-Disclosure of Religious Identity on Facebook," *Journal of Communication, Culture & Technology* 9, no. 1 (2008).

20. Curwen Best, "Cyber Reach: Caribbean Gospel (and Religious) Culture (Version 5.0)," In *The Politics of Caribbean Cyberculture* (New York: Palgrave Macmillan, 2008), 51–89.

21. Ibid.

22. danah m. boyd and Nicole B. Ellison, "Social Network Sites: Definition, History, and Scholarship," *Journal of Computer-Mediated Communication* 13, no. 1 (2008): 210–230.

23. Richard Elliott and Kritsadarat Wattanasuwan, "Consumption and the Symbolic Project of the Self," In *European Advances in Consumer Research* (Provo, UT: Association for Consumer Research, 1998), 17–20.

24. Nadine Dolby and Fazal Rizvi, *Youth Moves: Identities and Education in Global Perspective* (New York: Routledge, 2007).

25. Douglas Bourn, "Young People, Identity and Living in a Global Society," *Development Education and Research* 7 (Autumn 2008).

26. Ibid.

27. C. J. Coyne and P. T. Leeson, "Media as a Mechanism of Institutional Change and Reinforcement," *Kyklos* 62 (2009): 1–14.

28. Telecommunications Authority of Trinidad and Tobago, *The Digital Divide Survey: Trinidad and Tobago, 2013* (Barataria: Telecommunications Authority of Trinidad and Tobago, 2013).

29. Ibid.

30. The UWIIS at the St. Augustine campus of the University of the West Indies, in Trinidad, was formed in 1969. The society comprises a mix of undergraduate and postgraduate students, university staff members, and alumni. The UWIIS is open to Muslims and non-Muslims and hosts several religious, fund-raising, and social activities.

31. See the following articles for discussion on poverty and human rights in Islam: Ibrahim M. G. Sahl, "Challenging the Concept of Poverty: Does Islam Provide a Solution?," *Societal Studies*, no. 3 (June 2009): 217–248, http://societal.societystudies.org; and Allamah Abu al-'A'la Mawdudi, "Human Rights in Islam," *al-Tawhid Journal* 4, no. 3 (Rajab-Ramadhan 1407), http://www.islam101.com/rights/index.htm.

32. Fadwa El Guindi, *Veil: Modesty, Privacy and Resistance* (Oxford: Berg, 2003).

33. Ellison and boyd, "Sociality through Social Network Sites," 159.

34. Bobkowski, "Self-Disclosure of Religious Identity."

35. Bourn, "Young People, Identity and Living."

PART III

ISLAM LATINA/O

DIS-COVERING A HISTORICAL CONSCIOUSNESS: THE CREATION OF A US LATINA/O MUSLIM IDENTITY

HJAMIL A. MARTÍNEZ-VÁZQUEZ

FINDING MATERIALS ABOUT Latino Muslims is not always easy. As observed by Juan Galván (executive director of the Latino American Daʿwa Organization, or LADO), "Most information on Latino Muslims comes from Latino Muslim organizations instead of academia, which has essentially ignored them."[1] Given the absence of major academic research exploring US Latina/o Muslims, these Muslims' voices have been mostly absent from discussions about both US Latina/o religion and Islam in the United States. While some magazine articles have explored certain aspects of the social location of US Latina/o Muslims within the larger Muslim community, there was no in-depth analysis on conversions or the way they reorganize their lives after. Furthermore, since Latina/o religious experience in the United States up until now has largely assumed Christianity as the de facto religion, this community is hardly ever mentioned.

In the pages that follow, I introduce some details about US Latina/o Muslims, their conversions, and the way they revisit the past in order to make sense out of their decisions. As the centerpiece of this chapter, the dis-covery of this historical consciousness speaks to the identity reconstruction of this religious and ethnic group in the United States. I use "dis-covery" here to suggest a process of uncovering that which has been covered up by history and by those in power. Dis-covery is not the process by which someone finds for the first time a land or an idea. It should be understood as a process in which the subjects realize that covering up has been part of their past. As I have stated elsewhere concerning "dis-covery": "It serves the marginal, the subaltern, in the quest for an identity, a self-identity, different from that which has been placed upon her/him by the people who covered up the memory. It is a way of breaking away from the colonial heritage imposed on knowledge."[2] Thus, dis-covery becomes a process of uncovering and re-creating the subaltern's past and memory, and US Latina/o Muslims are the subaltern in this chapter.

LOCATING THE US LATINA/O MUSLIM COMMUNITY

US Latina/o Muslims constitute a group that even today is in its nascent stages; they are only beginning to construct their identities. While the American Muslim Council estimated that in 1997 there were forty thousand Latina/o Muslims in the United States, and while in 2006 Ali Khan, national director of the American Muslim Council in Chicago, claimed that this number had increased fivefold to two hundred thousand, most current conservative estimates suggest that the US Latina/o Muslim population is somewhere between seventy-five and ninety thousand. Not surprisingly, the densest populations of US Latina/o Muslims can be found in cities with higher US Latino populations, such as New York, Chicago, and Los Angeles. Though there are a number of US Latina/o Muslims who were born into Islam, for the most part this community is made up of converts. Juan Galván, executive director of LADO, describes this community as follows:

> Interestingly, Latinas are more willing to convert than Latinos, many of whom are too afraid to change. According to Samantha Sanchez's research, most converts are college-educated, between the ages of 20 and 30, and female. By far, the vast majority of Latino Muslims are Sunni. According to LADO's outgoing SLM project, most Latino Muslims are married and have more than one child. As is true of most Latino families, Latino Muslim families are traditionally larger than their American counterparts, which helps explain the community's rapid growth. It is not only about individuals converting; it is about entire families embracing Islam.[3]

While this is by no means a homogeneous group, US Latina/o converts do share common conditions of marginalization and stereotyping, or simply invisibility, both within their own ethnic and racial group as well as within the broader society. Their religious affiliation has opened the door to confront these conditions and has brought people together. This trajectory reflects what other US Latina/o communities usually experience when they arrive in the United States. Being misplaced, out of place, such individuals feel a sense of anomie, but they often find support within religious organizations that share their national or ethnic identity, including language, thus providing them with a community that offers nourishment and a sense of belonging. US Latina/os who have converted to Islam likewise typically felt religious anomie and disenchantment within Catholicism or other Christian churches, but after their conversion they create organizations, albeit sometimes virtual, that allow them to build and become part of a community.

In order to understand the present condition of the US Latina/o Muslim community and its growth in the past decade and a half, one cannot look into a single factor but rather must consider this growth as the result of multiple conditions and situations over the course of time. Khalil Al-Puerto Rikani in his article focusing on the Puerto Rican community in New York entitled "Latino Conversion to Islam: From African-American/Latino Neighbors to Muslim/Latino Global Neighbors" finds that there are five different ways US Latina/os come to Islam: Puerto Rican and African American interactions, the Internet, Latinos living among immigrant Muslims, prisons, and mar-riage.[4] He suggests that together these five ways explain the growth of the US Latino Muslim community.[5]

The first way is intrinsically related to the relationship between the Latino community and the African American community in the United States through the civil rights struggle and its connections to the Nation of Islam. While this connection to the Nation of Islam is less strong now than it was during the height of the civil rights movement, there are nonetheless some US Latina/o Muslims who come to Islam through the Nation of Islam. At the same time, some argue that, "on an ideological level, [US] Latino Muslims have been profoundly influenced by their African-American counterparts, adopting similar ideas of spiritual self-discovery and emancipation in their approach to Islamic theology."[6] This contact with African American Muslims during the civil rights era was particularly notable in big cities such as New York, where a group of Puerto Rican converts "involved in anti-war protests, civil rights protests, and Puerto Rican nationalist movements" founded la Alianza Islámica in 1975, the first grassroots Latina/o Muslim organization in the United States.[7]

Second, the boom of the Internet in the 1990s has connected individuals and communities that probably would not be in contact otherwise. This medium of communication has allowed for US Latina/os to make contact with Muslim groups and has allowed US Latina/o Muslims to actually create their own groups and establish *da'wa* (invitation to Islam through educa-tion) to other US Latina/os, especially younger generations.[8] This fits with anthropologist Karin van Nieuwkerk's argument that "many [US] American converts relate that the Internet was a very important medium in their search for information about Islam," and in some cases, "without the Internet they might not have become acquainted with Islam."[9] The Internet has thus proved to be an important mechanism in the establishment of US Latina/o Muslim communities across the United States, as it has provided a vehicle not only to learn about Islam but also to create a community.[10] Like other Muslims in Western societies, US Latina/o Muslims find in the Internet avenues to share their stories and as "converts can realize themselves not only by testifying to their conversion, but also by finding a place to belong."[11]

Third, interest in Islam among many US Latina/os increased at a time when the religion was at the forefront of the nation after the events of 9/11. Mainstream attitudes in the United States after 9/11 located Muslim immigrants at the margins of society, as "nonpersons." US Latina/os are quite aware of this condition of living as "nonpersons," so US Latina/os who converted to Islam after 9/11, especially in big cities, may have done so out of a sense of solidarity with these other immigrants and their religion. Rikani suggests that "most [US] Latinos have come to learn about Islam primarily from their interactions with immigrant Muslims" and that these interactions triggered conversions to Islam.[12]

Prison and marriage are other significant dimensions of conversion examined by Rikani, and they "are not restricted to any particular time period."[13] In prison most US Latina/o conversions to Islam are related to US African American conversions. This type of conversion, while not the most evident among the US Latina/os during my fieldwork, is important to understand because the conversion to Islam offers prisoners "an activity structure including such features as prayers and lessons, and an alternative social space within the confinement of the walls."[14]

Finally, in the case of marriage, while Rikani offers different examples of US Latinas who converted due to marriage, he finds that such conversions have "not occurred as often as marriage to non-Latino Muslims."[15] These conversions through marriage do not follow a single paradigm, as the conversions happen in different ways.

CONVERSION TO ISLAM

Growing up, I remember talking about (Christian) conversion as an event, a particular decision an individual makes.[16] But van Nieuwkerk makes the case that "conversion takes place in several stages and is usually experienced as a substantial transformation of religious, social, and cultural aspects of daily life."[17] In this sense, conversions to Islam should not be understood as a particular event, even when there is an actual moment when the convert officially becomes a member of the religion (*shahada*). "Conversion to Islam is embodied through taking up new bodily practices pertaining to praying, fasting, and food. In addition, important markers of identity are often changed, such as the name and appearance, including *hijab* or occasionally *niqab*."[18] US Latina/os who convert to Islam thus go through a process that cannot be explained as a simple change of religion.

Conversions to Islam are unlike many conversions within Christianity, specifically Protestantism, whose focus is on an event that took place at a particular place and time. They don't fit within "the Pauline paradigm of sudden, dramatic change," which "combines notions of an unexpected flash of revelation, a radical reversal of previous beliefs and allegiances, and an underlying assumption that converts are passive respondents to outside forces."[19] US Latina/o Muslims speak about their conversion—or what they call reversion—as a process of being involved in an active search.[20] This search takes many forms, and every path is different. "This warns us not to essentialize Islam [or conversion to Islam], but to systematically analyze whatever elements of Islam have to offer diverse groups of converts at different times."[21] The coming to Islam for these individuals is a path, a movement toward something new.

There are multiple reasons US Latina/os, or any individual, convert to Islam. The different motives for conversion that Yvonne Yazbeck Haddad identifies among US American women include an "intellectual connection to Islam," being "captured by the Qur'an," as well as "negative experiences the converts had had with Christianity."[22] US Latina/o Muslims refer to such motives to explain their conversions and likewise narrate them as a process.

In "Converting: Stages of Religious Change," Lewis R. Rambo and Charles F. Farhadian propose that since "converting is a process, a stage model is useful in portraying phases of a process that takes place over time."[23] This stage model is constituted by seven phases, and while I agree with the authors that "this stage model must not be seen either as unilinear or as universal," the model does nonetheless help us understand the process of conversion in a more organized way.[24] The first stage, *context*, speaks to the time and place where conversion happens. This is followed by the *crisis*, characterized by events or experiences of displacement. The third stage, *quest*, is a response to that crisis as it becomes a search to find locality and meaning. This ties into an *encounter* stage, defined by contact with someone who advocates a particular view that can help in the quest for meaning. This encounter acquires meaning as the *interaction* stage starts and the potential convert begins to relate to the newfound religion in order to reconstruct his or her identity. This reconstruction leads into the *commitment* stage in which the convert chooses to accept new religious ideals. Whether or not aware of the last stage, *consequences*, the convert measures the effect of his or her decision within a given social location.

Though this type of model helps us analyze the process of conversion, a more nuanced approach is necessary in order to examine the multiple narratives of conversion by US Latina/o Muslims. In particular, the encounter precedes the quest and not the other way around. For US Latina/o Muslims, the encounter with another person marks the start of a potential convert's quest. As a result, the interaction is another aspect of that quest, so I do not see it as a separate phase. With such changes in mind, let me offer a brief analysis of these dynamics in the process of conversion among US Latina/o Muslims.

There is no one particular context that serves as background to explain the bulk of the conversions to Islam since the individuals live not only in different places but also within multiple social contexts. Some conversions begin at school, work, or the military. But there are three particular characteristics that are important to mention, because while they are not universal, they indeed help us understand the general contexts in which these conversions happen. First is the relationship between urban space and conversion, as it is in this context where, regardless of their age, many entered a process of conversion. This is the setting where there is a higher contact and exchange between cultural or religious groups, so individuals are more exposed to this diversity.

The second aspect that facilitates the understanding of a general context is Christianity (mostly Catholicism, in the cases I document here). This milieu is critical because it has established particular norms within the members of this community about their religious identities. It is in contrast to these expectations that converts evaluate their process of conversion. Their new religious experience is compared with this Christian setting, and in many cases it is disenchantment with this milieu that prompts them to seek a new religious experience. Third, the function of movement should be recognized as an important aspect of the context. Movement does not only refer to migration across national borders, even though that is obviously a central aspect of it, but also refers to the aspect of constant movement by US Latina/os within their own cities or across states. Two major issues force these movements: family and work. This situation may create some instability in a person's life, and this in turn can open the door for considering new perspectives, like a new religion.

Within these contexts, most US Latina/os who convert to Islam experience a type of disenchantment within their established religious communities, mostly Christian, and that is what generates a crisis. While they sought concrete answers to questions about theological issues, they were often "troubled by confusing and complicated theological notions in Christianity."[25] They felt that Christianity, mainly Catholicism, and its leaders failed to address "the perennial doctrines that have set the two faiths apart: the concepts of incarnation and Trinity, the divinity of Jesus, crucifixion, and the doctrine of original sin."[26] For example, Sonia, a US Latina Muslim in Chicago, explains that she was Catholic, "muy católica" (very Catholic), and that after high school she entered a convent in order to become a nun.[27] After some months in the convent, she found herself more lost than before she entered, disenchanted not only with the convent but also with the church and its doctrines. She remembers often asking the priest about the Trinity and other mysteries within Catholicism and that not only did she get no particular concrete answers, but the priest also told her to accept the religion without questioning it.

Sonia looks back at that time as her crisis. Rambo and Farhadian refer to this stage as a "catalyst for change," as it forces the individual to look for something new.[28] A crisis develops from those experiences that disrupt one's status quo. In the case of US Latina/o Muslims, as shown by Sonia, crisis is often described as disenchantment that leads to spiritual anomie. Spiritual anomie refers to the feeling of an individual (or group) who can find neither tangible nor existential answers within her or his religious group, and this generates not merely doubts and suspicion but mostly a lack of meaning. People express this spiritual anomie through doubt regarding religious ideas and "mysteries," as well as through abandoning religious institutions.

After leaving the convent and visiting a Pentecostal church, Sonia started to work in a department store in Manhattan, where she lived at the time. Most of her fellow employees at the store were Muslims, and with that contact and exchange, Sonia became interested in learning more about Islam. Sonia's story is not uncommon; many US Latina/os have their first encounter with Islam through their workplace. For example, Elena and Carol, two US Latinas in Los Angeles, learned about Islam from Muslim colleagues in their respective jobs. This type of encounter represents the typical first contact most US Latina/o Muslims describe as they narrate their conversion stories. Their encounter with a coworker, a friend, or a family member who invites them to read the Qur'an and learn about Islam becomes the initial proactive phase in the process of conversion. These encounters should be seen as part of the da'wa in which Muslims are always engaged. Haddad explains the importance of the encounters, arguing that "while the articulation of Islam and its teaching for Westerners is important in appealing to seekers, crucial for many of the converts were their initial encounters with Muslims—friends, classmates, boyfriends, spouses, acquaintances, and neighbors who took the time and had the patience to explain, to mentor and guide."[29] For the most part, these encounters take place in private settings and not as part of some public activity—which is not to say that the encounters are not in some way proselytizing action.[30] The private setting is the essential aspect of this stage, as these interactions happen usually through close-knit relations and sometimes through one-on-one relations.

These encounters acquire significance because many US Latina/o Muslims, after their own encounter, began an examination of Islam, "a quest for knowledge or spiritual fulfillment."[31] For example, Marta, a US Latina Muslim from Chicago, narrates that after the initial shock of witnessing her daughter's conversion, she followed her daughter's advice and started to read the Qur'an, or, as she puts it, "no lo leí, me lo bebí" (I did not read it, I drank it).[32] She read it every day until she was done with it, and this provoked a process of searching. Through this search she became an active participant in a quest, as she sought "to maximize meaning and purpose in life."[33] After the encounter US Latina/o Muslims speak about a period when they not only read the Qur'an but also start studying Islam through reading other materials and especially through conversation with Muslims—in other words, through both personal and communal actions. It is because of such searching that this conversion to Islam could be considered "primarily intellectual" when compared to the emotional aspect of Christian conversions.[34] But this consideration does not do justice to the actual spiritual engagement within the quest. Yasin Dutton argues that this is one of the most difficult things to address because there is a tendency to argue "that Islam appeals by its 'rationality' and that an unbiased study of the texts will—or should in theory—lead to the reader becoming Muslim."[35] For US Latina/o Muslims, it is important to address the spiritual character of their conversion, because while they speak of the rational aspects of their decision, most maintain that it was "by a recognition of the heart."[36] In any case, the quest of US Latina/o converts to Islam becomes a process of searching, and the religion where they found some answers enables them to confront their crisis.

Once individuals find their way out of their spiritual anomie, they are ready to make a formal decision for a particular religious system, a commitment. As Lewis Rambo states, "commitment is the consummation of the conversion process," and it "empowers the convert with a sense of connection with God and the community."[37] Those converting to Islam affirm their commitment by taking the *shahada*, which consists of a public declaration of faith "in front of witnesses."[38] US Latina/o Muslims make this commitment after a long quest, but the ways these decisions are made vary considerably. On the contrary, most, if not all, individuals in my research talked about the *shahada* as something that they needed to do, but they did not all follow the same process. After all, the commitment to Islam involves more than the ritual of taking the *shahada*.

After conversion, "it is expected that anyone entering Islam will neither drink alcohol nor eat pork or meat of any incorrectly slaughtered animal, and will respect the basic prohibitions relating to such matters as stealing, committing adultery and/or fornication, murder, and so on."[39] At the same time, there is an expectation that individuals will adopt a Muslim name, participate "in transformative rites such as a Muslim pilgrimage to Mecca," and "particular clothes" will be worn by women in particular.[40] These expectations played out in different ways and at different times among converts. For example, people often adopt dietary restrictions as a first response to conversion and later change their names and plan a future pilgrimage. For women, wearing the *hijab* (head covering) is an important step, one unique to women; male converts do not have to so quickly and publicly make known their decision. As Haddad points out, "Consistently the *hijab* seemed to be a bigger issue for families and friends than the conversion itself," since "this visible display of Islam was seen as too radical," and their "family members were often concerned about what neighbors and other people would think about the change in wardrobe."[41] Even further, US Latinas who convert to Islam are aware of what will be expected of them as Muslim women, and these issues are part of their search and decision-making process before taking the *shahada*. They are ready for the stereotypical attitudes, exemplified in the common discourses about Islam and its treatment of women, that lead to the immediate marginalization of these women because of the way they look.

These changes may be seen with suspicion by the larger US Latino community, challenging those who consider converting. Transformations in diet and dress thus affect not only the spiritual aspects of converts' lives, but also their relationship with others, especially with their families and other US Latina/os. As consequences of taking the *shahada*, US Latina/o Muslims become aware of these issues during their quest and prepare to confront those outsider reactions to and stereotypes about Islam.

While the spiritual side is usually developed through prayer and conversation with the imam and other members of the religious community, the reactions of family and friends of the convert tend to focus on the convert's redefined identity. Most US Latina/o Muslims experience challenges (questioning, confrontation, even ridicule) from the larger US Latino community because of what it considers radical changes in lifestyle. They are seen, in many cases, as losing their culture and *latinidad*, their Latino/a identity. Hence, these individuals find themselves as outsiders within their own communities or, as Michelle Al-Nasr states:

> becoming estranged to the same people that you have known all your living years. All of the sudden, you are the outcast, the lost soul who doesn't have enough sense to know what you are doing, everyone is telling you that you are throwing your entire life away.[42]

They have become Other even to those with whom they consider themselves to be most closely affiliated. Public perspectives regarding Islam shape most of the responses by community and family members.

After the events of 9/11, the media's stereotyping and misrepresentations advanced the prejudice and marginalization of US Latina/o Muslims within the Latino community in the United States. They are looked at with distrust, especially by older generations of US Latina/os. Although many families respect one's decision to convert, most US Latina/o Muslims have to contend with suspicious responses from these and other societal domains. The responses of those closest to the convert vary considerably; some are extremely supportive, while others totally marginalize the convert, often simply buying into well-worn orientalist stereotypes. For example, the experience of Iris and Marta, in which the daughter's conversion led to the mother's, while not uncommon, portrays only one aspect of the consequences US Latina/o Muslims deal with after conversion within their families.

"¡Santísimo! ¿Y qué es lo que le pasa a esta muchacha?" (Holy! What is wrong with this youngster?).[43] These were the words Sonia heard her dad say the first time she came out of her room wearing her *hijab*. Her mother instantly stopped him and said, "No, déjala, que eso se le va a pasar" (No, leave her alone as that will go away).[44] Well, "it" did not go away, but as time went by, while still not totally on board with the change, her family did become accustomed to the idea of Iris's conversion. For Iris, the turning point came during her first celebration of Ramadan. When her family saw her fasting, they became much more conscious of her commitment and were so respectful that they would not allow anybody to eat in front of her. This is the type of experience most of the younger generations of converts speak about. Though at the beginning their family members would typically be surprised and would even make fun of them, after some time most of them would realize that it was a decision that transformed their loved one's life for the better.

Other individuals are forced to be silent and not discuss their new faith with family members. Yolanda, a young woman from the Bay Area in California who studied for two years before converting to Islam, struggled for a long time to tell her family. Before telling them, she wanted to learn as much as possible in order to be comfortable explaining her decision. Her family "wasn't very happy" when she revealed her decision, and even months after she told them, they still do not want to talk about the situation.[45] She observes that the problem is that they "don't understand about the religion yet," as "they view it from the media's perspective."[46] Yolanda confronted the same attitude among some friends, so she decided that it was better not to say anything.

Yolanda's story is not unique. Julio, who also converted after two years of reading the Qur'an and other literature on Islam, while reflecting on his family's reaction to his conversion, says, "They told me they don't want to know anything about it. So, I just respected that and we have a good relationship."[47] He reflected upon the situation and reached the conclusion that the principle of "don't ask, don't tell" would be the best way to keep a civil relationship within his household. This is how he lives his life even among friends: he does not tell them about his conversion unless they ask him. Sometimes he avoids hanging out with them in order to avoid the conversation and the awkwardness of the situation. This reaction seems understandable in light of the reaction many US Latina/o Muslims have experienced. I personally feel that for them, it is not a way of hiding who they are, but really avoiding unpleasant times and in some cases even argument.

BEYOND CONVERSION

The process of conversion to Islam for US Latina/os does not end with taking the *shahada* and its consequences. In fact, it is often then that the greatest challenges begin. As stated above, US Latina/os have become Others within their communities and families, and thus they are forced to reconstruct their identities in order to make sense of their decision.

After conversion—the path through which most US Latina/o Muslims come to Islam—Latina/o Muslims in the United States follow a process in the construction of their identities that is based on the dis-covery of cultural memory through religious experience. This dis-covery points to the fact that the act of remembering is not only an individual and social activity; it also incorporates a cultural aspect that in turn adds a dimension of "lived experience" to the representations of the past, much like a ritual does. Through the use of cultural memory, history is no longer a narrative of the past in a vacuum, but a link between the past and the present. This means that people look at themselves as part of a history and "passing on" (or transmitting) that history, those memories, to others. They look at the history of Muslim Spain as the source of those dis-covered cultural memories that serve in the process of identity construction. As Lisa Viscidi finds, "Many Latinos who convert to Islam believe they are reclaiming their lost Muslim and African heritage—which they view more positively than the legacy of Catholicism."[48]

The conversion to Islam offers the opportunity for US Latina/o Muslims to "remember" history in order to make sense of their culture and religion as nonexclusive. In other words, because US Latina/os are mostly identified by their Catholic (or at least Christian) roots, US Latina/o Muslims feel pressure to forge an identity that puts together their ethnic (or national) characteristics and their religious experience. As an outsider, it seemed to me that the members of this community do not have a choice, as they are forced to reidentify themselves. This reidentification alludes not only to the changes that conversion brings like eating habits, changing one's name, or wearing the *hijab*, but also to the process through which US Latina/o Muslims have to reinvent themselves as people. Conversion brings about a change in worldview, not just a transformation of practices. As Rebecca Sachs Norris acknowledges, "Conversion involves not just adopting a set of ideas but also converting to and from an embodied worldview and identity."[49] Since US Latina/o Muslim converts for the most part were raised within a particular Christian worldview that has informed the development of many US Latina/o identities, it is important for them to develop a historical consciousness and dis-cover a new cultural memory that serves as the core of their process of new identity constructions.

REVERSION: GOING BACK

Historian Alberto Hernández explains that US Latina/os "have looked back upon their Iberian cultural and family heritage with an ambivalence not easily understood by persons of Anglo-European or Germanic ancestry."[50] The ambivalence developed from the connection that the Iberian heritage has with "the trappings of Spanish conquest and colonial exploitation."[51] "Colonization" and "conquest," thus, have become the particular terms that describe the history of Spain's relationship to Latin America. On the other hand, US Latina/o Muslims, who do not dispute this colonial narrative, look to Spain in a different way because they look also at the history of Spain that comes before the colonization and conquest. They are interested in reconstructing the traditional and normative narratives to dis-cover cultural memories about Islam that have been hidden. These memories have been buried by the Catholic tradition imposed through the colonization and conquest of the Americas. When independence had been achieved by much of the hemisphere by the 1830s, "Spain and its history was marginalized by intellectuals and nationalists touting the racialized nineteenth-century discourses of Western European civilization."[52] The contact and exchange between three cultures—Muslim, Jewish, and Christian—generated a mixed society, a hybrid reality, which placed Spain outside of the paradigm that European modernity created. Describing this situation, Hernández states that "when the intellectual and literary canon of European civilization was constructed by nineteenth- and early-twentieth-century Euro-American intellectuals, Spain was marginalized for not being 'white' enough and still too mired in a latent 'medievalism' to have benefitted from the ideals and objectives of the Enlightenment."[53]

US Latina/o Muslims reinterpret the history of Spain beyond its relation to Latin America. They argue that the presence of Islam on the Iberian Peninsula, far from negatively impacting Spain, is what positively marks the country and the lands it colonized. The focus on the richness of this forgotten history not only allows for the reconstruction of historical consciousness through the dis-covery of cultural memories, but also leads US Latina/o Muslims to create a cultural identity that is itself perceived to be "hidden" or "covered." Thus, after conversion US Latina/o Muslims go through a series of steps that mold their identities in this way. They transform their personal lives, and they "go back" and re-member (or assemble) those silenced elements of the past in order to transform normative historical consciousness and help explain how their conversion actually fits their *latinidad*. Dis-covering the memories of the Islamic presence on the Iberian Peninsula, US Latina/o Muslims understand their conversion as a process of "going back" to the roots of what it means to be a Latina/o. For this reason, most US Latina/o Muslims refer to their process of conversion as a process of reversion, a process of returning. Even though "reversion" is a term that is used by most Muslim communities, for US Latina/o Muslims it takes on an added dimension in light of the historical reference to Islamic Spain. US Latino Muslim Yahya 'Abu Ayah' López explains this process:

> When we said that we "reverted" back to Islam, we therefore were, in effect, saying that we had returned, migrated back, or come home to our original condition from which we had been tragically separated in years past. After voluntarily returning to that primordial form, we then joyfully "embraced" it. We had realized, via our cognitive evaluation, its true worth and held it tightly within our arms, not wanting to let it go again.[54]

In other words, reversion represents not a stepping away from their cultural and historical background but an actual recovering of their past and the "forgotten" (dis-membered) heritage, a Muslim Spain. This "going back" tends for the most part to romanticize Moorish culture and history. As community leader Edmund A. Arroyo explains, "The Latino Muslim conversion can often be traced to this rediscovery of their ancestral roots."[55] This is a way of looking at the past in order to dis-cover a "new" cultural memory, hidden behind colonial discourses. Thus, the term "reversion" becomes essential in the way conversion folds into identity formation. It explains not only the religious "going back" to Islam, but also "going back" to the Muslim roots in the Latino cultural memory.

The concept of reversion allows us to see beyond the natural changes US Latina/o Muslims go through and understand how they go beyond describing their conversion. With this concept and understanding of "going back," they address the criticism of and challenge to their *latinidad* posed by other members of the US Latina/o community. US Latina/o Muslims typically find many similarities between Islamic and Latina/o culture, rather than seeing them as opposites or distant from one another, as do many outside this community. Establishing these connections is only the first step in the process of building an identity, which is founded in cultural memories that are in need of dis-covery. At the same time, there is a historical consciousness being developed out of these dis-coveries. When asked about how she reconciles her reversion with her Latina identity, María, a US Latina Muslim from New York, clearly establishes that reversion has actually reinforced her understanding of her *latinidad*:

> I feel it is reinforced because in my perspective I am actually going back to my roots. I think people who are Christian, who are Catholic, have gone away from their Latino roots because we have our roots in Spain. We have our roots in the Moors. Our language contains Arabic words. Our morality, our chivalry, the men, their protection, how they are with their women and with their families, that comes from the Arab, from the Moors. So, I think I am reinforced. I think I am in an uphill battle because some people's perspectives are now the norm and that is what I am dealing with. But I do not feel displaced or like I am going against my Latino roots.[56]

Many US Latina/o Muslims share this same perspective and look at this history as the basis of their new identity. Like María, some will challenge the Christian privilege within history and argue that it is in the Moorish tradition that one can find the actual roots of *latinidad*. This discussion regarding the role Muslim, and even Jewish, traditions play within the history of Spain has been a topic of dispute among historians and philologists since the nineteenth century. While I will not thoroughly analyze the entire dispute or manage to do justice to its complexity, even examining just a few aspects of it helps us to understand why this "going back" makes sense for US Latina/o Muslims' identity construction.

BUILDING ON THE PAST

US Latina/o Muslims focus their attention on such memories in order to demonstrate the central role Islam plays in their historical consciousness and for that matter in their identity formation. In this regard, Juan Galván states that "Latinos today are still influenced by Islamic Spain" and that, "for example, thousands of Spanish words are derived from Arabic."[57] This claim of Muslim Spain's continued relevance for many finds evidence in words like *ojalá* that derive from the Arabic *insha'allah* (God willing) and words that begin with *al* like *almohada*, which come from *almuhádda* (pillow). Raheel Rojas, a US Latino Muslim writing in the *Latino Muslim Voice*, focusing on this perspective about Muslim Spain being at the core of US Latina/o identity, makes a plea to US Latina/o Muslims who doubt their *latinidad*:

> What can be more Latino that being Muslim? Spain was predominantly Muslim for 800 years. The shining light of Islam belonged to people who spoke Spanish, mashallah. Europeans came to Spain to learn sciences. Spain brought the renaissance of Christian Europe. Islam spread in Spain through the reversion of the indigenous people not mass immigration of Moors as they have you believe.[58]

In this sense, Muslim Spain becomes the center in the process of the reconstruction of identity. Kenny Yusuf Rodríguez, a Dominican Muslim, argues that most Latina/os who criticize Islam do so because they may have "forgotten that Islamic and Spanish cultures were once closely knit," and he goes even further to link Islam in Spain and Latin America as he stresses the Islamic influences not only in language but also in architecture.[59]

In the same way, Ramón Omar Abduraheem Ocasio declares, "We are reclaiming our history after a 500-year hiatus" because "Catholics never successfully stripped the Moors of their identity," and thus "we are the cultural descendants of the Moors."[60] These claims help establish the importance of Islam for US Latina/o culture. While some, like María, offer a critique of Catholicism, most US Latina/o Muslims highlight Islamic culture in Spain as inclusive. US Latina/o Muslims seek this dis-covery: Islamic Spain as a culture of tolerance, which is part of Spanish identity and civilization. It has been hidden by the preponderance of Spanish narratives that emphasize only the "Occidental" aspects of its history, thus stressing Catholic perspectives. In discovering hidden stories and reconstructing narratives, US Latina/o Muslims seem to take a romantic approach to Islamic culture, but at the same time they try to underscore that the Spanish Catholic history of colonization cannot be understood without a full comprehension of the interactions between multiple cultures.[61]

Their attitude seeks to resonate with Spanish Muslims and Moriscos (Muslims or descendants who converted or were forced to convert), who after 1492 resisted the imposition by those in power (Christians) of a national myth that left Al-Andalus and Islamic tradition out of the picture, a myth that "veiled its divisive regionalism and sacralized its origin in the Crusades of the Reconquest."[62] Historian Mary Elizabeth Perry maintains that as part of the challenge to that national myth, Muslims "claimed their own myths of the past," which allowed them "to resist oppression and reclaim their position of honor and power."[63] The confrontation of these two myths created a debate regarding the legacies that served in the construction of Spanish identity, which resulted in the evolution of what Perry calls contested identities, each based on a different myth. The struggle between these contested identities forced those in power not only to expel Muslims and Jews from Spain but also to reinforce the myth of a Catholic, Occidental Spain, leaving the "Other" (Muslims and Jews) outside of the myth. US Latina/os, who after conversion to Islam no longer recognize themselves in the official history, reclaim that Islamic myth and create a space of contested identities among US Latina/os.[64] In the process of reconstructing their identity, they seek to dis-cover the Islamic tradition embedded within *latinidad*. This process of reconstruction is comparable to the process undertaken by US African American Muslims, who through their own *da'wa* search deeper into the past in order to make sense of their social condition and create new identities. This message "raised the consciousness of [US] African Americans about their history, including the fact that many of them were descendants of Muslims who had been forcibly converted to Christianity."[65] They look at the history of slavery in order to find a historical consciousness that makes sense and gives them meaning (cultural memory), in the same way that US Latina/o Muslims look at the history of Islam in Spain to obtain their own cultural memory.

After conversion US Latina/o Muslims no longer have legitimacy among the larger US Latina/o community. Because of the labeling and stereotypes created by those in power and internalized by the people, US Latina/o Muslims are left outside of the normative paradigm of what constitutes a Latina/o. While ethnically they fit the oversimplified conception of what a US Latina/o is, their conversion threatens to strip them of a historical consciousness, a past, that could support their actual "membership" within this community or that fits the traditional narratives. At the same time, because they have felt some marginalization among the larger Muslim community, US Latina/o Muslims find themselves "in-between." They see themselves as part of the two different communities, the Latino and the Muslim, yet they are at the margins of both. They become the "Other." This reality triggers their search of the past and the dis-covery of a historical consciousness. The normative historical narratives did not make any sense to US Latina/o Muslims because they were excluded, or at least marginalized, from them. As Guillermo Araya Goubet states, "History achieves its full meaning only when it creates an adequate awareness of the past in a community that recognizes that past as its very own."[66] Only through the "re-membering" of the Islamic past and the deconstruction of the normative narrative based on the colonial Catholic tradition can they see a history that actually makes sense and is comprehensible from their social and cultural location.

The act of remembering is essential in the process of identity construction, which is intrinsically related to the way stories are constructed and the knowledge they create. For example, for US Latina/os who are seeking identities independent from that imposed by normative stories fixed by stereotypes and labeling, the use of memory becomes essential. For US Latina/o Muslims, it becomes even more essential, since the process of remembering confronts not only the normative history but also colonial discourses embedded within the US Latina/o culture. The act of remembering and building a historical consciousness becomes a subversive enterprise when we use it to escape the stereotyping process and instead use it in our self identification process. Using memory as subversive activity uncovers the fragmentation within historical narratives. While normative historical discourses are portrayed as linear and continuous, memory breaks that illusion, not in order to create a new continuous discourse but to reveal history as an ever-changing discourse. As Juan Flores argues, since "the process of memory is open, without closure or conclusion: the struggle to (re)establish continuities and to tell the 'whole' story only uncovers new breaks and new exclusions."[67] The decision turns out to be between remembering and forgetting. Both are processes of selecting what to remember and what to forget, but the act of remembering works against the metanarratives used to label and marginalize people and, for that matter, to break down the power they convey.

US Latina/o Muslims decide to remember and "go back," dis-cover cultural memories, and create new representations that connect their new lives, after conversion, and a past that is not invented or somebody else's but their own. This uncovered past becomes a lived experience and the source of the creation of an identity that provides meaning to their conversion and legitimizes their religious experiences. US Latina/o Muslims argue that they should not be marginalized because some perceive them as "going against" their own culture, because they see themselves as essentially retrieving and then transforming that culture rather than abandoning it. Certainly, it would take some time to construct a clear US Latina/o Muslim identity, but through the dis-covery and the re-membering of the Islamic past, the path toward self-understanding is created, challenging the traditional understandings of US Latina/o identities.

NOTES

1. Juan Galván, "Who Are Latino Muslims?," *Islamic Horizons* (July–August 2008): 30.

2. See Hjamil A. Martínez-Vázquez, "*Dis*-covering the Silences: A Postcolonial Critique of U.S. Religious Historiography," in *Nuevas Voces/New Voices: Horizons in U.S. Hispanic/Latino(a) Theology*, edited by Benjamín Valentín (Cleveland, OH: Pilgrim Press, 2003), 55. I am using the term *dis-covery* following María Pilar Aquino's conception. See María Pilar Aquino, "The Collective 'Dis-covery' of Our Own Power: Latina American Feminist Theology," *Hispanic/Latino Theology: Challenge and Promise*, edited by Ada María Isasi-Díaz and Fernando F. Segovia (Minneapolis: Fortress Press, 1996). Writing from the standpoint of Latin American women, she states, "The five hundred years of European presence in Latin America have served not so much as an occasion for imagining what our history actually was or could have been but rather as an occasion for a continuing *dis-covery*." She goes on to say, "The great European invasions did not *discover* but rather *covered* whole peoples, religions, and cultures and explicitly tried to take away from natives the sources of their own historical memory and their own power" (241).

3. Galván, "Who Are Latino Muslims?," 29. SLM stands for Survey on Latino Muslims.

4. Khalil Al-Puerto Rikani, "Latino Conversion to Islam: From African-American/Latino Neighbors to Muslim/Latino Global Neighbors," *Latino Muslim Voice* (April–June 2008), http://www.latinodawah.org/newsletter/apr-june2k8.html#3.

5. Rikani forgets to mention that some US Latina/os are Muslims not as the result of conversion, but as the result of being the child of a Muslim parent. While these individuals are not the majority within the present US Latina/o Muslim community, in the next decade or so nonconvert US Latina/o Muslims will be a strong and larger part of this community.

6. Hisham Aidi, "Olé to Allah: New York's Latino Muslims," http://www.beliefnet.com/story/9/story_996.html?rnd=543. The clearest example of this connection is the focus on Africa as the place where their roots lie, even though ancestors of US Latina/os went through Spain before getting to northern Africa. We will analyze this focus on the Moors (Muslims in Spain) later in this chapter.

7. Ibid.

8. *Da'wa* refers to the dissemination of Islam, which compares to the term "proselytizing." But there are differences because, as Yvonne Yazbeck Haddad states, "the goal of da'wa is to win the individual to the truth, not to win the argument." See Yvonne Yazbeck Haddad, "The Quest for Peace in Submission: Reflections on the Journey of American Women Converts to Islam," in *Women Embracing Islam: Gender and Conversion in the West*, edited by Karin van Nieuwkerk (Austin: University of Texas, 2006), 22.

9. Karin van Nieuwkerk, "Gender, Conversion, and Islam: A Comparison of Online and Offline Conversion Narratives," in *Women Embracing Islam*, edited by van Nieuwkerk, 113.

10. The Internet is so important that even Juan Galván, executive director of the Latino American Da'wa Organization (LADO), wrote an article about the importance of the Internet, giving advice about how to use it for *da'wa*. See Juan Galván, "*E-Dawah*: Fun-

273 HISTORICAL CONSCIOUSNESS 273

damentals and Methods," *Latino Muslim Voice* (April–June 2006), http://www.latinodawah
.org/newsletter/apr-june2k6.html.

11. Van Nieuwkerk, "Gender, Conversion, and Islam," 114.

12. Rikani, "Latino Conversion to Islam."

13. Ibid.

14. Karin van Nieuwkerk, "Gender and Conversion to Islam in the West," in *Women Embracing Islam*, edited by van Nieuwkerk, 6.

15. Rikani, "Latino Conversion to Islam."

16. While I will be referring to the term "conversion," "It must be stressed that there is no such word as conversion in the Arabic language; rather, the emphasis is on the idea of becoming a Muslim, that is, 'submitting' to God in the form prescribed by his final revelation." See Haifaa Jawad, "Female Conversion to Islam: The Sufi Paradigm," in *Women Embracing Islam*, edited by van Nieuwkerk, 154.

17. Van Nieuwkerk, "Gender and Conversion to Islam in the West," 4.

18. Ibid.

19. Lewis R. Rambo, "Anthropology and the Study of Conversion," in *The Anthropology of Religious Conversion*, edited by Andrew Buckser and Stephen D. Glazier (Lanham, MD: Rowman and Littlefield, 2003), 213.

20. In the next section, I examine the concept of reversion and how it serves to explain US Latina/o Muslims' search for identity.

21. Van Nieuwkerk, "Gender and Conversion to Islam in the West," 7.

22. Haddad, "Quest for Peace in Submission," 28–29.

23. Lewis R. Rambo and Charles E. Farhadian, "Converting: Stages of Religious Change," in *Religious Conversion: Contemporary Practices and Controversies*, edited by Christopher Lamb and M. Darrol Bryant (London and New York: Cassell, 1999), 23.

24. Ibid., 24.

25. Haddad, "Quest for Peace in Submission," 30.

26. Ibid., 29–30.

27. Interview with a group of US Latinas in Chicago, July 26, 2006.

28. Rambo and Farhadian, "Converting," 25.

29. Haddad, "Quest for Peace in Submission," 27.

30. While the process of conversion to Islam is dissimilar to Protestant conversions, I can easily see similarities within the two groups. For example, the enthusiasm and effort both of these groups put into proselytizing are comparable, although US Latina/o Muslims do not consider their effort proselytizing but *daʿwa*, the process through which Muslims educate others about Islam.

31. Haddad, "Quest for Peace in Submission," 27.

32. Ibid.

33. Rambo and Farhadian, "Converting," 27.

34. Samantha Sánchez and Juan Galván, "Latino Muslims: The Changing Face of Islam in America," *Islamic Horizons* (July–August 2002): 25.

35. Yasin Dutton, "Conversion to Islam: The Qur'anic Paradigm," in *Religious Conversion*, edited by Lamb and Bryant, 163.

36. Ibid.

37. Lewis R. Rambo, *Understanding Religious Conversion* (New Haven, CT: Yale University Press, 1993), 168–169.

38. Dutton, "Conversion to Islam," 154.

39. Ibid., 155–156.

40. Rambo and Farhadian, "Converting," 32.

41. Haddad, "Quest for Peace in Submission," 31.

42. Michelle Al-Nasr, "A Letter to My Family," *Latino Muslim Voice* (October–December 2002), http://www.latinodawah.org/newsletter/oct-dec2k2.html.

43. Interview with a group of US Latinas in Chicago, July 26, 2006.

44. Ibid.

45. Interview with members of Latino Muslims of the Bay Area, in Hayward, California, July 30, 2006.

46. Ibid.

47. Ibid.

48. Lisa Viscidi, "Latino Muslims a Growing Presence in America," *Washington Report on Middle East Affairs* (June 2003), http://www.wrmea.com/archives/june2003/0306056.html.

49. Rebecca Sachs Norris, "Converting to What? Embodied Culture and the Adoption of New Beliefs," in *Anthropology of Religious Conversion*, edited by Buckser and Glazier, 171.

50. Alberto Hernández, "Hispanic Cultural Identity and the Recovery of Lost Memory: Response to Raúl Gómez-Ruiz's *Mozarabs, Hispanics, and the Cross*," *Perspectivas* 12 (Fall 2008): 41.

51. Ibid.

52. Ibid., 44.

53. Ibid.

54. Yahya 'Abu Ayah' López, "What's in a Word," *Latino Muslim Voice* (July–September 2002), http://www.latinodawah.org/newsletter/july-sept2k2.html#12.

55. Edmund A. Arroyo, "A Perspective from Chicago of the Latino Muslim Experience," *Latino Muslim Voice* (October–December 2002), http://www.latinodawah.org/newsletter/oct-dec2k2.html#4.

56. Interview with María in New York City, July 23, 2006.

57. Galván, "Who Are Latino Muslims?," 28.

58. Raheel Rojas, "In between Religions (Regressa a tu Senior y tu Cultura Latino)," *Latino Muslim Voice* (April–June 2006), http://www.latinodawah.org/newsletter/apr-june 2k6.html.

59. Kenny Yusuf Rodríguez, "Latino Muslims: Islamic Roots of Spanish Culture," *Islamic Horizons* (July–August 2002): 40–41.

60. Aidi, "Olé to Allah."

61. Américo Castro argues that Spanish attitudes toward indigenous populations and African slaves came as a direct result of their attitudes toward Muslims and Jews in Spain who were used as servants. At the same time, Castro also recognizes the Islamic style in the construction of churches (columns), which underscores the connection to Islamic culture. See Américo Castro, *Iberoamérica: Su historia y su cultura* (New York: Holt, Rinehart, and Winston, 1954), 9–12.

62. Mary Elizabeth Perry, *The Handless Maiden: Moriscos and the Politics of Religion in Early Modern Spain* (Princeton, NJ: Princeton University Press, 2005), 37.

63. Ibid.

64. This interest in dis-covering this history is present in the large amount of articles on the topic within newsletters dedicated to US Latina/o Muslims. For example, see Samantha Sánchez, "Islamic Resurgence in Spain and Beyond," *Latino Muslim Voice* (July–September 2002), http://www.latinodawah.org/newsletter/jul-sept2k2.html; and Mariam Santos Gar-

cía, "Musulmanes en la Peninsula Ibérica," *Latino Muslim Voice* (July–September 2003), http://www.latinodawah.org/newsletter/july-sept2k3.html; among others.

65. Haddad, "Quest for Peace in Submission," 21.

66. Guillermo Araya Goubet, "The Evolution of Castro's Theories," in *Américo Castro and the Meaning of Spanish Civilization*, edited by José Rubia Barcia and Selma Margaretten (Berkeley: University of California Press, 1976), 47.

67. Juan Flores, "Broken English Memories: Languages of the Trans-Colony," in *Postcolonial Theory and the United States: Race, Ethnicity, and Literature*, edited by Amritjit Singh and Peter Schmidt (Jackson: University Press of Mississippi, 200), 338.

CHAPTER 11

MAPPING MUSLIM COMMUNITIES IN "HISPANICIZED" SOUTH FLORIDA

MIRSAD KRIJESTORAC

DESPITE THE MUSLIM community's presence in the region since the 1960s, an undiscerning eye has often overlooked this still burgeoning aspect of South Florida's growth. Most information regarding Islam in South Florida comes from hollow media stories, surveys,[1] and various security and law enforcement reports, with little scholarly attention to the subject.[2] After the events of 9/11 and especially after the arrest of Jose Padilla,[3] South Florida is often portrayed in the media as a region with a growing number of Latino Muslims, but again without a systematic effort to account for it.[4] As an attempt to fill this gap, this chapter provides a historical overview and an ethnographic account of South Florida's local Muslim public sphere, composed of the Islamic centers and Muslim organizations, where Muslims are faced with the unusual dilemma of two-directional integration of Americanization and Hispanization that are often in tension with each other.[5]

Based on multiple interviews and participant observation, this chapter shows how past and present struggles have defined a growing and slowly adapting local Muslim public sphere and points of contact within and without Muslim groups. A key finding concerning this chapter is that, despite popular notions about the number of Latinos converting to Islam, there is not much evidence of a significant Hispanic Muslim community in "Hispanicized" Miami or South Florida. Instead, this chapter shows that not necessarily Hispanics, but more specifically Caribbean, South Asian, and African American subjects shape and reflect the complex social reality of Islam in southern Florida.

Since the definition of "public" is culturally constrained, in agreement with Wuthnow,[6] for this chapter "public" is a collective sphere that is open, accessible, and owned by many, if not all, local adult Muslims. Their public sphere is composed of Muslim places of worship, as well as locally based Muslim organizations, as places and situations where people can see and interact with each other, as part of a separate domain, on the basis of their performance and any role they have.[7] However, since the local Muslim public sphere grew spontaneously out of the individual sphere,[8] this inquiry will also note how that growth followed some of the ethnic and cultural lines of African American and South Asian Muslim groups. Therefore, the local Muslim public sphere *is* crosscut by different ethnic and cultural group lines, reinforced by the absence of an authentic US American Muslim *urf*.[9] This chapter looks at the making of this sphere through a historical overview of the growth of the two oldest *masjids*[10] and their congregations in South Florida, as well as some of the activities that take place around them. Although there are more local *masjids*, the two analyzed here are representative of the larger dynamics that define the Muslim public sphere in South Florida and the lack of interactions with local Hispanics.

Nowadays social scientists are referring to Muslims in the United States (even worldwide) as some sort of minority,[11] even as an ethnic group,[12] but only rarely as a religious community.[13] Following Geertz, however, this chapter views Muslims primarily as a religious community, which cuts across and includes other significations.[14] Such an approach provides an opportunity to note different places where various Muslim groups interact and come up with suitable solutions for themselves. What I observed is that the Muslims of South Florida are ready to "progressively rationalize" through compromises between the "ideal" and "real" in order to produce institutions that help them find solutions for religious dilemmas whether they come from social or religious structures.[15] Since those adaptations are mainly concerned about Muslims establishing themselves in the new situation and the new country,[16] they should be viewed as an effort to uphold or to attempt to shape "Americanization" by African American and immigrant Muslims, respectively.

The study starts with the oldest *masjid*, Al Ansar, established mainly by the African American reverts,[17] followed by the South Asians' Muslim Community Association's (MCA) two *masjids*, Flagler and Miami Gardens Masjid, and continues with the analysis of older Muslim social organizations and their interactions with the ever-growing Hispanic communities of South Florida. This chapter concludes that current trends where each community is preoccupied with itself will continue, especially among immigrant Muslims, who, as the result of external pressures from law enforcement agencies, increasingly cluster along more discrete ethnic lines in efforts to find their own definitions of Americanization.

LOCAL AFRICAN AMERICAN MUSLIM
GROWTH AND ADAPTATIONS

The first *masjid* established in South Florida was Masjid Al Ansar. It grew out of a storefront Nation of Islam (NOI) black community temple that traces its roots to 1958, when Elijah Mohammed[18] sent to Miami his first emissary, Clyde Rahman, from Chicago, followed shortly afterward by two other ministers, Lucius Beyah and John Muhammed.[19] They came and stayed in Miami for years, selling NOI newspapers and preaching on the street corners and in local parks until they established a regular congregation, which met in the house of one member. In 1966 the congregation moved into their present building[20] (formerly owned by the Church of Christ),[21] in the Liberty City neighborhood of Miami,[22] which became known as the Nation of Islam Temple 29,[23] purchased in cash by Elijah Mohammed. Some members of the *masjid* claim that he came to Miami with boxer Muhammad Ali and paid for the building in cash, while others deny that Muhammad Ali was involved in the original purchase. Either way, the connection between the establishment of the Masjid Al Ansar as the NOI Temple 29 with the legendary Muhammad Ali is often emphasized as an indicator of African *Americanness*. According to Imam Nasir, the NOI part of the history of the *masjid* matches other NOI places of worship that began in a similar way and with the same intention of establishing centers that are to serve locally as important markers of a *new* Black American identity. This Black *and* American orientation has been maintained since the beginning of the congregation.

Although Latinos began arriving in Miami in the late 1950s—few of them black—there was not much interaction between them and African American Muslims, except occasional flash points such as a 1989 incident when a Hispanic police officer, William Lozano, shot a black motorist[24] and the members of the *masjid* sided with local African Americans. In the "highly segregated city,"[25] the same social distance and weariness of subjects among the two communities persist, made evident by no Hispanic Muslim converts in the Masjid Al Ansar as well. Furthermore, since African American Muslims had their own ethnic community to which they could turn for their sexual interactions, there were few social contacts even through marriage.

From its inception, Temple 29 had a strong African American outreach program. Members were going to the local parks and street corners with the bullhorn, inviting bystanders into their religion and providing various classes and meals for the people of the neighborhood. The Hispanic population of Miami at this time was still small, and the temple did not have any specific outreach programs to attract Latinos. Membership grew exclusively among African

Muhammad Ali visiting Masjid Al Ansar in the late 1960s when the *masjid* was still a Nation of Islam temple. Seated (*left to right*) are Captain Sam (now Rodman), Muhammad Ali, and Charles X (now Charles Abdul-Malik). Standing (*left to right*) are Yusef X and Arlington X. Courtesy of Charles Abdul-Malik.

Masjid Al Ansar in Liberty City, Miami

Americans, and even early Muslim immigrants who arrived in the city during the late 1960s and early 1970s avoided the temple, as per their own accounts, at that time not recognizing it as a Muslim place of worship. With the death of Elijah Mohammed in 1975 and the new leadership of W. D. Mohammed, who reformed the NOI along the lines of Sunni Islam, Temple 29 became Masjid Al Ansar, and it began to have a more diverse membership, including some attendance from immigrant Muslims as well. This caused friction and division among the congregation, and one group eventually split, forming the new and separate Temple 29 (which still operates in Miami). This chapter, however, focuses on the majority group that followed W. D. Mohammed and stayed with the *masjid*. Even the new name they chose for the *masjid*, Al Ansar, which translates as "the helpers of those who emigrated," was a sign of change and an invitation for the greater cooperation among Muslims of increasingly immigrant, but not necessarily Latin American, origin. Though becoming more diverse, this *masjid* has continuously preserved its allegiance to W. D. Mohammed's organization and its approach to Islam, as well as an African American ethnic majority. The *masjid*'s first imam was a New York native, Imam Najiy, followed by Imam Nasir Ahmad who was sent in 1977 directly by W. D. Mohammed.[26] His direct connections with the national leadership meant greater support from the headquarters for the local community. An essential part of the *masjid* was the Miami chapter of the Clara Muhamed School,[27] where Imam Nasir assumed the position of director as well. Members note that Imam Nasir, who was previously the personal assistant of W. D. Mohammed, strengthened the outreach program within the South Florida community at large. He established good relationships with South Asian Muslim leaders such as Hamid Siddiqui, Tasnim Uddin, Muhamed Shakir, and Mian Subhani, who, in turn, significantly supported the Masjid Al Ansar.

Under his leadership members of the Masjid Al Ansar began weekly visitations to the jail in Belle Glade, while twice a month they also visited Indiantown jail as a continuous prison outreach effort. Congregants also began handing out bags of food to local residents on Saturdays as well as engaging with elected Miami officials and the ongoing participation in local interfaith events. Those interactions with the official sphere also became a strong meeting point between the Masjid Al Ansar with other South Florida Muslim communities, which often sought help from African American Muslims in negotiating relations with local US American officials, counting on their "Americanness" to show that Islamic religious identity does not exclude US American identity. As such, this was one of the rare local examples where the Muslim public sphere extended into the official sphere, while the cooperation between native and immigrant Muslims later decreased. All those *masjid* activities have brought many new converts from the local black and African American population. However, throughout those times few Hispanics joined either the religion or the Masjid Al Ansar's congregation.

Before assuming the local position, Imam Nasir traveled to the Caribbean, visiting some of its NOI temples, while also making television and radio appearances as a representative of W. D. Mohammed and introducing Islam to the general public. His appointment to Miami strengthened the Masjid Al Ansar's outreach programs in countries with a significant population of African origin such as Bermuda, Trinidad, Guyana, Puerto Rico, Haiti, and Jamaica. After 1984 the *masjid* also undertook an outreach program in Colombia that consisted mostly of providing printed materials about Islam and conducting fund-raising to support the local and indigenous efforts for the upkeep of or to establish Muslim places of worship locally. These kinds of activities continued after Imam Nasir departed. Although not much happened as a result of the outreach activities in the Caribbean and Colombia, which now have mostly ended, the Masjid Al Ansar kept the door open for those who would occasionally come and seek help in print materials for the outreach (*da'wa*) over there. The new imam Fred Nuriddin, who was also part of the W. D. Mohammed national group, came in 1987 and continued the same programs of activity and outreach. Imam Nasir returned in 2003, picking up from where he left the community. However, by that time Masjid Al Ansar was not the only *masjid* in South Florida. Although cooperation with other Muslims grew during Imam Nasir's leadership at the Masjid Al Ansar, a full merger of all the local Muslims did not occur. Other Muslims had already started their own *masjid* projects during the initial phase of the *masjid*'s growth as exclusively a Black American Temple 29 congregation.

Meanwhile, other Muslims in South Florida tended to view local "NOI outgrowth" the Masjid Al Ansar as a separate group, or with certain religious reservations,[28] and that may provide an important clue as to why those few local Latino coverts avoided the *masjid* as well. As they explained, it was NOI-originated specific religious practices—not race—that kept them away.[29] The same was noted to me by some of the African American Sunni Muslims from the Masjid Al Iman in Sunrise,[30] who reluctantly told me these misgivings explain why they don't pray together with Masjid Al Ansar.

Since South Florida, especially Miami, is now a region where the majority population is a US national minority (officially referred to as Hispanic Americans),[31] interreligious and interethnic relationships develop through slightly different conditions from the rest of the country. It led to more interactions between W. D. Mohammed–led African American Muslims and the rest of the Muslim community, which emphasize complementary versions of US

Americanness. However, both groups still inhabit separate dimensions of the local Muslim public sphere for their own social interactions, as we observed and as it was revealed to us by local Muslims themselves. Due to those separate social interactions, there was not much room left for outreach to other Muslims. In fact, since Al Ansar's congregation is so closely knitted around African Americanness, even the dozens of local nonblack, Hispanic reverts do not go to Masjid Al Ansar.

However, the continued effort to maintain a communal Islam of the African American–dominated *masjid*, with its own cultural views and practices, provided Masjid Al Ansar's community with ideological stability and so far without any major individual or official-sphere interventions. It appears that such stability and insistence on cultural specificity caused membership to decrease and gravitate more toward other local African Americans[32] or more international immigrant-run *masjids*.[33] Although the times have changed and Miami is now "Hispanicized,"[34] there is still not much contact with Hispanics, Muslim or otherwise.[35] Due to the economic uplift, induced by the effects of NOI's "Black puritanism,"[36] members had to adapt racial and cultural exclusivism to their new socioeconomic reality, which demands more interactions with other Muslims and the general population. Since that is still not happening in Masjid Al Ansar, membership started to grow older and dissipate, as observed by the significantly fewer members attending *jum'a* prayers[37] and not many outreach activities done by the *masjid*.

SOUTH ASIAN ADAPTATIONS TO MIAMI REALITIES

The interactions of immigrant Muslims with local Hispanics were not much different, as they focused energies to establish themselves and to negotiate their own internal needs and differences. The main group among immigrant Muslims came from South Asia and joined the few Muslim students who came earlier to study at the University of Miami (UM). They followed the general trends of other Muslim and South Asian immigrants who came to the United States after the 1965 passage of the Immigration Reform and Control Act.[38] Williams notes that "from 1820 to 1960, a total of only 13,607 people emigrated from the Indian subcontinent, and an unrecorded number of these departed."[39] Those numbers after 1965 increased from 371,630 persons in the 1980s to 919,626 in 1990.[40] Although there are no numbers to show how many of them came to South Florida, most of those early Muslim pioneers, mostly men,[41] who did were part of the "brain drain wave," which consisted of university graduates from Pakistan who were mostly civil engineers seeking their chance in the newly developing region of South Florida. Two of the most prominent among them were the late Hamid Siddiqui and Tasneem Uddin.

Muslim men gathering in the crowded apartment 6 of 3150 Northwest Twentieth Street in Miami. Courtesy of Asad Siddiqui.

Hamid, a geologist, was first hired by an American company, together with a group of civil engineers, all young University of Karachi graduates, to work on a highway project connecting Karachi to Hyderabad in Pakistan. Soon after that project was completed, Hamid moved to South Florida and joined a group of students led by Mohammed Shakir[42] and Badat Ayub, who also came from Pakistan to study at Miami-Dade College and the UM. As most of those students were attending the South campus of Miami-Dade, this is where they held the first *jum'a* prayers. Soon after Hamid and Tasneem, other engineers from Pakistan, such as Taj Sadiqi,[43] followed, as they all helped each other find jobs locally in South Florida. Most of them came as single men and eventually went back to Karachi, married, and returned to South Florida with their wives. The same marriage arrangements were followed by most other Muslim immigrants as well. For the reasons explained earlier, those immigrant Muslim pioneers initially did not join Temple 29, but rather they prayed at the Jackson Memorial Hospital, UM, Miami-Dade College, or together in the apartment complex where most of them initially lived as roommates. They first began holding their own *tarawih* prayers[44] in 1972 in their apartments at 3150 Northwest Twentieth Street in Miami. Since all of them were coming from religious families, and some of them, such as Tasneem and Seyeed Masroor, were even *hafiz*[45] of the Qur'an, they were concerned with community prayers. At that time, socially conservative America was accepting of such religious attitudes, and they had faced no problem holding congregational prayers in the apartments even from "their Jewish landlord," as they like to point out to show interreligious tolerance at that time.

Soon after attending the national Muslim Student Association convention in Georgia in the spring of 1971, Mohammed Shakir and Badat Ayub encouraged students to form a local affiliate MSA chapter. They elected the first group of MSA officers in 1972. In the absence of strong religious authority among them, that phase of local Muslim growth could be characterized as primarily being concerned with social and Muslim and less with theological and Islamic concerns. Such a situation allowed them not to be bothered by the sectarian divide, as they saw "Muslimness" primarily as a social and cultural category and they wanted to signify that with the ways they organized. So the first elected MSA president was an Iranian student, Ahmad Shazpot, along with Egyptian Yusuf, Pakistani Tasneem, and Ghulan Polani. All this concentration on establishing themselves precluded a concentrated effort in outreach to the other newly arriving migrants at the time, namely, Cubans fleeing Castro's regime.

Once a local community was organized through the MSA, they began the task of finding the property to establish a *masjid*.[46] Since Muslims are religiously restricted from using interest-based loans, the group also began with fund-raising in various ways. In that social phase of their formation, women were an important and welcomed part of the collective effort. As Mina Siddiqi remembers, a few women who were part of the group baked homemade food and cakes to sell during the weekend Indian film matinees and concerts that Muslim students organized at the UM. That progression from the formation of MSA to the establishment of a *masjid* could also be seen as a phase of gradual replacement of primacy from a social to more theological significations. So those types of initial stage fund-raisings were acceptable during the social stage, but not later when theological significations became more important, as no one will dare to do the same types of religiously unsanctioned fund-raising for any local *masjid* anymore.

The community eventually purchased a small two-bedroom, one-bath house at 7350 Northwest Third Street in Miami, in the mostly immigrant neighborhood near Flagler Street, and they began with prayer services there in 1975.[47] The place is popularly referred to as "Flagler Masjid," although the official name is the Miami Masjid.

The purchase of the house coincided with the time when the Muslim community in the United States began to organize on a national level in order to resolve their own challenges and create prospects for the future.[48] The local South Florida Muslim project followed the same path. First, they registered as

The Flagler Masjid, circa 2012 (without dome)

the local MSA. Next, when the national MSA became part of the newly formed "hierarchy" of the Islamic Society of North America in 1981, they did the same and became part of the MCA, a federation of community-based local organizations under ISNA. The participants of those developments explain that the tie with the national organization was primarily for practical reasons. The national organization was officially recognized as a nonprofit organization, and they as one of its chapters enjoyed the same privileges of tax exemption. Eventually, the national MCA wound down its activities, as the main ISNA branch took its intended role.

The South Florida chapter remained as the MCA, but later on registered its *masjid* property under the North American Islamic Trust (NAIT) to protect it in the case of civil litigation against any member of the *masjid* or its board of trustees. In the situation of a Muslim-majority country, believers will donate money or property for the *masjid* that then becomes *waqf*, a religious endowment as a voluntary and irrevocable dedication of property. Such property can then be used as investment to increase value or amount of the *waqf*, and laws in most Muslim-majority countries recognize dedications as such and do not tax it or pass litigations against it. However, this is not the case in the United States, and in order to dedicate a *masjid* as a religious endowment Muslims had to develop a particular legal category where they could achieve their aims and fulfill their needs as Muslims, albeit in an adjusted way. The NAIT was then formed in 1973 by ISNA, the largest Muslim organization in the United States.[49] As one of the local South Florida lawyers and an ISNA board member[50] explained, the original intent of NAIT was to provide financial support for the MSA activities, but it quickly grew into a trust that was to ensure perpetual Islamic use for the religious centers acquired by Muslims all over North America. The trust is organized to take over and hold the deed of any Muslim property that is registered under it.[51] However, so many places that originally wanted to protect their property by endowing it with NAIT now find it difficult to sell it in order to build a bigger facility or to relocate from places where Muslim don't live anymore. By its bylaws, which were enacted back in the early 1970s to ensure that a property remains to be used as it was originally intended, the NAIT is not allowed to permit the sale of it, unless the money is to be used in the buying of the new property, but again only under NAIT's name. This is what happened with the Flagler Masjid.[52]

At the time the house was bought for the Flagler Masjid, it was chosen because of its location, affordability, and convenience for many Muslims who worked in Miami and could, relatively quickly, come to it and return to work after *jum'a* prayer. This is different from traditional concepts of *masjid* as an abode for a *jam'at*, a basic unit of Muslim community around which a neighborhood of houses is established.[53]

The Flagler Masjid is an example where location is not chosen to be a geographic center of a *jam'at*, but a convenient place where people can come and attend *jum'a* prayer from work and, more important, a place that is both affordable for the community to buy without taking out interest loans but usually not a neighborhood where congregants' homes are.[54] Such a situation exemplifies where the border is between the individual sphere, where compromises can be made and a family home might be bought with interest, and the Muslim public sphere of a *masjid*, where such compromise could not be tolerated and the *masjid* has to be built with *halal*, or pure means, where no interest is allowed. Because of these reasons, Muslims in South Florida, in general, rarely live close to their *masjids*. Only some later *masjids* tried to correct this disparity and are established in residential areas where more of the congregants actually live, though still only few. The location convenience did not remove all of the problems for the new *masjid*.

The Flagler Masjid opened its door to Muslims in 1978, but it quickly became too small for the number of people attending. Initially, with minimal architectural adaptations the *masjid* could hold an estimated 150 to 200 people. Although still a large number for a single house in a residential neighborhood, the *jum'a* prayers did not disturb non-Muslim neighbors because prayer occurs during work hours.

But as the community grew, the members did some remodeling in order to enlarge the prayer space, and as part of it the Flagler Masjid got a dome. It was a dome discarded by the UM, and one of the Muslims, who worked there, obtained it and brought it to the *masjid*. Everyone loved the idea of a dome for the *masjid*, since most of them held the conception that a *masjid* has to have a dome and minaret[55] as visual representations of their identity, as they are "the undisputed signs, not only of Islamic cultures, but Islam itself."[56] The minaret was too much, but the dome was there. For the local Muslims, the possibility of having a dome on top of the house *masjid*, no matter how aesthetically difficult, not only was "a structural metonym of Muslim identity,"[57] but also provided the opportunity to display their identity. So there was not much of a discussion of whether it would be placed on top of the house. Once it was placed there, the fortuitous dome also served as a lightning rod for the mobilization of neighbors against the *masjid*.

An additional issue for the Flagler Masjid Muslims was that the *masjid* became frequented by the members of Tablighi Jam'at, "defensive pacifists"[58] who were coming from all over the world, dressed in their Pakistani outfits and with very modest means, eager to visit local, mostly Pakistani, Muslims in their *da'wa* efforts. As they came to Miami, they stayed in the *masjid* for three days before they moved on. During those three days, they would sometimes hand-wash their clothes and leave them on a clothesline to dry, and they would walk around the *masjid* property sometimes shirtless. Although this is not inappropriate in Islam, for the neighbors it was very strange. That, combined with the sudden appearance of the dome on top of the house *masjid*, sister Mina remembers, caused the neighbors to think that it was some strange cult that had moved into their neighborhood. In order to come to terms with the neighbors, *masjid* community members adapted once more to the situation in a very unorthodox way.

Generally speaking, Muslim men are not permitted to have girlfriends, and even if they do, the fact should not be publicly expressed or communally acknowledged. But since the growing tension with the neighbors demanded that they gather allies, some Muslim students who were attending the *masjid* asked their Spanish-speaking girlfriends to go around the neighborhood together with other Muslims, knocking on the doors of their mostly Cuban American neighbors and explaining to them that they were not part of any cult and telling the neighbors that they should have no reason for concern. Those efforts produced some positive effects, and at the city commission meeting new architectural adaptations were approved, but in the end the environmental logic of South Florida prevailed and the dome had to be removed, as it was declared not hurricane proof. Although this was an opportunity for Muslims to nourish those contacts with neighbors, they were too preoccupied with their own growth and the struggle to establish themselves locally, and these contacts were lost. As this "dome episode" shows, Muslims interacted with local Hispanic communities only when they were forced to do so. Even those few dating partnerships ended without marriage. The Flagler Masjid remained as the "strange foreigners'" house of worship for local Cuban American neighbors, who at that time were the most recent immigrants to South Florida.[59] The possibility for interactions with local Hispanics further decreased as the community found a new location for the bigger facility in the much less Hispanic neighborhood of Miami Gardens.[60]

MCA NEW HOME AND ADAPTATIONS
WITH THE MIAMI GARDENS MASJID

Soon after the controversy with the dome, the local Muslims outgrew the Flagler Masjid and began looking for a new larger property where they could build their own structure. They found it three years later, when they bought a small church at 4305 Northwest 183rd Street in Miami Gardens, known as the Miami Gardens or 183rd Street Masjid. At that point the Flagler Masjid became a secondary activity of the MCA, largely left to the Tablighi Jam'at to run and to serve as a place for *jum'a* prayer, while all attention and energy moved to the new location.

The MCA community initially used the old church building until they could agree on exactly what they were going to build and collected enough money to finally start the interest-free project of building the *masjid* in 1991. According to most of the participants, the key members of the community could not agree on the direction of the project, as to how and what should be built first, the *masjid* or the Islamic school. They actually began building the school,[61] but in the end they decided to erect the *masjid* first. Similar disagreements have followed the construction and subsequent existence of the *masjid* ever since.[62]

Because most of the energy was spent on the consideration of what to build first and raising funds for it, not much thought was given to the planning of how the *masjid* should functionally be organized, leading to some practical problems such as the absence of a lecture hall and any other official space for non-Muslim visitors. As has been noted by Rose, "Recreating the monumental mosque from back home is beyond the means of the community," yet it was difficult to renounce those elements that the community considered to be "markers of their Muslim identity."[63] So as a "proper" *masjid*, the Miami Gardens Masjid has both the dome and the minarets, albeit not for use to call the *adhan*[64] because the latter is not called aloud outside of the *masjid*, especially not from the minarets, even when a *masjid* has them. Calling the *adhan*

The 183rd Street Masjid in North Miami before recent renovations, with two minarets but without a dome

from the minarets is the ultimate sign of Muslim lands. Perhaps the most important element of architectural *da'wa* is "to make sure people would feel invited to visit"[65] the *masjid* and the most often expressed thing that people miss from "back home." As one of the local Muslims told us, "Home is where the *adhan* is being heard."[66]

According to the members of the community, prayer in the *masjid* started right after the structure was put up and almost two years before the certificate of occupancy was received from the county. As some of them joked, they prayed "illegally" until the certificate of occupancy for the building was received in 1997. The way the *masjid* was built reflects how the community was functioning "haphazardly," as some of the members saw it. Ultimately, the *jam'at* could not resolve the tension between the social and religious needs of the community. Religious needs meant a complete house of worship, which was somewhat better achieved.[67] Social needs were much less attended to, if any were, and those mostly through private initiative. They varied, from the need for a primary school for children, a shelter for women in distress, institutions for family counseling, an immigrant center to cater to the needs of newly arriving members of the community, and places where the youth and elderly could socialize to having open-house events and a space for interactions with non-Muslim neighbors and society at large; the *masjid* did not attend to any of them. Only after 9/11 did the community begin to plan its activities more carefully. The social versus religious battles were often played between the *masjid* imam and the *masjid* board. They were contentious because the board in the Miami Gardens Masjid, as in all other *masjids* in South Florida, did not have a specific job description for itself or for the imam. When conflict occurs, the imam will insist that the *masjid* is the house of worship, and his responsibility is to work as *da'i*[68] and work for Islam, while board members are more concerned about the needs of the local congregation. On the other hand, when one of the imams tried to undertake local outreach to African Americans, the board was not ready for that either. The Miami Gardens Masjid community failed to resolve these tensions, evident in the turnover rate of the imams at the *masjid* and hardly any interactions with the community at large.

The first imam from 1994 to 1996 was of Indian origin; the second was of the same origin, Imam Jamal Uddin from Hyderabad, who served for a year, from 1996 to 1997. They were followed by an imam from the West Indies, Sheikh Roshan, a graduate of Dar-ul-Ulum in India who served from 1997 until 2001 who was actively involved with the local Tablighi Jam'at. After the split with him, the community hired as an imam an African American revert originally from Tennessee, Rafiq Mehdi, who was a graduate of Medina University and served from 2001 to 2003. Because Imam Rafiq was American, he could not provide enough of those sociocultural connections with the "backhome" traditions.[69] He was followed by Dr. Abdul Hamid Samra from Syria, who served between 2001 and 2006. The problem with him was that he did not want to follow the ISNA proclamations for the days of Eid for North America, which most often differ from those in the "Muslim world." After Imam Samra the community appointed a temporary imam, Murrie, originally an immigrant from Saudi Arabia, to cover until a new permanent imam was hired. Imam Murrie served from 2006 until 2009,[70] when the community finally hired the Turkish Imam Ismet in 2010, a graduate of the Al Azhar University.

There was some optimism in the community that Imam Ismet might be able to provide the community with stability and that long-sought balance between social and religious needs. However, as we were concluding this chapter, Imam Ismet left after he fulfilled his two-year contract. So the community quest to find the appropriate imam continues. One encouraging sign, though, is that some of the community members who were strongly concerned about the social issues also found new avenues to work outside of the *masjid* to fulfill those needs, which will further reduce the social-religious tensions within the *masjid*'s community and possibly ease the job for the future imam. However, for the purposes of this inquiry, it should be noted that none of the imams spoke or understood the Spanish language, and neither did the community require them to know it. That can indicate that the present social distance between the Muslims and local Hispanics will remain for the time being.

The activities of the MCA community now go beyond the *masjid* structure, and it should be noted that some members started the project of a free

UHI Medical Clinic[71] for needy people. The clinic was first proposed to be part of the *masjid*, but then moved to its current location just a few blocks west on 183rd Street. Another project actively supported by the local South Asian Muslim community is the Sahara Asian Women's Group, which could play an important role in adjusting the local Muslims' traditional marriage relations. The group was established in 2005 as a joint project of the Asian American Advisory Board and the Women's Fund of Miami-Dade. Soon after they began work, they bought a property, which is located right next to the Miami Gardens Masjid, and converted it into a shelter for Asian, Muslim, and non-Muslim women in distress.[72]

DIASPORIZATION AND CONVERSION

During the time of initial "growth" from the Flagler to the Miami Gardens Masjid, the Muslim immigrant community split along sectarian lines. The split began to develop early, soon after the community acquired Flagler Masjid and visiting guest speakers began to deliver lectures. Some Shi'i members of the community in 1975 invited their scholar Hashim Amir Ali to talk. Muhammad Shakir, who was serving as the second president of the Flagler Masjid, agreed to it, but some of the other key community members objected and publicly walked out of the lecture, which caused tension.

The next big issue that encouraged the split was the occasion of the purchase of the first few graves for Muslims in 1978. A local South Florida doctor, who was one of the leaders of the Shi'i Muslim community, wanted to purchase the graves together, but the Sunni group did not. At that time the Sunni and Shi'i Muslims who were together in prayer began separating in death, with parallel graveyard projects. Still, they remained more or less together, until the Shi'i Muslim community of Miami began with their own *jam'at* formation in 1988. By 1989 they registered as the Islamic Jaffaria Association, Inc., bought their own land, and in 1991 completed the first phase of building.[73]

Splits began among the Sunni Muslim community as well. By then the original group of Pakistani civil engineers were accomplished,[74] and some of them began working on their own local Islamic projects. Tasneem in particular initiated the Islamic school in Miami, which eventually evolved into today's Miami Islamic School and Masjid Al Nur. Another direct split from the MCA of South Florida is Masjid Al Muttaqin, which separated from the Miami Gardens Masjid in 2009 and is mostly composed of Muslims of Guyanese origin.

Also by 1991, due to the growing diversity of the immigrant community, other projects emerged, such as the first full-time South Florida Islamic

School of Nur-ul-Islam in Cooper City, founded in 1996 by Amir Ali, also from Guyana, and other Muslims from the West Indies.[75] Another development was the Al Hikmat media service, with Darul Uloom Institute, and once a full-time school.[76] That project was led by Trinidad-born but Indian-educated Imam Shafayat Mohamed, who separated from Nur-ul-Islam. And there are more places, such as the Masjid Al Hijra in Miramar, established by the late shaykh Gulshair El'Shukri after his split with Darul Uloom. The weekend Islamic School of Broward in the city of Sunrise was founded in 1989 by Drs. Zahid and Samina Qureshi and led primarily by immigrant Muslims from India, which in 2000 then became the full-time Salah Tawfik Elementary and Middle School with a separate weekend Islamic school, all under the name of the Islamic Foundation of South Florida (IFSF).[77] The Egyptian-run Al Azhar Academy[78] used to be with the Islamic School of Broward but separated in 2000. The latest split from the IFSF is the storefront *masjid* the Islamic Center of Broward in Sunrise, led by Pakistan-born Imam Rashid. The Masjid Jam'at Al Muminum was founded in 1996 primarily by Guyanese Muslims, initially led by the late Imam Rustum, which eventually in 2006 built the small but functional *masjid* in northwestern Margate. Finally, we can add the latest ethnic addition to the South Florida Muslim community, the Turkish-run *masjid* and cultural (they emphasize cultural) Istanbul Center, which began in 2004 as the Anatolia Center[79] and now has changed its name and moved to Sample Road in Pompano Beach.

This list of South Florida Islamic projects is not exhaustive, but this growth clearly shows signs of the crystallization of the local Muslim public sphere, with increasing diasporization of Muslim immigrant communities that are closing upon themselves. These communities, after the initial clustering along religious lines in the 1980s, in the 1990s began and ever since continues to cluster around the lines of the "back-home" imagined *urf*, often masked as national or regional origins, as they grow smaller in size and community scope. In addition to an ethnic differentiation, this clustering is also the result of the increasing official-sphere interventions in the Muslims' public sphere. After the growing external pressure of police surveillance and infiltrations with so-called informants, Muslims are closing in among themselves in culturally tight communities where they feel safe from those interventions. Only in those smaller ethnic and cultural units do Muslims create room to behave in ways that conform to their identity, without great social and political cost.[80] As a result of these fragmentations, there is not much energy left to embrace the dozen or so new Hispanic reverts, who, as they told us, linger among different *masjids* but socialize primarily with other non-Muslim Hispanic friends and relatives, giving preference to their cultural and ethnic, rather than religious, background.

Another active Muslim organization is a local chapter of the Council of American Islamic Relations (CAIR), founded locally in 1999. Initially, this Muslim civil rights organization was successfully led by Altaf Ali of Guyanese origin, who worked diligently to establish it as a local umbrella Muslim organization. He largely succeeded in that mission. From its unique position in the local Muslim public sphere, CAIR served almost exclusively as a channel through which the individual and public interacted with the official sphere, especially after 2001. The organization slowed down significantly after Altaf Ali left the local leadership position and the country in 2009, in part because of the multiple anonymous threats to him and his family.[81] Due to the lull in CAIR activities, combined with ethnic clustering, and efforts of the official sphere to affect the internal dynamics of the Muslim public sphere,[82] lately some other similar Muslim activist groups started to form in South Florida.[83] However, they are smaller in scope and targeted different audiences (mostly South Asians) than CAIR. It remains to be seen what impact that will have on CAIR,[84] as well as on the joint South Florida Muslim–civil rights front in local and public interactions with the official sphere.[85]

Still another active local Muslim organization is the American Muslim Association of North America (AMANA). It was founded in 1997 as a local South Florida Muslim organization, which is not associated with any particular *masjid*, but is very active and part of the local Muslim public sphere, especially in regard to social issues. AMANA is locally based, with a national outreach, and one of its main activities is that it supplies many inmates with Islamic literature in different languages. The Palestinian-born Sofian A. Zakkout leads the organization, and it is thus far the only South Florida Muslim organization that has actively tried to reach out to South American Muslim reverts through contacts and Islamic literature in Spanish. They even have an active branch in Puerto Rico.[86] Their prison-outreach program has worked especially well in Puerto Rico, where a Muslim chaplain reported that there are now a few hundred reverts regularly attending Friday prayers in the several prisons, from just a few individuals several years ago. It all started when one of the prisoners was transferred from Chicago to Puerto Rico, and he contacted AMANA for literature and to help him to gain dietary rights. The local AMANA representative of Hispanic origin went to the prison several times and successfully negotiated on behalf of the inmate. The inmate got his religious dietary rights, while the island prison system got its first Muslim chaplain, who now attends to the spiritual needs of a few hundred prisoners across the island.

The inmates are the main group of Hispanic converts on the island. With them only a dozen or so local Hispanics became Muslims over time, either by marrying some of the Palestinian Muslims who came to the island or a few of them who converted on their own. A telling illustration of how small the number of Hispanic Muslims in Puerto Rico is is that only one of the local imams on the island speaks some Spanish, as one of the local Muslims pointed out. For that reason the Islamic Center of Montehiedra in San Juan is the preferred *masjid* for the island's Hispanic Muslims. Things might change in the future, since the Puerto Rican Muslim community is now actively looking to hire an imam who speaks Spanish. Such a person might change the dynamic and composition of the Muslim population of the island, since there are now the second and third generations of Muslims of Palestinian origin who were born and live in Puerto Rico and are very familiar with the local people and the local customs.

SOUTH FLORIDA AMERICANIZED MUSLIMS AND NON-AMERICANIZED HISPANICS

Despite the media sensationalization of growing Hispanic Muslim conversion rates,[87] research for this chapter shed evidence on only about a dozen Muslim reverts and converts who attend various South Florida *masjids*, most of whom do not know each other. Almost all of them turned to Islam through marriage with Muslims, but since both major Muslim groups reach out to their own groups for spouses, only a few such marriages actually happened. The media began to sensationalize Hispanic Muslim converts in 2002 due to the case of Jose Padilla. Originally from Puerto Rico, Padilla became a Muslim while imprisoned in South Florida,[88] but was always a locally marginal person even among Latino Muslims. In fact, most interviewees had become Muslims after he had already left South Florida. Few of the local Latino Muslims have families, and most are still closed into their own national non-Muslim Latino circles, where they feel most comfortable. As Latina Muslim Susan told us, even her children would rather play with other Latino immigrant children and not Muslims. When one of them tried to organize a picnic for those Latino Muslims, only two who already knew each other showed up. But the only thing they all have in common is that nearly all of them are of non-Cuban origin, which makes them a minority even among the local dominant Latino population. Only last year one person came from Cuba to Miami already a Muslim, and one women of Cuban origin allegedly first converted to Islam, but later it became unclear whether she stayed a Muslim. All other local Latino Muslims are non-Cuban. Furthermore, among the *masjid*-goers there are hardly any Muslims who married Cuban Americans, while there are a few families with one Latino spouse who became Muslim.

This points to the persistent construction of social distance between the two community formations. Furthermore, it signals that South Florida Muslims do not have many contacts with the local Latino-Cuban community, as observed by others as well,[89] and they learn about Muslims only through the mostly negative media coverage, which consistently eroticizes Islam as the religion of foreigners. As a non-Muslim Cuban American told me, his compatriots among themselves refer to all Muslims as "Talibanos." In such an atmosphere, it is no surprise that there are no converts and that there is no interest in Islam among local Cuban Americans.

On the other hand, both native and immigrant Muslim communities don't want to carry the stigma that Hispanics in the United States face.[90] Muslims are still preoccupied by their own struggles to establish themselves as individuals and as a community, while remaining under an ever-present watchful eye of various security agencies, causing them to further close in among themselves. Due to these pressures, most local Muslims want to "Americanize," either to showcase their patriotism as an expression of membership in the nation or because they believe that to be the best vehicle for social mobility and participation, which can possibly lessen the discrimination they face.[91] As Hobsbawm reflected, in a situation where Americanism is advertised as "an act of choice," any "un-American" signs present a doubt to the person's actual status in a nation's membership, which for Muslims anywhere in the United States carries a particularly heavy cost.[92] For South Florida Cubans, "Americanization was unnecessary and in some measure undesired,"[93] and in fact they engaged in what Portes and Stepick see as the "acculturation-in-reverse," and therefore these two communities are developing in different ways.[94] This Americanization choice makes even those Muslims trying to engage with the community at large become primarily concerned with "Anglos" who still hold political sway in the state of Florida or hold important positions in most security agencies. What could be another local "change without a blueprint"[95] of that reality concerns the college-age children of many naturalized Muslim Americans. They are beginning to interact more with Hispanic youth at South Florida universities, which are those rare local public spaces where all interactions are mainly done in the English language.[96]

CONCLUSION

The historical and ethnographic accounts here provide several conclusions worth reflection. As illustrated through the particular examples of the two oldest local communities structured around Masjid Al Ansar and MCA, Muslims in South Florida are preoccupied with their own social and religious needs and growing apart along the lines of their respective congregational ethnic majorities. In addition, the research conducted for this chapter also highlights the needs to dispel recurring journalistic accounts of growing Hispanic conversions to Islam in South Florida and relate South Florida to a larger world, namely, Latin American, Caribbean, and US Latino religious and ethnic landscapes. Besides a dozen or so Hispanic families and individuals, who often do not know each other, there seem to be no significant points of contact between the local Hispanic and Muslim *masjid*-going communities. Perhaps surprisingly, one of the main points of diversification of the two communities is their approach to Americanization, by which Muslims are actively trying to fit in with their religious and social practices and find the more permanent solutions for the realities of their new life, while local Cuban Hispanics have different aspirations and paths of adaptation. A sign that this situation will not change soon is that immigrant Muslim communities are not only disconnected from the local Hispanic community, but increasingly clustering along narrower ethnic lines, due to an increasing sense of insecurity caused by growing attempts of the official sphere to intervene in the development of the Muslim public sphere. As became evident in the process of research for this chapter, those interventions caused increasing religious diasporization of Muslim immigrant communities. Such situations could imply that development of Islam in South Florida is slowly getting into the same position as in some European countries where Islam, to a large extent, is expelled from the public sphere into ethnic circles or the privacy of homes and individual interactions. If this trend continues, ethnic and cultural communities will prioritize and seek their own solutions for missing rules of *urf* in the New World in an absence of wider public-sphere discussions. As religiosity leaves the Muslim public sphere, one's own religion becomes a personal struggle for the "expression of loyalty to a social order and its values."[97] In that way the situation in South Florida will begin to resemble the countries of the Old World, where Muslims are publicly urged to participate and integrate into the host societies, but actually are *being pushed* into situations where such interactions are impossible,[98] and where religion is the only thing left to counter these exclusionary tactics. It remains to be seen what kind of effect that will cause in the relationships between Muslim and Hispanic communities in South Florida.

NOTES

1. For example, the Association of Religion Data Archives conducted a survey, but of the five Islamic centers in Palm Beach County, their report notes only one. I note this example because it had three well-established centers at the time the survey was conducted (and now five). For more, see the Association of Religion Data Archives, http://www.thearda.com /mapsReports/reports/counties/12099_2000.asp.

2. With the exception of the Harvard "Pluralism Project." For the complete Pluralism Project list, see http://pluralism.org/directory/index/?flags=C&keyword=title&sort=title& state=FL&submit=Search&text=&tradition=Islam. However, even their report lists only a fraction (eighteen) of the total number of Islamic centers in South Florida (local Muslims note forty-seven centers, while I personally visited twenty-four).

3. He was initially alleged to be the "dirty bomber" with ties to South Florida. For more, see BBC, "Profile: Jose Padilla" (2007), http://news.bbc.co.uk/2/hi/americas/2037444.stm.

4. By South Florida, I mean the three counties of West Palm Beach, Fort Lauderdale, and Miami-Dade.

5. This tension is mainly due to the treatment of the US Hispanics in general as "illegal immigrants" or permanent foreigners, despite their longtime presence in the United States. For more, see Ruben Rumbaut, "Pigments of Our Imagination: On the Racialization and Racial Identities of 'Hispanics' and 'Latinos,'" in *How the United States Racializes Latinos: White Hegemony and Its Consequences*, edited by José A. Cobas, Jorge Duany, and Joe R. Feagin (Boulder, CO: Paradigm, 2009), 15–36.

6. Robert Wuthnow, *Producing the Sacred: An Essay on Public Religion* (Urbana: University of Illinois Press, 1994).

7. See Harald Eidheim, "When Ethnic Identity Is a Social Stigma," in *Ethnic Groups and Boundaries*, edited by Fredrik Barth (1969; reprint, Long Grove, IL: Waveland, 1998), 48.

8. In the sense that a particular Muslim public sphere is separate from local civil society, as was also noted by Eisenstadt, and is located between the individual and (in this case the non-Muslim) official sphere occupied by state institutions. See Miriam Hoexter, Shmuel N. Eisenstadt, and Nehemia Levtzion, eds., *The Public Spheres in Muslim Societies* (Albany: State University of New York Press, 2002), 140. Wuthnow additionally distinguished that the sphere forms a civil sector of political and public policy domain that we could consider more as part of an official but not public sphere. See Wuthnow, *Producing the Sacred*, 13.

9. Stulanovic notes, "In the legal limit pertaining to worship the [local] culture and doctrine has to accept Shariʿa norms, and *urf* has no legal force in the regulation of those principles. However, this branch of Shariʿa law is mostly applied in the practical [everyday] life of Muslims, where its regulatory power remains positive, and where those guidelines are practically observed, performed and applied as long as one remotely counts oneself as Muslim in ideological and practical terms" (my translation). An example of this regulatory power is the issue of a "Muslim name." There is no Qur'an or Sunna category for a "Muslim" name, but Muslims make sure to name their children with, and reverts often change their own first names to be, Muslim-sounding names. Such rules are regulated by local *urf* and are expected to be followed by the community members. Muharem Stulanovic, *Islamski Sarti (ruknovi) u BiH Obicajima i Tradiciji: Etnolosko Serijatska Studija* [Islamic pillars (conditions) in Bosnian customs and tradition: Ethnological Shariʿa study; my translation from Bosnian language] (Bihac, Bosnia and Herzegovina: IPA Bihac & Medresa Dzemaludin Causevic Cazin, 2002), 7–8.

10. I am going to use the Arabic term *masjid* (plural *masjids*, in English) for the Muslim place of worship, since this language is used by most Muslims themselves.

11. Ilyas Ba-Yunus and Kassim Kone, *Muslims in the United States* (Westport, CT: Greenwood Press, 2006).

12. M. Arif Ghayur, "Muslims in the United States: Settlers and Visitors," *Annals of the American Academy of Political and Social Sciences* 454 (1981): 150–163.

13. Michael S. Merry and Geert Driessen, "Islamic Schools in Three Western Countries: Policy and Procedure," *Comparative Education* 41, no. 4 (2005): 411–432.

14. Clifford Geertz, "Conjuring with Islam," *New York Review of Books*, May 29, 1982, 25–29.

15. Earle H. Waugh, "Muslim Leadership and the Shaping of the Umma: Classical Tradition and Religious Tension in the North American Setting," in *The Muslim Community in North America*, edited by Earle H. Waugh, Baha Abu-Laban, and Regula B. Qureshi (Edmonton: University of Alberta Press, 1983), 13–14.

16. For more on Muslims in the United States, see Kambiz GhaneaBassiri, *A History of Islam in America: From the New World to the New World Order* (New York: Cambridge University Press, 2010) and *Competing Visions of Islam in the United States: A Study of Los Angeles* (Westport, CT: Greenwood Press, 1997).

17. Since they refer to themselves as reverts, I use the same term. The term "revert" comes from the Islamic belief that every human being is born in a state of purity, or *fitra*, which is the primordial state of a human being from which people later in life could diverge due to their upbringing. So people who become Muslims will call themselves reverts to refer to that original state of being. With such a name, reverts also try to elevate their own position in the community and put themselves at the more even position with immigrant Muslims who usually come from Muslim families. For more on the term, see *The Oxford Dictionary of Islam*, s.v. *fitra*, http://www.oxfordislamicstudies.com/article/opr/t125/e666?_hi=7&_pos=1.

18. According to some former members of NOI, he changed the spelling of his name before he died and preferred Mohammed.

19. As explained to us by the current imam Nasir, who was highly positioned in the NOI hierarchy at the time, and other early pioneers of the community.

20. For more details, see Michael Kenneally and Kathleen Siesnick, "Report on the Potential Designation of the Masjid Al Ansar Mosque as a Historic Site," report of the City of Miami preservation officer (2006), http://www.historicpreservationmiami.com/pdfs/2011 %20designation%20reports%20updates/Masjid_Al-Ansar_Mosque.pdf.

21. In this sense, "native" American Muslim groups are similar to Muslim immigrant groups because, for both, the first places of worship were storefront spaces or modified buildings. In fact, Khalidi notes that "of nearly 1000 mosques and Islamic centers in the United States surveyed in the mid-1990s, fewer than 100 had originally been designed to be mosques and, of those, the older ones had not been designed by architects." See Omar Khalidi, "Import, Adapt, Innovate: Mosque Design in the United States," *Saudi Aramco World* 52, no. 6 (2001): 24–33.

22. Perez refers to Liberty City as the new center of Miami's black community after the Overtown was destroyed by the 1950s construction of the Miami expressways. Lisandro Perez, "Racialization among Cubans and Cuban Americans," in *How the United States Racializes Latinos*, edited by Cobas, Duany, and Feagin, 142.

23. Not to confuse it with the current Mosque 29, which is now located a few blocks

away from the Masjid Al Ansar as a storefront NOI temple at 5660 NW Seventh Avenue that in 1995 also became Miami's NOI headquarters. Currently, the minister of the Temple 29 is Elijah Mohammed's son Rasul Mohammed—younger brother of W. D. Mohammed. For more, see Ted B. Kissell, "Two Faces of Islam: Two Distinct Factions of a Religion—One Extremist, the Other Orthodox—Are Vying for the Minds and Souls of Miami's Muslims," *Miami New Times*, September 4, 1997, http://www.miaminewtimes.com/content /printVersion/237880/.

24. As mentioned by Alejandro Portes and Alex Stepick, *City on the Edge: The Transformation of Miami* (Berkeley: University of California Press, 1993). For more on the story, see Lisa Yanez, "Miami Police Officer Charged in Overtown Cyclists' Deaths," *Fort Lauderdale Sun Sentinel*, January 24, 1989.

25. Perez, *Racialization among Cubans and Cuban Americans*, 141–143.

26. As noted in the invitation for the event honoring Dr. Nasir Ahmed.

27. Formerly the Muhammad University of Islam NOI schools, renamed by W. D. Mohammed after his mother, Clara Mohammed. Some members of the *masjid* claim that the Miami chapter of the school began its work before 1970, while others claim that it was actually later.

28. Also noted by Steve Johnson in "The Muslims of Indianapolis" about the group's strained relations with the Islamic Society of North America (ISNA), in *Muslim Communities in North America*, edited by Yvonne Haddad and Jane Idleman Smith (Albany: State University of New York Press, 1994), 264.

29. Similar general tendencies to overcome racial divide among blacks and Latinos in the South were shown by Barreto and Sanchez, when mutual negative attitudes among the members of the two groups decrease if they have a common point of reference, such as when Latinos self-identify as Americans. Matt A. Barreto and Gabriel R. Sanchez, "A 'Southern Exception' in Black-Latino Attitudes? Perceptions of Competition with African Americans and Other Latinos," in *Latino Politics en Ciencia Politica: The Search for Latino Identity and Racial Consciousness*, edited by Tony Affigne, Evelyn Hu-DeHart, and Marion Orr (New York: New York University Press, 2014), 221.

30. Built in 1982, the Masjid Al Iman is the oldest *masjid* of Broward County and possibly the oldest purposely built *masjid* in the state of Florida. The Masjid Al Iman community was founded by African Americans Muslim reverts in the late 1970s in the historic black neighborhood by the Swap-shop, in the city of Sunrise. Some people from Miami's Masjid Al Ansar claim that they formed the congregation and point out that W. D. Mohammed came to the grand opening of the Masjid Al Iman. However, in an effort to reaffirm the Sunni Islam roots of the Masjid Al Iman from the beginning, a few original members dispute that Miami's community started the Sunrise congregation. Masjid Al Iman now has the most diverse congregation in South Florida, composed of immigrants from Africa, South Asia, the Middle East, and a large number of local African American Muslims. A few local Latino reverts I talked to note this *masjid* as their favorite, even though they are not part of that congregation since they live far away from it. Masjid Al Iman has had several imams, mostly of African American origin. The last one was also African American, Imam Rafiq, a Medina University graduate who came after he parted with the Miami Gardens Masjid. He left Masjid Al Iman recently to move to another state for family reasons, as he explained during one of the Friday prayer sermons. For more on the *masjid*, visit their website, http://www.masjidaliman.com/mosque_fort_lauderdale/.

31. Rumbaut, "Pigments of Our Imagination," 15–36.

32. Like Masjid Ibrahim. For more on the *masjid*, see http://pluralism.org/profiles/view /73317.

33. During the late 1990s and early 2000s, it was hard to find parking and a place to sit during Jum'a prayer, while lately Masjid Al Ansar is only half full on Fridays.

34. Samuel P. Huntington, *Who Are We? The Challenges to America's National Identity* (New York: Simon and Schuster, 2004).

35. Hispanic immigrants "often lack knowledge of the social and political histories of the South and often find it difficult to empathize with the life experiences of their coworkers and neighbors who are often African American." Barreto and Sanchez, "'Southern Exception' in Black-Latino Attitudes," 209.

36. Lawrence H. Mamiya, "From Black Muslim to Bilalian: The Evolution of a Movement," *Journal for the Scientific Study of Religion* 21, no. 2 (1982): 138–154.

37. Weekly congregational prayers that Muslims hold on Friday around noon.

38. Ali A. Mazrui, "Islam and the United States: Streams of Convergence, Strands of Divergence," *Third World Quarterly* 25, no. 5 (2004): 793–820; Raymond Brady Williams, "Asian Indian and Pakistani Religions in the United States," *Annals of the American Academy of Political and Social Science: Americans and Religions in the Twenty-First Century* 558 (1998): 178–195.

39. Williams, "Asian Indian and Pakistani Religions," 180.

40. Ibid., 181.

41. They were mostly men because Muslim culture is more restrictive toward women going that far away from home, especially at those times. Still, few of them were with their wives, but most of them brought them from "back home" later after they realized they were not going back.

42. Mohammed S. Shakir now serves as the director of the Asian American Advisory Board of Miami Dade County Commissions.

43. Taj Sadiqi later became the director of the city of Pembroke Pines' Department of Public Services. See Joe Kollin, "Retiring Official Dedicated to Pines: He Helped Build Solid Infrastructure," *Fort Lauderdale Sun Sentinel*, December 5, 2004.

44. *Tarawih* are congregational prayers that are not compulsory, though many Muslims pray them as an effort to increase worship during the nights of Ramadan, the month of fasting.

45. *Hafiz* is the honorary title of a person who has memorized the entire Qur'an with a proper *qirat* (particular method of recitation). Such a person holds special respect in the Muslim community and is usually chosen to lead prayers, especially *tarawih*, and other religious rituals.

46. Learning from the example of the Prophet Muhammad who, upon immigrating to Medina, first built the *masjid*, Muslims around the world replicate that tradition, and as soon as they establish a community anywhere, they work hard to establish a *masjid* as an axis of the community and prime public sphere for their interactions.

47. For more, see the Muslim Communities Association of South Florida (MCA) website, http://miamimuslim.org/mca_code/site/?q=node/27.

48. Ilyas Ba-Yunus, *Muslims in North America: Problems and Prospects* (Takoma Park, MD: Muslim Student Association of the United States & Canada, 1975).

49. For more on the reasons for the formation of ISNA, see ibid.

50. The same person also served as an assistant state prosecutor for Miami from 2000 to 2004.

51. Once that happens, "the property is possessed, used, and operated by the beneficiary (the Islamic center) exclusively for religious, educational, and similar activities in compliance with Islam, [without any interference of NAIT, but] the value of these properties become restricted on a perpetual basis, to serve the Islamic objectives prescribed at inception," and it cannot be used as collateral or to increase the value of it. For more, see Nait.net.

52. As many other early *masjids* around the country at that time, Flagler Masjid was one of the four local *masjids* endowed under the NAIT: Masjid Al Iman, Miami Masjid, MCA, and the Islamic Center of Southeast Florida.

53. This is not the only way the word *jamʿat* is used nowadays, since the Tablikh group, or the even larger group of Ahlus Sunnah wal Jamʿat, also refers to itself as *jamʿat* to show the closeness of the same principles among group members.

54. Being a sacred place, a *masjid* is to be bought for cash, with no interest involved, while many people compromise and buy their own houses using bank loans with interest. Many of those people who buy homes in such a way justify it as a necessity, *darura*, which is a Shariʿa concept that allows Muslims to break the Islamic rule. However, houses bought that way are rarely modest homes in less affluent neighborhoods, but rather comfortable houses in middle-class neighborhoods.

55. A minaret is a tall tower adjacent to the *masjid* from which the call for the five daily prayers is made. Although it is a later addition to the sacred space, it is widely assumed to be an integral part of the *masjid*, especially among Muslims of the Hanafi school, which is the vast majority in South Asia.

56. Nebahat Avcioglu, "Identity-as-Form: The Mosque in the West," *Cultural Analysis* 6 (2007): 101.

57. Ibid., 92.

58. Larry Poston, "Da'wah in the West," in *The Muslims of America*, edited by Yvonne Y. Haddad (New York: Oxford University Press, 1991), 125–136.

59. Cuban neighborhoods along Flagler Street grew in the 1960s and 1970s. Perez, *Racialization among Cubans and Cuban Americans*, 143.

60. The real estate website demographics information for the zip code 33055 show that more than 30 percent of residents are African American, while 60 percent are Hispanics. In contrast, the Flagler Masjid 33165 neighborhood is 1 percent African American, while Hispanics are an overwhelming 90 percent. For more, see http://www.city-data.com/zips/33055 .html or the bit less precise http://www.movoto.com/neighborhood/fl/miami-gardens/33055 .htm. This also shows that Muslims in South Florida historically gravitate more toward African American neighborhoods when it comes to *masjid* cites. The new location for Pompano Masjid (still under construction) is also a predominantly African American neighborhood in Pompano Beach.

61. They even laid down the foundation for the school, but then as a result of the board leadership's sudden decision, they rather quickly built the *masjid* first. Similar discussions and clashes were ongoing at the other local Islamic centers, where they are trying to build or establish Islamic schools, like the Islamic Foundation of South Florida in Sunrise, since local communities inexperienced at being the religious minority could not agree on how important Islamic schools for the children are in the new world.

62. At one point members of the *masjid* sued its president Hamid Siddiqui over his

leadership style. According to *all* of the interviewed people, Hamid Siddiqui was one of the South Florida Muslim pioneers and an important pillar of the community and certainly most often mentioned by everyone with whom I talked, but nevertheless even he encountered problems.

63. Eric Roose, *The Architectural Representation of Islam: Muslim-Commissioned Mosque Design in the Netherlands* (Amsterdam: Amsterdam University Press, 2009), 17.

64. In most of the *masjids* in the United States, the *adhan*, or call for prayer, is called only inside of the building, or sometimes from the doorstep of the *masjid*, but extremely rarely from the minarets or loudly, as is the case in Muslim-majority countries.

65. Roose, *Architectural Representation of Islam*, 14.

66. Hearing the *adhan* is explicitly tied to certain Muslim everyday activities, and it is mentioned in many hadith and several places in the Qur'an—for example, Sura 62, Al-Jumu'ah, ayat 9: "O you who believe! When the call is proclaimed for the Salat on Friday [Jum'a prayer], come to the remembrance of Allah and Salat and leave off business" (translated by al-Hilali and Khan).

67. Somewhat, this is due to some limitations in religious practices such as the issue with the call of the *adhan* and impermanence of the imams, which cause a lack of the sense of *jam'at*.

68. One engaged in *da'wa*, that is, one who calls to Islam.

69. After the Miami Gardens Masjid, Imam Rafiq was hired as the imam for Sunrise, Al Iman Masjid, where he fitted in much better and stayed with the community until recently, when he moved out of state.

70. Imam Murrie then became the imam for another South Florida *masjid*, Al Muttaqin. Such practice is common across the South Florida community, wherein one imam is hired by another community once he leaves the first one.

71. For more on the Universal Heritage Institute (UHI) Clinic, see http://universalheritage.org/.

72. For more, see Sahara's web page: http://www.saharafl.org.

73. See the Islamic Jaffaria Association, Inc., website, http://ijamiami.org/ijaglance.html.

74. By then Tasneem Uddin had become well respected and very successful in his business. Among many local projects, he worked on the building of the additional terminals of the Miami Airport and a section of Interstate 595. He was also an instrumental part of many other South Florida Islamic building projects as well as a silent backer of many South Florida Muslim families who purchased their first homes with his help. His financial support to some of those people became known to a few of his family members only after he died in 2007. However, even now his family is not sure how many people and how many projects he helped build. Many of the people interviewed confirmed that he was an important pillar of the South Florida Muslim community.

75. For more on Nur-ul-Islam, see http://www.nuia.org/.

76. For more on Al Hikmat Services and activities, see http://www.alhikmat.com/who orwhatisalhikmat.html.

77. For more about IFSF, see http://www.ifsf.net.

78. For more on Al Azhar Academy, see http://www.edline.net/pages/AlazharSchool.

79. For more on the Anatolia Center, see http://www.anatoliacenter.org/.

80. Eidheim notes the same for a different minority, which also has to find a way to function in a limited public sphere. See Eidheim, "When Ethnic Identity Is a Social Stigma," 52.

81. Ruth Morris, "Muslim Leader Gets Death Threat," *Fort Lauderdale Sun Sentinel*, May 3, 2007.

82. See US Attorney's Office press release, May 9, 2011.

83. Such as the Coalition of South Florida Muslim Organizations Community (COSMOS), Emerge USA, and various FBI and police individual meetings and training efforts. For more on individual efforts, see U.S. Department of Justice, "Arab and Muslim Engagement: U.S. Attorneys' Outreach Efforts in the Southern District of Florida," http://www.justice.gov /usao/briefing_room/crt/engagement.html.

84. In a 2009 Gallup poll conducted among American Muslims, they expressed that CAIR represents them more than any other national Muslim organization. However, it will be interesting to observe whether the effects of the official sphere and increased clustering of Muslim communities made a dent in those feelings.

85. Some implications of it are also hinted at in NPR's piece on the case. For more, see D. Temple-Raston, "Imam Arrests Show Shift in Muslim Outreach Effort," July 19, 2011, http://www.npr.org/2011/07/19/137767710/imam-arrests-show-shift-in-muslim-outreach -effort.

86. For more on AMANA, see http://al-amana.net.

87. One local South Florida imam commented that the media is "pushing the jockey before the horse" with a "growing number of Muslim converts" stories, possibly to scare the non-Muslim population that knows nothing about Islam, yet it is being fed stories about "the fastest growing religion in the US" in terms of the number of followers.

88. Padilla was actually from Chicago. See BBC, "Profile: Jose Padilla."

89. Huntington, *Who Are We?*; Portes and Stepick, *City on the Edge*.

90. Joe R. Feagin and Jose A. Cobas, *Latinos Facing Racism: Discrimination, Resistance, and Endurance* (Boulder, CO: Paradigm, 2014).

91. Farida Jalalzai, "Anxious and Active: Muslim Perception of Discrimination and Treatment and Its Political Consequences in the Post–September 11, 2001, United States," *Politics and Religion* 4 (2011): 71–107.

92. Eric Hobsbawm and Terence Ranger, *Mass-Producing Traditions: Europe, 1870–1914* (Cambridge: Cambridge University Press, 1992), 280.

93. Huntington, *Who Are We?*, 249.

94. Portes and Stepick, *City on the Edge*, 9.

95. Ibid.

96. To further underline the point about the divergence among the two communities, it should be noted that, as of now, none of the local Islamic schools offers in-class Spanish-language courses to its pupils, while some of them even offer in-class instruction in Mandarin. All of the schools have in-class Arabic instruction, while in addition to Arabic some of them direct students to take online classes in different foreign languages of their choice.

97. Ernest Gellner, *Postmodernism, Reason and Religion* (London and New York: Routledge, 1992), 3.

98. The onus for integration is on the larger, host, society and not on a "minority," and in the case at hand South Florida Muslims face the unusual and simultaneous dilemma of two-directional integration of Americanization and Hispanization, which often sit in tension with each other. Such a dilemma is especially hard for Muslims who, on the one hand, have to prove their patriotism in a larger national setting by unquestioningly adopting Americanization while, on the other, locally accepting Hispanization as well.

CHAPTER 12

DOUBLE-EDGED MARGINALITY AND AGENCY: LATINA CONVERSION TO ISLAM

YESENIA KING AND MICHAEL P. PEREZ

IN THIS POST-9/11 ERA, Islam has been viciously distorted in the context of the U.S. "War on Terror," whereby racialized images of Muslims have occupied public consciousness. Such backlash is not unlike the long history of anti-immigrant and anti-Latino U.S. sentiment and politics. In fact, the two phenomena are historically intertwined and rooted in a racialized history. Interestingly, there has been a steadily increasing trend of Latina/o converts to Islam.[1] Latina/o Muslims in the United States approximate twenty-five to forty thousand and up to seventy-five thousand. These figures are possibly much higher at two to four hundred thousand.[2] However, academic research on Latina/o Muslims is nearly nonexistent. Yet this phenomenon is significant in terms of understanding double-edged marginality, multilayered identities, and multiple consciousness, themes that are present and noteworthy of articulation with respect to the intersectionality of this relatively understudied population and phenomenon. These themes are precisely central to the analysis in this chapter and the scholarly niche of this volume. This analytical endeavor is not only relevant to give voice to this understudied Latina Muslim population and experiences. The wider significance of this chapter is to contribute to the expanding literature on intersectionalities and enhance the visibility of historically understudied and invisible populations whose experiences meet at the intersection of multiple dimensions of marginality.

Indeed, the double-edged marginality of the Latina Muslim meets at intersecting locations where the converging positions of marginality among the larger community of Muslims are comparable to her experiences within her minority status as a woman of color in the United States. As these women navigate unfamiliar places by way of conversion, they are once again relegated to a marginal status among the majority Arab, South Asian, and Orthodox Muslims in this new community. This double-edged collision presents an array of paradoxical identities inhabited and applicable to the multiple otherness of being on the margins of U.S. society, their own ethnic culture, and Arab and South Asian Muslim communities. Understanding the struggles and double-edged experiences of being Latina Muslim relative to U.S. society and Muslim groups, respectively and simultaneously, is important in tracing the navigation of their borderlands.

Drawing on Gloria Anzaldúa's borderland perspective,[3] this chapter contextualizes, explores, and analyzes the experiences of Latina Muslim converts, in regard to marginality, gender politics, and resistance to patriarchy. In so doing, this chapter specifically engages the following:

- Given the paucity of literature on Latina Muslims, Latina/o conversion is first juxtaposed relative to black conversion to Islam.
- Latina Muslim experiences are situated within Islamic feminist and borderland notions of mestiza consciousness.
- Latina Muslim narratives are analyzed in terms of the formations, negotiations, and navigation of identities with respect to marginality and borderland experiences at the convergence of Latina and Islamic feminist sensibilities.

The last section is grounded in semistructured, in-depth interviews of ten Latina Muslim converts and participant observation of sites of Latina Muslim interactions, including Spanish Qur'an classes and *platicas* (discussions) conducted at several Southern California mosques for a period of two months.[4] Ultimately, this work demonstrates the flexible agency involved in the conversion process of the Latina Muslim.

JUXTAPOSING LATINA/O AND BLACK CONVERSION TO ISLAM

In the past decade, Latina/o conversion to Islam has been on the rise in the United States and Latin America. Hishaam Aidi refers to this conversion as "the other September 11 effect," the principal "effects being anti-Muslim and anti-immigrant backlash and infringements upon civil liberties."[5] According to a report from the First World Congress of Spanish-Speaking Muslims held in Seville in April 2003, there were 10 to 12 million Spanish speakers among the world's 1.2 billion Muslims.[6] Aidi further argues that since September 11, Islam has provided an anti-imperial outlet for many Latinos, as "Islamic" culture permeates the West.[7] While Westerners of various backgrounds are drawn to Islam, it is more commonly the racially and ethnically marginalized "mostly black, but nowadays also Latino, and Native American minorities who, often attracted by the purported universalism and colorblindness of Islamic history and theology are asserting membership in a transnational *umma* and thereby challenging or 'exiting' the white West."[8]

Consequently, many contemporary political movements have Islamic undercurrents, as minorities in the West protest the launching of the War on Terror, the invasion of Iraq, and the colonial similarities between the Middle East and Latin America. Aidi adds that political leaders and activists in Latin American countries have been wary of U.S. imperialistic aims, hence declaring solidarity with the Arab world, emoting their Moorish roots.[9] For example, the growing rate of conversion to Islam among indigenous Mayan communities in Chiapas, Mexico, has been explained as a historical remedy for the oppression and conquest by the Spanish hundreds of years ago. As with various other groups who have in many ways indigenized major forms of Christianity,[10] Latinos are arguably doing the same within Islam. Aidi notes that in an interview with *El Pais*, a Mayan convert stated that "five hundred years ago, they came to destroy us. . . . [N]ow [Islam] came to return a knowledge that was taken away from us."[11] In light of northern or Western imperialism in the South and East, political and cultural models of Islam have emerged in re-creating identities and cultural ties for Latinos within a Muslim context.

Given the lack of literature on Latina/o Muslims, the longer history of black emancipation and conversion to Islam is informative to Latina conversion specifically. African Americans have (re-)created a distinct Afrocentric identity within Islam as a means to navigate their marginality. Jamillah Karim analyzes African American Muslim women's experiences of discrimination within a common religious community, or *umma*, with immigrant Muslims in the United States.[12] She notes that the *umma* in America, ideally a symbol of religious unity and solidarity, is marked by ethnic and racial divides. Her research shows a level of privilege and power of immigrant Muslims over African American Muslims. She states that African American women's struggle to define and express their experiences as "black, female, and Muslim positions their voice within the broader tradition of black feminist thought and resistance."[13] In her study African American Muslims regularly expressed how immigrants exclude and discriminate against them. However, their determination to express their voice positions them within the "tradition of black feminist struggle: a struggle marked by the overlap of race and gender oppression," which has led to the development of African American cultural expressions of Islam in their thought, practice, dress, and communities.[14]

Furthermore, Tinaz analyzes the Nation of Islam as a global ethnoreligious movement that appeals to the black diaspora.[15] Tinaz examines how the NOI's ethnic, racial, political, social, and religious teachings appeal to African and

Caribbean peoples in the United States, Canada, West Africa, the Caribbean, and western Europe. The NOI cultivates transnational ethnoreligious identities and transcends ethnic and national boundaries, hence appealing to a diversity of diasporic African peoples across the globe, who become spiritually connected based on their shared historical experiences with colonial displacement via the transatlantic slave trade. As Elijah Muhammad described more than forty years ago, Islam is the "the original religion of all black mankind."[16]

ISLAMIC FEMINIST PARADIGM SHIFT
AND OPPOSITIONAL CULTURE

Given their similar colonial experiences, Latina/o conversion to Islam follows a path akin to postcolonial appropriation and rearticulation. Juxtaposing black and Latino conversion in this context is analytically useful in terms of the emancipatory effects of conversion to Islam for Latinas in particular, especially in light of their multiple marginalities as Latina Muslims at the intersection of patriarchy, whiteness, Judeo-Christian norms, and Arab and South Asian Muslim communities.

The identity formation and gender politics of Muslim women reflect a new paradigm shift within Islamic thought. Events such as the First International Conferences on Islamic Feminism in Spain and New York indicate the emerging global movement of Islamic feminism.[17] The conferences convened well-known Muslim and non-Muslim scholars, activists, and feminists who critiqued male interpretations of Islam to promote equal rights for Muslim women. McGinty defines Islamic feminism as a struggle "against patriarchy and gender inequality, challenging traditional, patriarchal gender systems, which promote segregation between men and women."[18]

In revisiting the Qur'an and hadith, feminist Muslims resist cultural traditions limiting women's freedom. They draw on Qur'anic belief in gender equality and social justice and argue that the Qur'an does not justify patriarchy.[19] Muslim feminists stress the importance of working within the system that marginalizes them, as well as the implementation of multiple ideas and positions. While several studies on Islamic feminism exist, many have only discussed issues of how the sacred texts should be interpreted and revisited from feminist perspectives.[20] Connections between feminism, identity, and conversion to Islam have not been rigorously analyzed.[21]

Bonnie Mitchell and Joe Feagin's theory of oppositional culture is additionally useful to the understanding of Latina Muslim identity formation and suggests that marginalized groups draw on diverse cultural resources to resist and survive oppression by creating oppositional cultures that provide "a coherent set of values, beliefs, and practices which mitigates the effects of oppression and reaffirms that which is distinct from the majority culture" and "models for coping with and reversing the oppressive excesses of the dominant culture."[22] In other words, oppositional cultures preserve dignity and offer alternative constructions of identity.[23] Gloria Gonzalez-Lopez applies a similar notion to articulate the migration process of Mexican women itself as a form of oppositional culture.[24] She argues that many women resist, survive, and actively escape gendered violence through the migration process and formation of new relations.

Similarly, the spiritual and political thought of Latina Muslims via their conversion signifies a new form of oppositional culture that can be described as a critique of their own culture. In rejecting the gendered practices and foundations emanating from their previous faith, Latina Muslims create a "culture of resistance" in opposition to multiple dimensions of oppression.

BORDERLAND THEORY AND MESTIZA CONSCIOUSNESS

In observing social activism in Maclovio Rojas, a settler community near the U.S.-Mexican border between Tijuana and Tecate in northern Mexico, Michelle Tellez documents the realities of this border and the role of women in building a sense of community while simultaneously defying "the neoliberal state, transnational corporations, and abusive partners, highlighting the importance of viewing women's activism as linking public and private forms of subjugation," hence shedding light on women's agency in the form of resistance and survival in a literal borderland.[25]

Anzaldúa's borderlands concept offers insight into Latina Muslim identities, specifically the shifting between resistance and agency from the margins of dominant structures and cultural arrangements.[26] Borderland theory provides an analytical framework to contextualize, historicize, and analyze Latina Muslim experiences at the edge of patriarchal and colonial hegemony. This notion of borderlands uncovers discursive spaces that transcend the border areas these women must adapt to, resist, and appropriate as new strategies to transcend their marginal locations.[27] Moreover, Anzaldúa conceptualizes the border as "a dividing line, a narrow strip along a steep edge . . . a vague and undetermined place created by the emotional residue of an unnatural boundary. It is in a constant state of transition. The prohibited and forbidden are its inhabitants."[28] In other words, the border is a place where two or more cultures, classes, races, and ideologies collide. This collision presents a multiplicity of contradictory identities inhabited by marginalized others.[29] This view of a border is applicable to the multiple otherness for Latina Muslims, of being at the margins of dominant U.S. society, Latina/o communities, and Arab- and South Asian–dominant Muslim collectivities.

Mestiza identity emanates from a straddling of cultures that create alternative identities for Latina Muslims.[30] This alternative identity is dialectically in flux with respect to negotiating the pressures of spiritual and cultural borderlands. This dialectic is part and parcel to a transitional and tension-filled state of "mental nepantilism," that is, of being torn between opposing forces.[31] Mestiza consciousness enables adaptability and flexibility of Latina Muslims to negotiate their identities to both belong and not belong. For instance, Latina Muslims can switch between different codes of conduct and language as part of their borderland positionality.

Yet Latina Muslims must also contend with an internal fear of exclusion from family, friends, and fellow Muslims. Anzaldúa refers to this fragile state of being as the "shadow beast," or facets of the "rebel in me."[32] Confronting the shadow beast, or coming to terms with themselves, is a process that Latina Muslims must undergo in order to bring together their multiple forms of belonging.

Anzaldúa further states that "the ambivalence from the clash of voices results in mental and emotional states of perplexity. Internal strife results in insecurity and indecisiveness. The Mestiza's dual or multiple personality is plagued by psychic restlessness."[33] Mestiza consciousness is similar to W. E. B. Du Bois's classic notion of "double consciousness" of African Americans' "two warring ideals in one dark body."[34] Martínez claims that both concepts are connected, as they both describe systems of oppression,[35] Du Bois's being one that includes race and class, while Anzaldúa adds the dimension of gender. Returning to the phenomenon of oppositional culture, Martínez argues that African and Mexican American experiences with U.S. racism have led to "significant forms of oppositional culture and consciousness" situated within a larger matrix of domination or intersecting oppressions.[36]

In response, marginalized people tend to challenge and appropriate the exclusionary structures and practices of the borderlands to assert their inclusion.[37] These "hierarchically organized settings" can be examined as interactional settings of "contested terrain where subjects negotiate how they are regarded and treated."[38] Application of this feminist mestiza borderland perspective potentially contributes new insights to the experiences and interactions of Latina Muslims, in spite of and precisely because of their marginalized and intersectional locations. Though not the sole purpose of this work, this research thus expands the application of and moves Anzaldúa's theory into the contemporary moment with respect to Latina Muslim experiences. The final section of this chapter empirically explores and analyzes the narratives of Latina Muslims in terms of their identity formation and expressions of agency.

LATINA MUSLIM NARRATIVES AND IDENTITY FORMATION

The complexity of Latina Muslim identity formation stems from multiple vantage points and pressures to negotiate and rationalize their conversion at the intersection of being Latina and Muslim. The narratives of ten Latina Muslims enable us to empirically explore the themes in the literature and gain a greater understanding of their double-edged experiences. Given the relative scarcity of Latina Muslim converts, networking and snowball sampling techniques were incorporated, thus yielding the ten interviewees. These interviewees were selected to ensure some level of similarity and variation in their conversion experiences, with respect to life-course timing of conversion, Latina/o family structure, Catholic religiosity and Latina/o cultural pluralism and assimilation, and educational levels. In applying and integrating Islamic feminism, oppositional culture, borderland theory, and mestiza consciousness, Latina Muslim narratives are analyzed in terms of Latina appropriations of Islam, forms of devaluation and empowerment, Latina Muslim feminist sensibilities, oppositional culture, and mestiza Muslim identity.

APPROPRIATED ISLAM AND HISTORICAL "AUTHENTICITY"

These Latinas expressed a common view that Muslim identity is multidimensional, and their appropriations played a key role in navigating their multiple marginalities. They voiced an understanding of Islam as a spiritual site of practical alternatives and solutions to real problems. Built on a linguistic and political premise, their conversion to Islam was seen as an enlightening return to their ancestral faith with pre-Columbian ties to their people. Although these Latina Muslims entered a new site of gendered expectations, they were explicitly conscious and active in navigating their identities to the pressure to conform, which specifically surfaced in their appropriations of *hijab*.

In rationalizing their decisions to convert, these Latina Muslims expressed an understanding of the historical convergence of Islamic and Latin American countries in their belief that Muslims were in the Americas long before Christopher Columbus left a colonial imprint. This was specifically articulated in Latina beliefs in the Arabic roots of the Spanish language. For instance, the comments of Jennifer, a twenty-three-year-old Mexican Salvadorian, typified the sentiments of these women in her claim of the historical connection to Islam:

Yes, of course, Muslims were traveling to Latino America long before
Columbus ever came. I've read this proof in different books. . . . [H]ave you
read *They Came before Columbus*? There are even similarities in our language,
as you know. Spanish has so many words that come from root Arabic words.

Comparative understandings of Islam and Latin America were also expressed politically. Consistent with Aidi in her article "Let Us Be Moors,"
these women saw Islam as an anti-imperial outlet. Their insights to transcend
anti-Islamic sentiments are grounded in their postcolonial mestiza consciousness. For instance, Yadira, a thirty-three-year-old Mexican American, expressed herself as a Latina Muslim with a keen sense of indigeneity in drawing
similarities between Palestine and Latin America:

My community was already a Muslim community from my organizing.
You know because of my work in relating the occupation of Palestine in
the struggle of the indigenous people of the Middle East to the indigenous
people of the Americas and both of our fight against this concrete colonization and the reclaiming of indigenous ways as well as the evolution and birth
of new ways. They were excited for me, of course, and embraced me. . . .
I was now a part of an international *umma* who understood the struggles
me and my people have faced very similar to theirs.

Yadira identified the political and social struggles of Palestinians with her indigenous community's struggles and personal marginality in the West. This
comparison between the colonization of Palestine and Latin America by the
United States surfaced in several interviews. These women united within a
larger *umma* based on a shared indigeneity and colonial history as a perceived
awareness of sharing a common struggle against colonial powers.

Given the history of Latina/o appropriation of Catholicism, in spite of imperial intentions, cultural symbols were articulated in ways that add another
layer of appropriation to their conversion to Islam. For instance, Miriam, a
twenty-six-year-old Mexican, expressed a connection between the *hijab* and
Jesus's mother, Mary, hence identifying continuity in cultural practices between Islam and Catholicism:

Well, Mary the mother of God wore the cover, so it makes sense that we
should wear it too, because if she was the most pious woman ever, we should
wear it. Many Catholics in the older days used to wear it. My grandma still
wears it when she goes to church. . . . [S]o it's something that is connected to
our culture anyway.

In contrast, Iman, a thirty-year-old Mexican, voiced more explicit opposition to double-edged reactions to *hijab*. In light of her *mestizo* consciousness regarding her dual marginality from inside and outside of the *umma*, Iman was critical of both the misconceived assumption that all Muslim women are required to wear *hijab* and the reduction of a women's religious authenticity to the *hijab*:

> You have to take the *hijab* in the context it was presented in. The message of it was revealed during a time where women wore it even before Islam. Now women think they still have to wear it, but they don't; it depends on their interpretation, but just because women wore it back then doesn't mean we have to wear it now. And just because the Prophet's wives used to wear it don't mean we have to wear it; it don't say that anywhere in the Qur'an. I mean, if people want to wear it, they can, but they don't have to; or, in other words, Islam doesn't force them to wear it. I mean, women in other cultures and religions wear it too, and they aren't even Muslim. It just sucks that your piety or how religious people think you are gets judged according to your use of it. I used to wear it — I thought it was mandatory — but now I don't, and I noticed how people treated me differently.

Similarly, although the spiritual messages of peace and respect for women were the impetus for Rabia's conversion, she found the "requirements" of dress after conversion impractical. Rabia, a twenty-nine-year-old, consciously decided to dress in her own practical style to reflect her hybridized identity as a Mexican and Muslim, hence taking active ownership in voicing "my Islam."

> I chose to wear the *hijab* and the *jilbab* like most converts usually do eventually. What I started to realize was that I didn't have to wear it the way others wear it, all wrapped around and covering the neck and all, because I'm not Arab. I love the *hijab*. I don't ever want to stop wearing it, nor do I plan to, but I wear it like this now. Sometimes I wear it other ways, but I realized a long time ago I could still be me and keep my identity, my culture. My *wipiles* cover me perfectly because they're loose and my traditional skirts like my mom's and my grandma's. . . . Islam really emphasized for me the importance of my culture and my own relation to it. I used to see how proud of their culture my Muslim friends were, and I'd be like wow . . . My *wipiles*, my skirts, my *hijab* wrapped like this, this is all a part of me and a part of Islam and a part of my Islam. . . . I really think the *wipiles* were inspired by Islam at some point because look at how similar they are to *abayas*. You know they were. But in my Islam I can dress and be and look how I want. I can be Mexican

and Muslim and traditional and cultural, because I decide what all this means to me at the end of the day.

These narratives demonstrate that Latina practices of Islam are rationalized through their recognition of the historical, linguistic, and political parallels between Islamic and Latin American countries. In spite of the Orientalist claims regarding alleged divides between the Muslim and Western worlds, Latinas turn to Islam not as a break from but as an attempt to rethink their cultural roots. In addition to their constructed authenticity and appropriation of Islam, religious identification provides Latina Muslims with an emotional shield to the inequalities of everyday life, as they "feel that they are the objects of prejudice and discrimination."[39] In contrast to Western liberal feminist views, these women see Islam as a source of opposition to patriarchal oppression.

MULTIPLE DEVALUATION AND EMPOWERMENT

A prominent experience among a majority of these women upon conversion involved multiple inter- and intragroup devaluations in U.S. society, devaluations that stemmed not only from their families and U.S. Latina/os, but also from immigrant Muslims. Nonetheless, these intersecting dimensions of devaluation foregrounded their path toward an empowered sense of self.

One woman converted and married a Muslim man in secret from her Catholic family because she feared they would disown her. Although she maintained that she loved her family and her religion, having to choose between the two was a difficult decision she had to make that ultimately came down to her new lifestyle. A large majority of the women also expressed negative reactions from their families and friends. Similarly, Rabia recalled the encounter with her family upon revealing her conversion, as she wore the *hijab* for the first time following months of studying Islam:

> After having studied it, I felt like I was already Muslim, so my friends took me to the mosque and I said my *shahada* and that's that: I was now officially a Muslim. . . . I decided I wanted to wear the *hijab* that day, but I was scared. I knew I had to tell my family, especially my mother. I knew she'd get mad, but I didn't think like that—she was so pissed. She yelled and cried and made me feel horrible. I tried explaining, but she kept telling me I was going to hell and reminding me of my communion and all that and kicked me out. It was like she felt I was deserting the family and my traditions, like I was committing cultural treason or something.

Several of the women lost many friends as a consequence of their conversion. Although she expected some disagreement, to her surprise Jennifer recalled the loss of close friends: "Some of my best friends stopped talking to me. I didn't expect for them to, not them, other friends that I wasn't so close to, yeah, but not them." In other words, the devaluation of Islam in the United States can be so intense as to result in backlash that severs close friendships. Jennifer further commented:

> She had been avoiding me and wouldn't answer my calls. I would go to her house, and her mother would say she wasn't home when she was obviously home because her car was there. Then one day she called when I was out, and she left me a message telling me that she couldn't be my friend anymore because she didn't understand why I had done that (convert) and that I was basically confused and all that. . . . I was so hurt because I had known her since third grade, and she was supposedly one of my best friends. But, you know, it happens. I've heard other stories like that—oh, well. I can't say— she must not have really been my friend because she was, she was just willing to throw everything away because to her it was more important to go out and drink and go clubbing and not accept me as the same person I was only someone who was changing. . . . It happens.

These Latinas also endured discrimination from fellow Muslims after their conversion. For instance, Luz experienced racial devaluation from her husband's Muslim family. Being a dark-skinned Mexican was not ideal for her husband's family, of Lebanese descent. Luz, a forty-year-old, also experienced racialized marginality by her fellow Muslims: "Even though I wear *hijab* and pray to the same God and everything, they see me as a Mexican first, then a Muslim. They are no better than people in this country."

Another form of devaluation involved gender-role expectations. Those who deviated from the gender script in the Muslim context were outright rejected or treated as outsiders. In response to gendered pressure to wear *hijab* in the mosque, Yadira displayed a sense of resistance to patriarchy:

> So what does this mean to me when things that I'm told that, oh, this is what you believe and how you act that contradicts and counters what I believe, or the way other people practice it contradicts what I feel. . . . [T]o me that was the most difficult thing, is being like very much respectful of other people's home. . . . [Y]ou don't go into other people's homes and tell them it's dirty or this should be moved to the left or to the right, you know. Or tell them you know, well, I disagree with that . . . That's just rude and disrespectful,

and at the same time it's like you don't understand why things were built up a certain way. And in certain ways, you know certain things need to be called out, but a relationship and trust needs to be built before you can make those call-outs. And to me I think that was the hardest part, when these conflicts started occurring, was what does this mean for me? I know what I am doing is not wrong, you know. Trying not to idolize Muslims and being like, oh, no, no, no, there is nothing wrong, the community has no flaws, the be-all-end-all, answer for everything, no, don't talk bad about it publicly. . . . [I]t's like, wow, you know, how can I be true to what my soul knows? What do I need to do to take care of myself?

Discrimination and unequal treatment associated with obtaining work in Muslim-owned establishments either because of the women's dress, difference in beliefs, or ethnicity were echoed by a few participants, including Iman, who was not hired by her friend's husband at a real estate office because of her ethnicity. "She told me her husband was racist and then tried to sweep it under the table like it was no big deal." Immigrant Muslims thus reproduce dominant U.S. hierarchies that subjugate Latina/os, including those who converted to Islam, but such a reproduction is critiqued by Latina Muslims.

Latina resistance to gendered pressure and patriarchal expectations of dress frequently led to marginalization, and hence disengagement by these women from their mosques. Interestingly, this isolation served as a means to cope with devaluation. However, withdrawal from a community space that emphasizes unity resulted not only in emotional and spiritual anguish, but also in denial of access to collective resources such as marriage prospects, inclusion in cultural or religious events, as well as jobs. For instance, Yadira also recalled a double-edged experience when she chose to not wear the *hijab*, which led to being fired from her job at a Muslim-owned retail store.

You know, I couldn't believe I was being fired for choosing to take off the *hijab* and not wear it anymore. I was discriminated [against] at non-Muslim establishments for wearing it, and discriminated against at [a] Muslim-owned business for not wearing it. It was the same thing. I just thought there would be some understanding from my boss, but there wasn't. Every Muslim establishment I went to apply for work at asked me to wear *hijab* while at work. Tell me, what the hell is that?

Due to devaluation and discrimination, some women developed a separatist mentality, by both physically and emotionally withdrawing from established Muslim communal spaces that influenced them to locate and create a surrounding that nurtured their spiritual and material needs. Hence, they expanded their understanding of Islam and negotiated their identities to fit their intersecting experiences. In other words, the marginality of their borderland experience sparked their mestiza imaginations to delve deeper into Islam and appropriate the spiritual space. In turn, Latina Muslims displayed agency at the intersection of multiple sites of oppression and transformed their struggles into a source of empowerment drawn from their mestiza roots. Therefore, in spite of being marginalized by Muslims and non-Muslims, these Latinas embraced Islam in creating a communal sense of empowered identity, as explored in subsequent sections. As Smith's subcultural identity theory contends, cultural tension serves to strengthen group commitment, which seems to ring true in the case of these Latina Muslims.[40] For them, the fact that Islam offers a means to empower themselves against the discrimination faced within their own cultures, communities, and experiences is very appealing. Thus, a prominent theme was that of a communal sense of individual empowerment among these Latina converts. For them, Islam offers a way to gain a perceived sense of "respect" as women otherwise not acquired throughout their lifetimes, within their own culture, or within that of Islam.

LATINA MUSLIM FEMINISMS

As noted, identity formations of Muslim women in general bring together feminist and Islamic thinking, which create new space for struggle "against patriarchy and gender inequality, challenging traditional, patriarchal gender systems, which promote segregation between men and women."[41] Islamic feminism is a trajectory of empowerment for Latinas to transcend what one respondent called "the roles that suppress our womanhood all around." Conducive to the borderland experiences of Latina Muslims, Islamic feminism embraces the flexibility and negotiation of identity in contesting patriarchy. Furthermore, Islamic feminism offers a female-centered refashioning of Islam. For instance, most of the women pointed to Islam's matriarchal view of mothers. As Rabia stated, "In Islam it says that heaven is at your mother's feet, so like it means that you have to have the utmost respect for your mother and women." Likewise, the U.S. irony in the patriarchal distortion of *hijab* is that whereas in the Western world the *hijab* may be viewed as an oppressive tactic to control women, Latina Muslims view it as an opportunity to free themselves of what Maricella, a twenty-seven-year-old Mexican, calls "the annoying perversion of men in this country."

Islamic feminism is also keen on intersecting oppressions. As noted, Latina Muslims simultaneously endure sexism within Latino and Muslim communities and racialized sexism within U.S. society. Among (non-Muslim) Latinos and immigrant Muslims (overwhelmingly Middle Eastern and South Asian), they contend with socially conservative, middle-class ideologies that define "true" womanhood in patriarchal terms with double standards in general. As a participant stated, "When a man converts to Islam he may be considered eccentric, perhaps even brave, but when a woman does it, it's like she committed cultural treason." The female convert to Islam, much more than her male counterpart, becomes the rope in a cultural tug-of-war, as multiple interests—Western, Latina/o, and Islamic—fight to claim her. However, Latina Muslims are active agents in their decision to convert to Islam, while maintaining their Latina identity.

Through Islamic feminism Latinas integrate seemingly irreconcilable gender discourses and explore alternative femininities. Thus, their new religious identity as "Muslim" represents an alternative to Western and Islamic patriarchy and Western feminism. In fact, the majority of the women criticized Western feminist assumptions that all Muslim women are hopelessly oppressed. For example, Mouna, a forty-three-year-old Bolivian, stated, "I'm not a feminist in the Western sense. I don't like that they think we are poor little oppressed women or that they think a woman should be above a man. I don't believe in that. I believe what Islam teaches us, that women and men are equal, and that is what I believe."

For Muslim feminists themselves, their religious identity and belief in social justice and equality for all women are at the heart of their struggle. That said, there were some differences in the feminist approaches of Mouna and other respondents concerning gender issues in Islam. Although Mouna internalized male patriarchy and privileged Orthodox Muslims, she also expressed an Islamic value for gender equality. Her explanation echoed a dominant discourse among Orthodox Muslims who rationalize certain sexist practices due to so-called natural differences between men and women. Yadira, on the other hand, was keen on the sociocultural foundation of gender:

> Men and women are the same in Islam and will be accountable the same way when they die. It's people who have twisted Islam and have interpreted the Qur'an to mean this or that, but no, because it doesn't say that anywhere, it's only because of the person's culture or country they come from that decides what a man and a woman should be like, you know, it says nowhere that just because we have children and they don't or they are stronger than us they should have more rights or stuff than us.

The differences in opinion between these two perspectives on gender and Islam signal the plurality of Latina Muslim feminisms. Just as there are many understandings of feminism in the West, there are also numerous views within

Latina Muslim feminisms. Nonetheless, the narratives show that these women all emphasize their right as women to choose their faith regardless of external pressures.

LATINA MUSLIM OPPOSITIONAL CULTURE

In addition to the appeal of Islamic feminist sensibilities regarding patriarchy and racism, Latina conversion to Islam is often spurred by spiritual and political discontent as well. Consistent with Mitchell and Feagin's notion of oppositional culture, discussed above, Latina Muslims form an oppositional culture and borderland space of transcendence, creativity, and cultural production. Miriam expressed her conversion in these terms: "It represented the way I was already wanting to live my life, but because of all the issues I was going through and all the things that happened to me when I was younger and as an adult, I never could. But Islam was like an outlet for me to rebel and say enough—I will finally live how I want to live."

These women also shared their political work in organizing around Latina Islamic feminist interests and women's rights. Through their emergent political consciousness, these women sought to critique inequalities within Latina/o and Muslim communities as well as construct safe spaces to resist and survive various marginalities. Yadira explained why she participates in a support group with other Latina Muslims:

It's not just with me, you know, because the Muslim community exists in the world. The world is antiblack, the world is anti-queer, women, poor, and Islam is comprised of people who live in a world with their own specific cultures and in their own culturally specific ways where misogyny comes out and white supremacy comes out, homophobia, classism. And it comes out in the Muslim community because we are all raised within this global hegemonic reality that operates on different principles. And so for me I'm like this is real . . . You know, look at the mannequins. They're dressing the mannequins in *hijab*, and they have white skin and blue eyes, but I don't know many people that look like that. I'm looking down the streets, and I don't see anyone who looks like that. But once again this notion of what it means to be beautiful or this is what it means to be a good Muslim . . . It's all fake. I mean, they're human too, so I understand, but when they see my brown skin and accent and traditions and experiences and look down on me, it makes no sense because they have brown skins, accents, and traditions too. But oh, we have to fight twice as hard to be noticed sometimes, and even when you bring it up to them, they act like we are wrong or like it's us that have the problems.

It's so much easier to get together here with other Latinas because we understand; they understand what I go through, and I understand them, so it's just
so much easier, and we are able to be noticed and make our presence felt and
respected like we should be because we're Muslim too. . . . So it's like we get
discriminated against by our people for converting, and then we get discriminated against [by] these people just because we are Latina, well, then, excuse
me, you tell me where do we belong. It's not supposed to be like that, and
it's hard to deal with sometimes and it's just easier to get together with my
Latina sisters, you know.

Maricella's reasons for attending Latina Muslim Qur'an classes and support groups resonate with Yadira's response in that she also mentioned a
higher level of comfort because of the shared language with other Latinas, the
linguistic barriers with other immigrant (Middle Eastern and South Asian)
Muslims, as well as the past marginality they experienced at the hands of Muslims themselves:

I've been a part of other *halaqus* before, but I feel way comfortable here with
my sisters because it's in Spanish and they understand me more because at the
other classes the other women would dominate the conversation and make
me feel like I wasn't qualified to teach any of the classes because I hadn't been
Muslim as long as they were.

The agency of these women converts is exercised to endure subjugation,
organize, and create space. Latina Muslim oppositional culture develops at
the borderlands of intersecting oppressions. In resisting multiple oppressions,
Latina Muslims actively shape their identities and spiritual surroundings on
their own terms. In turn, Latina Muslims effectively navigate the borderlands
at critical crossroads of their lives. The oppositional culture of Latina Muslims
is made up of alternative stories, blends of languages, and the notion of communal action as transformative empowerment.

THE FLUIDITY AND FLEXIBILITY
OF MESTIZA MUSLIM IDENTITY

The ability of Latina Muslims to be flexible, adaptive, and transformative with
their multiple identities is part and parcel to their empowerment. Latina Muslims fluidly move between various languages and different cultural codes in the
borderlands. At times, Latina Muslims must shift to living at a "crossroads"—
a space of travel and habitual change between the many cultures they exist

within.[42] Leila, for instance, articulated this mestiza sensibility with respect to familial celebration of holidays:

> We celebrate Christmas, Thanksgiving, kind of ironic; that's pretty much it. That's my family, like what I grew up with. You know, I'm not going to deny my family their celebrations and their heritage just because I don't believe what they believe or because people don't like those holidays. I watch what I do personally, you know, like I don't toast the wine anymore and I don't cut the ham. But I mean, I'm not going tell them, "No, I'm not going to celebrate this holiday with you because you're not Muslim." You know what I mean, like to me it's about holding on to those people that are close to you, and I don't see anything Islamically wrong with taking things as long as I watch the religious worship. It is my culture after all, you know.

Although more Orthodox Muslims do not generally celebrate holidays such as Christmas and Thanksgiving, Leila, a twenty-four-year-old Cuban Puerto Rican, described her decision to hold on to certain practices because it exemplifies an essential part of her identity before conversion. Similarly, Somaya, a thirty-five-year-old Mexican, was also keen on the nuances of the borderland experiences with respect to her value for all oppressed groups, including lesbian, gay, bisexual, and transgender (LGBT) communities:

> Well, the way I describe Islam, Islam is a guideline then; it doesn't contradict my life. I believe in full rights for all oppressed, suppressed, people in the world to self-determination and growth; the ability to create a reality in which our loved ones have the resources, emotional, physical, spiritual, mental, cultural, capital, we need to not only survive but to live and thrive . . . as not only a people but as a humanity and a human being. So that includes full and absolute rights for the LGBT, queer community, full rights for the women community, full rights for the people of color, full rights for suppressed and religious minorities. Full rights, you know, for all people who have always been subjected to this idea that you are different and difference needs to be eliminated and destroyed and made more like us, us being those with power. To me there's nothing in Islam that supports that notion that you have to be like us, like those who try to tell me how I should live and what to believe in. You know, to me Islam's very much just a general outline of how you live your life in justice and in justice means to walk in love and create a reality in which people have those basic human needs and human rights we so deserve so that we can actually have conversations of what does it mean to be a human, exist, and to thrive and flourish and nourish. To me

those things aren't counter to Islam or counter to what I believe. There are people within the Muslim community who do have those beliefs and who are very much afraid of difference and who are afraid and perpetuate systems and cycles of violence, dominance, oppression, brutality, subjugation, forced submission. That to me is counter to the very principles of which we subscribe to in Islam, and I don't participate in it.

Even though homosexuality is generally not approved by Muslims (or Christians), Somaya does not find her promotion of rights for all groups as a contradiction to Islam. The flexible negotiation of their identities in an Islamic feminist context enables Latina Muslims to stay true to their social selves and embrace their intersectionality. Anzaldúa captures this idea in her definition of identity as "an arrangement or series of clusters, a kind of stacking or laying of shelves, horizontal and vertical layers, the geography of selves made of the different communities you inhabit . . . a process in the making."[43]

Latina Muslims are highly conscious of their shifting locations and challenges. Power struggles often manifest internally as part of a transitional phase where Latina Muslims must cope with their perpetual state of ambivalence. Nonetheless, their ability to switch between borders constitutes the Latina Muslims' mestiza consciousness. Islam, at its core, provides a space for these women to transcend borders and maneuver intersections.

CONCLUSION

Grounded in oral histories and feminist epistemologies, this chapter explores the shifting layers of Latina Muslim experiences on the edges of multiple oppressions. Incorporating a feminist borderland sensibility, Latina Muslims make sense of their own conversion and appropriation in terms of an oppositional culture that challenges the many subjugations they experience from within and outside of U.S. society, patriarchy, Latino/a cultures, and Muslim communities. In turn, the spiritual connection to Islam allows Latina Muslims to cope with several forms of marginalization; in other words, Islam is a foundation of empowerment. Furthermore, their empowered sense of self enables a flexible negotiation of their identities, termed flexible agency.

Moreover, as part of a new feminist paradigm shift, Latina Muslims successfully integrate ostensibly conflicting discourses and explore alternative femininities, prompting a critical commentary of both Latina/o and Islamic discourses. Thus, from their Latina Muslim feminist standpoints, Islam offers alternative ways of articulating their experiences as women and to take charge of their social, personal, and spiritual lives. Latina Muslims, therefore, follow the tradition of feminists of color, occupying a safe space where counter-narratives are possible.⁴⁴ Latina Muslim mestiza identity crystallizes in this context. In an era of the devaluation of Muslims, Latina Muslims have hybridized Latina/o and Islamic sensibilities in embracing Islam without abandoning their culture and actively expressing themselves as at the crossroads of their insider and outsider experiences. As Anzaldúa states, "To survive in the Borderlands you must live *sin fronteras* [be a crossroads]."

NOTES

1. Lisa Viscidi, "Latino Muslims a Growing Presence in America," *Washington Report on Middle East Affairs* (June 21, 2003), 22; Daniel Wakin, "Ranks of Latinos Turning to Islam Are Increasing: Many in City Were Catholics Seeking Old Muslim Roots," *New York Times*, January 2, 2002, 1; Lindsay Wise, "In a New Light," *Houston Chronicle*, June 14, 2008, 1.

2. Ihsan Bagby, Paul M. Perl, and Bryan T. Froehle, *The Mosque in America: A National Portrait: A Report from the Mosque Study Project* (Washington, DC: Council on American–Islamic Relations, 2001), 19; ISNA, "Latino Muslims Growing in Number in the US" (2003), http://www.isna.net/articles/News/Latino-Muslims-Growing-in-Number-in-the-US.aspx; Pew Research Center, *Muslim Americans: Middle Class and Mostly Mainstream* (Washington, DC: Pew Research Center, 2007), 17.

3. Gloria Anzaldúa, *Borderlands/la frontera: The New Mestiza* (San Francisco: Aunt Lute Books, 1987).

4. The names of our participants have been changed; included are their pseudonyms.

5. Hishaam Aidi, "Let Us Be Moors: Islam, Race and Connected Histories," *Middle East Report* 229 (2003): 43.

6. Mansur Escudero, speech at First World Congress of Spanish Speaking Muslims in Seville, Spain, April 9, 2003; Aidi, "Let Us Be Moors."

7. Aidi, "Let Us Be Moors."

8. Ibid., 44; Hishaam Aidi, "Jihadis in the Hood: Race, Urban Islam and the War on Terror," *Middle East Report* 224 (2002): 36–43.

9. Aidi, "Jihadis in the Hood"; Aidi, "Let Us Be Moors."

10. Heung Kim, "Is Christianity a Korean Religion? One Hundred Years of Protestant Churches in Korea," *Evangelical Review of Theology* 30 (2006): 162–168; William Liu and Beatrice Leung, "Organizational Revivalism: Explaining Metamorphosis of China's Catholic Church," *Journal for the Scientific Study of Religion* 41 (2002): 121–138.

11. Aidi, "Let Us Be Moors," 229.

12. Jamillah Karim, "To Be Black, Female, and Muslim: A Candid Conversation about Race in the American Ummah," *Journal of Muslim Minority Affairs* 26, no. 2 (2006): 225–233.

13. Ibid., 225.

14. Ibid., 232.

15. Nuri Tinaz, "Black Islam in Diaspora: The Case of Nation of Islam (NOI) in Britain," *Journal of Muslim Minority Affairs* 26, no. 2 (2006).

16. Elijah Muhammad, *Message to the Blackman in America* (Newport, VA: United Brothers Communication Systems, 1965), 80.

17. Anna McGinty, "Formation of Alternative Femininities through Islam: Feminist

Approaches among Muslim Converts in Sweden," *Women's Studies International Forum* 30 (2007): 474–485.

18. Ibid., 481.

19. Margot Badran, "Feminism and Conversion: Comparing British, Dutch, and South African Life Stories," in *Women Embracing Islam: Gender and Conversion in the West*, edited by Karin van Nieuwkerk (Austin: University of Texas Press, 2006), 192–229; Na'eem Jeenah, "The National Liberation Struggle and Islamic Feminisms in South Africa," *Women's Studies International Forum* 29 (2006): 27–41; McGinty, "Formation of Alternative Femininities."

20. Asma Barlas, *"Believing Women" in Islam: Unreading Patriarchal Interpretations of the Qur'an* (Austin: University of Texas Press, 2002); Amina Wadud, *Qur'an and Woman: Rereading the Sacred Text from a Woman's Perspective* (New York: Oxford University Press, 1999).

21. Badran, "Feminism and Conversion," 192.

22. Bonnie Mitchell and Joe R. Feagin, "America's Racial-Ethnic Cultures: Opposition within a Mythical Melting Pot," in *Toward the Multicultural University* (Westport, CT: Praeger, 1995), 65–86.

23. Theresa Martínez, "Double-Consciousness and Mestiza Consciousness Raising: Linking Du Bois and Anzaldúa," in *Gender, Race, and Class: Central Issues in a Changing Landscape* (Los Angeles: Roxbury, 2005).

24. Gloria Gonzalez-Lopez, *Erotic Journeys: Mexican Immigrants and Their Sex Lives* (Berkeley: University of California Press, 2005); Gloria Gonzalez-Lopez, "'Nunca he dejado de tener terror': Sexual Violence in the Lives of Mexican Immigrant Women," in *Women and Migration in the U.S.-Mexico Borderlands: A Reader* (Durham, NC: Duke University Press, 2007).

25. Michelle Tellez, "Community of Struggle: Gender, Violence and Resistance on the U.S./Mexico Border," *Gender and Society* 22, no. 5 (2008): 546.

26. Anzaldúa, *Borderlands/la frontera*.

27. P. Zavella and Denise Segura, "Introduction: Gender Borderlands," *Gender and Society* 22, no. 5 (2008): 537–544.

28. Anzaldúa, *Borderlands/la frontera*, 3.

29. Zavella and Segura, "Introduction: Gender Borderlands."

30. Anzaldúa, *Borderlands/la frontera*.

31. Ibid., 100.

32. Ibid., 38.

33. Ibid., 78.

34. W. E. B. Du Bois, *The Souls of Black Folk* (New York: Penguin Books, 1995), 44; Theresa Martínez, "The Double-Consciousness of Du Bois and the Mestiza Consciousness of Anzaldúa," *Race, Gender & Class* (New Orleans) 9, no. 4 (2002): 158.

35. Martínez, "The Double-Consciousness of Du Bois and the Mestiza Consciousness of Anzaldúa."

36. Ibid.; Patricia Collins, *Black Feminist Thought: Knowledge, Consciousness, and the Politics of Empowerment*, 2nd ed. (New York: Routledge, 2000).

37. Denise Segura and Patricia Zavella, introduction to *Women and Migration in the U.S.-Mexico Borderlands*, 1–32.

38. Ibid., 539.

39. Arnold Dashefsky, Bernard Lazerwitz, and Ephraim Tabory, "A Journey of the 'Straight Way' or 'Roundabout Path': Jewish Identity in the U.S. and Israel," in *Handbook of Sociology of Religion* (Cambridge: Cambridge University Press, 2003), 244.

40. Christian Smith, *American Evangelicalism: Embattled and Thriving* (Chicago: University of Chicago Press, 1998).

41. McGinty, "Formation of Alternative Femininities," 481.

42. Anzaldúa, *Borderlands/la frontera*.

43. Gloria Anzaldúa, *Interviews: Entrevistas* (New York: Routledge, 2000), 238.

44. Collins, *Black Feminist Thought*.

CONCLUSION

JUST AS THE PLURALITY of Islam is thoroughly intertwined with and constitutive of the Caribbean, Latin America, and U.S. Latinos, this hemisphere abides in an Islamic world far more expansive than heretofore acknowledged. In the sixteenth century, Iberians and North Africans with Muslim ancestry, often labeled *moros/mouros* (Moors) or *moriscos/mouriscos* (Moorish descendants), were implicated in the Spanish colonization of the New World. From that time to the mid-nineteenth century, enslaved Muslims from West Africa were brought to Iberian and northern European colonies. Beginning a decade later, British, Dutch, and similar imperial interests contracted Muslims from northern South Asia as indentured laborers to toil in the Caribbean. From the late nineteenth century to today, Muslims from Arab lands known as *al-sham* (present-day Lebanon, Palestine, and Syria) started to migrate to what they called *Amrika* (the Americas). And especially from the late twentieth century to today, U.S. Latinos and *latinoamericanos* who are new Muslims positioned themselves in relation to such histories and peoples.

The first part of our volume traced some of these secretive, forced, coerced, and voluntary flows into Latino America from Africa, Iberia, and South Asia. The three chapters in this part drove our historical rethinking of the *umma* in this hemisphere, and this hemisphere in the *umma*. Drawing on court records and personal documents, Karoline P. Cook's focus on *moriscos* in Spanish imperial domains provided solid evidence of their presence in initial waves of settlement and conquest in the post-1492 Americas. Her chapter showed that *moriscos* worked as enslaved subjects, skilled artisans, as well as *encomienda* lords, negotiating their place in colonial societies through either dissimulating an "old Christian" status or turning themselves in to the Inquisition. Overlapping with the time period of Cook's chapter, John Tofik Karam provided a synthetic, comprehensive mapping of African Muslims in the so-called New World through a formidable body of scholarship already published about their captivity and agency under Iberian and northern European powers. Karam argued that African Muslims were very much part of the imperial rifts and shifts that took place across the Atlantic, from the fifteenth century to the close of the nineteenth century. The chapter by Ellen Bal and Kathinka Sinha-Kerkhoff focused on the connections and detachments fostered by Muslim Hindustanis between British-ruled India and Dutch-rule Surinam, vividly capturing the ways that ethnic formation was historically emphasized over religious difference, which nonetheless mattered as well. Together, these three chapters historically situated a Latino American horizon of a broader Islamic world, which reveals Islam within the formation of this hemisphere and these Americas within the making of an Islamic world.

Unevenly proceeding from the very genesis of the so-called New World to the first half of the twentieth century, the plurality of Islam continued to shape and reflect these multiple Latino Americas in the late twentieth and early twenty-first centuries. This dialectical interplay between a Latino America and a broader Islamic world was further developed by our book's second part, "Contemporary Cartographies." Silvia Montenegro addressed multiethnic politics and civil society formations in Argentine national contexts. She traced a shift from the early and mid-twentieth century when religio-civic associations formed around *shuyukh* and philanthropy to the late twentieth century when Muslim migrants, descendants, and reverts in both Sunni and Shiʿa organizations cultivated stronger ties with varied state powers and became far more visible in the Argentine public sphere. Paulo G. Pinto likewise revealed new dynamics of Islam in Brazil that emerged through globalizing notions of class privilege, family regime, and civil society. At the same time he attended to the politics of authenticity among Middle Eastern Muslims and (non–Middle Eastern) Brazilian reverts, Pinto mapped the linguistic and cultural flexibility of Islam in Brazil. The chapter by Camila Pastor Maria y Campos focused on the symbolic capital that conversion to Islam affords everyday Mexicans, enabling them to "step outside of local ideologies of dominance and difference." Luis Mesa Delmonte's chapter contextualized the rising numbers of Cuban reverts since the 1990s in relation to dynamics of liberalization as well as the geopolitics of solidarity emanating from the self-proclaimed revolutionary government of the island. Liliane Kuczynski's chapter focused on ethnically diverse Muslims in creole Martinique, contending that Islam provides a way for Afro-Martinicans as well as Martinicans of Middle Eastern and South Asian origin to identify in terms of a broader cosmopolitanism. Shifting from institutional contexts to virtual spaces on the Internet, Halima-Saʿadia Kassim's chapter addressed Trinidadian Muslim uses of social networking sites. She argued that these kinds of technologies enable individual and plural forms of Muslim identity and belonging, in addition to more conventional spaces. Each of these six chapters elucidated how the plural beliefs and practices of Islam dovetail with the uneven social and cultural processes in the hemisphere. They also revealed the imagined and institutional ties cultivated between these Muslim Americas and Islamic-majority spaces, whether through Argentines or Brazilians traveling to Iran or Saudi Arabia, Mexicans and Cubans associating or distancing themselves in relation to diplomatic representatives or actual migrants from Islamic-majority states, or Martinicans and Trinidadians who, through personal and virtual networks, connect their islands into a far more expansive *umma*.

Of course, these historical and contemporary patterns in the Americas can also be seen in the dialectical construction of U.S. *latinidad* and Islam. Our volume's third part attended to not only the ways that U.S. Latino reverts engage with plural Islamic beliefs, practices, and histories, but also how ethnically diverse Muslim publics take shape in an increasingly *latinoamericanisado* United States. Hjamil A. Martínez-Vázquez's chapter narrated the "historical consciousness" honed by U.S. Latino reverts, exploring the ways that Puerto Rican, Dominican, Mexican, and other Central and South American subjects in the United States are drawn to Islam and envision their own spiritual journey. In stark contrast, Mirsad Krijestorac's chapter found little overlap between "Latinos" and "Muslims" in the institutional histories of mosques and Islamic centers in the Latino-majority city of Miami. Revisiting the shared and contested connection between *latinidad* and Islam, Yesenia King and Michael P. Perez's chapter took an intersectional approach to the "double-edged marginality" that Latina Muslims experience in relation to both non-Latino Muslims and non-Muslim Latinos. Although these chapters made distinct arguments, they similarly underlined Latino and Latina Muslims' drawing upon memorialized histories of Andalusian and African Muslims. Whether attending to U.S. Latino Muslim affinities or detachments, Martínez-Vázquez, Krijestorac, and King and Perez foregrounded not only their integral position in these Muslim Americas, but also their imagined ties and social distances across a more expansive Islamic world.

Through these three parts, our volume's dual purpose was to trace how Latin American, Caribbean, and U.S. Latino Islam stemmed from distinct regions around the world, including Iberia, West Africa, South Asia, the Middle East, as well as the Americas itself, and to map these geographies of Islam within and from key Latin American, Caribbean, and U.S. Latino historical processes and experiences, including colonialist and nationalist ideologies as well as ethnic and transnational forms of belonging. With a sweeping scope, our point was that the plurality of Islam was shaped by and helped to animate Latin American, Caribbean, and U.S. Latino configurations of identity and belonging since the late fifteenth century. By situating in the same frame of analysis Iberian settlers, enslaved Africans, indentured South Asians, migrant Arabs, as well as Latin American, Caribbean, and U.S. Latino reverts, this volume revealed the global breadth of Islam and its intrinsic multiplicity in the making of these Americas.

In exploring how Islam helped to shape this hemisphere, and was in turn shaped by it, our work built upon and advanced the present-day reformulation of area studies. As noted in the introductory chapter, Appadurai's call for a "new architecture of area studies" that employs a more processual approach to the making of regions was answered by Latin American, Caribbean, and U.S. Latino studies scholars, who, long before, began to think beyond the given boundaries of their respective fields. Well aware of the histories of circulation of peoples and beliefs across the Americas, they sought to conceive of a hemispheric unit of analysis that foregrounded the connections between Latin America, the Caribbean, and U.S. Latinos. In a parallel fashion, specialists in fields conventionally considered Middle Eastern, South Asian, and Southeast Asian studies also began to map out alternative geographies, such as the Mediterranean, the Indian Ocean, and the Malay world. These rubrics better capture the experiences of those who actually inhabit and move across such terrains. *Crescent over Another Horizon* built upon these novel scales of interpretation by tracing the long-standing presence of Muslims from five distinct points of origin in these Americas, as well as these Americas in an Islamic world.

Our edited volume also advanced scholarship on Muslims in non-Muslim-majority countries and regions. Engaging with work that has problematized the position of Muslim migrants and converts "as minorities," we show that "the place" of Latin American, Caribbean, and U.S. Latino Muslims is defined and contested through colonial, ethnic, national, and racialized histories. In the colonial period from the fifteenth to the nineteenth centuries, Islam was an ethnic religion and, even, defined a discrete ethnic identity beyond the specific religiosities of the agents, whether they were Iberian *moriscos/mouriscos*, Muslim African slaves, or Javanese and Indian indentured laborers. From the late nineteenth century to the early twenty-first century, Middle Eastern migration to the Americas continued this tendency of ethnicizing religion, but came to establish many of the Islamic institutions and community formations in Latin America and the Caribbean today. However, these historical patterns began to shift from the last decade of the twentieth century to today, especially with regard to the growing conversion to Islam of non-Arabs in Latin America, the Caribbean, and Latino USA. These new Muslims reject the ethnic overtones that Muslim identities had acquired in the Americas, claiming and advancing a more universal definition and understanding of Islam. Nevertheless, as was stated in the introductory chapter, new ethnic classifications appeared, not as markers of the boundaries between Muslim and non-Muslims, as was the case in the previous periods, but rather as indexes of the discrete histories and cultural identifications of the various groups that compose the *umma* in this part of the world. Studying Islam through these and other horizons enables a fuller understanding of the range of Muslim identity politics and community formation processes in non-Muslim-majority spaces.

Most important, this volume sought to counteract the idea that Islam is new or foreign to this hemisphere. Transmitted through Iberians, Africans, South Asians, Arabs, as well as Latin American, Caribbean, and U.S. Latino reverts, Islam has helped to define colonial and slavocrat orders as well as ethnic and national publics today. In positioning Islam in Latin America, and Latino America in an Islamic world, our purpose was not to call for the mere inclusion of "Muslims" in a conventional multiculturalist or pluralist narrative. Put another way, this volume was not just about adding Islam to Latin America or Latin America to an Islamic world. The far more ambitious goal was to critique the boundaries of knowledge that both separate them and downplay the more than five-hundred-year history of their mutual entanglements. The need for this kind of approach cannot be emphasized enough. We find that recent U.S.-inspired calls for the respectful recognition or selective inclusion of Islam remain complicit with long-standing ahistorical visions that artificially separate these geographies. Our book showed that Muslimness has been historically intertwined with and constitutive of the colonial, racial, national, and ethnic formations of this hemisphere that require us to globalize our notion of an Islamic world as not only "over there" but also "over here," and this Latino America as not only "over here" but "over there" as well. Perhaps more consequential for those based in area and ethnic studies, this book will help us "politically articulate," to borrow the words of Juan Poblete, "the new types of transnational communities emerging today."[1] By locating Islam at the core of this hemisphere, and this hemisphere in the currents of an Islamic global ecumene, this volume advanced the much wider transnational turn in history and the social sciences. This turn will enable area and ethnic studies scholars to broaden the "particular" positions they were historically assigned by the disciplines and lay bare the ingrained provincialism in the latter's seemingly "universal" knowledge.[2]

NOTES

1. Juan Poblete, introduction to *Critical Latin American and Latino Studies*, edited by Juan Poblete (Minneapolis: University of Minnesota Press, 2003), xv.

2. In this regard, Mitchell writes that "the future of area studies lies in their ability to disturb the disciplinary claim to universality and the particular place this assigns to areas." See Timothy Mitchell, "The Middle East in the Past and Future of Social Science," in *The Politics of Knowledge: Area Studies and the Disciplines*, edited by David Szanton (Berkeley: University of California Press, 2004), 98.

CONTRIBUTORS

Ellen Bal is associate professor in the Department of Anthropology, VU University Amsterdam. She studied history at the Erasmus University in Rotterdam and the Jawaharlal Nehru University in New Delhi. She received her doctoral degree from the Erasmus University in 2000 with a dissertation on ethnicity and minority issues in Bangladesh. Bal specializes in South Asia, with a focus on Bangladesh and India. Her main fields of research include ethnicity, migration, transnationalism, and human security. She has conducted research on a wide variety of issues, including migration from British India to Surinam and the Netherlands, diversity and conflict in Bangladesh, and migration of high-skilled Indian migrants to the Netherlands. She has published widely on these issues.

Karoline P. Cook received her PhD from Princeton University in 2008. She currently teaches at Washington State University, where she is revising her book manuscript tentatively titled "Forbidden Crossings: Muslims and Moriscos in Colonial Spanish America." She specializes in the history of the early modern Iberian world. Prior to her current position, she has held Andrew W. Mellon postdoctoral fellowships at the University of Southern California Huntington Early Modern Studies Institute and at the Illinois Program for Research in the Humanities. In 2010–2011 she also held a National Endowment for the Humanities fellowship at the John Carter Brown Library in Providence, Rhode Island. She has presented papers at the annual meetings of the American Historical Association, the Conference in Latin American History, the Latin American Studies Association, the Middle East Studies Association, the Society for Spanish and Portuguese Historical Studies, and the Fifty-Second International Congress of Americanists. Cook has published several articles, including "Navigating Identities: The Case of a Morisco Slave in Seventeenth-Century New Spain," *Americas: A Quarterly Review of Inter-American Cultural History* (July 2008): 63–79; "'Moro de linaje y nación': Religious Identity, Race, and Status in New Granada," in *Race and Blood in the Iberian World*, edited by Max Hering Torres, María Elena Martínez, and David Nirenberg (Berlin: LIT VERLAG, 2012); and "Muslims and the Chichimeca in New Spain: The Debates over Just War and Slavery," *Anuario de Estudios Americanos* (June 2013): 15–38.

John Tofik Karam is an associate professor in the Department of Spanish and Portuguese at the University of Illinois, Urbana-Champaign. His ethnographic and archival research advances the transnational turn in cultural and historical studies by reframing South America and the Middle East through their mutually entangled imaginaries and histories. His first book, *Another Arabesque: Syrian-Lebanese Ethnicity in Neoliberal Brazil* (2007), won awards from the Arab American National Museum and the Brazilian Studies Association, and it was translated into Portuguese (2009) as well as Arabic (2012). His essay "Muslim Histories in Latin America and the Caribbean," which first appeared in *Istor: Revista de Historia Internacional* (2011) and was later reprinted in Aminah McCloud's *An Introduction to Islam in the 21st Century* (2013), helped shape this coedited volume as well. Karam is now working on his next book, tentatively titled "Manifold Destiny: Arabs at the Tri-Border and U.S.-South American Politics." With Akram Khater and Andrew Arsan, he coedits the online peer-reviewed

Mashriq & Mahjar: Journal of Middle East Migration Studies, http://faculty.chass.ncsu.edu /akhater/Mashriq/. Published in the journal's inaugural issue in 2013, his "The Lebanese Diaspora at the Tri-Border and the Redrawing of South American Geopolitics, 1950–1992" was awarded the best article prize by the Brazil Section of the Latin American Studies Association in 2014. He has published in both the *Journal of Latin American Studies* and the *International Journal of Middle East Studies*.

Halima-Saʿadia Kassim holds a PhD in history from the University of the West Indies, St. Augustine, and publishes on women in the Muslim community in Trinidad and Tobago. She is currently a senior planning officer at the University Office of Planning at the University of the West Indies and has previously held the positions of deputy program manager for gender and development at the CARICOM Secretariat in Guyana, head of Continuing Studies at Cipriani College of Labour and Cooperative Studies, and special adviser to the president of the Republic of Trinidad and Tobago.

Yesenia King is a faculty member in the Sociology Department at Los Angeles Harbor College. She received her master's degree from California State University, Fullerton, in 2009. Her thesis, "Latina Muslims: In the Borderlands," argues that Latina Muslim women's conversion can be viewed as a form of oppositional culture in the borderlands as they use their borderland experiences to move past and form new empowering identities. By drawing on both their Latina and their Islamic ideas, the converts arguably produce a feminist commentary, criticizing both Western ideals of femininity and patriarchal practices within "Islam."

Mirsad Krijestorac is a doctoral candidate in Florida International University's School of International and Public Affairs, Department of Political Science, where he also teaches a course on ethnicity and nationalism. He holds a master's in political science and a bachelor's degree in journalism. His research interests are nationalism, identity, religion, conflict and peace studies in comparative politics, and international relations. Mirsad's main regional concentration is on Southeast Europe and the Middle East–North Africa region, while his secondary interest is ethnic relations in the United States. He is currently conducting research on the development of the modern Bosniak identity.

Liliane Kuczynski is a researcher at the National Centre for Scientific Research in Paris and a member of the Institut Interdisciplinaire d'Anthropologie du Contemporain. A specialist in the study of Muslim practices in urban contexts, Kuczynski completed a research program on African Muslim healers (*marabouts*) in Paris. Her book *Les marabouts africains à Paris* was awarded the Carlier Prize from the Academy for Ethical and Political Sciences (Paris) in 2003. In 2006 she was in charge of a lecture program on the flexibility of religious practices in urban contexts. She has recently published a study of the celebration of the main Muslim festival, Eid al-Kabeer, in different towns of Senegal, *La Tabaski au Sénégal: Une fête musulmane en milieu urbain* (2009). Her areas of expertise also include the development of Islam in cross-cultural urban contexts, especially in the French Caribbean, where she has carried out ethnological studies for some years. She has published several articles on this topic. Recently, she extended her research interests to new forms of religious practices and co-organized the first international conference on "Religion on the Web," held in Paris (February 2013).

María del Mar Logroño Narbona earned a PhD in modern Middle Eastern history from the University of California, Santa Barbara. She is currently assistant professor of modern Middle Eastern history at Florida International University in Miami. She has codirected two research and dissemination projects on Islam in Latin America funded by the Social Science Research Council–Carnegie Foundation that laid some of the ground for this collaborative volume. As part of this research, she wrote and produced a short documentary on the topic, *Being Muslim in Latin America* (2010). She has conducted extensive original archival work in Syria, Lebanon, Jordan, Brazil, Argentina, France, and Spain on Syrian and Lebanese migrant communities to South America and their transnational political and cultural connections to the Middle East. She has authored several articles on this topic, among them "Information and Intelligence Collection among Imperial Subjects Abroad: The Case of Syrians and Lebanese in Latin America, 1915–1930," in *The French Colonial Mind*, edited by Martin Thomas (2012); "The Making of a Lebanese Pan-Arab Nationalist in the Argentine Mahjar," in *Politics, Culture and Lebanese Diaspora*, edited by Paul Tabar (2010); and "De emigrantes a embajadores: Un análisis del nuevo papel de los emigrantes sirios en la política exterior de Siria," in *Política Exterior Siria*, edited by Luis Mesa Delmonte (2013).

Hjamil A. Martínez-Vázquez, PhD, is an independent scholar and serves as an online instructor for institutions such as the University of Phoenix and Azusa Pacific Online University, as well as bilingual elementary teacher in Fort Worth, Texas. He is the author of *Latina/o y Musulmán: The Construction of Latina/o Identity among Latina/o Muslims in the United States* (2010) and *Made in the Margins: Latina/o Constructions in US Religious History* (2013). His research has focused on postcolonizing criticism, Latina/o religions and identities, and theories of knowledge.

Luis Mesa Delmonte is associate professor and researcher in the Center for Asian and African Studies, El Colegio de México, Mexico City. He received his PhD (2000) and master's (1987) in Middle Eastern studies from El Colegio de Mexico. He also earned a master's in contemporary history from Havana University (1996) and graduated with a bachelor's degree in international affairs from the Higher Institute of International Relations, Havana (1981). Additionally, he holds two diplomas in conflict resolution as well as peace and security from the Department of Peace and Conflict Research, Uppsala University, Sweden (1999 and 2007, respectively). He carried out Arabic-language studies at King Saud University, Riyadh, Saudi Arabia (1988). His most recent books are *Las relaciones exteriores de Siria* (2013), *Protestas sociales y conflictos en África del norte y en Medio Oriente* (2012), *Las guerras de Israel con Hezballah y Hamas: Retos asimétricos y déficit disuasivo* (2010), and *El debate sobre la seguridad nacional en la República Islámica de Irán* (2009). He lectures on Middle Eastern contemporary history, international relations of the Middle East, political Islam, military affairs, conflict management, and security studies. He has published numerous articles and book chapters on these topics in academic journals from Argentina, Canada, Colombia, Cuba, Mexico, Spain, Turkey, the United States, and Venezuela. Before moving permanently to Mexico in 2003, he worked for twenty years at the Center of African and Middle Eastern Studies (Havana, Cuba), and he served as director of that institution from 1994 to 1998. He was the secretary-general of the Latin American Association of African and Asian Studies from 2006 to 2013.

Silvia Montenegro is a full professor in the College of Arts and Humanities of Argentina's Universidad Nacional de Rosario and a researcher of the Consejo Nacional de Investigaciones Científicas y Técnicas (National Council of Technical and Scientific Investigations). She received her PhD in sociology from the Universidade Federal do Rio de Janeiro in Brazil. She undertook postdoctoral study in Morocco and is an affiliated researcher in the Institut des Études Hispano-Lusophones of the Université Mohammed V. Rabat. Her areas of interest are religious identities, the relations between religion and ethnicity, the practices of transnationalism, and diasporic communities (of Arabs and Muslims). Two of her many publications include the coedited volumes *Musulmanes en Brasil* (2013) and *Repensar las fronteras* (2011).

Camila Pastor de Maria y Campos joined the History Division of the Centro de Investigación y Docencia Económicas (CIDE) in Mexico City as professor and researcher after receiving her PhD in sociocultural anthropology from the University of California, Los Angeles (UCLA). Her research lies at the crossroads of various disciplines and contemporary debates: transnational processes, mediation, representation, and hierarchy in postcolonial settings. Her first book project turns to historical anthropology to explore the trajectories of migrants circulating between the Middle East and middle America since the late nineteenth century, with an emphasis on processes of racialization and the intersection of various transnational frames generated by migrants in transit, French imperial practice, and Middle American postcolonial societies. She is the author of multiple articles and book chapters. She has taught graduate and undergraduate seminars at UCLA, CIDE, the Colegio de Mexico, and Instituto Mora. She is currently carrying out an ethnographic census of the Muslim population in Mexico and launching a new research project on performance and prostitution as labor in the Mandate Mediterranean.

Michael P. Perez is a native diasporic Chamorro/Chamoru ancestrally rooted in Guam and born in Long Beach, California. He is a professor of sociology and the faculty athletics representative at California State University, Fullerton. He was previously an assistant professor of sociology at the University of Guam. He received his PhD in sociology at the University of California, Riverside, after conducting fieldwork and completing his dissertation on indigenous identity in Guam. His teaching and scholarly interests include critical race studies, race, ethnic and indigenous relations, Native Pacific studies, sociology of sports, social justice, education and critical pedagogy, and deviance and delinquency. Perez's published work has appeared in *Amerasia Journal*; *Critical Criminology*; *Deviant Behavior*; *Ethnic Studies Review*; *Faculty of Color Teaching at Predominantly White Institutions* (Anker Publishing); *Global Processes*; *Local Impacts: The Effects of Globalization in the Asia Pacific Region* (University Press of America); *Pacific Studies*; *Social Identities: Journal of the Study of Race, Nation and Culture*; *Social Science Quarterly*; *Sociological Spectrum*; and *Sovereignty Matters: Locations of Contestation and Possibility in Indigenous Struggles for Self-Determination* (University of Nebraska Press).

Paulo G. Pinto earned his PhD in anthropology from Boston University. He is a professor of anthropology at the Universidade Federal Fluminense, Brazil, where he is also director of the Center for Middle East Studies. He did ethnographic fieldwork in Syria in various periods from 1999 to 2010. He has also done fieldwork with the Muslim communities in Brazil since 2003. In 2012–2013 he did ethnographic fieldwork of the *Ziyara al-arba'iyyn* in

Najaf and Karbala, Iraq. He is the author of articles and books on Sufism and other forms of Islam in contemporary Syria, as well as on Arab ethnicity and Muslim communities in Brazil. His recent publications include *Islã: Religião e civilização, uma identidade antropológica* (2010), *Árabes no Rio de Janeiro: Uma identidade plural* (2010), and *Ethnographies of Islam: Ritual Performances and Everyday Practices* (2012), which he coedited with Baudoin Dupret, Thomas Pierret, and Kathryn Spelman-Poots.

Kathinka Sinha-Kerkhoff did her PhD in the social sciences at the University of Amsterdam in 1995. She resides in Ranchi (India), where she was director of research at the Asian Development Research Institute until 2010. Since 2011 Sinha-Kerkhoff has been the South Asia regional representative for the International Institute of Social History. She has been involved in several research projects in eastern India, Bangladesh, Nepal, Surinam, the Netherlands, and Mauritius. She has published widely, reflecting her broad interests, which include migration and diaspora issues, commodity history, history of the colonial development state, minority and refugee issues, youth studies, gender issues, and the agrarian history of South Asia. Her latest book concerns the social history of the tobacco plant amid sugar cane and indigo in colonial Bihar (India).